I0652175

ACCLAIM FOR DES...

"*Desilu* was written by two gentlemen I trust implicitly. They researched that book within an inch of their lives, and have recorded dozens of interviews in connection with it. . . . I think that book is one you can trust for the big picture on the studio and the relationship between all parties."

—Lucie Arnaz

"A terrific book. It reads itself."

—Joan Rivers

"The best of the *Lucy* books."

—Carole Cook

"Excellent."

—*Entertainment Weekly*

"Definitive."

—*Orange County Register*

"A valuable new perspective. . . . A poignant portrait."

—*Variety*

"A page-turner of the first order. . . . *Desilu* is good, gritty, fair but strong and—bottom line—a gripper."

—Robert Osborne, *Hollywood Reporter*

"Lively and informative. . . . A thoughtful, candid look at one of the world's most loved, most watched comedy teams."

—*Houston Post*

"Fans of the *Lucy* show will find *Desilu* fascinating."

—*San Francisco Chronicle*

"In the well-researched and toughly sympathetic *Desilu*, Coyne Steven Sanders and Tom Gilbert have given us a Lucy and Desi that aren't as lovable as the couple frozen in reruns. But they're twice as fascinating."

—*Boston Globe*

"It's their numerous interviews with friends and relatives that tell the real story, one that is disturbing but nevertheless intriguing."

—*Bergen Record*

Desilu

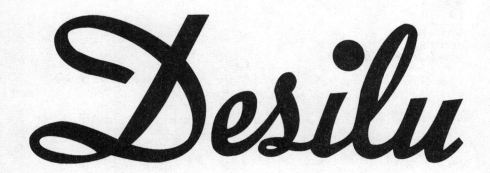

Desilu

THE STORY OF LUCILLE BALL AND DESI ARNAZ

COYNE STEVEN SANDERS AND TOM GILBERT

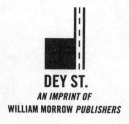

DEY ST.
AN IMPRINT OF
WILLIAM MORROW *PUBLISHERS*

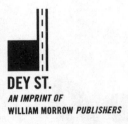

DEY ST.
AN IMPRINT OF
WILLIAM MORROW *PUBLISHERS*

Quotations from the unpublished memoirs of Vivian Vance granted by special permission of Serge Matt, 1878 Union Street, San Francisco, California 94122.

This work was originally published in 1993 by Quill, an imprint of William Morrow and Company, Inc. Reissued by HarperEntertainment in 2001.

DESILU. Copyright © 1993 by Coyne Steven Sanders and Tom Gilbert. Preface copyright © 2011 by Coyne Steven Sanders and Tom Gilbert. New foreword copyright © 2011 by Tom Shales. Foreword copyright © 2001 by Madelyn Pugh Davis and Bob Carroll, Jr. All rights reserved. Printed in the United States of America. No part of this book may be used or re-produced in any manner whatsoever without written permission except in the case of brief quotations embodied in critical articles and reviews. For information address HarperCollins Publishers, 195 Broadway, New York, NY 10007.

HarperCollins books may be purchased for education, business, or sales promotional use. For information please e-mail the Special Markets Department at SPsales@harpercollins-.com.

Designed by Michael Mendelsohn

FIRST IT BOOKS PAPERBACK EDITION PUBLISHED 2011.

The Library of Congress Cataloging-in-Publication has catalogued the 2001 HarperEntertainment edition as follows:

Sanders, Coyne Steven.
　Desilu : the story of Lucille Ball and Desi Arnaz/by Coyne
Steven Sanders and Tom Gilbert.
　　p. cm.
　Includes index.
　ISBN 0-688-13514-5
　1. Ball, Lucille, 1911–1989. 2. Arnaz, Desi, 1917–1986.
3. Entertainers—United States—Biography.　I. Gilbert, Thomas W.
II. Title
PN2287.B16S26　1993
791.45'028'092273—dc20
[B]　　　　　　　　　　　　　　　　　　　　　92-30490
　　　　　　　　　　　　　　　　　　　　　　　CIP

ISBN 978-0-06-202001-7 (It Books edition)

16　17　18　　OV/RRD　　10　9　8

For Richard and Margaret O'Malley
—C.S.S.

For Bert and Jack
—T.G.

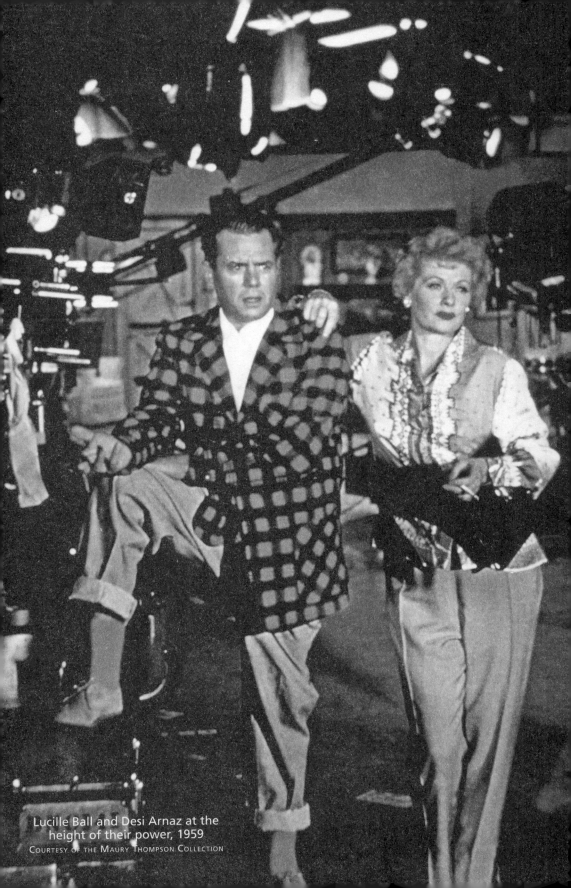

Lucille Ball and Desi Arnaz at the
height of their power, 1959
COURTESY OF THE MAURY THOMPSON COLLECTION

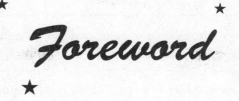

Foreword

FOREWORD TO THE NEW EDITION
by Tom Shales

*I*n 1993, when the first edition of this eminently readable book was published, you couldn't Google Lucy. You couldn't watch her on your iPod, either, or your iAnything. And you weren't likely to be downloading her to your hard drive, unless you were a bit ahead of your time computer-wise. All you could do really was love her—or, naturally, adore her, admire her, and watch her faithfully or intermittently in reruns long since gone re re re re re re re re, all the way home. For all those re's, there still seemed many a run left in them, and there still does today.

I Love Lucy, the mother of all sitcoms—almost literally—has survived the transition from analog to digital, from twentieth century to twenty-first, from a three-network universe to a multichannel maelstrom, and so has *Desilu: The Story of Lucille Ball and Desi Arnaz*, which tells her story, as artist and businesswoman, better than anyone else has. The not-very-mysterious reason for *Lucy*'s own longevity is that, quite simply, it's funny. And the reason it was so funny, and still is, are many, from the good-to-brilliant scripts by some savvy young pros to the directorial touches made possible by the three-camera film technique that Desi himself helped create and perfect (combining the best of "live" TV with the longevity and pliability of film) to the miraculous if quixotic alchemy of the supporting cast—and most of all, it's so pitifully obvious to note—the titular and eponymous star at the center of it all.

But the book is also very much Desi's story, because whatever his temperament, he was a man with uncanny affinity for the new medium. He was full of ideas and determination, both of which helped immeasurably in making *I Love Lucy* the classic that it is and the hit that it was.

Lucille Ball was apparently not an intrinsically hilarious human being but, more impressively, a gifted actress whose cool, keen comic instincts enabled her to take what was on the page and wring every drip and drop and dab of laughter (or, in some cases, poignancy) from it. The unique thing about *Desilu*, among the plethora of *Lucy* books that have been published (everything but the *Lucy* diet book, and don't rule that out), is that it encompasses both the practical and the mercurial, the nuts and bolts that went into the building of an entertainment empire as well as the defiantly indefatigable mystery of talent that is at its center—and, indeed, its heart.

Tom Gilbert and Coyne Steven Sanders clearly and affectionately appreciate the show, the company, and the other hits that took shape there—including pop-cultural classics like *The Untouchables, Mission: Impossible,* and *Star Trek,* all of which proved the soundness of their foundations much later when made into successful motion pictures, or whole series of movies. The authors also tell a complex tale, however, of all-too-human shortcomings among the principals in the story. The details are fascinating, whether they glorify or incriminate; whether they increase one's affection for Ball, Arnaz, and company, or remind us of their very human foibles and fallibilities. Lucy could be a bitch and Desi, alas, a bellicose drunk. And that's just for starters.

TV critics should probably, as a rule, avoid the people they scrutinize and analyze for a living, but given the opportunity to interview Lucille Ball, I could hardly say no. As it turns out, when the day came for the interview, I was bugged big time by one of the innumerable viruses always floating around Los Angeles. I thus spent a few prefatory minutes in, yes, Lucy's bathroom. This was when she was making her ill-fated comeback attempt, *Life with Lucy,* at the Samuel Goldwyn Studios on Formosa.

There, in that bathroom, I was hugely amused to see them for myself: cans and cans of henna rinse, the very chemical that gave Lucy the red hair so often mentioned and lampooned on the show.

Maybe I should have tried to sneak one out of the place and taken it home as a souvenir. Later, as I interviewed her, Lucy ate a sad-looking little white-bread sandwich she'd brought from home and apparently made herself—the Queen of Comedy and the greatest star in television history still very much a commoner with common tastes, not that there's anything wrong with that; it seemed ingenuous, in fact. There was, of course, nothing common about what she did in front of a camera, or about the joy she inspired through laughter in city after city, country after country, generation upon generation as *I Love Lucy* filled hour upon hour.

During a later trip to L.A., while Lucy was hospitalized for the aortic aneurysm that would take her life, I drove by the Hard Rock Café and saw, in large letters on its marquee, something along the lines of "Get Well Soon, Lucy." The café was across the street from Cedars Sinai, the fashionable celebrity hospital where Lucy was being treated. It seemed so touching that a generation many decades removed from hers was reaching out in deep affection to express the debt it felt.

The era in which *Lucy* and *Desilu* were born is long gone but touchingly evoked in *Desilu*, and of course it's touchingly evoked whenever and wherever a *Lucy* rerun re-runs—whether Lucy is trapped on a rooftop with her friend Ethel Mertz, or staggering down a staircase under the weight of a giant headdress, or posing as a bust of herself to fool an art critic, or, yes, rehearsing a commercial for 80-proof Vitameatavegamin and getting sweetly pickled in the process.

That aneurysm didn't really "take" her life. We still have it. It's ours. And it's there for us to relish in the million moments of Lucy's capers and antics, in the huge laughs and warm smiles they inspire—and in the pages of this ever-loving book.

Tom Shales is the Pulitzer Prize–winning television critic and columnist for the Washington Post.

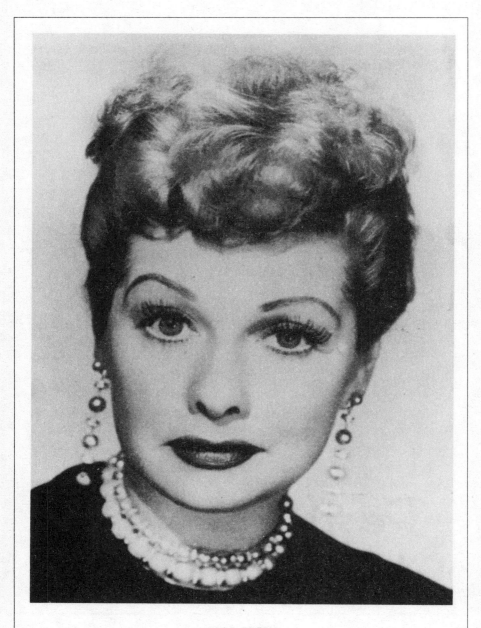

1911-1989

LUCY DIES

NEW YORK POST

A poster announcing the death of Lucille Ball that appeared on
newsstands throughout New York City

PersonalityPhotos.com

Authors' Preface to the New Edition

★

It is with great pride that we present this new, updated edition of *Desilu: The Story of Lucille Ball and Desi Arnaz*, commemorating the sixtieth anniversary milestone of *I Love Lucy* and the posthumous one hundredth birthday of Lucille Ball.

That our *Desilu* has been continually in print since its initial hardcover edition release in 1993 is a telling testament to the ongoing appeal and popularity of Ball and Arnaz and *I Love Lucy*, overwhelmingly hailed as the greatest situation comedy in broadcasting history. This pioneering series, created at the dawn of the television era, is no less than a comic masterpiece, with Lucille Ball often lauded as "the greatest female clown in history."

Desilu received decidedly positive reception from critics, readers, and *Lucy* fans, and, most important, from family members, friends, colleagues, and members of Lucy and Desi's inner circle—many of whom had never previously spoken on the record about life with Lucille and Desi and the Desilu era—who entrusted us to share their stories.

However well our book was received, our most personally meaningful and gratifying review came from the couple's daughter, Lucie Arnaz. We sent the galleys to Lucie prior to publication; aside from our editor, Lisa Drew, and her assistant, Robert Schuman, no one else had read a word of the book. We believed in our work, but had no idea how Lucie would react to what later would be called by one reviewer a "toughly sympathetic" look at the lives of her parents.

Lucie Arnaz did not ask us to delete a single sentence. "It's the first time the truth has ever been told about my parents," she told us privately after having spent a weekend reading the final manuscript in 1993. "It says all of the things we can't say."

Lucille Ball and her universally appealing Lucy Ricardo character have inspired an astonishingly rare and unconditional affection—there's really no other word for it than "love"—among audiences around the world that in no small measure has fueled the longevity of our book, which spans the original hardcover release, more than twenty paperback reprints, and this new, expanded 2011 version.

The sixty-year-old phenomenon that is *I Love Lucy* shows no sign of abating as it continues to touch hearts and generate laughter. *I Love Lucy* consistently captivates both familiar and new viewers, even in this shifting communications landscape that has evolved through home videotape, DVD, and high-definition Blu-ray (and, no doubt, whatever new viewing platforms are introduced in future years). *I Love Lucy* not only survives, it thrives.

In the years since Lucille's death on April 26, 1989, which was the ending point for the original edition of *Desilu*, the ongoing worldwide fascination and acclaim for Lucille and Desi, and the series and the empire they created, has manifested in myriad ways.

On September 15, 1989, the forty-first annual Emmy Awards ceremony featured a posthumous tribute to Lucille, who had been chosen to receive the Academy of Television Arts & Sciences' top honor, the Governors Award. It was presented by Bob Hope to Lucille's widower, Gary Morton, during the awards telecast.

In his acceptance speech, Morton spoke of the star's love for her public, noting that "it was one of the great joys of her life that they loved her back." He recalled their relationship spanning more than two decades, saying, "Our marriage was blessed with laughter, which is a priceless bond for any couple." He concluded, with noticeable emotion, "Ladies and gentlemen, you made the Lucy I loved very happy. Thank you very much."

In the wake of Lucille's death—and the surge of renewed interest it generated in the *I Love Lucy* series—CBS went to the Viacom vaults and dusted off the long-since-retired 1956 Christmas episode, a clip show consisting of early-in-the-series flashbacks woven together by newly filmed holiday-themed footage.

"The I Love Lucy Christmas Show" special aired in CBS prime time December 18, 1989, eight months after Lucille's death and thirty-three years after it was first broadcast on the network. Once again, ratings-charmed *Lucy* ran true to form: the special rated sixth place for the week, one of the highest-ranking CBS entertainment shows of the season.

It was a much-needed pivotal boost for the network, which at the time was mired in third place among the Big Three broadcast networks. As esteemed TV critic Tom Shales observed in the *Washington Post*, "At last—a way for the once-proud network to crawl out of the ratings subcellar where it has languished for two whole seasons: All CBS has to do is keep finding lost episodes of *I Love Lucy*! Lucille Ball had helped build the network in life; maybe she could help rebuild it in death."

Around the time the Christmas special was broadcast, a film of the series' thirty-four-minute pilot—long believed lost—was discovered to be hiding under a bed at the home of Joanne Pérez, widow of José "Pepito" Pérez, the Spanish clown who had appeared in the episode with the Arnazes. A deal to air the original kinescope was quickly made with CBS, and "I Love Lucy: The Very First Episode," an hour special hosted by Lucie Arnaz, was presented on the network to lead off the May sweeps period on April 30, 1990.

This time, the erstwhile CBS champion performed beyond all expectations, confirming the stunning durability of the series' appeal. Thirty-nine years after it was first shown to potential sponsors in a bid to secure its place on the network's 1951–52 prime-time schedule, the grainy, black-and-white "lost" pilot of *I Love Lucy* tied with ABC's *Roseanne* for the number one spot in the ratings for the week—and the entire sweeps month.

CBS's *Lucy* juggernaut continued into the following season. During the February 1991 sweeps, it presented the made-for-TV movie *Lucy & Desi: Before the Laughter*, a biographical dramatization of the couple's life together from courtship up to the premiere of *I Love Lucy*. It was produced by Larry Thompson, a personal manager who had once represented Lucie Arnaz's husband, actor Laurence Luckinbill.

Lucie and Luckinbill—who also had teamed professionally as producers with their Just Arluck Productions—at one time had pitched a Desi Arnaz biographical TV movie to CBS, which twice had nixed the idea. The couple was immediately disenchanted with the Thompson project and its focus on Desi's relationship with Lucille, thinking it was too soon after the beloved icon's death for such an exploitive movie. Lucie took the bold step of denouncing the TV movie publicly as soon as it was announced.

Marilyn Beck reported in her syndicated column in early 1990, "[Lucie] Arnaz was very surprised to learn two weeks ago that CBS was planning to make a two-hour [telefilm] for the 1990–91 season. And that it will be produced by Larry Thompson, who recently managed Luckinbill's career. The official line from CBS is: 'Lucille Ball's family is aware of the project, and doesn't wish to participate at this time.'"

"That was my mother's network for so very many years—and the people there promised me they would never do the Lucille Ball story without the family's involvement," Arnaz told Beck. As the February 10, 1991, airdate approached, Lucie became increasingly vocal in her objections to the TV movie on talk shows and in the press, despite the fact that she was starring in the same network's fledgling month-old series *Sons and Daughters* at the time.

Shortly before *Lucy & Desi: Before the Laughter* aired, Thompson rather arrogantly defended the project to a reporter for Canada's *Globe and Mail*. "I, fortunately, have the luxury of being more objective than Lucie is about her parents. I fantasize that when she and her husband watch the movie they'll say 'we were wrong.' Lucy and Desi came into the living rooms of the American public for four decades and they are truly TV icons. I would do nothing to tarnish that memory."

The telefilm, which drew substantially negative reviews, did not perform up to its subject matter's usual chart-topping standards; it nonetheless ranked in the top twenty for the week, leading the *Los Angeles Times* to conclude, "Despite some negative reviews and criticism from their daughter, Lucie Arnaz, the dramatic biography of Lucille Ball and Desi Arnaz drew strong ratings on CBS Sunday night. It was seen in about 15.3 million households and ranked seventeenth on the list of ninety-four prime-time programs that were broadcast on the four networks last week."

The TV movie's critical pans and less-than-stellar performance constituted sweet victory for Lucie, who later said on her website, "[The movie

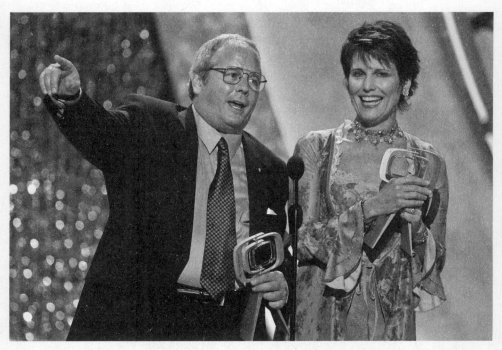

Desi Arnaz Jr. and Lucie Arnaz accept the Legacy of Laughter Award on behalf of their mother Lucille Ball at the 2007 TV Land Awards.
TV LAND

CBS did in 1990] was dreck. But I didn't have to do or say much—the reviewers and the audience said it all for me."

On Monday, September 23, 1991, Desi Arnaz finally took his place in the Academy of Arts & Sciences' Television Academy Hall of Fame alongside Lucille, who had been inducted during the first such ceremony in 1984. And, in a first for a television series, *I Love Lucy* was also named into the Hall of Fame pantheon, as were Leonard Bernstein, James Garner, Danny Thomas, and Mike Wallace.

Desi was cited "not only for making an indelible impression on audiences worldwide through his portrayal of Ricky Ricardo on *I Love Lucy* but also for his innovative off-screen advancements, particularly the development of the three-camera setup still in use today by many television comedies as well as the idea of shooting on film rather than kinescope, thus creating the 'rerun.'"

In its accolades for *I Love Lucy*, the Academy described it as "the classic situation comedy whose worldwide popularity has been unmatched in television history," adding that "its inventive comedy has been frequently imitated but rarely equaled."

The Arnaz children were on hand at the Beverly Hills ceremony to accept the award for their father; and producer-head writer Jess Oppenheimer's widow, Estelle, and series cocreators Madelyn Pugh Davis and Bob Carroll Jr. accepted the award for the show.

In 1992, Desi Jr., who had been residing out of the limelight in Boulder City, Nevada, with wife, Amy, and stepdaughter, Haley, returned to Hollywood to take on the role of his father in the film adaptation of the 1990 Pulitzer Prize–winning novel *The Mambo Kings Play Songs of Love* by Cuban-American writer Oscar Hijuelos. In the film, two Cuban musician brothers seeking fame and fortune in the U.S. during the 1950s are invited by Desi Sr. to perform on *I Love Lucy*, actual scenes of which were intercut with new black-and-white footage of Desi Jr. and the film's other actors, enabling them to play against the "real" Lucille Ball.

Reflecting her displeasure with CBS at this juncture, Lucie took her own documentary version of her parents' story to another network, NBC. On Valentine's Day 1993, the two-hour special, *Lucy & Desi: A Home Movie*, a dual biography featuring interviews with family members, close friends, and coworkers, and exclusive, never-before-publicly-seen family home movies, was produced by Lucie and husband Luckinbill's now-rechristened ArLuck Entertainment.

The documentary, which went on to win an Emmy for Outstanding Informational Special, suffered in the ratings against the debut of CBS's six-hour highly publicized miniseries presentation of *Alex Haley's Queen*, which drew a 22.7 rating and a 35 percent share of that night's audience. Despite this formidable competition, *Lucy & Desi: A Home Movie* averaged a 14.1 rating/21 percent share, landing in solid second place.

A year later, on Valentine's Day 1994, the team of Lucille Ball and Desi Arnaz proved its durability yet again when the cable network Nick at Nite began airing a week-long marathon of restored-to-original-length *I Love Lucy* reruns that led into a regular 9 P.M. weekday berth for the show starting February 21.

But it wasn't until 2003 that a major broadcast network again dipped into the Lucy pond for sweeps fodder. On May 4 of that year, CBS aired the three-hour TV movie *Lucy*, which chronicled Lucille's life, including her personal and professional relationship with Desi, up to the time of their divorce. The old ratings magic proved elusive for the network: less than well-received critically, the TV movie managed to be only a modest success, ranking twenty-first among the week's programs and drawing close to thirteen million viewers.

In 1995, the manuscript of Lucille's unpublished autobiography, *Love, Lucy*, written in 1964 with the aid of magazine journalist Betty Hannah Hoffman, was discovered packed away among the personal possessions of the star's longtime director of publicity, the late Howard McClay. It was put up by Lucille's estate for bids from publishers shortly thereafter. At the time, Lucie Arnaz said in a statement: "I was just as shocked as everyone else when the book was first discovered. I never even knew it existed. She never talked about it. I think she just forgot about it, or maybe she got cold feet."

Lucie further described her mother's autobiography as "the absolute best account of her childhood I have ever read or heard anywhere," adding that "it's fascinating to see how her version of the divorce differs from the one that my father wrote in his book." Lucie ended up writing a foreword to the book, which was ultimately published in 1996 by G.P. Putnam's Sons and peaked at number seven on the *New York Times* best-seller list in October of that year.

Interest in Lucille Ball—and the *Lucy* phenomenon—never waned following the star's death. Lucy: A Tribute, a permanent, 2,200-square-foot heart-shaped exhibit that housed an assortment of Lucille's awards, costumes, personal items, and even her home backgammon table, opened in early 1991 at Universal Studios Hollywood, which once featured Lucille's dressing room on its famed studio tour. Such a huge draw for theme park attendees of all ages, the following year, a counterpart attraction filled with similar artifacts was opened at the studio's Orlando, Florida, theme park.

And in memory of its most famous daughter, Lucille's hometown of Jamestown, New York, hosted the first Lucille Ball Festival of New Comedy, LucyFest, on Memorial Day weekend 1991, presented by the Arts Council for Chautauqua County.

At a news conference promoting her appearance at the second LucyFest in 1992, Lucie Arnaz announced a plan to move her mother's and grandmother's remains from their side-by-side niches at Forest Lawn Cemetery in the Hollywood Hills to Jamestown.

"I haven't told my brother this yet, but my husband and I decided today that we really don't think it's necessary to have my grandmother, DeDe, and my mother in this Forest Lawn place all by themselves over there, when their whole entire family is here," she reasoned. "I'm going to sort of bring it up to the family that we try and move their stones, so everybody can sort of be together. I think they should have a resting place with the rest of the family."

It took more than a decade to accomplish, but the remains of Lucille and her mother were finally reinterred alongside their relatives at Jamestown's Lake View Cemetery in 2003.

By 1994, LucyFest had grown to include an auction of 120 of Lucille's personal items that raised almost $57,000 toward the Chautauqua County Arts Council's establishment of a permanent comedy center in the star's honor in Jamestown. Helped along by proceeds from a second auction and a grant from local office furniture manufacturer Bush Industries, it became a reality two years later, when the sixth annual LucyFest served as the May 25 opening celebration of a 2,100-square-foot museum at 212 Pine Street. By December, attendance had exceeded expectations, topping 8,500.

Named the Lucy-Desi Museum, the concept had been expanded to encompass the life and career of Desi Arnaz as well. Lucie donated more than 2,000 items from the estates of her parents to the museum, including the guestbook from Desi's Corona, California, ranch, a mosaic-patterned dress Lucille wore in *I Love Lucy*, her letters to friends, one of her wigs (still in curlers), her gold 1972 Mercedes-Benz, and a can of henna used to dye her hair.

The new museum also proved a showcase for the Arnaz siblings' other endeavor: Lucy merchandising. Heralding back to the "Desiloot" merchandising glory days of the 1950s, the museum's gift shop offered new lines of Lucy and Desi books, clocks, mugs, T-shirts, dolls, puzzles, and other collectibles, including a $250 music box featuring Lucy Ricardo hawking Vitameatavegamin and a $130 cookie jar shaped like the 1955 Pontiac convertible that took the Ricardos and the Mertzes to California—complete with occupants.

With the Internet boom of the early '90s, sales of unlicensed *Lucy* products such as refrigerator magnets, greeting cards, and bootleg videos proliferated. In response to such pirating, Lucie and Desi Jr. formed their own company—cleverly dubbed Desilu, too—to stake a claim in the control and quality of merchandise bearing their parents' likenesses, sharing the image rights to the Lucy and Ricky Ricardo characters with CBS.

"When Dad struck the deal years ago, he had in the contract certain likeness rights for the characters, too. It was in place from the 1950s," Desi Jr. told the *Miami Herald* in August 2004. By that time, *Lucy* merchandising had become big business.

"It's huge," Bruce Bronn, president and CEO of Unforgettable Licensing, the Illinois entity also representing Desilu, told the *Herald* in the same report. "It does well over $100 million a year retail. And it always goes up because we keep adding products." DVDs, dolls, salt-and-pepper shakers, clothing, a line of candy, and even Las Vegas slot machines were among the nine-hundred-plus products being licensed at that time. Bronn also noted that children between the ages of eight and twelve, who watch reruns on cable and on video, comprised the largest consumer segment for the products.

A ten-year agreement between the Arts Council and Lucille's estate to use the names and likenesses of Lucille Ball and Desi Arnaz expired in March 2002, and after a brief legal battle during which the operation was temporarily closed, control of the museum was transferred from the county to the private not-for-profit Lucille Ball-Desi Arnaz Center, the board of which included Lucie, Desi Jr., and Lucille' longtime secretary Wanda Clark.

The strong continuing appeal of Lucille, Desi, and their legacy was such that in July 1996, an annual gathering in celebration of the iconic star's life and career, was launched in Burbank, California, in time to mark the forty-fifth anniversary of the *I Love Lucy* series. It was organized by Lucille's latter-day public relations representative (and "We Love Lucy" fan club president) Thomas J. Watson.

Called Loving Lucy—billed as the first-ever national Lucy convention—it had lofty aspirations to attract some five hundred fans; by its second day, at least twice that many had packed the event, held at the Burbank Airport Hilton. Featuring auctions, an exhibit floor for merchandisers and collectors, and screenings of the works of Lucille Ball and Desi Arnaz—and anything related to them—the multiday event attracted a global audience and was staged annually until 2001. At its final stanza, a recently unearthed print of the long-shelved *I Love Lucy: The Movie*—the amalgamation of three first-season episodes stitched together with specially shot interstitial footage and intended to play in movie theaters—was screened.

Lucille and Desi's enduring place in the public consciousness was re-affirmed in 1997, when Apple Computer, on the cusp of the legendary comeback that put it in the forefront of personal technology, launched its "Think Different" ad campaign featuring some of the world's most-admired figures portrayed as larger-than-life icons in striking black-and-white photographs. Lucille Ball and Desi Arnaz were featured, along with such out-of-the-box thinkers as Pablo Picasso, Albert Einstein, Alfred Hitchcock, Thomas Edison, Martin Luther King Jr., Amelia Earhart, and Frank Lloyd Wright.

A close-up photo of Lucille and Desi in profile, about to kiss, originally taken as a publicity shot for 1953's *The Long, Long Trailer*, was used extensively in the campaign and for a time dominated a segment of Los Angeles's legendary Sunset Strip, where an award-winning "tall wall" billboard carried their enormous image as a reminder to Hollywood of the great heights that can be scaled in the entertainment business with a little innovation.

The late 1990s brought the beginning of a steady stream of *I Love Lucy*, *The Lucy Show*, and *Here's Lucy* DVDs that continues in the present, among the most recent being the Lucille Ball specials that aired in the 1970s and Desi's *The Mothers-in-Law* series from the late 1960s.

This period also brought the death of Gary Morton, who had been re-married to former golf pro Susie McAllister since 1996. Morton died of lung cancer on March 30, 1999, at the Palm Springs home built by Lucille and Desi at the peak of their popularity, and which Morton had shared with Lucille from their 1961 marriage until her death.

On May 26, 1999, a thirty-three-cent *I Love Lucy* stamp, featuring a black-and-white circa-1955 photograph of Lucille Ball and Desi Arnaz, was issued as part of the United States Postal Service's "Celebrate the Century" stamp series. It was among the public's fifteen selections for stamps commemorating the 1950s. The show was again honored with a stamp—this one featuring Lucille with Vivian Vance in a still from the iconic chocolate factory scene—was issued ten years later as part of the USPS's "Early TV Memories" set of forty-four-cent stamps.

The year 2001 brought with it appropriate hoopla surrounding the ninetieth anniversary of Lucille's birth and the fiftieth anniversary of *I Love Lucy*. Things kicked off in Milwaukee in June with the debut of an *I Love Lucy* Fiftieth Anniversary Tour, a four-room touring county fair exhibit. For a three-dollar premium, fairgoers could tour re-created sets and see authentic costumes and props from *I Love Lucy*.

After its run, the exhibit ended up permanently housed at a newly annexed Desilu Playhouse extension of the Lucille Ball-Desi Arnaz Center in

Jamestown, New York, which during the first part of the new decade would continue to blossom under executive director Ric Wyman. The Jamestown-based museum eventually broadened its scope in the mid-2000s armed with the stated mission "to preserve and celebrate the legacy of Lucille Ball and Desi Arnaz and enrich the world through the healing powers of love and laughter."

On what would have been Lucille's ninetieth birthday on August 6, 2001, the U.S. Postal Service honored the star with the issuance of the thirty-four-cent Lucille Ball commemorative postage stamp. The first day of issue ceremony took place at the Hollywood History Museum, located in the historic Max Factor Building in Hollywood. Lucille's eighty-six-year-old brother, Fred, traveled to Los Angeles from his Cottonwood, Arizona, home to participate in the proceedings.

At 9 P.M. on Monday, October 15, 2001, fifty years to the minute after *I Love Lucy* debuted on CBS, TV Land telecast the first episode aired of the series, "The Girls Want to Go to a Nightclub," as part of a week-long, fifty-episode prime-time marathon of favorite episodes as selected by TV Land and *TV Guide*. For the occasion, the show's original animated Lucy-Desi stick-figure opening credits were re-created, the new versions replacing the Philip Morris branding in the old cartoons with a TV Land logo. The series assumed a regular 9 P.M. weeknight slot on the nostalgia-steeped network's schedule the following week.

Nearly a month later, on Sunday, November 11—an optimal November sweeps berth having been chosen over the actual anniversary date—CBS broadcast the two-hour *I Love Lucy's 50th Anniversary Special* featuring a top-ten countdown of the public's favorite episodes as determined by an online poll. Lucie and Desi Jr., who were executive producers of the show, took their licks for appearing in it as well.

Under the headline "*Lucy* Special Has Some 'Splainin' to Do," the New York *Daily News* review groused, "the most gratuitous segments of the special are explained because the famous couple's children, Lucie Arnaz and Desi Arnaz Jr., control the licensing rights to *I Love Lucy* and are the special's executive producers. What they say goes, so this two-hour special includes way too much Lucie and Desi Jr. when it ought to be Lucy and Desi, period. We see Lucie and Desi Jr. touring their mother's house, singing a song dedicated to their father and—most painfully of all—jumping to the stage with conga drums to join Jorge Moreno in a version of 'Babalu.' That's a lot of *babaloney*."

Not surprisingly, the Arnaz clan, who had provided so many laughs over the decades, had the last one. *I Love Lucy's 50th Anniversary Special* returned the TV's royal family to the top ten, tying CBS's own *Survivor* with an 11.8 rating and an 18 percent share. Hardly the audience numbers of yore, but nevertheless a reflection of the fragmentation of viewership the multichannel universe had wrought on the major networks.

The late 2000s were marked by surprise and tumult for the Arnaz heirs. In September 2008, a report surfaced in the *New York Post* about Cassandria Lucianna Carlson, a thirty-eight-year-old woman claiming to be the granddaughter of Lucille Ball and Desi Arnaz, contending that her deceased mother had been put up for adoption by the famed couple in 1947 for fear that a baby would "derail Ball's plans for stardom."

Carlson had been pursuing her claim for a number of years, and was reportedly in possession of a 2004 letter from Lucie Arnaz saying, "I must inform you we're almost certainly not related. In 1947, my parents were married and wanted nothing more than to have a baby together. They struggled for ten years with infertility and miscarriage until I came along in 1951. My mother would never have given up a child of hers, nor would my father have let her."

The *Post* report also brought to public awareness the existence of Julia Arnaz, another woman who had successfully made a similar assertion—in this case that she was the out-of-wedlock child of Desi Jr.—and whose heritage apparently had been verified by a DNA test. Julia had withdrawn an offer to provide a DNA sample to help verify Carlson's claim, the report said.

As the *Post* explained it, "Julia Arnaz, 39, denies her dad played any role in changing her mind about giving Carlson a DNA sample. However, the Connecticut resident confirmed she initially offered the genetic material to Carlson 'because she's in the same position that I was a long time ago'— referring to a court-ordered paternity test Julia obtained in 1991 from Desi Jr., who impregnated her model mom when he was just 15."

"We're really working on me threading back to the family," Julia told the *Post* at the time.

Lucie Arnaz created headlines in July 2010 by taking legal action in a Los Angeles Supreme Court against Gary Morton's widow, Susie, in an attempt to halt a planned auction of items from Morton's estate.

The cache being put on the block at Heritage Auction Galleries in Beverly Hills included a number of items that had belonged to Lucille; Lucie specifically sought to take possession of seven love letters from her mother to Gary, an address book, some portraits, and several lifetime achievement awards.

Lucie's attorney, Ronald J. Palmieri, in a statement issued to the Associated Press, said, "It is clear these are personal effects earned by a lifetime of work by someone of great stature in the entertainment community. To demean their true nature, and prostitute their value in monetary terms,

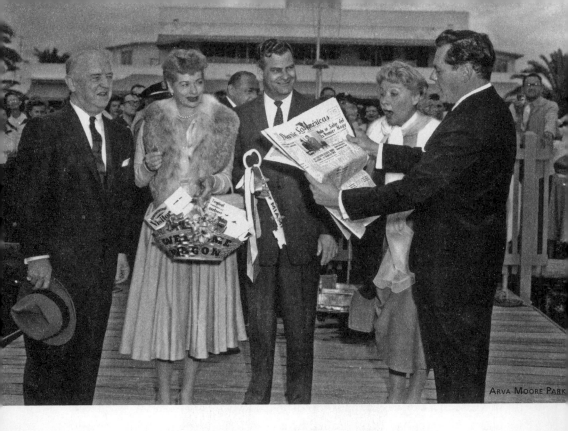

ARVA MOORE PARK

is insulting to Ms. Ball's memory and contravenes her express desire that these items were to belong to her daughter after her death."

An agreement was reached at the eleventh hour, and the awards were returned to Lucie, who planned to have them displayed at the Lucy-Desi Center or another museum, her lawyer said.

At the end of 2008, TV Land, which as the decade progressed had grown less about classic TV and more about attracting a younger demographic, said good-bye to *I Love Lucy* after seven years, sending the venerable series off with a twelve-hour News Year's Eve marathon. Two days later, another marathon kicked off its arrival at its new network home, the Hallmark Channel. In addition, the series still runs in syndication around the country, most notably in Los Angeles, where it is carried multiple times daily by two stations, KTTV and KCOP.

And it's not just the show that has defied the confines of its time. In August 2010, as the series approached its sixtieth anniversary, Desilu Productions was honored with the Philo T. Farnsworth Award at the sixty-second Primetime Emmy Engineering Awards in recognition of its pioneering use of the multiple-camera system of shooting on 35mm film in front of a studio audience, allowing for distribution on high-quality prints and helping establish the syndication business.

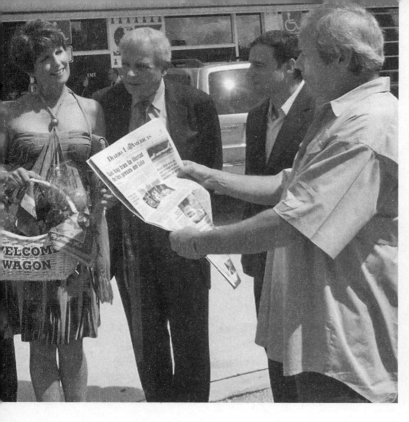

At a 2010 City of Miami ceremony held in conjunction with a show celebrating the music of Desi Arnaz, Lucie Arnaz and Desi Arnaz Jr. (far right) pose with city officials to re-create a photo taken during a visit the *I Love Lucy* cast made to the Florida city in 1956.

JORGE PEREZ/CITY OF MIAMI

And on it will go as long as little children continue to become enchanted by TV's funny woman-child with the harebrained schemes, who is often playfully at odds with her hotheaded Cuban husband. That's because it's a cinch that *I Love Lucy* will transcend for them from an ancient 1950s situation comedy into a lifelong constant that embodies loyalty, laughter, love, and above all, the human condition.

Coyne Steven Sanders and Tom Gilbert
August 2011

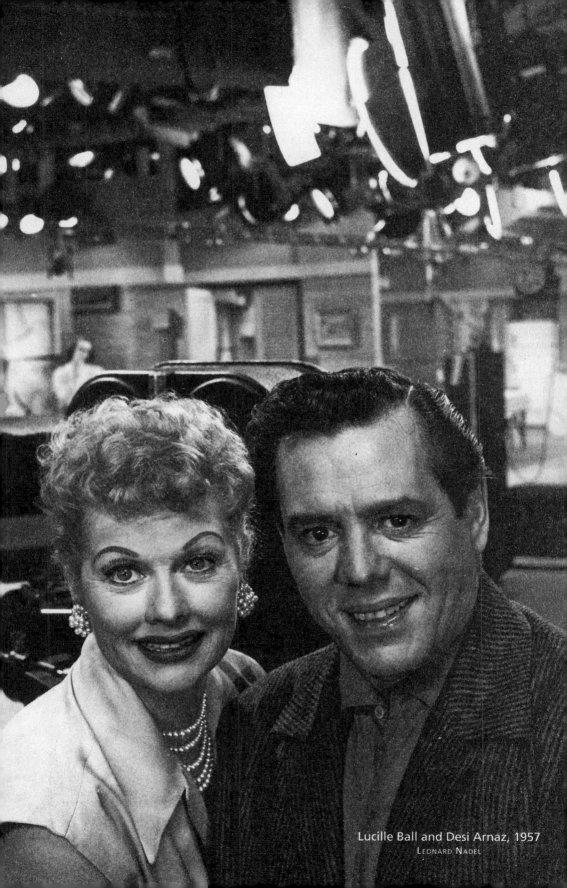

Lucille Ball and Desi Arnaz, 1957
Leonard Nadel

Foreword

★ ★ ★ ★

Foreword to the Fiftieth Anniversary of *I Love Lucy* Edition

**by Madelyn Pugh Davis and Bob Carroll, Jr.,
co-creators and writers, *I Love Lucy***

*T*om Gilbert and Coyne Steven Sanders have done a wonderful job of telling the amazing story of Lucille Ball, Desi Arnaz, *I Love Lucy*, and the Desilu empire. We worked at Desilu for more than twenty years, but Tom and Steve's book told us things we never knew. We say "amazing" story because even though it has been fifty years since *I Love Lucy* first aired, it is still playing in seventy-six countries and has been seen by more than one billion viewers. That's certainly more than those fourteen people in 1951 who stood outside the window to watch the show on that new gadget in the appliance store window.

The huge popularity of *I Love Lucy*, while very gratifying, has always astounded us. People tell us they watch the show over and over. There is an *I Love Lucy* convention every summer in Burbank, California, attended by more than a thousand fans who know all sorts of *Lucy* trivia. One young man at the convention knew all the words and gestures for the "Vitameatavegamin" routine. Others knew the lyrics to *The Pleasant Peasant*, the operetta that Lucy wrote. People have told us that their parents learned English from watching *Lucy* reruns, although we're not sure what kind of English they learned from a man who lives in a "parmen" and keeps asking his "ret-hetted" wife to "'splain."

People often ask why we think *I Love Lucy* has lasted so long. Well, of course, the obvious answer is the incredibly talented Lucille Ball, a beautiful clown and the funniest woman in the whole world. She was a great joy for writers to work for because she would do anything. We'd ask her if it was okay to hit her in the face with chocolate, or if she would set her own nose on fire or minded stamping on grapes. And all Lucy wanted to know was, "Is it funny?"

Someone once queried Desi why the show was so incredibly popular and his answer was, "The credit should be divided among a lot of people. Ninety percent should go to Lucy and the rest of us can split the other ten percent." No one would argue with his evaluation, but he was discounting his own contribution to the success of the show. He proved to be not just a handsome bongo player but an astute businessman who built an empire.

Lucy was in awe of her husband's business ability. We were filming *The Lucy-Desi Comedy Hour* at a small studio called Motion Picture Center. We used two soundstages for the sixty-minute show to accommodate the many sets. We would film the first part, have an intermission, give the audience soft drinks and sandwiches, and then move them into the second stage. During intermission, Desi took a business call. He was negotiating for more studio space, which he now needed for the many new series being produced at Desilu. When he hung up, Lucy announced, "How do you like that! While the audience was out having cold cuts, Desi bought RKO!" This, of course, was the old RKO Studios, where Lucy got her start as a bit player.

We were lucky enough to be writers on *I Love Lucy*, the *Lucy-Desi* hours, *The Lucy Show*, and *Here's Lucy*, and we're glad that Tom and Steve wrote their book telling about these shows and Desilu, so that they can all be preserved as part of television history.

"What does Desilu stand for? It sounds like a past participle of a French verb."

—Thornton Wilder

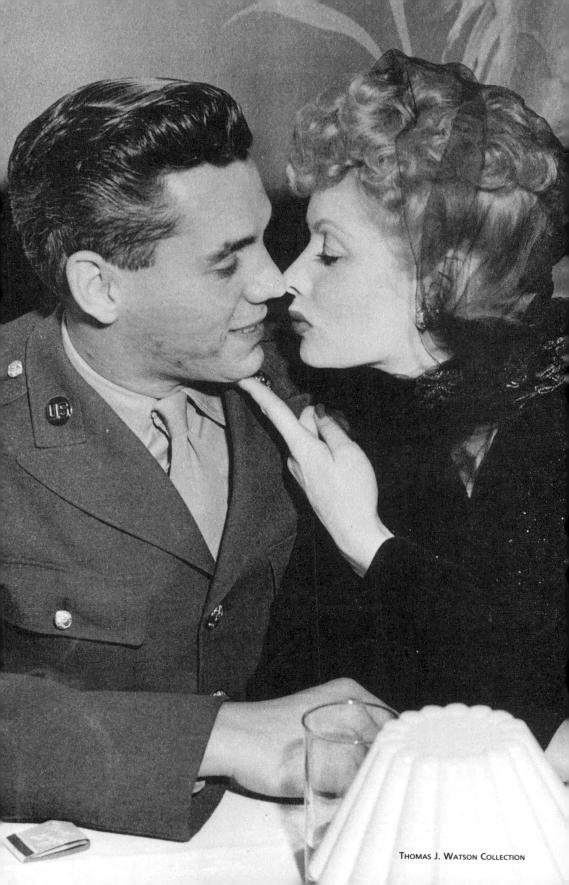

THOMAS J. WATSON COLLECTION

Chapter One

"I am a real ham. I love an audience. I work better with an audience. I am dead, in fact, without one."

—Lucille Ball, 1953

⭐

*T*he year 1947 was a time of great uncertainty for thirty-six-year-old Lucille Ball. A fourteen-year career in mostly mediocre motion pictures had left her financially rewarded but artistically frustrated. With a film actress's greatest opportunity—a shot at major MGM stardom—behind her, not exactly a failure but certainly not a success, she was faced with the brutal reality that odds were she had nowhere to go but down. With no film offers forthcoming—and almost against her will—Lucille would make what would prove to be a very significant choice: to go "legit," or perform in a play, onstage, an area where she had had very little experience.

Dream Girl, a Walter Mitty-esque mixture of comedy and fantasy written by Elmer Rice, was the vehicle that would bring Lucille to the boards. A smash hit on Broadway during the 1945–46 season, it presented the vivid romantic daydreams of a prim bookshop owner. The tour-de-force—and very demanding—part of Georgina Allerton was a plum role Rice had concocted as a gift, of sorts, for wife Betty Field. Lucille, however, would make her debut as Georgina in a less auspicious place than Broadway—she would bow in a summer-stock production one hundred miles away, in Princeton, New Jersey.

The events leading up to Lucille's appearing in *Dream Girl,* however, were not quite the result of her own determined efforts for a stage career. In the early months of 1947, Herbert Kenwith was scouting talent for his upcoming production of the show, which would reopen the McCarter Theater under his auspices that June as part of the Princeton Drama Festival. Lucille had often complained that she was a second-string film actress, losing good parts to Ann Sothern and Ginger Rogers. True to form, she was not Kenwith's first choice for the stage; he originally opted to cast the then-popular Martha Scott. When that actress proved unavailable, the young director happened to read that Lucille was visiting New York, and began a zealous pursuit.

Lucille was staying at the posh Hampshire House on Central Park South, so Kenwith phoned her suite, only to be told by her maid, Harriet, that "Miss Ball was out shopping." When Harriet mentioned that Lucille would return to the hotel very briefly to dress for the theater, Herbert asked which play she would be attending. Harriet revealed Lucille's theater-going plans for the next three nights.

Kenwith hatched a plan. He called in some favors and managed to secure a house seat for each play on the same night Lucille planned to attend. "House seats are usually down in front, and I assumed she had house seats, too, so I'd be sitting near her," recalls the director. "As it turned out on that first night, I was not sitting directly in front of her, but sort of checkerboard in front of her. I kept turning around and looking at her. Every time I'd look at her, she'd catch my eye and look away. She was becoming annoyed, but I wanted her to remember my face. During intermission, we both walked out to the lobby. I kept moving around in front of her. The second night, I was seated about three rows away, so I made a deliberate error and walked into the row in front of her, as if I were looking for my seat. This time I said hello to her. She said hello, nodded her head, and ignored me. The third night, in the lobby, she grabbed me by the arm and said, 'Who the *hell* are you?' I said, 'I'm Herb Kenwith. You don't know it yet, but you're going to do a play for me.' "

"You're out of your *mind,*" she told him. "I'm not going to do a play for anybody."

"Yes, you are. You are going to do a play."

"*What* play?"

"It's called *Dream Girl.*"

"Oh, I wouldn't do *that,*" said Lucille, who had seen the Broadway production. "It's longer than *Hamlet.*"

Despite her protestations, Lucille was intrigued by Kenwith and invited him to lunch with her in her suite the following afternoon. "We had lunch. There were a lot of carrots on the plate. I commented that the carrots matched her hair. 'Well,' she said, 'That was the inspiration for the hair.' " At that moment, two local reporters arrived and began to interview Lucille, asking her what she was doing in New York. When at first she hesitated, one reporter said, "We can't believe you'd come to New York without any plans. Is there some plan that you have?"

Trapped, Lucille—merely in New York on pleasure—stammered, "Well, as a matter of fact, I'm going to do a play." The announcement surprised Kenwith as much as it did the newspapermen. Lucille deftly tossed the ball in Kenwith's direction. "By coincidence, this is my producer. He's going to produce and direct a play for me." Kenwith announced that Miss Ball's upcoming play would be *Dream Girl*. "The next day I got a copy of the paper and went to Actor's Equity. I said, 'I don't have a contract with Miss Ball, but will this interview constitute a contract?' They told me that it might not stand up but, on the face of it, it was like a contract because she was quoted about doing the play and had made a commitment." He visited Lucille later that week.

"Here's a copy of *Dream Girl*," he said as he handed her the script.

"What the hell for?" she retorted.

"You're going to do the play at Princeton."

"You're crazy."

"No, you're going to do it. You have to do it. You made a commitment in the newspaper to do this play."

"You know this is blackmail?"

"Yes, I know it. But I want you to do this play."

As Kenwith recalls, "It was all done with a sense of humor. There was no anger at all. I think she was amused because, as young as I was, I had trapped her into something." She told him she would do it only if she could memorize the script in "three or four days." A Columbia University professor worked with Lucy around the clock. "Lucy did learn it very quickly," recalls Kenwith, "in less than the three or four days she said she wanted to learn it. It was remarkable. She became intrigued with it. Finally, she consented to do it."

She signed a contract with theatrical producer Jules J. Leventhal at two thousand dollars a week-plus 50 percent of any profits to star in the Herbert Kenwith–Harold Kennedy production directed by Jus Addis. Also in the cast were Scott McKay, Hayden Roarke, and Barbara Morrison. Launching a six-month tour, the play opened June 10 at the McCarter Theater in Princeton, New Jersey. "In rehearsals, she was wonderful," Kenwith remembers. "Nervous as could be, but very sweet. She didn't have the kind of tension that she developed later. She was always onstage, marking it for herself and, without other actors, doing her lines and moving into positions." Her calm demeanor dissipated opening night. "She was so nervous and so frightened that she became very short with everybody. Myself included. But I understood her tension. All the tension she had saved all week just came out, yelling at everyone, being unreasonable—on the surface. She started yelling at me, and I said to her, 'Miss Ball, you must remember one thing—I don't work for you. You work for *me*.' "

Her anger turned to sheer panic for a moment when the curtain went up opening night. "When the cue was given to roll the bed she was in

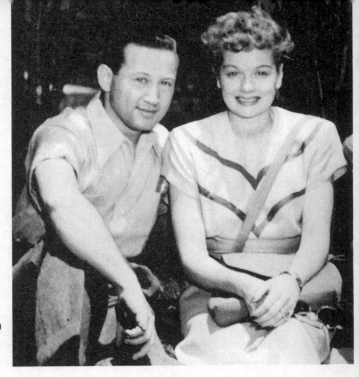

Herbert Kenwith with
his *Dream Girl*,
Lucille Ball, 1947
COURTESY HERBERT KENWITH

forward, she said, 'Oh, Christ!' as soon as she saw the audience. Eleven hundred seats. She just stared for a few moments. At one point in the bar scene, she went up on her lines. Scott McKay was sitting with her. She picked up a drink and said to him, 'Well, don't just sit there. Say something.' She had such presence. So, of course, he led her back into the dialogue. And she got great reviews. She was marvelous."

The experience proved invaluable to Lucille, prompting her to remark during the tour, "You haven't been in show business until you've been on the stage. I know what it is to experience poor houses in remote sections and big audiences in major centers. And I've learned how you have to modify and key everything that you do to the public you're playing for."

Lucille displayed a rather extraordinary amount of loyalty to her fellow cast members. At one point in the tour, the box office took an unexpected slump, and the producers asked cast members to take a salary cut. She insisted that, as the highest-paid performer in the troupe, she alone take a pay reduction, and told the producers to charge her for any deficit incurred in maintaining the other actors' salaries. The production arrived at the Biltmore Theater in Los Angeles the first week of January. It was then that *Dream Girl* turned into a nightmare. It started out well enough. The *Los Angeles Times* gave the play—and particularly Lucille—a rave notice: "Here is a young lady of the films who could, if she would, have a dazzling footlight career . . . she is, in a sense, wasting her talents in pictures . . . Miss Ball is a striking presence in the footlight world." The

12

production, concluded the reviewer, was "completely satisfying." *The Hollywood Reporter* added more praise for Lucille: "That she defines her current many-sided stage role with so much meaning and conviction is another way of saying she is an actress with a capital 'A'—something the studios should realize."

Reviewers were unaware that, as the show prepared to open in Los Angeles, first, the rest of the company—and finally Lucille—were stricken with the so-called "Virus *X*," a mysterious malady for which there was no treatment. An urgent call went out to June Havoc (a replacement in the original Broadway production) to step in for the ailing star, but by the next day she, too, was stricken with the virus, and further performances were canceled. "I went back, but we'd lost a week then," said Lucille. "All the people around town that we'd wanted to see the show came, but I wasn't there. We could have run for weeks, but the show closed shortly after I went back."

Further alarming Lucille was the fact that her own marquee value was not particularly potent. *Variety* noted, "Lucille Ball in *Dream Girl* drew rave notices but unaccountably failed to do business . . . only about half-full, despite raves." The Los Angeles experience was particularly disappointing because Lucille had been driven throughout the entire tour by the knowledge that a good performance there could revitalize her stalled film career. And, as she neared forty, Lucille Ball's prolific if not distinguished film career—giving her the dubious distinction of being known around town as "Queen of the B's"—was now precariously on the edge of taking a sharp downward slide.

Her sometimes tempestuous off-camera life offered little comfort.

Lucille had, by this point, weathered several often stormy and head-line-bannered years of marriage to Cuban bandleader Desi Arnaz. The two first met in June 1940, when both were cast in the RKO film version of the hit Richard Rodgers–Lorenz Hart musical *Too Many Girls* in which Arnaz had appeared on Broadway. The handsome, extroverted twenty-three-year-old Arnaz was already infamous for his generous appetites for women, fast living, fast cars, and high-stakes gambling. He also, from the start, possessed a highly developed flair for showmanship and self-promotion.

Wanting to make a splash upon his arrival on the West Coast in 1940, Desi drove into Hollywood, first buying a flashy Buick Roadmaster convertible in Detroit. After stopping to ask directions to the studio, Desi, accompanied by a valet in full uniform, headed down Gower Street toward the RKO Studios lot. Spotting a huge archway, they turned in and asked to be directed to the casting office. The man at the gate wryly remarked that he was "a little early," Arnaz having driven into the Hollywood Memorial Park Cemetery. Finally locating adjacent RKO, Desi with great authority told the studio guard at the entrance gate that he was "Mister Arnaz from New York" and was waved right in. By the next day, however, the guard had been alerted to Desi's ploy, flatly telling him to park "where all the other goddamned actors park."

Lucille and Desi first met in the RKO commissary. Expecting a typical ingenue, Desi was startled to see Lucille, looking "like a two-dollar whore who had been badly beaten by her pimp, with her hair all over her face and a black eye, and she was dressed in a cheap costume." For a knock-about catfight scene with Maureen O'Hara in *Dance, Girl, Dance,* she had been costumed as third-rate burlesque queen. Lucille stopped by to greet George Abbott, seated with Desi Arnaz. After she left, Desi asked, "Who the hell was that?" When the producer told him it was Lucille Ball, the ingenue in *Too Many Girls,* Desi retorted, "That's Lucille Ball, and she's gonna do the ingenue thing? You gotta be kidding."

That same afternoon, Desi was rehearsing a number for the picture with a pianist when Lucille strolled in. As he recalled, "She was dressed in a pair of tight-fitting beige slacks and a yellow sweater, with beautiful blond hair and big blue eyes. I said to the piano player, 'Man, that is a hunk of woman!' " Desi was unaware that it was the same woman he had met earlier until told by his accompanist. Turning on his consid-erable Latin charm, he cooed, "Would you like me to teach you how to rumba? It may come in handy for your part in the picture." She accepted his invitation to join him and other cast members to visit a "swinging Mexican restaurant" where, he later recalled, "we danced all night, had dinner, and everybody got loaded."

The following Sunday, Desi and his date, Renée DeMarco, nicknamed "Freckles" and half of the Dancing DeMarcos team, were invited to a party in Malibu hosted by *Too Many Girls* costar Eddie Bracken. During the party, Desi deposited "Freckles" with Van Johnson, and strolled along the beach. He found Lucille sitting alone near the shore. It was the first time they had seen each other since their night on the town. "I did not go back to the Hollywood Roosevelt," said Desi. "I went to Lucille's apartment, and that was our first night together."

However much of a tough-talking, brittle demeanor Lucille had cul-tivated to survive in Hollywood, she was, in many ways, highly con-servative, insecure, and quite shy. Born on August 6, 1911, she was a beautiful child blessed with an arresting mix of Irish, Scottish, and French ancestry. Her birthplace was Jamestown, New York, a farming and man-ufacturing town about sixty miles south of Buffalo. In 1915, Lucille's father, Henry Dunnell Ball, who worked as a telephone lineman, contracted typhoid fever at the age of twenty-three and died. At the time of his death, Lucille's mother, Desirée (DeDe) Evelyn Hunt, was pregnant with another child, born on July 17, 1915, named Fred after Lucille's grandfather. After Henry's death, the family moved in with DeDe's parents, Fred, an eccentric Socialist, and his wife, Florabelle. Lucille formed a close bond with "Grandpa Hunt," who became a substitute father figure and instilled in young Lucille her first interest in show business by taking the family to three-a-day vaudeville shows that traveled through Jamestown. Lucille and her friends put on short revues, and Grandpa Hunt lavishly praised his granddaughter for her many performances in school plays.

In the summer of 1926, fifteen-year-old Lucille abandoned high school and ventured to Manhattan, where she enrolled in the Anderson-Milton School, founded by Broadway producer John Murray Anderson and stage director Robert Milton. Lucille's stint as a student lasted only six weeks. ("I was a tongue-tied teenager spellbound by the school's star pupil— Bette Davis.") Lucille fared so poorly that her instructor wrote to Mrs. Ball: LUCY'S WASTING HER TIME AND MINE. SHE'S TOO SHY AND RETICENT TO PUT HER BEST FOOT FORWARD.

Lucille briefly went back to Jamestown, but at the age of sixteen was determined to return to New York City and try her luck in breaking into show business. Lucy eventually landed a job with designer Hattie Carnegie as a twenty-five-dollar-a-week dress model at her salon on East Forty-ninth Street near Fifth Avenue. While working at the salon, Lucille suddenly collapsed one afternoon before being diagnosed, as she would later claim, with a form of crippling rheumatoid arthritis. She returned to Jamestown, using crutches for several months. She graduated to the use of a cane and six months later was able to walk unassisted. "I used to get up in the middle of the night and practice walking around in my room without the cane, figuring that if I fell on my face, no one but I would know it," she later confessed.

Lucille returned to New York City and got her first big break. She was chosen by Liggett & Myers as "the Chesterfield Girl." Her next big break came not long after. "Walking up Broadway past the Palace Theater building one boiling hot July day, I ran into Sylvia Hahlo, a theatrical agent. 'How would you like to go to Hollywood?' she asked. 'I'd do anything to get out of the heat!' She had just come from the office of Jim Mulvey, Sam Goldwyn's New York representative." Lucille immediately visited Mulvey, who offered her the opportunity to go to Hollywood as one of of twelve "Goldwyn Girls" set to appear in, and promote, the upcoming Samuel Goldwyn production of *Roman Scandals* starring banjo-eyed comedian Eddie Cantor.

Lucille was given a six-week guarantee at seventy-five dollars per week, with transportation and living expenses paid for by the studio. The dozen girls (including Barbara Pepper, who would remain a lifelong friend) were sent on the Twentieth Century Limited from Grand Central Station to Hollywood the following Saturday. While Lucille jumped at the chance to move to California, her subsequent year and a half with Goldwyn found her growing increasingly impatient. "I was tired of being a bewigged and bejeweled mannequin, posturing and posing. I wanted *action*." She asked for her release and signed with Columbia Pictures as a stock player. "It was one continuous shower bath of Vichy water and lemon-meringue pie. I was the 'she-Stooge' to the Three Stooges, and I loved every minute of it."

After an absence from Jamestown of several years, she missed her family terribly. On the strength of her $125-a-week Columbia paycheck (which often amounted to triple that with overtime), Lucille sent for them, first bringing in her nineteen-year-old brother, Fred, who at the time was working in the nightclub at New York's Waldorf-Astoria Hotel. The day after she wired the money for Fred's move, however, Columbia's stock company was suddenly dissolved, and she found herself out of work. Fortunately, a showgirl call at RKO "an hour and a half after being let out of Columbia" led to a fifty-dollar-a-week contract as a stock player. Eventually, Lucille also sent to Jamestown for her mother, her eccentric grandfather, Fred Hunt, and her cousin Cleo Mandicos—Florabelle had died of cancer in 1921—and they all lived together, for a time, in a rented "tiny house" on North Ogden Drive above Sunset Boulevard in West Hollywood.

Film roles expanded from work as an extra to bit parts to featured roles. Yet despite churning out dozens of films during her early RKO days, Lucille found time for a number of romances, with, among others, director Alexander Hall, RKO mogul Pandro S. Berman, tough-guy actor Broderick Crawford (resulting in a brief 1938 engagement), William Holden, actor-gangland figure George Raft as well as Raft's friend and bodyguard, Mack ("Killer") Grey, who reportedly also had strong ties with organized crime. "It was not until I met Desi that I knew I was in love and with the man I wanted for the father of my children," she later noted.

Desiderio Arnaz y de Acha III was born on March 2, 1917, in Santiago, Cuba, where his father was mayor. His mother, Dolores (known as "Lolita"), was said to be one of the "ten most beautiful women in Latin

America." By the age of sixteen, Desi had his own boat, automobile, and a stable of horses. "The world was my oyster," said Desi. "What I wanted I only needed to take." The 1933 Batista political revolution shattered Desi's world, stripping his family of wealth, property, and power. His father was jailed in Morro Castle along with the entire Cuban Senate. His mother was forced to flee with young Desi to the home of an aunt in Havana—"I had to run for my life from a Cuban firing squad," he claimed. Desi and his mother spent six months and their remaining five hundred dollars in a successful attempt to free his imprisoned father, released only because U.S. officials believed him to have remained "neutral" during the revolt. The elder Arnaz then fled to Miami, Florida, followed not long afterward by Desi, with Dolores later joining them.

Tiring of a succession of menial odd jobs—including cleaning bird cages—Desi decided to exploit his amateur singing and guitar-playing experience and bluffed his way into a drum-playing gig with a band at a jai-alai fronton. He got his first break of any consequence in 1937, when he successfully auditioned with his most popular number, "Babalu," at the Roney-Plaza Hotel for an opening as a singing guitarist. He was spotted by bandleader Xavier Cugat, "king" of Latin dance music, who hired Desi to join his orchestra as vocalist. He soon left Cugat to form his own Latin band and launched the conga craze that swept America. While appearing at New York's LaConga nightclub in the summer of 1939, he was approached by lyricist Lorenz Hart (who had reportedly seen Desi's act at the Miami Beach version of the LaConga club) and his partner, composer Richard Rodgers. They expressed interest in casting Desi as the Latin lover third-male lead in their upcoming college-football musical, *Too Many Girls*. Upon the Broadway opening at the Imperial Theater on October 18, 1939, the inexperienced but charismatic Arnaz was an immediate hit with a show-stopping conga routine, and was brought to Hollywood to recreate his role in the RKO film version of *Too Many Girls*.

It was not only his exploits as a real-life Latin lover but also separations caused by Lucille's Hollywood commitments and his constant on-the-road bookings with his band that caused inevitable separation and friction first in their courting and later in their marriage. Both were temperamental, volatile, and stubborn, and at first such obstacles and spirited battles only acted as a powerful aphrodisiac, further intensifying their almost overpowering passion. His possessive nature prompted Desi to begin calling her "Lucy"—"I never liked 'Lucille,' " said Desi. "That name had been used by other men. 'Lucy' was mine alone."

"Lucille always said that she had fallen in love with my father, who was Greek—and tall, dark, and handsome with an accent," recalls Lucille's cousin Cleo. "That was her role model. So when Desi came along, that was her 'Uncle George.' "

And, notes Lucie Arnaz, "There's something in the kind of man you choose, the strength of the kind of man you choose. She knew what she was doing when she chose my father. She knew that he was a man who loved women, a 'Latin lover.' She always went after people like that, and kind of liked the challenge. It made her feel really womanly to have a guy who is clearly the 'lover boy,' and 'lover boy' falls in love with you, the clown. How fabulous that would make you feel."

Desi was quite aware of the publicity value of their tempestuous romance. During one interview immediately following their marriage, he turned to Lucille and said, with great passion, "Darling, I love you more than Antony loved Cleopatra, more than . . . " Abruptly, he turned back to the reporter and asked, "Did you get that down? I'll repeat it. 'Darling, I love you more than . . . ' "

Long-distance telephone calls between the two—which Lucille later estimated to cost more than $29,000 and mostly comprised of the shouted word "WHAT?" during bad phone connections—contained equal mixtures of incredible longing and inflamed jealousy, each often accusing the other of rampant infidelity. During Lucille's publicity jaunt to Milwaukee to promote *Too Many Girls,* Desi accused her of having an affair with the town's handsome mayor. During Desi's four-week engagement at New York's Roxy Theater, Lucille, in turn, burned up the telephone lines, saying, "You Cuban son of a bitch, where were you all last night? What are you trying to do, lay every goddamned one of those chorus girls in *Too Many Girls?* No wonder they picked you for the show!"

After several months of escalating passion, accusations, and separations, to promote *Dance, Girl, Dance,* Lucille arrived in New York in late November during Desi's Roxy engagement. Between shows, Desi ran over to visit Lucille at the Pierre Hotel, where he found her concluding an interview with fan-magazine writer Eleanor Harris. Lucille detailed all the reasons why she and Desi would not marry, insisting, "It could never work—I wouldn't want to end up one of those neglected musician's wives who sit home doing needlepoint while their husbands are barnstorming around the country." Despite Lucille's protestations, her cousin Cleo remembers her sole motivation: "She went to New York to corral the Cuban."

When they were finally alone, Desi proposed, revealing he had already made all arrangements for them to elope—they would leave for Connecticut the next morning at 6:00 A.M., just enough time to tie the knot before his first eleven o'clock show at the Roxy. Justice of the Peace John P. O'Brien performed the wedding ceremony on Saturday, November 30, 1940, at the Byram River Beagle Club. The marriage license had Lucille list her age as "twenty-six" (when she was actually twenty-nine), while Desi, twenty-three, added two years to reduce the six-year age difference of the couple.

"My friends gave the marriage six months," said Lucille. "I gave it six weeks." For his part, Desi offered, "It's amazing that two people from such different backgrounds and geographical origins ever got together. That was perhaps part of our attraction and also, I am sure, the cause of many of our arguments, fights, and other problems."

The Arnaz marriage crumbled to such a point that Lucille separated from "Staff Sgt. Arnaz" on September 6, 1944, and filed her divorce suit the next day. While Lucille told Hollywood columnist Louella Parsons the estrangement was due to "a clash of temperaments," she privately told Desi years later her divorce action was actually the result of her firm belief that he was "screwing everybody at Birmingham Hospital" near Van Nuys, California, where he was stationed with the Army Medical Corps.

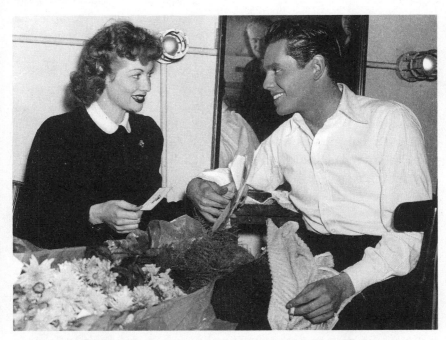

Just married: the Arnazes backstage at the Roxy Theatre, November 30, 1940

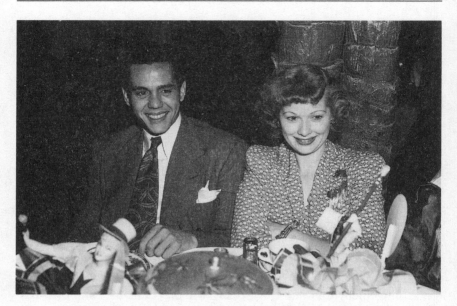

Newlyweds Desi and Lucille on their honeymoon, 1940
RICK CARL COLLECTION

Despite the pending divorce, the couple spent the night together on October 15, 1944. Although her interlocutory decree was granted the very next day, it was void since California law at the time stipulated that if the parties cohabitated during the one-year waiting period, the final divorce decree would not be granted.

Soon after, Desi and Lucille returned to their five-acre ranchito in Chatsworth, California, which they had purchased during Lucille's RKO tenure several years before. Taking a cue from Mary Pickford and Douglas Fairbanks, Sr.'s famous estate, "Pickfair," they christened the spread a combination of their given names, "Desilu," an appellation they would apply to a number of their possessions, including a cabin cruiser and, ultimately, to the studio that would symbolize the great success of their union. The couple managed to purchase the San Fernando Valley property—complete with house, pool, and 350 orange trees—for only $14,500, but, as Lucille later quipped, "It's just big enough and not small enough so that we lose money on it all the time."

Their deep love and continuing passion managed, for a time, to keep the spectacularly mismatched couple together. "I knew there was never anyone in the world for me but Desi," said Lucille, "and that we might have our ups and downs, just as many people have. But I'd rather quarrel and make up with him than anyone else in the world."

"They just had so much stacked against them from the beginning," notes *Hollywood Reporter* columnist Robert Osborne, who befriended Lucille in the late 1950s. "I met Desi's mother. His father had long since died. She used to sit quietly in the corner and knit. That's the whole culture he came from. So when Desi hit New York, and was such a sensation with Cugat, and then café society, dating debutante Brenda Frazier, the success of *Too Many Girls*—he was a hotshot who goes out to California. He meets Lucille Ball, who gets bigger billing than he does in the movie. She's the star of the film. That was something that his Cuban culture upbringing just couldn't handle. He was used to the little woman sitting there while the man went out, tomcatting around, and got his woman pregnant. Lucy's a dynamo, a bigger star at RKO than he was. The war comes along, she moves to MGM, he goes to MGM, does a sensational role in *Bataan* that probably would have made him important, but he's in the service at this point. He comes back, and she's an even bigger star.

"I know some of the scrapbooks she had. I remember reading them and wondering why they would keep some of the reviews. They were supposedly his reviews, but they would say things like, when he opened at Ciro's, the big draw of the night was not bandleader Arnaz, but Lucille Ball, sitting front and center. And predicting that if she showed up a lot, it would help keep Ciro's filled. And when he came back from the war, he was nothing, doing *Hollywood in Havana* and *Cuban Pete*—all those 'B-minus' [late 1940s] pictures. With the male ego—particularly a Latin male ego—I don't think there's any way she could have won."

"Both of us have been sickened and frustrated many times by conflicting careers," said Lucille candidly of these years. "I lost him once and got him back. I have had to plot, scratch, and connive to hold a husband."

Lucille plotted to keep her career on track as well. Although by 1947 she could still often command in the neighborhood of $75,000 per picture, the actress was already in danger of losing coveted leading roles to younger, fresher ingenues. Her much-publicized ascent in 1942 from RKO contract player to featured Metro-Goldwyn-Mayer star—after a critically acclaimed dramatic performance as a nightclub singer crippled by a gangster in *The Big Street*—resulted in only nine film roles during her tenure at that studio, most of them ill-suited to her innate though largely untapped comedic skills. And while Lucille would be rewarded with good reviews in pictures clearly wasting her talents, MGM seemed unable to find the proper vehicles to showcase her and dropped her option after only three years.

By 1945, she was eager to free-lance upon the expiration of her contract. She made a number of pictures of varying quality, including the romantic comedy *Lover Come Back* and two melodramatic thrillers, *Dark Corner* and *Lured*. Upon completion of *Lured* in January of 1947, Lucille reported to Columbia, where she and Franchot Tone costarred in the frothy but belabored comedy *Her Husband's Affairs*. No immediate film offers followed the Columbia release, and Lucille Ball's career neared a standstill. It was then that she focused her attentions on developing a radio career.

"Desi was on the road with his band," Lucille recounted. "I was on layoff at the studio at the time, and if I didn't get paid for doing a radio show, they couldn't do anything about it. I must have done thirty or thirty-five shows in two weeks." One such appearance in this period had her guesting on a special May 27, 1947, Bob Hope broadcast emanating from Detroit. Desi was also on the same program, having augmented his nightclub engagements by serving as musical director on Bob Hope's weekly radio series during the 1946–47 season.

Desperately wanting to salvage a marriage once again on the verge of collapse, Lucille joined Desi as often as possible at various locales across the country as Hope presented special broadcasts of his weekly program from such cities as Toledo, Atlanta, Philadelphia, Washington, and New York. After the Hope show folded for the summer, Desi and his band set out on engagements across the country. A lonely and frustrated Lucille—desperately wanting to have a baby—frequently lamented, "You can't have children on the phone."

"We'd either make love like mad or fight like hell," wrote Desi of this period. "Lucy and I had two of the worst years we ever had."

January of 1948 brought Lucille a "one-picture" deal at Columbia. The film, titled *Pink Lady,* was to roll in February. Columbia mogul Harry Cohn was said to be "thinking out loud" about how good Lucille Ball would be in his film version of *Born Yesterday,* but she was once again rejected in favor of a bigger-name star—Rita Hayworth, for whom Cohn had originally bought the property. Cohn's momentary indecision on choosing Ball or Hayworth for *Born Yesterday* cost Lucille *Pink Lady;* ironically, Hayworth's battles with Cohn cost Rita the part, and Judy Holliday eventually was cast. A team of Jack Benny's radio writers concocted expressly for Lucille and Desi a Broadway-bound play, *Hey, Señorita,* "full of South American, Broadway and Hollywood stuff." The theatrical impresario Shubert brothers reportedly sought the Arnazes to star in a proposed new musical, *Casa McClusky.* United Artists considered Lucille and Desi to costar in a film based on roving war photographer Robert Capa's autobiography, *Slightly Out of Focus,* Desi playing Capa and Lucille "as the gal who does *not* wind up with him." Ultimately, nothing materialized on any front.

Lucille was alerted that a Bob Hope comedy, *Sorrowful Jones* (a remake of the Damon Runyon tale *Little Miss Marker*), was to begin shooting at Paramount on April 7, with no leading lady chosen only days before filming was to commence. Paramount wavered on casting Lucille until Bob Hope publicly campaigned on her behalf. "She'd be tops," he said. "I want her to get it." *Sorrowful Jones* was a huge hit and grossed double of any Hope picture to that time.

When *Sorrowful* finished shooting in June, Lucille again turned her attentions to radio, signing with Columbia Broadcasting System to star in a one-shot pilot episode for a domestic situation comedy titled *My Favorite Husband,* the brainchild of CBS vice president Harry Ackerman. On one of his frequent business flights from New York to Los Angeles, he had read the amusing novel *Mr. and Mrs. Cugat.* "It was a funny look at a marriage between two wildly different types," recalled Ackerman. "I thought it had terrific possibilities as a radio show and it seemed like a great vehicle for [Lucille]." CBS executive Martin Leeds, however, remembers that Lucille wanted the part so badly that her agent, Don Sharpe, offered his client's services at no cost so that she would be cast in the *Husband* pilot. "You have nothing to lose," Sharpe said to Leeds. "I'll give you Lucy for *free.*"

The novel was adapted for radio by *Ozzie and Harriet* writers Frank Fox and Bill Davenport. Lucille was cast as Liz Cooper, a slightly daffy—but intelligent—housewife. Husband George (Lee Bowman) was the fifth vice president of a midwestern bank. CBS aired the pilot as a "one-shot filler" on July 15, and the network, said *Variety,* "hit the situation comedy jackpot," the program enriched by "adult, smart scripting." The success of *My Favorite Husband* caught CBS by surprise, the episode rushed on the air due to production delays on another new radio comedy, *Our Miss Brooks.* The role of wisecracking high school teacher Connie Brooks was first rejected by Shirley Booth (for whom it was originally conceived), passed over by Joan Blondell, and then, reportedly, offered to Lucille, who also declined. Eve Arden was chosen so late that *Our Miss Brooks* missed its proposed premiere by one week, prompting CBS to air the *My Favorite Husband* pilot. Although sans sponsor, CBS announced that it would produce new episodes and air *Husband* beginning July 23, confident it would soon attract advertisers.

Lee Bowman dropped out due to other commitments and was replaced by thirty-four-year-old Richard Denning, a second-string leading man

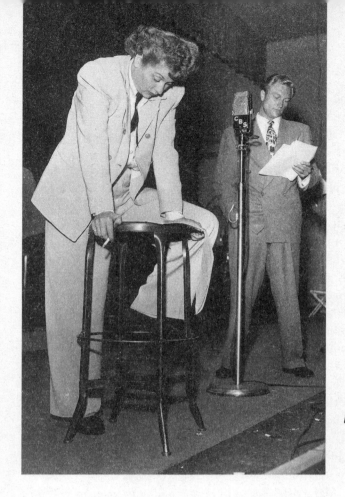

My Favorite Husband: Lucille and Richard Denning
THOMAS J. WATSON COLLECTION

best known for his role opposite Dorothy Lamour in *Beyond the Blue Horizon.* The teaming of Ball and Denning on the premiere show, noted *Variety,* "was admirable and effective." The show, said the trade paper, was "good and fast entertainment." New supporting-cast members included Gale Gordon and Bea Benaderet as an older, more affluent couple. Gordon was cast as Denning's bank-president boss; Benaderet played his wife, Liz's best friend and coconspirator in their running battle of the sexes.

After the first ten installments, writers Fox and Davenport had to return to *Ozzie and Harriet* in September for the new radio season. Based on the strong recommendations of the *Ozzie* writers, Ackerman assigned the CBS staff writing team of Madelyn Pugh and Bob Carroll, Jr., to *My Favorite Husband.* The two already had to their credit *The People Next Door* radio series "which was about a married couple," recalls Pugh. "We found we liked to do domestic comedy." At the time of the departure of Fox and Davenport, Bob and Madelyn were writing domestic comedy segments for Steve Allen's half-hour radio show, *It's a Great Life.* So eager were they to write *Husband,* the pair paid Steve Allen one hundred

24

dollars to write his own material for his show one week to allow them time to write a free-lance script for Ackerman's consideration. The CBS programming executive was so pleased with the results that he assigned Pugh and Carroll to the Ball program.

Already Lucille's strong personality had manifested. According to her brother, Fred, Lucille was always "up-front—a family trait." And, adds Lucie Arnaz, "She wasn't very tactful. She would use a defensive way of getting something across. Maybe she was just terrified of hurting someone's feelings, so she'd just crash on ahead and get it over with."

"They had a lot of problems," admits Madelyn. "The producer-director [Gordon Hughes] was not strong—he just couldn't handle Lucy. She was very apprehensive, and so she was being troublesome. This went on for about six weeks." Ackerman moved to replace Hughes and brought in writer-producer Jess Oppenheimer, who had managed successfully to handle the formidable Fanny Brice on her radio series. "He had the knowledge we didn't," says Pugh. "We were just green as grass. He came on, and they put us with him, and from then it worked."

Oppenheimer described his first several weeks on the program as "idyllic," the calm suddenly shattered when the three writers submitted a script, he recalled, "that just didn't work. And it was the only one we had. Bob and Madelyn and I worked through the night. We were confident that we had saved the script. We weren't too proud of the very last line, but the rest of it was good, and we had all day to work on that one last line. We were happy."

The next day Jess, Lucille, and agent Sharpe met in Oppenheimer's office to read the revised script. "She was delighted as she read along," Jess recalled. "Time after time, she laughed uproariously, in that wonderful, abandoned way she had, and we all laughed with her. I thought we were home free, until she came to that last line. She screamed and she yelled, and she swore, and she threw the script across the room. Then she got it and tore it up in pieces and threw it again. She roared—in that horrible, abandoned way she had. She bellowed, 'I won't do this shit!' After she finished this nonstop salvo, I walked over to her and said, 'Lucy, I thought we had a team effort going here. We're happy to stay up all night or all week, and break our butts to make the script right for you. But not if you're going to ignore a major rewrite which you loved, and crucify us over one little line, which can easily be fixed. We need quite a bit more respect than that.' I took her hand and shook it and said, 'I can't say it has been a pleasant experience working with you, but at least it's over.' "

Oppenheimer stormed out with Don Sharpe in pursuit. "She's crying and hysterical," the agent told Jess. "She knows she was wrong. She agrees with you and wants to apologize." Jess accepted Lucille's apology, but insisted she apologize to Bob and Madelyn. They went down to the studio and found the two, who knew nothing of what had transpired. "Lucille put her arms around their shoulders, and as she walked them across the stage said, 'I've been a shit.' After the rehearsal, Bob and Madelyn came up to me and said, 'What the hell was that all about?' "

Madelyn remembers a moment when Lucille took her to the side of the stage for a private moment "because I was a woman, I guess. She said, 'I've been awful, and I'm sorry.' I said, 'Oh, that's all right.' I was just so scared. She had some bad advice. People told her to come in and be strong, so she came in telling everybody what to do. I was twenty-six and had never met a movie star. I was terrified."

The rehearsal and taping schedule of *Husband* was flexible enough to allow Lucille freedom to accept outside roles until the series went off the air on March 31, 1951. On December 8, 1949, she made a leap into television playing a dance hostess in a sketch teaming her with Peter Lind Hayes in *Inside USA with Chevrolet,* which aired on local Los Angeles station KTTV. She returned to Columbia to star with William Holden in the comedy *Miss Grant Takes Richmond.* Lucille's excellent reviews for *Sorrowful Jones,* released in June, prompted Paramount to team her again with Bob Hope in *Fancy Pants,* a remake of *Ruggles of Red Gap.* Opposite Victor Mature, Lucille was cast—and her talents largely wasted—as a wisecracking secretary in the football drama *Easy Living.* Lucille's facile comedic performance ("first-class," said *The Hollywood Reporter*) in *Miss Grant Takes Richmond,* however, so pleased Columbia that the studio quickly cast her with Eddie Albert in *The Fuller Brush Girl,* which *Variety* deemed a "rollicking, slam-bang, slapstick comedy with Lucille Ball at her very best."

Always searching for a property to do together, she and Desi did their best to salvage their strained marriage, their efforts largely undermined by circumstances. Desi spent much of both 1948 and 1949 on the road, and when they were together, they fought incessantly. During the filming of *Fancy Pants, Variety* leaked news of heated verbal battles between the two when Desi would visit Lucy on the set. Hoping a religious ceremony might bless and strengthen their union, Desi asked Lucy to marry him again, this time in the Catholic Church to supplant the couple's first civil ceremony. The June 19 rites were witnessed by only a handful of close friends; Lucille was escorted to the altar by her MGM mentor, director Edward Sedgwick, with mother-in-law Dolores serving as matron of honor, and Ken Morgan, cousin Cleo's husband, Desi's best man.

One month later, the trade papers reported a "good chance that Lucille Ball's *My Favorite Husband* will be videoed this fall." The idea to transplant the program from radio to TV no doubt came to Harry Ackerman by observing Lucille's sharp delivery and skillful interplay with her live studio audience—the result of Oppenheimer having coached his cast "to loosen up and act out the jokes and reactions." Jess had not long before sent Lucille to Jack Benny's radio broadcast and told her to "go to school" and observe Benny's masterful "takes" and keen comedic-timing sense. Her recent *Dream Girl* tour—combined with studying Benny's technique with audiences—had immediate, tremendous impact. "The next time I saw her, she was so excited, she couldn't stand it," said Jess. "She couldn't wait to get started trying this new, emancipated attitude she had discovered." Her revitalized performance was so improved that *The Hollywood Reporter* noted, "Too bad that her funny grimaces and gestures aren't visible over the radio."

Lucille was quite interested in CBS's offer of a television version of *My Favorite Husband,* perhaps not viewing the offer as a particularly good career move, but rather a means to save her marriage. While Lucille did not object to playing opposite Richard Denning on the radio version, she actively campaigned for Desi to play her husband on television—which she viewed as an excellent opportunity for the couple to not only work as a team but allow them to finally live together on a sustained basis and, with luck, have children.

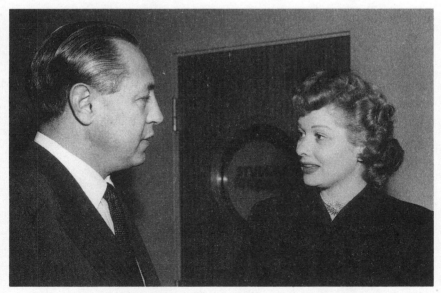

CBS founder and chairman William S. Paley with *My Favorite Husband* radio star Lucille Ball

Her plans met with immediate opposition. ("They thought Desi was just a bongo player," said Lucille.) Although Desi and Lucille had already successfully appeared together on a December 1949 Ed Wynn television show, CBS executive Hubbell Robinson immediately vetoed the idea, assuring them television audiences certainly would not accept the notion that the "All-American typical redhead" Lucille was married to, as Desi put it, "a Latin bandleader with a 'Cuban Pete' conga-drum 'Babalu' image."

"What do you mean, nobody'll believe it?" Lucille shot back. "We *are* married!"

The Arnazes suddenly hit upon the idea of embarking on a vaudeville tour that summer to prove to CBS—and perhaps themselves as well—that the American public would accept them as a husband-and-wife team. "If no one will give us a job together," Lucille vowed to Desi, "we'll give ourselves one."

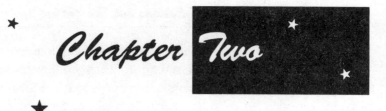

Chapter Two

★

"How *I Love Lucy* was born? We decided that instead of divorce lawyers profiting from our mistakes, we'd profit from them."

—Lucille Ball, 1952

★

*O*n March 24, 1950, *Variety* leaked news of Desi and Lucille's plans for an "Eastern vaude string." Although no mention was made that the personal-appearance tour was, in essence, a city-by-city audition for a proposed network-television series, the Arnazes were keenly aware that the success of this public experiment might well salvage their marriage and perhaps resurrect waning careers.

The gamble was indeed an expensive one, the act costing an estimated twenty thousand dollars. Desilu Productions—essentially an extension of the company Desi had created for his band tours—was formed with Desi as president and Lucille as vice-president to mount the tour and handle the receipts. The actual tab was considerably higher when including the potential earnings from film roles Lucille had to reject in order to appear on the road. After her *Fuller Brush Girl* success, she campaigned for Columbia to purchase expressly for her a slapstick yarn about a female softball player. Also unrealized were plans to team her with Larry Parks in another Columbia comedy, *Two of a Kind.* Along with Joan Crawford and Claudette Colbert, Lucille rejected a tour-de-force lead role in *The Star,* ultimately cast with Bette Davis. *The Star*— perhaps the script too uncomfortably reminiscent of Lucille's real-life scenario—presented a largely unromanticized, often harsh look at a fading middle-aged Hollywood actress clinging to a career irrevocably on the downslide.

Desi moved quickly to assemble a first-rate vaudeville act and called in an old friend, the renowned international Spanish clown Pepito, to devise some physical-comedy sketch material. Pepito rigorously coached the couple, as Desi recalled, "eight to ten hours a day" at the Coronado Hotel in San Diego. For Lucille, Pepito created a xylophone and, as she put it, "an incredible cello"—an elaborate Rube Goldberg–like prop— based on his own invention that had been part of his own act. "I pulled a stool out of it, a toilet plunger, gloves, flowers, a violin bow," recalled Lucille. "I put on a fright wig and an ill-fitting swallow-tailed coat that dragged on the floor and pretended to be a serious cellist. I must admit that bit appealed the most to the ham in me." For the sketch, she would come out of the audience as a baggy-pants character, meet "Dizzy Arnazy," and imitate a seal.

Other routines in the act included a Pugh-and-Carroll-scripted skit and a musical routine based on Desi's trademark "Cuban Pete" number, Arnaz creating new, playfully suggestive "Sally Sweet" bump-and-grind lyrics for Lucille to join him on the second chorus. In addition to Desi's solo warbling of several Latin-accented tunes, he joined his wife for a comedy sketch illustrating a married couple's hurried meetings in an airport between separate professional engagements, based on a real-life predicament often suffered by the Arnazes.

"We tried out the act in Long Beach, California," Lucille said. "I wouldn't let my friends come to the show. Desi already had proven himself as a vaudeville entertainer. I had done all right in *Dream Girl,* but that was, although a comedy, a straight play. If I fell on my face, I wanted to do it in front of strangers."

The tremendous gamble in taking their husband-and-wife act on the road—in the months during her summer hiatus from *My Favorite Husband*—paid off handsomely from the start. As *Variety* said of their twenty-

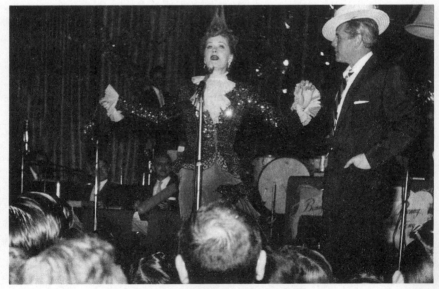

"Cuban Pete"/"Sally Sweet"

minute routine, first premiered on June 2, 1950, at Chicago's Paramount Theater, "It is top fare for vaude houses and niteries."

Lucille and Desi's two-weeker at New York's Roxy Theater opening June 9 found *Variety* a bit more reserved but still enthusiastic: "Perhaps some of the material she does is reaching for laughs, but there is, nevertheless, a keen sense of audience values in everything she does . . . there is always evidence that whatever the medium, Miss Ball knows her way around a script. Arnaz . . . conducts himself with taste and simplicity."

On June 13, the couple enjoyed an early celebration of their tenth wedding anniversary, occuring on the same site where Desi had carried Lucille over the threshold after their first wedding ceremony in 1940. Only a few days after opening at the Roxy, however, Lucille suddenly fell ill. Both husband and wife, for a time, attributed her condition to fatigue or the result of the great demands put upon Lucille by the strenuous physical-comedy routines she was required to repeat on the average of seven performances daily. Desi and Lucille, however, became alarmed when her condition did not improve. Her physician, Dr. Sym Newman, administered a complete physical examination as well as a "rabbit test," suspecting that she might be pregnant. Although Lucille had for years wanted to have a child, she did not suspect pregnancy— she was, after all, nearly forty years old at this point and had miscarried on at least one occasion.

The results of her "rabbit test" arrived in a most surprising manner. According to Lucille, "When we opened in Chicago, I was feeling a little sick, and when we got to New York, I had some tests made. It was on a Friday, and I was to get the results Monday. Well, Sunday night I was in my dressing room at the Roxy Theater waiting to go on, and I had turned on Walter Winchell's program. He said we were going to have a baby! I ran out of my dressing room, and Desi ran out of his, and both of us yelled, 'We're going to have a baby! Winchell says so!' I know Walter had spies everywhere—but in the *lab?*"

The couple officially announced Lucille's pregnancy in late June. They told reporters they were hoping for twins, since Desi wanted a boy and Lucille hoped for a girl. Her pregnancy prompted them to cancel the second half of the tour. Desi asked Dr. Newman to observe their act and recommend any changes in the physical routines to protect Lucille's health. The slapstick sketch having Lucille imitating a seal and performing belly flops was somewhat modified so she no longer "wiggled around on my stomach—but I still did backflips and barked." She reasoned, "When you're pregnant, you're supposed to keep doing what you've been doing all along."

After a successful Wisconsin engagement, the Arnazes flew back to the Desilu ranch. "For the next three weeks, we were as happy as it is possible for two people to be," said Lucille. "Almost before we unpacked, I began to shop for the layette. We made plans to add a wing—bedroom for the baby, bath, and nurse's room—to the house." Added Desi, "We even thought ahead many years and put in a separate front door on the kids' wing, so that when they got to the age where they were dating they could come in and out without disturbing the old folks."

In late July, Lucille and Desi hosted a large-scale costume party at Desilu. During the gala, Lucille was stricken with agonizing pain. She ran to her husband and said, "I think I'm having a miscarriage, Desi—what can we do?"

Yet, in the midst of this tragedy, an incident occurred giving the event a macabre Keystone Kops quality as she steeled herself for the thirty-minute ride from Chatsworth to Hollywood's Cedars of Lebanon Hospital. Lucille recalled, "Desi says I put both my hands on my stomach as if to hold the baby tight, while he ran for the telephone. I don't know how long it was before the ambulance got to our house. The ambulance men dashed in, put me on a stretcher, and shoveled me into the back of the car. We took off with the siren screaming. Ninety miles an hour through our quiet valley! Chickens flew to either side of the road. We missed a couple of cars by inches. Desi and the intern were in the ambulance with me, and Desi was holding my hands. Then, all of a sudden, there was a big wind inside the ambulance, and Desi wasn't holding my hands anymore. I opened my eyes to see that the door had burst open, and the intern was outside. Only his feet were in the ambulance, and Desi had hold of those. The intern's body was at right angles to the machine, and his head was barely missing the parked cars as we whizzed by.

"Somehow, Desi managed to hold down the intern's feet with one hand and to pound on the glass behind the driver with the other to make him stop. But the driver never even turned around. He just nodded his head and stepped on the throttle, pushing it all the way down to the floor. So there we were, tearing through the valley in an ambulance, with an intern sticking out the door. And Desi was trying to pull him back but couldn't, and every time Desi knocked on the window, the driver would nod and go faster. I don't know how Desi did it, but he hauled the intern back inside the ambulance."

Lucille suffered the miscarriage on July 27. "After it was over, I lay in the hospital with the tears rolling down my face," she recalled. "We had proved that the public wanted us as a team, and there was big interest in our proposed TV show. But we had lost our baby. So what difference did anything make?"

The Arnazes did their best to cope with the loss of the baby and continued with plans to mount a television series. To further acquaint himself with the new medium, Desi signed with Snader Telescriptor Corporation to appear in a series of three-minute filmed commercials; other talents to appear in separate spots were Lionel Hampton and Herb Jeffries. Lucille signed for solo September guest appearances on programs headlined by Bob Hope and Dinah Shore. Newly formed Desilu Productions planned on entering independent feature-film production, announcing plans to produce a "Technicolor comedy western" titled *Blazing Beulah of Butte,* Lucille and Desi costarring under the direction of Edward Sedgwick.

Lucille's bargaining power at CBS escalated when Harry Ackerman, her powerful champion at the network, was promoted from West Coast network programming chief to executive in charge of production for CBS radio and television. Ackerman offered Arnaz his own CBS showcase—albeit a low-budget one—as the host of *Tropical Trip,* a nonsponsored Sunday afternoon musical radio-quiz show. "Lucy had that kind of power even then," revealed Ackerman. "CBS didn't want to lose her. Even though it wasn't certain that she and Desi would be right together on a television series, the network wanted to make it clear that it respected Desi, too. Of course, the then-host of the series had to be persuaded to step aside for Desi. He was a young, up-and-coming comedian—Johnny Carson."

Word had reached Desi and Lucille that CBS's primary rival, NBC, was also interested in a Ball-Arnaz television series. Aware that such interest only enhanced their overall bargaining power, Desi commissioned a number of free-lance writers to create show concepts and scripts; the Arnazes were aware that their prized writers, Jess Oppenheimer, Madelyn Pugh, and Bob Carroll, Jr., were all under exclusive CBS contract and therefore unavailable for outside projects.

The best of the lot had the Arnazes play fictionalized, glamorized versions of themselves, Desi a "highly successful" bandleader and wife Lucille a top-rank film star. However, as Ackerman later recounted, "I okayed the Ball-Arnaz project and was one of those who worked in the creation and development of the show along with Don Sharpe and Jess Oppenheimer. I convinced Lucy and Desi they should do a fictional series rather than portraying themselves as they had intended to do. I assigned Oppenheimer to the project."

Lucille and Desi briefly resumed their vaudeville act in mid-November at San Francisco's Paramount Theater. The engagement proved "disappointing," said *Variety,* adding "the six day run shapes to only an average $20,000 despite price-upping to $1.25 from the regular 95-cent scale." Conversely, Desi took Hollywood's Ciro's nightclub by storm later that month and, stated the *Reporter,* "opened to a full house with enough fireworks to last his entire two-week stand."

The outlook for Lucille's film career brightened upon Cecil B. DeMille offering her the role of "the elephant girl" in his upcoming all-star circus epic, *The Greatest Show on Earth.* Aware that this would be her most important film role in years, she begged Harry Cohn at Columbia Pictures to allow her to appear in the DeMille Paramount production, arguing, "Why won't you let me make this picture? You have loaned me out for lousy ones before, when it didn't matter!"

She had one picture remaining on her Columbia contract. Cohn— disenchanted with the high-priced actress—banked on her desperation to secure the *Greatest Show on Earth* role and spitefully sent her a script for a low-budget Arabian Nights–themed potboiler titled *The Magic Carpet.* The studio mogul fully expected her to reject the assignment, which would break her Columbia contract and spare the studio her $85,000 per-film salary.

The Arnazes then received news even more exciting than DeMille's offer: Lucille was again pregnant. Along with her delight of having conceived again so soon after the July miscarriage, Lucille was faced with the disturbing realization that she would be forced to drop out of *Greatest Show,* her pregnancy certain to be apparent as the picture first went before the cameras on January 19, 1951. She and Desi decided Lucille would accept *Magic Carpet,* which would net her a sizable salary collectible after a lightning-fast six-day shooting schedule. And, further reasoned Desi, "The thing is so lousy I'm sure nobody will ever see it, so it can't do you much harm. Go ahead and do the goddamned thing." Lucille stunned Cohn when she agreed to do the film. And not wanting to provide Columbia with contractual means to drop her from the high-paid *Magic Carpet* assignment, she told neither Cohn nor DeMille of her condition until completion of filming.

Lucille openly defied Cohn and refused to read the *Magic Carpet* script a moment before she went on studio salary November 27. When she did finally appear at Columbia to begin work on the picture, she was met by four anxious producers as she drove past the Columbia studio gates. "I know there's a small budget on this picture," she quipped to them, "but do we have to have our first conference in the *parking lot?*" Her lack of enthusiasm for *The Magic Carpet* was clearly evident in the final product, so much so that *The Hollywood Reporter* in its review cracked, "Lucille Ball and John Agar deliver particularly undistinguished performances—Miss Ball wouldn't, Agar couldn't."

When he finally learned of Lucille's pregnancy, Harry Cohn was vitriolic, and heatedly snapped at her, "Why, you bitch. You screwed me, didn't you?" Desi ran into DeMille at a Hollywood party not long after. "Congratulations, Mr. Arnaz," said the producer. "You are the only man who has ever screwed his wife, Cecil B. DeMille, Paramount Pictures, and Harry Cohn, all at the same time."

CBS inaugurated negotiations with agent Don Sharpe for a Ball-Arnaz series shortly after Christmas. The deal would be launched—despite Lucille's increasingly obvious pregnancy—with a pilot episode to be kinescoped early in the new year. According to Jess Oppenheimer, "Lucy and Desi were unhappy with the scripts they bought and told CBS they would make a deal if I would produce it and be head writer. The basic notion that I had was that of a performer who was born into a show-business home life, who is married to a girl who had a normal, average, nontheatrical life and is dying to get into show business." For his services, Oppenheimer negotiated a 20 percent royalty and reportedly gave 5 percent of his percentage to Madelyn Pugh and Bob Carroll.

Bob and Madelyn cut short a European vacation to return home and write the pilot episode with Oppenheimer. With the pilot to be shot in a matter of weeks, the writers worked quickly to assemble a script, ultimately recycling much of what was used on the vaudeville tour, including the broad physical "cello" comedy sketch. First mention came in *Variety* on February 7, 1951, noting that the Arnazes would be presented in a "Mr. and Mrs." format, "set up as a situation comedy with music, in which Arnaz will play an orch leader and Miss Ball his wife who is a frustrated singer." On February 15, *The Hollywood Reporter* announced CBS's plans for preparing "a raft of both live and filmed TV shows to originate here next season. First to audition, on a closed-circuit kine February 23, will be a Lucille Ball–Desi Arnaz starrer." The trade paper amended this report on February 20, announcing that the Arnaz "TV tryout" had been rescheduled for March 2, 1951, at Columbia Square, headquarters of CBS West Coast Radio and Television divisions.

The day of the pilot performance, Jess Oppenheimer—for a fee of one dollar—registered the concept for the new series with the Screen Writers' Guild:

> He is a Latin-American orchestra leader and singer. She is his wife. They are happily married and very much in love. The only bone of contention

between them is her desire to get into show business and his equally strong desire to keep her out of it. As show business is the only way he knows to make a living, and he makes a very good one, the closest he can get to his dream is having a wife who's out of show business and devotes herself to keeping as nearly a normal life as possible for him.

Of the pilot episode, Oppenheimer stated:

> The first story concerns a TV audition for Ricky, where Pepito, the clown, due to an accident, fails to appear and Lucy takes his place for the show. Although she does a bang-up job, she forgoes the chance at a career that is offered her in order to keep Ricky happy and closer to his dream of normalcy.

A myth has persisted over the years that the Arnazes dipped into their own pockets and produced five thousand dollars in order to partly fund the pilot. However, as Oppenheimer recalled, "On the night of the shooting, we were set to go. Lucy, six months pregnant, was already onstage, waiting for the curtain to rise. Desi and Hal Hudson from CBS were still arguing about some items on the as-yet-unsigned contract. Hal suddenly said that the contract must be signed as is or the show would not go on. Desi, furious, asked, 'How much will the kinescope cost to shoot?' My memory says that Hal told him it would cost nineteen thousand dollars. 'Okay,' Desi yelled. 'I'll pay for it myself, and it will belong to us.' 'No,' Hal told him. 'We'll go ahead and shoot it, and thrash out the contract details later.' So," concluded Oppenheimer, "it never got away from CBS." CBS executive Martin Leeds confirms, "The pilot was paid for by CBS. It was a risk. If the show wasn't sold, we lost the money."

Leeds also recalls that the contracts remained unsigned and, as head of the network's West Coast business affairs, he had warned Desi the pilot show would be halted without the signatures: "During the kinescope recording of the pilot, somebody kicked the plug, and the lights went out. Desi was in one bed and Lucy was in another. He said, 'That son of a bitch pulled the plug!' and she said, 'Why?' 'Because I didn't sign their fucking contracts!' He was serious. The lights went on three seconds later."

CBS immediately sent a kinescope of the pilot to New York to be shopped around the powerful Madison Avenue advertising agencies. Oppenheimer remembered initial reaction being far from positive, not only from advertisers but from CBS as well. "When the pilot film was sent back to CBS in New York, the head of the programming department—who later remembered a little differently and claimed that he loved it from the first moment he saw it—actually called me up and said, 'What are you sending me? This is the worst thing I have ever seen. How can I possibly sell that?' " CBS provided no fanfare whatsoever when previewing the pilot for the press. *The Hollywood Reporter's* Dan Jenkins recounted, "CBS called me and said, 'Come on over and see a pilot.' They screened it for us at an empty storefront right next to Columbia Square at 6121 Sunset Boulevard. They had tacked up a sheet up on the wall. They had a sixteen-millimeter projector on an orange crate."

By mid-April, the Ball-Arnaz show was still without a sponsor, and the network, along with Lucille and Desi, was beginning to panic. Although Milton H. Biow of the Biow advertising agency seemed to be one of the very few at this point to see real potential in the series, he nevertheless remained hesitant to recommend to any of his clients that they assume the hefty $26,500 per-show price tag demanded by Sharpe. Finally, on April 24, it was announced that a Biow client, Philip Morris Cigarettes, would assume sponsorship of the series "in excess of $20,000 per week"—indicating that Sharpe was forced to reduce the asking price somewhat in order to secure a sponsor. *The Reporter* added that the show would "originate live from Hollywood on Monday nights." Philip Morris dropped bandleader Horace Heidt's filmed TV show in order to assume full sponsorship of the Ball-Arnaz program, now titled *I Love Lucy*.

"I got a call from New York and was told the show was sold," said Martin Leeds. "Desi was rehearsing *Tropical Trip*—Lucy had asked Ackerman to give him something to do during the summer. I went down to his studio, and he stopped the number at one point, and I said, 'Desi, congratulations. Your show has been sold!' Desi thought I meant *Tropical Trip*. It's not unbelievable. He would have loved to have the show sold, instead of being sustained for the summer. I said, 'The *television show's* been sold—*I Love Lucy!* ' "

Philip Morris, however, insisted on a weekly series, while Desi and Lucille had from the start envisioned the program as a biweekly enterprise. "We contracted to do a live show every other week, in the naive delusion that Lucy could continue her film career if she only had to do one little television show every two weeks," recalled Oppenheimer. Sharpe discussed the matter with the Arnazes at the Desilu ranch to determine whether they were willing to take the full plunge into television and do a weekly series. "If he's willing to give up traveling with his band, I'm willing to give up film work," said Lucille. Desi firmly told

Sharpe, "We'll gamble everything on this show. The answer is yes." Lucille said later, "Everybody was telling us, 'You're crazy to give up sure things like nightclubs, radio, and the movies for a risky thing like television,'" adding, "but it was now or never. We had come this far, and we were ready to risk everything to be together. We could, in fact, risk going broke, because we knew something nobody else knew. We knew, having risked so much, that we *had* to be a success."

Soon after the Arnazes agreed to the weekly format, Oppenheimer received a call from Biow, asking him, "When are you and your gang coming to New York?" Jess told the advertising executive that they "had no intention" of relocating the show to the East Coast. "I bought a show that's going to be done from New York," retorted Biow. "I am not about to put on a program where 15 percent of the audience sees it clearly and 85 percent see it through a piece of cheesecloth." The trade papers bannered Philip Morris's discontent with the Arnazes' demand to broadcast the series live from Hollywood, with an inferior-quality kinescope recording to be supplied to the much larger East Coast market (CLIENT NIXES KINE ON LUCI AND DESI, headlined *Variety*), and the deal seemed on the verge of falling apart. Further confusion ensued with the sponsor insisting that the series "kick off" in New York and then "anchor" in Hollywood. The only recourse, noted *Variety,* was to film the show, "which is acceptable to Morris though budget-swelling to CBS, which owns the package." A mid-May summit meeting between Harry Ackerman and the sponsor proved to be the turning point—in the Arnazes' favor—and it was shortly announced that the series would originate on film and from Hollywood. As Lucille logically concluded, "If I had to go to New York to do TV, I'd stay here and do pictures instead."

To show-business insiders, Ackerman's position was not altogether surprising. As early as November of 1950, *The Hollywood Reporter* noted that Ackerman and fellow CBS executive Hubbell Robinson decided that "CBS, in the future, will produce its comedy TV shows from Los Angeles as much as possible, both live and on film." Yet despite his support, filming TV shows was not first pioneered by CBS. Jerry Fairbanks, head of NBC's film department during 1947–48, first utilized a three-camera film technique when using his 16mm Multicam system for the 1947– 48 *Public Prosecutor* television series; he also filmed episodes of *Silver Theater,* among other programs, between 1949 and 1951. Fairbanks reportedly introduced the three-camera technique to Ralph Edwards when he filmed the April 1950 *Truth or Consequences* pilot. Al Simon was hired by Edwards several months later and is credited with making several improvements to the Fairbanks system, including dropping the

16mm format in favor of higher-quality 35mm film stock and devising a more sophisticated intercom system to enhance communication between the studio floor (which held a live studio audience) and the control room. CBS essentially utilized the Fairbanks-Simon technique beginning in 1950 for its *Amos 'n' Andy* series. And, by June 1951, television-filmed productions were booming. *The Hollywood Reporter* announced that a record 118 "tele-film programs" were set for the upcoming 1951–52 season.

The decision to film the Ball-Arnaz series caused the project to once again hit a snag in negotiations. Martin Leeds, among other network heads, determined that filming the show, instead of producing episodes "live," would double the per-show cost, since, because of film-union requirements, the shows could not be shot at CBS-TV facilities. Philip Morris refused to ante up additional money, and CBS, in turn, proved equally stubborn and refused to put up the five-thousand-dollar projected per-episode difference.

Don Sharpe suggested to Desi that CBS might allow them to do the series on film if he and Lucy would take a salary cut of one thousand dollars per week, thereby reducing their total combined pay to four thousand dollars weekly and 50 percent of the profits. Desi countered with, "Okay, Don, we'll take the thousand-dollar cut for the first thirty-nine shows, if you can get them to agree that we will then own all the shows of this year and all the shows of all future years, if any, one hundred percent." And, as Desi further reasoned, "In our bracket, another thirty-nine thousand dollars in income would mean that, after taxes, we could keep only four thousand dollars, or possibly five thousand dollars at the most. In reality we would be buying the other fifty percent of the films for five thousand dollars or less."

Sharpe approached Martin Leeds, who summarily rejected Desi's proposition. "He said, 'I want to own it all, Martin.' I said, 'You're not going to be able to afford [to produce] it. Where are you going to get the money? I'm sorry, but I can't give it to you.' 'Then we'll go back to [CBS] New York, and I'll get it there.' Hubbell Robinson, in business affairs, New York, gave him the other fifty percent—the whole ownership of the films—and it didn't cost them one nickel." Desi had, in effect, at that moment, created the television off-network "rerun" market.

Complete ownership of the show meant Arnaz had to expand Desilu Productions into a full-fledged production company, and it proved a financial challenge. "Two weeks before they were supposed to begin shooting, Desi came to my office and said, 'I have no money,'" Leeds remembers. "I said, 'What do you want from me? You own the show.'"

Leeds ended up advancing Arnaz sixty thousand dollars against future revenues and, as a bonus, included CBS lighting equipment.

In 1973 Oppenheimer addressed the still-raging controversy surrounding the commonly held belief that *I Love Lucy*—and specifically Desi—"invented" the revolutionary three-camera film technique: "The truth is that no particular person came up with the idea. It developed in conferences and was dictated by necessity. Milton Biow refused to let it be done live, as there was no transcontinental cable at the time, and it would mean going on live on the West Coast for fifteen percent of the audience and by kinescope, and unsatisfactory picture, for the other eighty-five percent of the country in the East. We were in a quandary, and all manner of ideas were suggested. The fact surfaced that Ralph Edwards was doing his television show with moving-film cameras. We called in his production manager, Al Simon, who saw no reason why a comedy show couldn't be done that way."

Marc Daniels was an ideal candidate to direct the new situation comedy, having directed a number of New York-based anthology television programs before relocating to Hollywood. Daniels met with Willard Josephy, a fellow ex-serviceman and business associate of Lucille's film agent, Kurt Frings; Frings recommended Daniels for the Arnaz project, and at his initial meeting with Arnaz, Oppenheimer, and Ackerman, Daniels won the directing assignment.

Performing live before audiences in *Dream Girl* and *My Favorite Husband* sharpened Lucille's innate comic abilities and prompted her keen desire to film the TV series before studio spectators. "Lucy was dreadful without an audience," Ackerman once said. "She absolutely bloomed in front of an audience." CBS scouted film studio locations around town but soon discovered that motion-picture moguls wanted nothing to do with new rival television. Desi appraised several vacant theaters, but, recalled Lucille, "they seemed too formal and cramped. He thought of doing it in a supper club, but they seemed too *informal* and cramped."

While Desi, Jess, and the others worked to solve the many logistical problems, Lucille temporarily retired to the Desilu ranch to prepare for the birth of their first child, and on July 17 had seven-pound, six-ounce daughter Lucie Desiree Arnaz. And, as proud mother Lucille later recalled, "That was one of the greatest moments of my life. I began to cry from sheer happiness when Lucie was put in my arms. I kept saying to myself, 'This is *ours*. This is our baby.' "

In the meantime, Oppenheimer, Pugh, and Carroll made show-concept adjustments in the leap from the isolated pilot episode to scripting weekly installments. "We rethought the pilot and realized that we had written it for Lucy and Desi only, omitting anyone for our stars to speak with and plot with, as we had in the radio show with Gale Gordon and Bea Benaderet," said Oppenheimer. "We decided that we would get an older couple, whose only asset was they owned the building. In this case, the younger couple would be better off financially. But we could still pursue the examination of marriage from two age levels and two economic levels. And we could pair them off as couple against couple, women against men, or haves against have-nots—all setups which had worked for us on the radio series."

This, in essence, was a reversal of the somewhat older, more affluent couple on radio's *My Favorite Husband* played by Gale Gordon and Bea Benaderet. Not surprisingly, Lucille wanted those same actors to be cast in the television series, but both proved unavailable; Gale Gordon was under CBS contract for the radio and television versions of *Our Miss Brooks* ("Mister Conklin") and Bea Benaderet was already a regular cast member ("Blanche Morton") on *The George Burns and Gracie Allen Show*. Character actor James Gleason was another Ball choice, but his asking price of $3,500 per week was far too steep. Cantankerous sixty-four-year-old character player William Frawley heard that the Arnazes had not cast the part and directly called Lucille at the Desilu ranch, asking her, "I'm wondering if there's a role for me in your TV show." Lucille, Desi, and Jess decided that Frawley would be right for the role but encountered resistance from CBS and Philip Morris, based upon reports that he was an alcoholic and therefore unreliable. Such fears proved groundless. "He never missed a day's work nor was he even a few minutes late during all the years he was with us," said Desi.

Candidates to play Frawley's wife included *Husband* supporting-player Ruth Perrott, character actress Mary Wickes, and Lucille's close friend Barbara Pepper, reportedly rejected by CBS due to her severe alcoholism. It was director Marc Daniels who suggested thirty-nine-year-old, relatively obscure actress Vivian Vance for what would become the "Ethel Mertz" role. He had directed her in *Counselor at Law* with Paul Muni and knew that she was then appearing at the La Jolla Playhouse in a revival of the Broadway hit-comedy *Voice of the Turtle* with Mel Ferrer. Having just given birth to little Lucie, Lucille was unable to travel with Desi, Jess, and Marc Daniels on Saturday, July 28, to see Vivian in the play. "I think we've found our Ethel Mertz," Arnaz told Oppenheimer and Daniels by the first-act intermission. They met with her backstage, and Daniels told her she was up for the part. Vivian, however, was far from enthusiastic: "I laughed when Desi and Jess suggested me for the part of Ethel. I said, 'Do a TV series? Ha!' It seemed ridiculous. I didn't know what a TV series meant in those days, but it did seem promising if a star like Lucille Ball was going to take a chance, so I agreed to give it thirteen weeks."

Vivian had recently suffered a mental breakdown and, although on the road to recovery, was still somewhat fragile. As she said later at the height of her popularity on the *Lucy* series, "As Ethel, I memorize a full speaking part each week. But in the year 1947 I would not leave my room without first writing my name and address on a piece of paper and putting it in my bag. This was so someone would know who I was if I went crazy, which I firmly thought I was going to do." She added, "To put it bluntly, I flipped." Her illness first manifested in 1945 during a Chicago production of *Voice of the Turtle;* fearing a relapse, she had nearly turned down Mel Ferrer's invitation to appear in the same role. Intense ongoing psychotherapy for Vivian proved to be a key to her slow but eventual recovery. Analysis was so liberating to her that she once quipped to her therapist, "How can you go through adolescence and the menopause at the same time?"

Time was running out as the production staff continued the search for a suitable location to film the show. A cinematographer still had not been hired. Upon Lucille's prompting, Al Simon contacted the legendary Oscar-winning Karl ("Papa") Freund, who had photographed her for the MGM's *DuBarry Was a Lady* in 1942. Freund at first refused the offer to embark on a television career, retorting, "I'm not interested in TV. I'm an Academy Award winner."

Al Simon met with Freund, who remained adamant in rejecting Arnaz's offer and furthermore advised Simon that filming the series with the proposed simultaneous three-camera method would be impossible. "Every shot requires different lighting," Freund told Simon. Only when Lucille and Desi personally prevailed upon "Papa" did he relent and accept the job—and the formidable task ahead of him. According to *I Love Lucy* historian Bart Andrews, Freund's "true contribution" to the show was his "revolutionary overhead lighting system that lit the entire set uniformly." Expressly for the forty-year-old Lucille, he devised a clever lighting system. According to Martin Leeds, "Lucy had, shall we say, slight beginnings of wattles under her neck, which would have made her look older, so he designed putting lights up at the foot of the camera, removing all the shadows on her face. That was *really* his major contribution."

Finally, in late August, General Service Studios owner Jimmy Nasser contacted Al Simon and suggested that his eight-soundstage, seven-and-one-half-acre Hollywood studio lot was the perfect filming site. Simon visited the studio and thought that, with some modifications, General Service would indeed be suitable. He envisioned tearing down a wall to create an audience entrance and building a number of permanent sets on the largest soundstage, which could also be used for rehearsals. Desi agreed with Simon's choice as well as his inspired suggestions. Nasser approved the necessary remodeling, and Arnaz, to comply with fire regulations, installed a special audience entrance as well as a new over-head sprinkling system. The soundstage's badly warped and damaged wood floors were removed and replaced by smooth cement and a Masonite finish, allowing cameras to glide about the floor. Permanent sets were constructed, and 35mm Mitchell BNC cameras and "crab dollys" (pro-viding the cameras mobility on the stage floor) were ordered. Desilu stage manager Herb Browar ingeniously complied with fire regulations barring wooden bleachers on the soundstage when he suggested the installation of steel grandstand seats. A new sign bannering DESILU PLAYHOUSE was mounted above the exterior of Stage 2.

With CBS supporting the General Service renovation with a $25,000 cash infusion, the ever-expanding production staff was headquartered in their new studio by the end of that same month. August 27, 1951, brought the "official" announcement that *I Love Lucy*—"the first regular TV series to headline a top current Hollywood actress"—with Philip Morris as sponsor had a premiere date of October 15. The writers hurredly completed the script for the first episode, "Lucy Thinks Ricky Is Trying to Murder Her," to be filmed on Saturday, September 8, 1951.

Despite the camaraderie that had developed among the dedicated group, script clerk Maury Thompson recalls Lucille—and Desi, though to a far lesser degree—clearly separating themselves from the others that first day of rehearsals: "The call was at ten in the morning. Jess was there, Madelyn and Bob and Bill Frawley. I had already set up the scripts and the pencils around the table. Here comes the balloon skirt, the big long coat, and dark glasses and I thought, 'Omigod, that's her!' Desi's smoking a cigar. And Willie Mae, the nurse, with a long basket with napkins over it. So I assumed it was lunch. They sat it down, right between the two chairs. Lucille took off her coat. Jess introduced her to me and told me to 'Sit right by her. Anything she wants, you get it. If they make a correction in the script, write it down so we can read it back.' In comes Marc Daniels and his wife, Emily, the camera co-ordinator. Then Vivian. Desi said to Lucy, 'This is Miss Vance.' Viv said, 'Oh, hi.' Lucy said, 'What part are you trying out for?' And Desi said, 'For the landlady, honey.' 'She doesn't look like a landlady,' Lucy said. 'Her hair's the same color as mine.' Viv said, 'Well, Miss Ball,

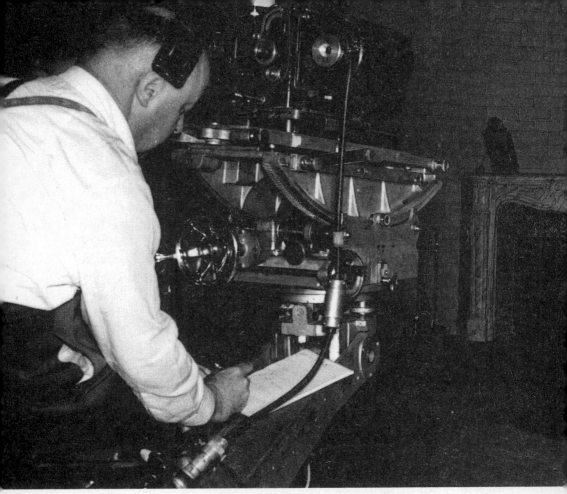

Rehearsing the first *I Love Lucy* episode
ARCHIVE PHOTOS

I can dye it. I don't care. It doesn't matter to me.' 'Well, I know. But you're not heavy.' Viv said, 'Well, I'm round-shouldered, Miss Ball, and I do photograph dumpy.' Lucille says, 'I don't know. I want a dumpy, peroxide-blonde with curlers in her hair and a terry cloth robe and fuzzy slippers. That's what I want.' Viv says, 'You got her. I look just like that in the morning when I get out of bed.' Lucy was not too convinced, so Desi said, 'Well, honey, let's read it through and see what happens.' 'Alright,' said Lucy. 'But I don't know.' "

The group began to dissect the script. "Lucy makes a big checkmark right *through* the paper," recalled Thompson. "She'd break the pencil and grab another one. 'Who *wrote* this shit?' she said [in admiration]. It comes noon, and she peels back her linen and gives Desi some chicken. And she takes some. She tears into it, holding on so she won't drop it. It comes to be about one-thirty, and we're just starved, especially with them eating right in front of us. So Bill Frawley says, 'May I ask a question? When the hell do the peons put on the feedbag around here?'

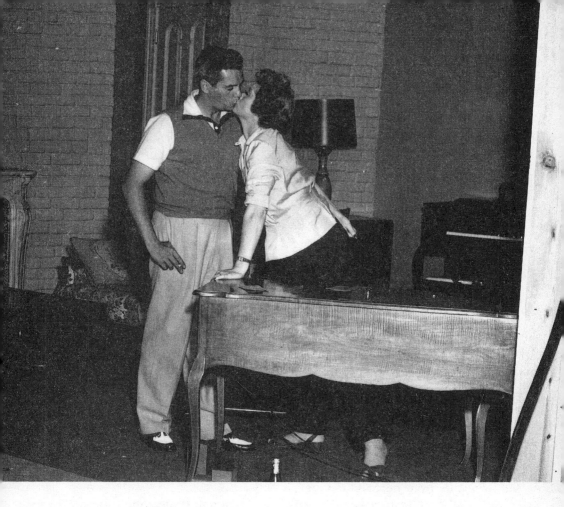

'Haven't you had your lunch?' they ask. He says, 'Hell, I don't eat lunch at ten o'clock in the morning.' Lucille says, 'Okay, let them have forty-five minutes and go to the commissary.' "

A similar incident occurred early on. According to Lucy's longtime makeup man Hal King, "One day she went over to Vivian Vance and pulled off Vivian's false eyelashes. Lucy said, 'Nobody wears false eyelashes on this show but *me*.' " (Vance, a year younger than Ball, was contractually obligated to remain twenty pounds overweight during the filming season; over the years, Lucy would often call up Vivian during their summer hiatus and quip, "Okay, start eating and putting on the flesh again, dear—we'll be shooting again soon!")

Echoing the sentiments of many fellow Desilu employees, Marc Daniels once remarked, "I found Desi very good to deal with. He was brighter and more talented than most people gave him credit for. Most people assumed he was riding on Lucy's coattails. It's hard for me to talk about

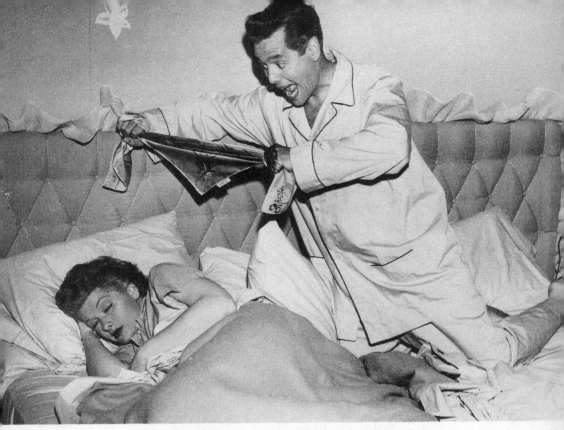

"Lucy Thinks Ricky is Trying to Murder Her"
THOMAS J. WATSON COLLECTION

Lucy. I never felt I got close to her. She preferred to keep her social life separate from her working life."

"All I remember about that night was trying to protect my stomach," said Lucille of the first *I Love Lucy* filming. "Lucie had just been born by cesarean section, and I was wearing one of those big skillet bandages. I was more concerned with that than anything else. When the laughs started coming in, I was very relieved. I remember going, 'Whew! It worked!' I remember that, and my stomach, and very little else."

Reportedly because of technical glitches—including a cumbersome and unnecessary fourth camera not used after the first episode—the first half hour to air was actually the second one filmed, "The Girls Want to Go to a Nightclub." The premiere program, however, was not greeted with uniformly positive response. *Weekly Variety* deemed it "one of the slickest TV entertainment shows to date . . . here is a film that has all the Grade A qualities of major studio production, achieving a depth and visual values that pertain to theater presentation, yet encompassing the desired intimacy for TV." The trade paper added that "if the storyline wasn't exactly inspiring, nonetheless it had a flexibility that permitted for a full-blown exposition of Miss Ball's comedic talents. On this score alone, Monday's preem was a resounding click." Sister publication *Daily*

Variety offered an entirely different perspective: "The laughs were there and plentiful but not quite so raucous as the audience made them out to be. . . . The writing and plotting should be more inventive and less contrived just for the sake of laughs."

The Hollywood Reporter praised, "The outstanding pertinent fact about *I Love Lucy* is the emergence, long suspected, of Lucille Ball as America's number-one comedienne in her own right. . . . She is a consummate artist, born for television. Half a step behind her comes husband, Desi Arnaz, the perfect foil for her screwball antics and possessing comic abilities of his own more than sufficient to make this a genuine comedy team rather than the one-woman tour-de-force it almost becomes . . . a comic triumph of the first order . . . Desilu Productions has scored with this one, and scored heavily."

However, an earlier *Hollywood Reporter* "On the Air" column by Dan Jenkins dated June 28, 1951, was eerily prophetic:

> We saw the audition kine of CBS' *I Love Lucy* yesterday and are happy to predict the immediate ascendancy of Lucille Ball and Desi Arnaz to TV stardom come airing of the first filmed show in the fall. And by stardom, we mean in the top five of everybody's rating system in every area. . . . Keep your eyes peeled for this one—it's a honey.

Lucille Ball herself apparently did not possess such powers of prediction or have as much faith in her show as did columnist Jenkins. "I expected to work for a year, maybe two. I said, 'I'm having a baby, and I'd like to have it like home movies for the baby.' *That's* how long I expected it would last."

Chapter Three

"We had a generous share of ongoing feuds simmering during *I Love Lucy,* but not a hint of it is
to be seen on the screen. Actors might be eccentric,
but they're not crazy."

—Jess Oppenheimer, 1986

"*W*e just took ordinary situations and exaggerated them," said Lucille Ball in an attempt to explain the phenomenal popularity of *I Love Lucy.* "The believability of all of our unbelievable situations is what made it funny. It wasn't just slapstick comedy. People identified with the Ricardos because we had the same problems they had. We lived in a brownstone in Manhattan, and paying the rent, getting a new dress, getting a stale fur collar on an old cloth coat, or buying a piece of furniture were all worth a story. It wasn't my genius. It was the genius of craftsmen behind the scenes, and rehearsing over and over again until we had it down perfect."

The top rating winners at the very start of the 1951–52 television season did not include *I Love Lucy,* but instead programs headlined by Arthur Godfrey, Milton Berle, Dean Martin and Jerry Lewis, Red Skelton, Sid Caesar and Imogene Coca (*Your Show of Shows*), Jimmy Durante, and Jack Benny. The October 15 *I Love Lucy* premiere episode registered a 38.7 rating and a 56 share, the latter indicating the percentage of all television sets tuned in to the program. Only a month later, newcomer *I Love Lucy* jumped into the Top Ten and, noted *The Hollywood Reporter,* "pulled a 40.8 national Nielsen to rank fourth behind Berle, Godfrey, and *Your Show of Shows.* And Lucy, incidentally, hasn't come up with a bad show yet." Said Jess Oppenheimer of this newfound success, "There was magic in the air. The audience fell in love at first sight. Once the spell was cast, laughing at the jokes wasn't enough for them. They started laughing at the straight lines, and then at any line as long as it came from that particular cast."

The *I Love Lucy* ensemble, however, was not necessarily the cozy bunch presented over the airwaves. Notes Oppenheimer, "Just because a cast loves to work together as professional performers doesn't mean that, as individuals, they can't hate each other's guts."

From the start, Vivian Vance and William Frawley disliked each other intensely. After meeting Vivian, Bill asked Desi, "Where did you find this bitch?"; not helping matters was Frawley's overhearing Vance complaining that her on-screen husband was, in fact, "old enough to play my *grandfather*." When "the Mertzes" were to do a soft-shoe routine on one episode, Vivian told the choreographer that Bill would not be able to master the number, later saying, "He was always half a beat behind us in a dance routine. When the three of us marched around the stage, we'd find ourselves running into him." Incensed, vaudeville veteran Frawley complained to Desi, "I guarantee you I'll wind up teaching old fat-ass how to do the fucking thing." Vance, often snarled Frawley, had a figure "like a sack full of doorknobs," frequently referring to her as "that dried-up old cunt."

Vivian once admitted, "My first concern was to flip through the mimeographed pages every Monday morning, praying, 'Please, God, I won't have to climb into bed this week with that square-headed little Irishman.' His constant complaint on the set was 'You're wasting my time.' Desi to him was 'that Cuban heel.' Lucille and I were brass-bound bitches. Playing Fred Mertz on the top-rated show in television was a nuisance to Bill—it interfered with his hobby of sitting in bars, chewing the rag with baseball players."

Frawley occasionally vented his wrath on star Lucille Ball. As she once recalled, "He prided himself on being one of the old song-and-dance men. He *never, ever* read the script. We were all singing at the piano, and I'm in the kitchen, cooking, Viv playing as Bill and Desi were singing one of the old songs. I was never allowed to hit the right note. I had to sing off-key. I came in behind them, and I joined in the song. This was for rehearsal. And he was singing, and he was enjoying it so much because it was one of the old songs. And I walk in behind him and hit this off-note. 'What the hell was that?' he asked the director. He said, 'Bill, that's the story. She hits the sour note.' He said, 'There's only one way to describe her singing—it's like a shovel of shit on a baked Alaska!' "

It was quickly learned by the *I Love Lucy* cast and crew members that Frawley had a well-deserved reputation for thrift. Herb Browar recalls, "He lived with his sister in the Knickerbocker Hotel. He used to watch his pennies. I was in [Hollywood restaurant] Musso & Frank one day for lunch. He didn't know I was there. I hear this bombastic voice. Bill was yelling. He used to have lunch there every day. He'd have the same sandwich, and they would always charge him sixty-five cents. They had raised it a dime to seventy-five cents. He didn't know it because he never saw the menu. When he got the check, he saw it was seventy-five cents. He started raising his voice, saying, 'I'm *never* coming back!' He started eating at the Brown Derby."

Lucy and Vivian had a complex relationship, an often uneasy blend of personal friendship and professional rivalry. "She was tough on Viv," Maury Thompson states. "She picked [at] every little thing that Viv did. Viv could read a script cold like a professional. And of course Lucille realized this as time went on. She'd say, 'You *like* green?' Viv would say, 'Yeah.' 'You gonna wear *that?*' 'Yeah.' 'Oh.' 'Why? I can wear anything you want. Just tell me.' 'Oh, no, that's *fine*. That's okay.' I was driving Viv home, and I said, 'What are you going to do about her?' She said, 'Honey, if this show should be a hit, it'll be the biggest thing that ever happened in my career. So I made up my mind. I'm going to *learn* to love the bitch.' It had to be done Lucy's way. So Viv would say to her, 'Okay, honey, you own the store. It's all right with me.' Lucille would fall apart, laughing. And that's what Lucille needed. You needed to break her down." As Vivian once admitted, "We fought like sisters and made up the same way."

Vivian, however, insisted—perhaps a bit too often—that she never

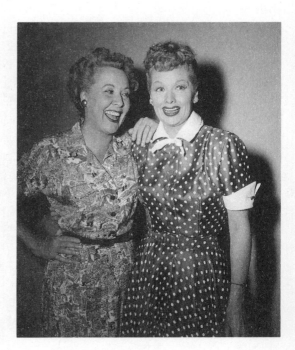

Lucille and Vivian Vance
THOMAS J. WATSON COLLECTION

particularly wanted to be a top-rank star herself. "As working women, we had great respect for each other's talent, without a twinge of jealousy. I was tickled to death to go along with a star who was willing to work as hard as she did. I personally wasn't that willing."

Vivian also fancied herself as a rather glamorous, ex-Broadway trouper, an image in direct contrast to her dumpy Ethel Mertz characterization. Consequently, one incident occurring in the early days of *I Love Lucy* remains particularly vivid to Hal King: "We were all standing backstage. Lucy and Vivian were dressed for a party scene. I looked over at Vivian and said, 'Lucy, I better go over and tell Vivian that her stockings are wrinkled.' She said, 'Yeah, why don't you.' So I went over to her and said, 'Vivian, I want to fix your hose.' She said, 'I'm not *wearing* any.' Fat legs. I didn't know which way to turn."

To the nearly one hundred Desilu employees who comprised the *I Love Lucy* cast and crew, Lucille proved herself to be a determined, disciplined perfectionist demanding the very best from herself and her coworkers. Unpredictable, contradictory, extremely blunt, often abrasive and aloof, she was capable of displaying incredible loyalty or, conversely, dismissing someone instantaneously if she felt betrayed or disobeyed. Maury Thompson was subject to both excesses in his two-decade relationship with the star. "As a script supervisor, I'm not supposed to have anything to do with wardrobe, not even touch it. It was just before the show started. She had on a big, full skirt. She sat down, and it got

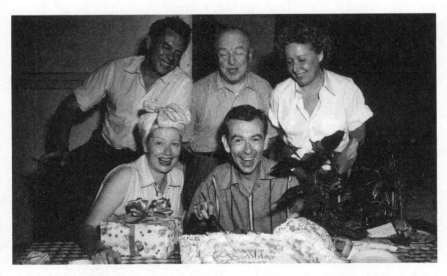

Desi, William Frawley, Vivian, and Lucille celebrate Maury Thompson's birthday on the set.
THOMAS J. WATSON COLLECTION

caught under the chair. And I thought, My God, when she gets up, that will tip over the chair.' The cameraman says, 'All right. Everyone ready.' I said, 'Wait a minute.' I said to Lucille, 'Honey, get up just a second,' and I adjusted the skirt. She says, 'Thanks, Maury.' Normally, she never thanked you for anything. She said, 'I want to see you after the show.' I thought I overstepped my bounds. After the show, I stuck my head in the trailer and said, 'Miss Ball, you wanted to see me?' She said, 'Yeah. How much are they paying you?' I told her seventy-five dollars a week. She said, 'I'm going to *double* it. I'd appreciate it if you keep your eye on the money—and *I'm* the money.' Once you proved your loyalty, then you got her."

"I'm *not* funny. I don't *think* funny," Lucille insisted over the years. Concurs Bob Carroll, Jr., "Physically, she was great, acting things out. Sometimes she would kill you showing what happened on a plane last night, when some drunk got on and they threw him off. You suddenly became the drunk, and she would grab you and hustle you around." Her "inability to express herself," and a certain lack of warmth, offers Carroll, made her appear insensitive or abrupt. "Sometimes during a run-through, there would be a really great scene. We'd all applaud, and she'd be off-camera, saying, 'Who *writes* this shit?' That was her highest compliment. That meant, God, this is great." Adds Herb Browar, "I'd be standing on the stage, and all of a sudden, she'd whack me on the shoulder. I wouldn't call it affection, but that was one of the ways she was showing that she considered you a friend."

Lucille, however, did occasionally display flashes of refreshing good humor about her newfound television celebrity. "Desi loaned me six hundred dollars for a down payment on my first house, [near the Desilu ranch] in Reseda," recalls Maury Thompson. "Lucille would say, 'Are you going home? I'll ride with you.' I said to myself, 'Oh, God, we'll get hit, with people looking at her in the car, they'll drive right into us.' So we put a highball [cocktail] between her legs and drove off, and of course, other cars drove up alongside us when they spotted her. Then they'd drop back and drive up on *my* side of the car, because they saw her talking to *me,* and they'd get another good look at her."

Of Lucille on *I Love Lucy,* Oppenheimer once astutely observed, "The entire project rode on the radiant talent of that woman. The Lucille Ball of the 1950s was a simply incredible, stunning performer. In every sense, she was a star. Unexpected qualities appeared out of nowhere. Little human, ordinary, recognizable values. Inflections that were exactly the way your sister or your mother or the lady bus driver used to sound. She was everywoman. Ask her to be a tough showgirl, and you got back a broad who simply could not look and move like that unless she'd been pumping out bumps and grinds for years. Ask her for royalty and she became a queen. And she kept astounding us that way each week.

"She didn't know what the hell she was doing—at the first reading. Lucy stumbled through the first reading and then took the material to the mat. She fought with it, examined it, internalized it, and when it reappeared, she owned it. There was no feeling that the audience was watching her act. She simply was Lucy Ricardo. And if you looked carefully, you would marvel that every fiber in the woman's body was contributing to the illusion. Did Ricky catch her in a lie? She wouldn't be just a voice denying it. Her stance would be a liar's stance. Defensive. There would be a telltale picking at a cuticle, or a slight, nervous jerking of an elbow, or a finger brushed against an upper lip, which is the first place you feel the perspiration of anxiety. Her hands, her feet, her knees, every cell would be doing just the right thing."

Lucille's abilities were nurtured and honed with a great deal of encouragement from her old friend Edward Sedgwick, who, having directed Buster Keaton and Joe E. Brown, recognized the depth of her comedic talent but realized it was often very difficult for her to drop her natural reserve and tackle a role with abandon, constantly advising, "Let yourself go, Lucy." But it was, in fact, Desi who was ultimately crucial in coaxing Lucille to blossom and dispel her inhibitions. Cleo Morgan notes, "She didn't trust, really let go, put herself in someone's hands and do what they told her to do. But she had total trust in Desi. She thought he was just brilliant—and he was."

I Love Lucy—and the stimulating, guiding, and artistic hands of such gifted talents as Desi, Jess, writers Pugh, Carroll, and the others—finally allowed Lucille to tap into the deepest, purest resources of her innate comic abilities; furthermore, she showed herself to be a far better actress than revealed in her past film performances. She now possessed an extraordinarily keen sense of comic timing, the means to express layer upon layer of "microreactions" within the space of a second, shining with a particular magic that somehow had never before manifested—and, sadly, would largely become elusive in later years. "It is so important to have what I like to call the enchanted sense of play," she once explained. "Many, many times you should think and react as a child in doing comedy. All the inhibitions and embarrassments disappear. We did some pretty crazy things on *I Love Lucy,* but we believed every minute of them."

"She was the best there was. The greatest female clown ever, or ever will be. You didn't have to tell her anything," Maury Thompson notes.

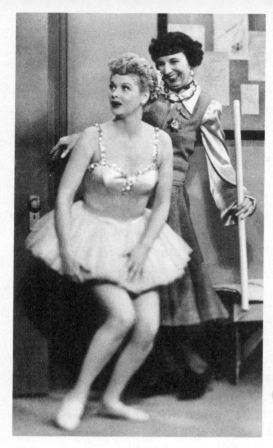

Lucy with dance instructor
Mary Wickes in "The Ballet,"
one of the first season's
classic episodes
THOMAS J. WATSON COLLECTION

"Even Bob and Madelyn would say that they never expected it to be as funny as when they put it on the floor and she did it." And, adds, Bob Carroll, Jr., "She never said, 'I can't do that.' 'Would you mind milking a cow, work with an elephant, whatever.' She would say, 'Yeah, sure, just give me time.' We told her once we heard she played saxophone in high school. She said her group was called the Four Balls. She said, 'Give me a few weeks.' We said okay. She learned to play the violin. She played it so well, we said, 'Lucy, hold it. You're playing *too* good. Back up to where you were *last* week.' She was such a student of things, rehearsing at home."

Yet she could also be remarkably insecure, even at the very height of her popularity. One *Los Angeles Times* profile on the star had the telling headline LUCILLE BALL UNHAPPY ABOUT HER TOP TV RATING. "When people come up to me and congratulate me for being a part of the top show in television it makes me unhappy. I don't know how anyone can say one show or another is the best on TV. As long as we're in the first ten on the ratings we'll be happy. I'd rather let someone else be on top of the pile. That way one can't get pushed off." Another key to the enormous popularity of *I Love Lucy* certainly was the extraordinary writing team of Pugh, Carroll, and Oppenheimer, who in the earliest days of *I Love*

54

Lucy faced the daunting task of churning out more than thirty episodes each season. The best *I Love Lucy* scripts adroitly combined broad physical comedy, sparkling dialogue, quieter moments of sentiment and vulnerability wrapped in story lines containing universal truths, all the while maintaining logic of character and plot development—allowing the most outrageous comedic situations to retain believability. As Madelyn once remarked, "When Lucy first met you, she tended to be a little wary, a little challenging. But once you convinced her you knew what you were doing, she would trust you all the way. Some of the stunts we wrote for her could have been dangerous. Yet never once did Lucy back off from any of them, although Desi frequently wanted her to because he was concerned for her safety. She trusted us enough to know that Bob and I had worked out every piece of business ourselves beforehand to make sure it could be done. If the script called for her to hide dozens of uncooked eggs inside her dress, she knew that I'd tried it myself first to see if it was possible and if it was funny."

"We were busy, those little fingers, tapping away at the typewriter, weekends," says Bob Carroll, Jr., about the formidable workload. "We loved it, being dramatic, saying, 'We're working all night again!' We'd work on New Year's Eve, until ten or eleven o'clock, then put on our little tuxedos and formals and go to a party."

Bob Carroll cites many real-life incidents spawning inspiration for later episodes: "Desi and Lucy had the same body-heat problems that a lot of couples have. He liked air, and she liked the windows closed. We used a lot of those little things. We'd always keep notes. We'd meet on Monday and say, 'What do you got?' 'Well, I did this—I went to my reunion. . . . ' 'Ah, ha! We'll do a reunion someday.' Also, the routine where Lucy changed her mind about her order at the Brown Derby actually happened. Madelyn said she'll have a ham sandwich. I said, 'I'll have the veal chops.' She said, 'Wait, that sounds good. I'll have the veal chops.' So Jess said, 'I'll have the roast beef.' She says, '*Forget* the veal chops. I'll have the roast beef.' So we did a whole routine out of that. Those were the best ones, things that people could identify with."

Adds Madelyn, "We all get strange about money. We used money a lot. We learned that Vivian could say anything she wanted to about Fred, but no one else could. We found out the audience didn't like it if someone made fun of Desi's accent. Only Lucy could. We learned that the audience couldn't really think that Lucy was in danger. Once time, she was on a ledge, supposedly, although the [studio] audience could see it wasn't really a ledge. She slipped, supposedly, and grabbed onto the drainpipe, and the audience gasped and did not laugh because they

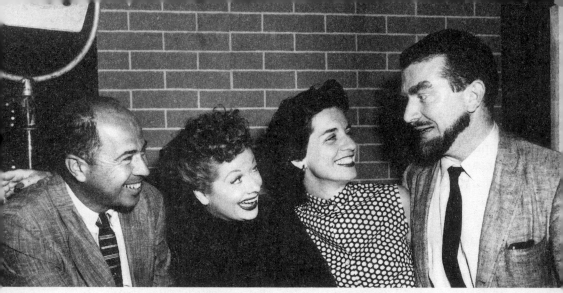

Producer—head writer Jess Oppenheimer and writers Madelyn Pugh and
Bob Carroll, Jr., flank Lucille.
ARNAZ FAMILY ARCHIVES

thought Lucille Ball was going to be hurt. So we learned very quickly
that you had to be careful with the audience. We learned all the funny
things that we could use of Desi's English. We learned that if we wrote
it correctly, he would say it incorrectly. If we wrote it like he talked, he
wouldn't say it, he'd say it correctly. So we'd never write it in. He didn't
know sometimes what we were talking about. He told us much later, 'I
didn't know—when everybody laughed, I figured, well, it was okay.'
Little Americanisms he didn't know. He had no idea, he never let on.
And that must have been difficult for him."

Desi summed up the show, and its success, by noting, "Our TV story
is not just a comedy. It's also a romance. It even has sex in it—with a
sense of humor."

An appreciation of Desi's abilities—both on *I Love Lucy* and behind
the cameras—grew steadily within the industry, if not by the average
television viewer of the day. "His talents as an actor never received the
public recognition they deserved," Vivian Vance stated. "The three of us
seemed so much funnier than Desi. The contribution that Desi made!
The secret lay in his Cuban point of view, which he brought to three
clods, who didn't know what to make of it. That was the crux of so
much of the laughter." *The Hollywood Reporter* in January 1952 proclaimed Desi Arnaz "the most underrated performer on network
television."

As a Desilu executive, he inspired an unusual amount of dedication
and affection among his fellow workers. "He had great enthusiasm, which
he's always had for everything that we've ever done," states Bob Carroll,
Jr. "He never said no. He never said anything was too expensive. He

would do anything, pay for anything." And as Lucille offered in 1952, "He's the brains of our Desilu Productions company and is always working at either filming, editing, or shipping the programs we've already done." He had an uncanny, innate rather than intellectual, business sense, which bloomed along with the success of *I Love Lucy*. "Desi has a mathematical mind, but he had never used it much up to that point," said Lucy. "Then CBS sent over this budget, and he began to study it. He said to me, 'They've made a million-dollar mistake.' I said, 'That's impossible.' 'No,' he said, 'I know there's a million dollars more in here for us to spend on production. They've got their figures wrong.' The next day he took the papers in to CBS and said, 'You've made a million-dollar mistake.' They said, 'That's impossible. Look, Desi, stick to your acting. We'll handle the business details.' So then he spread their papers out all over their office. He proved to them that they were wrong. There was an extra million in there to be used for production. From then on, when he talked, they listened. That gave him a boost of self-confidence. Over the years, I've watched a brilliant mind blossom. He surprises me— I think he even surprises himself. He's intuitive. He lives from minute to minute. But I call him Nostradamus—he seems to know what'll happen next. And he learned every job in our setup before he hired anybody else to do it."

Early in filming *Lucy,* it was discovered that an average of seventy-five hundred feet of 35mm film stock was shot for each episode via the three-camera simultaneous-filming method. Editing the final product was particularly laborious, the film editors delayed by having only a standard one-screen Moviola from which to work. Desilu film operations head George Fox designed a unique synchronized four-headed Moviola, nicknamed "Desilu's Four-Headed Monster" within industry circles. This was the direct result, said Desi, of his finding himself "spending five, six, seven, hours a day and night in the projection room with our film editor, Danny Cahn. . . . The guy who built it wanted to rent it to us. I said, 'No, I don't want to rent it, I want to *buy* it.' Al [Simon] said, 'It'll cost us thirty-five thousand dollars.' 'Okay, buy it.' Unbelievably, that was the only four-headed monster in town until the demands for it were so many we built the second one."

At the close of 1951, *I Love Lucy* was in seventh place according to the Arbitron Top Ten ranking. January 1952 found *Lucy* catapulting to the near-top of the ratings heap with a 43.9, beaten only by Arthur Godfrey's *Talent Scouts*. Following *Lucy* were Skelton, *Your Show of Shows,* and Berle's *Texaco Star Theater*. The unparalleled impact Lucille Ball and *I Love Lucy* were making upon television was reflected at the Academy of Television Arts and Sciences' fourth annual Emmy Awards dinner (honoring achievements for the year 1951) held on February 2, 1952, at the Coconut Grove of the Ambassador Hotel. In his acceptance speech for his "excellence in comedy" honor, Red Skelton graciously said, "Ladies and gentlemen, you've given this to the wrong redhead. I don't deserve this. It should go to Lucille Ball." *The Reporter* noted, "There wasn't a dry eye in the house when Red Skelton did his best to give his second Emmy to Lucille Ball and Lucy herself, technically a loser, won more friends than a dozen Emmys could ever compensate for." That same month, *I Love Lucy* reached the pinnacle of popularity when, for the first time, it became the number-one show on the air.

Hollywood quickly took notice of Desilu's burgeoning success. *Newsweek*'s February 18 edition noted that such stars as Rosalind Russell, Eve Arden, Arlene Dahl and Lex Barker, Laraine Day, and Leo Durocher and Bing Crosby toured the Arnaz soundstages. Crosby, said *Newsweek,* "would probably use the Desilu technique when he makes his long-awaited television debut. The Durochers were so impressed that they had Desilu film a baseball series for them. Red Skelton uses the facilities for his [Tide] commercials. And last week Eve Arden was making a pilot film of *Our Miss Brooks*." Others in the *Brooks* cast included Jane Morgan, Richard Crenna, Robert Rockwell, and Lucy's first choice as her Fred Mertz, Gale Gordon. "We aren't at all alike," said Eve Arden when reporters noted a similarity in style between her and Lucille Ball. "She

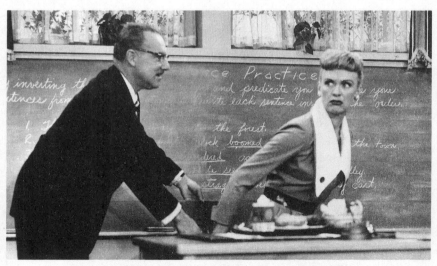

Gale Gordon and Eve Arden in *Our Miss Brooks*
THOMAS J. WATSON COLLECTION

has a great show, and we don't even know what we've got yet." For her part, Lucy countered, "Don't forget that I'm vice president of Desilu Productions, which means the better *Miss Brooks* does, the better off I am. That's not exactly competition, if you see what I mean."

With *I Love Lucy* as the linchpin, Desi's acquisition of *Our Miss Brooks*—to be produced by his company for CBS-TV—signaled the beginning of Desilu's expansion. CBS's Harry Ackerman first announced plans to film a television version of the concurrently airing radio hit in November 1951, with "the production organization to be announced at a later date." By April of the following year—with *I Love Lucy* now solidly installed as television's top-rated show—Desilu not only won the bid to film the pilot but the series as well, already sold to sponsor General Foods. Furthermore, the network at first had envisioned *Brooks* filming at its just-opened multimillion-dollar Hollywood CBS Television City office and studio complex, but Desi, of course, brought the new series to Desilu's General Service Studios headquarters. To bring the Arden show to Desilu, he had turned down very lucrative personal appearances with Lucy scheduled for that summer in Boston and at New York's Roxy Theater, where they were to be paid $57,000 for the two-week Roxy stint alone, with a similar "guarantee and percentage basis" in Boston, said *Variety*. Lucille was suddenly a hot ticket for feature films; she had to turn down a Warner Bros. bid to star in the comedy *Stop, You're Killing Me* during her summer hiatus from the series, saying, "I'd like to, but I don't know whether I'll have the strength." Indeed, the Arnazes's longtime friend and physician, Dr. Marcus Rabwin, advised Lucy that she was at a state of near-exhaustion near the end of the first season and insisted that she rest before resuming her strenuous activities for the 1952–53 season.

"I got so nervous and keyed up I went to a psychiatrist," Lucy once admitted. "But she only saw me for three weeks. Then she told me that there was nothing psychologically wrong with me, I was just worn out from having a baby and a television show at the same time. She taught me how to rest in a roomful of people, to hold all my emotions in, instead of talking about them. That's why people sometimes complain that I'm staring at them deadpan. I'm trying to be deadpan inside, too, so that I won't fly apart."

May 1952 brought news that *I Love Lucy* had already made television history. *Variety* reported that the series "was now seen by an average of 29,000,000 viewers each week—and that's more than double the number of persons who see the average Hollywood 'A' film during its total domestic first run." The news report further noted that, according to the most current American Research Bureau statistics, Lucy became the "first [show] in TV to reach over 10,000,000 homes. ARB estimates that an average of 2.9 viewers now watch each TV screen, which gives a total of well over 29,000,000 viewers for the show each week." *The Hollywood Reporter* chimed in—upping those already astounding numbers—stating Lucy "now sits atop TV's highest peak with a total audience never before reached by any show, including Milton Berle. Total number of people now watching Lucy every week: 30,740,000, including an estimated 7,377,600 children. Anyone for competition?"

Not surprisingly, Philip Morris signed to sponsor *Lucy* for a second season. Rumors circulated in the trades that it was "entirely possible"— but ultimately untrue—that the series would be broadcast in color for the 1952–53 season. The trades also circulated another unfounded story that Desi was on the brink of purchasing the old Chaplin Studios in Hollywood, planning to construct a hotel for the Sunset Boulevard side and the actual studio behind the property.

At the end of the first season, in a profit-percentage deal, Al Simon departed the series to produce *I Married Joan,* a *Lucy*-like sitcom starring Joan Davis. Herb Browar and Marc Daniels soon followed. *The Hollywood Reporter* on May 9 announced director Daniels's "entirely amicable" departure from the show, the result of a salary dispute. Lucille's clashes with the director, however, reportedly contributed to his departure from the show after the first season. "I had to handle a pop-up toaster, and during rehearsals he had me use balsa wood instead of real bread," said Lucille in 1974, "and it was popping way up in the air. So I said, 'I'm going to have to eat this bread. Don't you think we ought to start working with the real thing?' By the second day of rehearsal with the balsa wood, I said, 'Sir, don't you think we should be working with the bread?' 'For what?' he asked. 'Because of the weight,' I explained. 'The balsa's taking off like a Ping-Pong ball.' So he got a little miffed. And I said, 'May I use the bread?' 'No.' So I insisted, 'It's *my* bread, bring it in!' And what a helluva difference."

The item added that a replacement for him was expected to be "signed over this weekend"; *Variety* added that Desilu "refused to meet his demands for upped coin." Three days later, the *Reporter* brought news of Edward Sedgwick joining Desilu, brought aboard to "work with Desi Arnaz in developing and coordinating original television productions." *Variety* on May 12 stated that Sedgwick had been signed to direct the upcoming season of *I Love Lucy* as Marc Daniels's replacement; another item in the same issue, however, noted that Bill Asher "will reign a coupla" episodes. Adding to the confusion was an item in the *Reporter* the following day, claiming that Sedgwick "will have no part of *I Love Lucy*." In the end, Sedgwick was given the task of converting three *Lucy* programs into a theatrical feature for the United States and Latin America; he directed several days of new footage, including opening and closing sequences as well as necessary continuity bridges. (Apart from a preview in Bakersfield, California, the film was ultimately shelved, prompted by MGM signing the Arnazes in early 1953 to star in the comedy *The Long, Long Trailer;* the studio felt that the *Lucy* theatrical film would provide undue competition.) A few months later, another old Arnaz friend, Argyle Nelson, departed RKO and joined Desilu Productions as general manager in charge of production.

William Asher had been hired by CBS to direct the *Our Miss Brooks* pilot, with the understanding that he would direct the series as well if the project was sold to a sponsor. Asher had known Lucy and Desi "very slightly" during their MGM days, his older sister, Betty, having once worked in the studio's publicity department. "Lucy and Desi were having problems [with Daniels]," recalls Asher. "Eve Arden didn't know that I had any connection at all with Lucy and Desi, and she kept raving to them about this young director. It all played into the fact that they asked me to come over and do *Lucy*. The problem was, the *Brooks* pilot sold, and I was committed to do the first ten episodes. Desi arranged the schedule so that I could do both. I was working in the morning with *Lucy* and in the afternoon with the other show, two of the days without crew, so I could arrange working early morning on one and in the afternoon with the other. And overlap the physical days of the crew, and use the same crews. So it worked very well. We had a four-day schedule. We would rehearse two days and then have four days on camera." Desi, says Asher, later "called me in and said, 'A lot of people are going to be coming to us. How do you feel about directing all of our pilots?' And I did."

Asher maintains a high regard for Arnaz. "Desi was invaluable. He didn't necessarily take any creative credit. But he was a big contributor to all those shows. All of them. And he was very highly respected by the creative forces that worked on those shows. His skills were never fully appreciated. He contributed from the time we sat down to have a reading on the script. Nobody saw a script until we read it on that Monday morning. And the most meaningful notes would come from Desi, far more than from Lucy."

Desi proved to be an increasingly formidable opponent in his dealings with CBS. As network executive Martin Leeds recalls, "We gave *Our Miss Brooks* to Desilu. CBS owned the show. I took a vacation. My wife and

I drove to Vancouver Island. We're there for about two days. It's dinnertime. The waitress comes over and says, 'There's a phone call for you.' I said, 'Nobody knows where I am.' 'Somebody's asking for you.' I get to the phone. It's Bernie [Weitzman from CBS's Business Affairs Department]. 'How did you find me? What's the big problem?' He said, 'Hubbell Robinson, the executive vice president of programming, New York, is pissed off that Desilu is charging CBS for the use of the lights on *Our Miss Brooks!* He said, 'What can we do about it?' I said, 'Pay it. We *gave* them the lights. Now they're entitled to charge for it.' "

Desi shrewdly began recruiting the best people he could find, starting with Martin Leeds, who he hired away from CBS to run Desilu on a day-to-day basis as executive vice-president. "That son of a bitch had given me so much trouble arguing about the CBS money we were spending on *I Love Lucy,*" Arnaz quipped, "I figured it would be better to have him fighting on my side," In what seemed to be a raid on CBS executives, Leeds in turn lured Bernard Weitzman away from the network, with Edwin E. Holly joining Desilu the following year. As Holly, who became financial vice-president, notes, "*Our Miss Brooks* enabled us to do two half-hour shows per week with the same crew, so it started basically as a mutual cost-sharing concept. Argyle Nelson developed a staff of good production people, and we could hire them for part of the year. It was tremendous employment [for them] if they became part of our 'almost-permanent' staff. One supervisor would be servicing maybe four shows. Instead of allocating the salary over four shows, we sold his services, at a flat rate, to each show that he serviced. So we developed these profit centers through spreading the services around."

Holly recalls Arnaz seizing upon a previously untapped means to increase Desilu's revenue: "Desi got shaken up every time he would look at a *Lucy* show and see the end of a scene come up and then the screen would go to black and then up would come the commercial with all different music, different lighting, different everything. He thought this was wrong. He thought the commercial should be done as part of the show, not filmed at the same time or using the same people, but laid in so there was no break in the music, there was no break in the picture. The music would bridge, the *I Love Lucy* orchestra would continue the score right onto the bridge and into the commercial. It made a smooth transition. Desi insisted that as part of the *Lucy* deal with Philip Morris and CBS that we take their commercials and integrate them in the show that way—for an additional fee, of course. After they developed it to a point, other producers in the industry started saying, 'Hey, I want my show to look like the *Lucy* show does.' So we then had people lining up to use our services, and we were the only ones in the industry integrating commercials. We had a handsome business going doing an operation that cost us pennies, and for many years were running a huge profit just on 'Integration.' "

Bill Asher found it initially difficult to integrate himself into Lucille's increasingly dominating presence on the *I Love Lucy* set. As had Marc Daniels before him, Bill Asher clashed with the headstrong redhead: "Being a young director, I knew what my function was. Lucy was getting the cast behind the sets and giving them readings and contradicting staging, and had a general kind of 'takeover' flavor. She would stop the rehearsal and say, 'Wait a minute. No, I don't *want* to go over here. I'm gonna go over *there* and then she can do *this*—Vivian, do *that*.' In the middle of a rehearsal, I stopped it. I finally said, 'This is unacceptable. If I'm going to direct these shows, then *I'm* going to do it. Now, if *you* want to do it, then you don't have to pay me. You guys would save money.' Well, Lucy burst into tears and ran off the stage. Everybody else disappeared. I'm standing on an empty stage wondering, What the fuck have I done? I didn't have an office there, so I had no place to go. I went into the men's room and sat in the stall for about half an hour wondering what was going to happen. And when I came back onto the stage, Desi was there. The stage was empty. He said, 'What the hell did you say to Lucy?' And I told him. He said, 'Well, you're absolutely right. You can't let her do that. She's in the dressing room, crying. Go in there and have a talk with her, because you're right.' I went in, and she was crying. The first thing you know, I'm crying. And it was all hugs and back to work. And I must say, from that time on, I never had that kind of situation."

He adds, "I can't say that we were ever that close. It's difficult when you're working with a major star. They may appear friendly, but you have to be aware just how far you can go in offering friendship in return. It can appear presumptuous, so there's always that barrier. She was great to work with, but no matter how zany her antics were, she was very conscious of the fact that she was an attractive, sexy woman. She didn't want anything she did to appear ugly. That sometimes meant working with her at night after the crew had gone home because she found it easier to come to grips with some of the broader and outrageous things she had to do when no 'outsiders' were watching. She wanted to get it right without people laughing at her, instead of with her. Sometimes, she would balk at my suggestion. She'd say, 'Bill, would you ask your *wife* to do what you're asking me to do?' "

Proof that Asher made the grade came in *Variety* on June 9 when the trade paper reported he had been signed to direct the full 1952–53 season of *Lucy*. The item also noted, without explanation, that production would commence early on July 28, instead of the originally announced date of August 14. The actual cause for the rush to begin production on the new season came from gossip columnist Louella Parsons on June 18: "Lucille Ball is expecting a second baby this winter. She and husband, Desi, are vacationing in Sun Valley and it was their plan to keep this a secret until they return to their TV show this fall. They hoped to break the story on their *I Love Lucy* show. . . . I am sorry to have to break the news ahead of them, but I am sure they'll understand that it is difficult to keep the expected arrival of such a famous baby a secret."

"The *Lucy* show was doing unbelievably well," recalled Lucille. "We were among the first ten on the popularity polls after our fourth show. Twenty shows later, we were the number-one show. I began feeling tired again. No energy. All tuckered out. I told Desi about it, and he grinned. 'Lucy,' he said, 'maybe we're going to have another baby.' Well, it was true. We were. After waiting so long for one, there were going to be two. A lot had been asked of us, but not nearly so much as was now being *given* us."

Lucille's pregnancy was already known to several insiders. Jess Oppenheimer first learned of Lucy's condition in May, just as the current season was to conclude filming: "I could see that whatever the news Desi had, it could only be bad. Swallowing hard, he said, 'We've just been to the doctor. Lucy's going to have a baby.' He looked to me for answers to questions: What could we do? How long would we be off the air? How much would it hurt the show?

"Without thinking twice, I said, 'Congratulations! This is wonderful. It's just what we needed to give us excitement in our second season. Lucy Ricardo will have a baby, too!' "

Chapter Four

★

"We now had our daughter, our son, and two people couldn't have been more in love or happier than we were. Then the shit hit the fan."

—Desi Arnaz, 1977

★

*T*he celebration of Lucille's pregnancy was short-lived when it became alarmingly apparent that the birth of her baby might well cause the demise of *I Love Lucy*. Despite Jess Oppenheimer's conviction that Lucy Ricardo's pregnancy would indeed be part of the show, both CBS and sponsor Philip Morris adamantly opposed the idea. The Biow advertising agency flatly told Desi, "You cannot show a pregnant woman on television," and further advised that, during filming, Lucille's figure had to be somehow completely disguised. "There's no way I can hide Lucy's pregnancy," Desi countered. "By the time fall comes around, she'll be as big as the Goodyear Blimp. And I still don't see what is so wrong if she has a baby in the show as Lucy Ricardo."

Finally, the agency offered a "compromise," allowing only one or two episodes about Lucy's condition. Desi insisted that perhaps eight to ten shows were needed "to do them honestly." Desi then wrote a letter to Philip Morris chairman Alfred E. Lyons saying, in part, "We have given you the number-one show in the country and, up till now, the creative decisions have been in our hands. Your people are now telling us we cannot do this, so the only thing I want from you, if you agree with them, is that you must inform them that we will not accept them telling us what not to do unless, in the future, they will also tell us what to do. At that point . . . we will cease to be responsible to you for the show being the number-one show on television and you will have to look to your people, to the network and to the Biow agency for that responsibility."

Soon after Desi sent Lyons the heartfelt—but carefully composed—letter, no more objections to Lucy Ricardo's pregnancy were raised. Years later Desi discovered what action the Philip Morris executive had taken to still the complaints when Lyons's secretary showed Desi a confidential memo he had issued: *To whom it may concern: Don't fuck around with the*

Cuban! Lucille's pregnancy shortened the summer hiatus, with production to commence July 29. Jess, Bob, and Madelyn were faced with the challenge to develop story lines for the first pregnant actress to portray a pregnant woman on television. "We decided at once to give every script concerning pregnancy to a three-man committee consisting of a priest, a minister, and a rabbi," said Lucille. "If they found anything objectionable in the script, we would abide by their decision." Nothing objectionable was found in any of the submitted scripts, although the group was admittedly puzzled by CBS's edict that the word "expectant" be used to describe pregnancy, asking to no avail, "What's wrong with the word *'pregnant'?*"

It was decided that seven episodes would detail Lucy's pregnancy and birth, with Philip Morris requesting that for those particular programs Lucille not smoke on the air. While she was pregnant, nine "nonexpectant" half hours were shot, five of them to be used later as "postbirth" installments via flashback segments to allow her sufficent time to recover after giving birth before returning to work.

Reviews of the second-season premiere were glowing. *The New York Times*'s Jack Gould said the series was "a triumph of familiar nonsense beautifully tuned." Praised *The Hollywood Reporter,* "The show came back last night with a whoop and a holler to prove, all over again, that TV comedy can be done on film, that good writing spells the difference between the average and the superior and that Lucille Ball has no peer in the difficult realm of slapstick. Nor is Desi Arnaz far behind. . . . Heaven help the competition faced by this one."

Indeed, *I Love Lucy* set an all-time high Nielsen tally—"Seen in more homes than any other regular scheduled program in the history of TV," stated *Variety*—viewed by more than 12,324,000 homes, posting an astounding 66 rating; Berle's *Texaco Star Theater* was in distant second place, seen in 9,454,000 homes.

The first pregnancy episode (borrowing the French word for pregnant, "Lucy Is Enceinte") was filmed on Friday, October 3. The story line featured Lucy's discovering her condition, wanting to tell Ricky but thwarted when the right moment to break the news fails to materialize throughout the day. Finally, Lucy decides to go to the Tropicana nightclub to tell her husband. As Oppenheimer recalled in 1954, "Lucy and Desi got to this point in acting out the script, and then this strange thing happened. Suddenly, they remembered their own real emotions when they discovered at last they were going to be parents, and both of them began crying and couldn't finish the song. It was one of the most moving

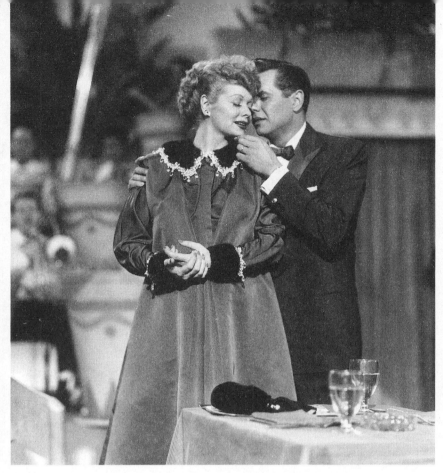

"Lucy Is Enceinte"
THOMAS J. WATSON COLLECTION

things I've ever seen." Asher asked for another, less emotional take of the same scene, but it was ultimately decided to use the original, far more poignant and touching version. During her last filming before temporary retirement, between scenes Lucille told the audience the expected date of birth, January 19, pointed to obstetrician Dr. Joe Harris, and flashed, "Be sure you're right!"

Lucille's physician had scheduled her cesarean procedure for Monday, January 19, and it was decided that the birth of Lucy Ricardo's baby would be broadcast that same evening. Her doctor routinely scheduled cesareans at Cedars of Lebanon Hospital on Mondays, so the Arnazes, said Dr. Harris, had a "fifty-fifty shot" of actually having the baby the same night the episode aired. The only male of the Arnaz family of his generation, Desi was very much hoping for a boy. It was decided, for a different reason, that the Ricardos would have a male child as well—for the benefit of young Lucie, whom her parents felt might feel confused or resentful if another little girl appeared on television with her mother and father. Desi also told Jess Oppenheimer, "Look, Lucy gave me one girl, she might give me another. This is my only chance to be sure I get a son. You give me a boy on TV."

At the time, Lucille appeared a bit defensive that she was to undergo a cesarean procedure, and not long after delivery said, "I believe word has gotten around that some Hollywood actresses have their babies by cesarean because they are afraid of pain or because they fear normal delivery will do something to their figures. My first baby had to be born by cesarean, and so my second was also delivered by cesarean because normal delivery would not have been possible." She added, with rather surprising candor, "I shouldn't like to be accused of saving my figure. Because of young Lucie and her new brother, I've hardly had a figure for the last few years. I still feel like a cumulus cloud in a cloak."

Any concerns that CBS or Philip Morris harbored over Lucille's "delicate condition" were dispelled when it became clear that the public loved *Lucy* just as much, if not more, than before impending motherhood. *The New York Times* commented, "Miss Ball and Mr. Arnaz not only handled the topic of their approaching baby with a great deal of taste and skill but also have been thoroughly amusing in the process. Far from ridiculing motherhood, *I Love Lucy* has made it appear one of the most natural things in the world."

As the date of delivery drew nearer, the entire country seemed transfixed by the event. "We'd expect interest, but not that much interest," said Desilu public-relations man Kenny Morgan, then-husband of Lucille's cousin Cleo. "All day Friday, Saturday, and Sunday I was trapped at my telephone. Newspapers ran hourly bulletins, they ran pools betting on the baby's sex, you couldn't turn on your radio without hearing the question would it be a boy or a girl. Man, it was bedlam!"

Lucille Ball—in what Desi called "the most unbelievable bit of timing I know"—was taken by Desi on Sunday night, January 18, to Cedars of Lebanon and wheeled into surgery the following morning and given a spinal anesthetic allowing her to remain conscious during the procedure. At 8:15 A.M., Dr. Harris announced, "It's a boy!"

Associated Press reporter Jim Bacon—the only newsman allowed to be with Desi in the hospital waiting room—remembered, "Suddenly I heard voices from the operating room yell, 'It's a boy!' Then I heard Lucy say, 'His nose is turned up so much he'll drown if it rains—oh, Desi will be so happy!' "

Desi, upon hearing the news of Lucy giving birth to an eight-pound, nine-ounce son—to be named Desiderio Alberto Arnaz IV—gleefully shouted, "That's Lucy for you. Always does her best to cooperate. Now we have everything!" Lucille's real-life birth, said Hollywood writer Eleanor Harris, caused "world-wide hysteria. Headlines all over the world carried the news. Flowers poured into the hospital in a giant stream, filling up Lucy's room, the entire hallway on her floor, the stairway leading down to the floor below and finally its corridor as well. The switchboard at the hospital lit up like a Christmas tree. Hospital authorities angrily refused to permit the crowd of photographers pressing at the outside doors to enter at all." Thirty thousand viewers wrote fan letters to Lucy offering good wishes, only twenty-seven of them expressing disapproval of her on-air pregnancy. "Counting letters, telegrams, gifts and telephone calls, she and Desi received over one million indications of public interest—a figure never before even approached in the entertainment world."

Lucy writers Pugh and Carroll seemed astonished at its popularity, having installed a sign in their office reading IT'S ONLY A SHOW. "If we ever stopped and asked ourselves why forty million people watch the show, we'd shake with fear all week," said Madelyn. "We try not to think about it too much," concurred Bob Carroll. "The scripts are just as good or bad as they ever were. We bought books on how to write for TV but got so busy writing *Lucy* scripts that we never did have time to read them."

"Lucy Goes to the Hospital" resulted in an yet another ALL-TIME HIGH TRENDEX RATING set by the series, bannered *Variety,* winning a "shattering" 71.1 rating, CBS estimating that more than 44,000,000 viewers tuned in; the program had even been seen by more viewers than Dwight D. Eisenhower's inauguration as the thirty-fourth president of the United States, which attracted an audience of only 29 million. Yet *The Reporter* on January 29 noted, "Despite that top *I Love Lucy* rating, Philip Morris is rumored pulling out, claim being that sales haven't increased enough to warrant the cost." Philip Morris sales had dropped to fifth place, company revenues dropping $2,371,990 in the past year.

Despite that ominous rumor, the Arnazes seemed to be at the very peak of popularity. On February 2, MGM announced that the couple would star in the Technicolor comedy *The Long, Long Trailer,* based on the novel by Clinton Twiss, which amusingly detailed a honeymooning couple's various comedic adventures driving a gigantic 947-foot New Moon trailer across the country. Arnaz had unsuccessfully attempted to buy the property for some time, but was outbid by the studio. The one-picture deal with Metro brought Lucille and Desi the combined flat-figure salary of $250,000, with production to commence in June during *Lucy*'s summer hiatus. Vincente Minnelli signed on as director, with a former

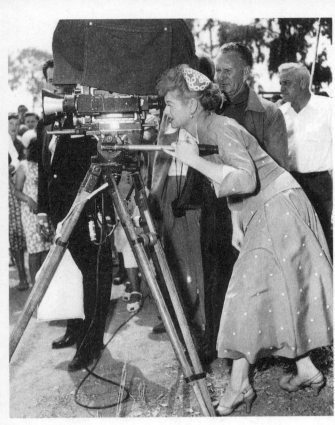

Lucille checks an upcoming shot while on location for *The Long, Long Trailer.* Desi is behind the camera.
THOMAS J. WATSON COLLECTION

flame of Lucille's during her RKO days, Pandro S. Berman, already set as producer. Reports of the Arnaz-MGM deal were quick to point out how television had very recently caused Desi and Lucille's salary to jump to a combined $40,000 per week, Desi having made a meager $650 a week during his brief stint at Metro, Lucille faring much better at $3,500 weekly. Agent Don Sharpe at MGM's lavish "welcome home" bash for the Arnazes cracked, "It wasn't long ago that these movie guys were predicting Lucy had killed her career by appearing on TV every week."

The Long, Long Trailer—although often too reminiscent of *I Love Lucy*—was a great popular and critical success. *Saturday Review* called it a "very funny movie," and *Time* deemed *Trailer* "a wonderfully slap-happy farce." *The New York Times,* on the other hand, countered, "It is an hour and a half of the sort of nonsense you might get in one good, fast *Lucy* show... the wife is still a nitwit... and the spouse is still a good sport with more patience than passion—or brains."

At the same time the Arnazes finalized the MGM deal, despite any reservations about continuing its association with the show, Philip Morris began preliminary negotiations to continue sponsoring *I Love Lucy* in a new two-and-one-half year deal. Perhaps the change of heart was prompted by *Variety*'s Jack Hellman, who chided, "Al Lyons, prexy of Philip Morris, and his agency brain, Milton Biow, are disturbed because *I Love Lucy* doesn't supply the sales surge expected of their high rating. . . . This is unfair to Desilu for the academic reason that *Lucy* is being paid for just one thing—to deliver an audience, which it is doing at the lowest cost per thousand viewers. For somewhere around $55,000 a week, *Lucy* delivers roughly 40,000,000 lookers every Monday night, easily the best record of any top show. If P. Morris can't sell this vast audience there's something wrong with the selling copy or the cigarette and certainly *not* with *Lucy*."

Later that same week, eight days after Lucy was released from the hospital after giving birth, on Thursday, February 5, *I Love Lucy* won an Emmy Award as "best situation comedy" (accepted by Lucille and Desi), with Lucille also singularly honored as "best comedienne." When Lucille appeared on the Statler Hotel ballroom stage to accept the first award, presenter Art Linkletter quipped, "It looks like Lucy and Desi get something every month." Indeed, the Lucy phenomenon hit new heights. A *Lucy* newspaper comic strip and a series of comic books appeared. The birth of the Arnaz child prompted almost unlimited merchandising possibilities, prompting many to refer to Desi IV as "Lucy's $50 million baby." Thousands of stores soon carried Lucille Ball clothing, Desi Arnaz casual attire, "Ricky, Jr." dolls, *I Love Lucy* dolls, aprons, bedroom suites, nursery furniture, games, costume jewelry, and desk and chair sets, among other items. While Lucy grumbled at public criticism of her and her husband pulling in huge amounts of "Desiloot," *Variety* cracked, "Aren't Lucille Ball and Desi Arnaz carrying their endorsements a little too far? Their caricatures even adorn 'potty' seats."

If the Arnazes thought that February 1953 could bring no more good news, the middle of the month brought the announcement that Philip Morris had indeed agreed to continue sponsorship of Lucy in a record $8 million two-and-one-half-year, ninety-eight-episode deal spanning the remainder of the current season through 1955. The unique "no option" contract meant that it was not subject to normal cancellation privileges by the sponsor. Approximately half of that amount was paid to CBS for on-air charges, agency commissions, and production, with about $4 million actually paid to Desilu. While the previous season's half-hour installments were budgeted between $36,000 and $38,000, the new deal called for "in excess of $40,000" per episode, far beyond the initial $19,500 1951–52 season per-show estimate.

"It couldn't happen to a nicer pair of kids," said Lucille, who hastily added, "I mean our two children, of course."

The Philip Morris deal, recalls the Arnazes's tax attorney, Art Manella, was simple to negotiate: "I went down with Martin Leeds to Palm Springs.

I went down there all prepared. I had done my homework and met with a CBS executive. I thought we were going to have a business meeting. Nobody wanted me to talk about the meeting. All they did was drink and have fun. It went on for two days, Friday and Saturday. Finally, Sunday afternoon we started talking about it. They picked up the phone and called Bill Paley. The whole deal was made in five minutes."

At the Philip Morris signing, Desi emotionally said, "The people really blessed by this are Lucy and myself. We're really happy. I can't tell you how much the program means to Lucy and me." When he sat down after his speech, Desi had tears in his eyes, prompting the far less demonstrative Lucille to crack, "Boy, he can top me any time." Arnaz also quipped that "after everybody gets their cut, we'll wind up with eight dollars and sixty-seven cents saved."

If *I Love Lucy*'s budget was escalating sharply upward, so was a simmering behind-the-scenes feud between Desi Arnaz and Jess Oppenheimer. According to Martin Leeds, upon his Desilu hiring in February 1953, Arnaz "offered me five percent of the net of *Lucy*. I said, 'You're out of your mind.' He said, 'No, I want you to have it. I have to be able

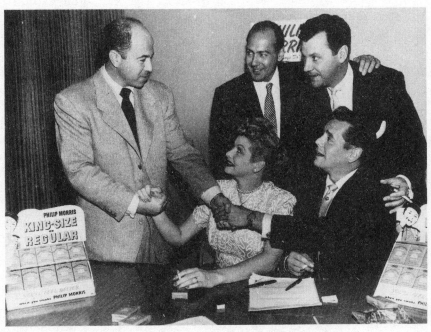

Jess Oppenheimer congratulates Lucille and Desi at the signing of the Philip Morris contract while CBS vice-president Harry Ackerman (left) and Philip Morris executive Harry W. Chesley look on.
ARNAZ FAMILY ARCHIVES

to trust you. I have my own problems. Now the first thing you have to do is make peace between me and Jess Oppenheimer. We're fighting onstage, and that's no good.' " Shortly after Leeds joined Desilu as second in command, "Jess came into my office and said, 'The show will be dead in six weeks. It'll never make it.' Jess hated the show. There was a dispute going on between him and Desi [as to] who was running the show."

The deterioration in Arnaz's and Oppenheimer's relationship apparently was triggered by Desi's assuming "executive producer" credit in the second season of the series. "Desi and I had a running set of problems," admitted Jess, "stemming from the fact that although he was 'El Presidente' of Desilu, I had creative control contractually. The only person who could override me was Lucy. Desi got even in a strange way. Every time I did something newsworthy, like enlisting a priest, minister, and rabbi to approve each unborn-baby script before it was shot, I would find it in the trade papers the next day attributed to Desi."

A purported example appeared in *The Hollywood Reporter* on April 21, 1952. Dan Jenkins, in his "On the Air" column, indicated credit for the success of *I Love Lucy* went "above all to Desi Arnaz, the crazy Cuban whom Oppenheimer insists has been the real producer all along and who in two weeks reluctantly starts taking screen credit as executive producer. Arnaz, whom most people seem to think of as a bandleader, period, has emerged not only as a fine comedian in his own right but as an exceptionally astute businessman."

However, an Oppenheimer intimate insists Desi's elevation to "executive producer" was "meaningless—his contract did not change one bit. Desi came to him at a party. It was Desi's birthday party in 1952. Lucy wanted Desi to have more credit as the brains and production talent. Everyone was saying she was the real talent, and he was just on the show with her. And Jess was exhausted. He was doing so many things at the time. Desi said to him, 'You know, after the show's over, I'm not going to get a job as an actor. So I need some production credits. So would it be okay with you if I had the credit, executive producer?' And Oppenheimer said okay. It was the worst decision he ever made in his life. Then Desi puts out this press release—which Jess reads in *The Hollywood Reporter*—that Desi is 'reluctantly' taking credit now as executive producer, that according to Jess Oppenheimer, Desi's been the real producer all along. And Jess couldn't do anything. He couldn't issue a denial, because Lucy would hit the roof. And it would cause tremendous problems in their marriage."

"Desi doesn't get a lot of credit," states Madelyn Pugh. "For some reason, people play down his part, like he was some lucky Cuban. He wasn't. I mean, he was a lucky Cuban, but he deserved it. He was marvelous to writers. He loved writers, and he liked working with us. We never had arguments. We never had harsh words. I could call him on the phone, I could walk down the hall and say, 'We've got this crazy idea, and can we do that?' He never said no. He never said it would be too expensive. He never said it would be impossible. He never said, I don't want to get a guest star. So we could do anything we wanted. He didn't stifle our enthusiasm, which I think was very important. He'd say, 'That sounds great. Well, let me call the guys.' He'd call Special Effects or he'd call John Wayne, or anybody. It was a new medium, and we did wild things, all those props and all those special effects in front of an audience. I never asked how they worked—to this day I don't know how they did it. That was not my problem.

"He was just terrific because he had a lot of charm. If he wanted us to change something, he would say, 'This is great. Oh, boy, this is funny . . . just a few little thin's . . . ' And 'the few little thin's' could quite often be a *lot* of 'little thin's.' But by now you're saying, 'Oh, well, I don't mind changing a *few* things. Lucy herself said, 'Desi can tell you one thing and it's fine, and I say something and I say it all wrong.' Because she'd say, 'This doesn't work.' We'd say, 'Oh, *God,* the whole script?' He'd say, 'Now, honey, they said it would work and they tried it, so let's try it, and then if it isn't right, they'll fix it.' I can see why she was hesitant— I wouldn't have wanted to do them. But I did a lot of them."

Recalls Bill Asher, "[For rehearsals] it became routine for me to play Desi's part, because he wasn't available. We'd have a reading and then after the reading, the discussion, Desi would be there. Then he'd take off, and I'd do his role. He would come in at the end of the day and watch. I'd go through the scene, and he would just step in and do it. The routine got so that I would block a scene playing Desi's part. I'd call Desi. He'd come in, no matter what he was doing, look at it, step in, try it, and then, after the second day, we had the full run-through with Desi. Oddly enough, when Lucy became pregnant, it reversed itself, because Lucy couldn't be on her feet. So I'd play Lucy's part, and then Desi had to come in, and I would play her part. And then she would look at it and step into it."

While Lucille tempered her tendency to direct the show—and override Asher—she still was confrontational. "When I would start to stage a scene—'Do this, go to the couch, go to the fireplace'—she'd say, 'Why?' In the very beginning, I thought, Is she dumb? I thought, Why is she saying, 'Why?' It was as simple as saying, Why do I breathe in and breathe out? It was obvious. But she kept doing that. Then I realized what it was, why she started every scene asking, Why, why do I do this? Actors can't really trust anybody. It's your face up on the screen, and it's very hard to give yourself to somebody. And that was her way of knowing that I knew what I was doing. And yet she always did it."

Asher fondly recalls the teaming of Ball and Vance. "They did stuff working together that was pure gold. I could get it started and get them in the right direction, but those two got a rhythm going that a director could only sit back and take credit for." The director largely dismisses the continuing off-camera strain between Vivian and Bill Frawley, stating, "Vivian and Bill became an extension of Fred and Ethel. They really did. Vivian and Bill were beginning to act like Fred and Ethel. She'd call him a dirty old drunken slob, and he'd say, That old *cunt,* but it was just an extension of those two characters. Maybe it got to the point where he hated her and she hated him. He'd complain about her. But I was always amused by it. And I think anybody else that was close to her was always amused by it."

The success of *I Love Lucy* and the rapid growth of Desilu Productions, however, continued to be the talk of Hollywood. At the close of the 1952–53 season, *I Love Lucy* remained the top-rated show on television for eleven consecutive months, winning an average 66.3 rating of more than 45 million viewers. Although the project ultimately never materialized, the trades announced that several *Lucy* pregnancy episodes would be repackaged as a feature film titled *Lucy Has a Baby;* also aborted were plans for the Arnazes to costar that summer in *Camp Fire,* a co-venture with Twentieth Century–Fox, or *Main Street to Broadway* with Ethel Barrymore. RKO, Columbia, and United Artists were engaged in a fierce bidding war for Desilu's package of three nonpregnancy shows for theatrical distribution until MGM's *Long, Long Trailer* deal scuttled the entire project; Desilu originally planned to "launch a one-a-year picture" based on several TV episodes of *Lucy,* despite the death of sixty-year-old Ed Sedgwick in May 1953.

Desilu also offered Philip Morris the choice of *The Eddie Quinlan Show* or the musical-comedy series *Those Whiting Girls* as the summer replacement for *I Love Lucy;* Philip Morris, though, chose a non-Desilu show, *Racket Squad,* with *Those Whiting Girls* finally chosen as Lucy's summer replacement for the 1955 and 1957 seasons. Jack Benny also chose Desilu to film five episodes of his program during the summer months, the filmed installments to be interspersed throughout the season's bulk of live broadcasts. In a career slump, Frank Sinatra signed with Desilu to star in *Blue in the Night* (alternately titled *Downbeat*), a dramatic filmed series about a musician, the project abandoned when Sinatra was cast in his blockbuster comeback film *From Here to Eternity.*

Desilu's three-camera filmed technique was utilized for Danny Thomas's pilot of his new series *Make Room for Daddy,* directed by Bill Asher; when the Marterto Enterprises production sold to ABC-TV for the 1953–54 season, Desilu's General Service Center was chosen as the filming site, along with programs starring Loretta Young and Ray Bolger. Arnaz at the same time established a "commercial division" of Desilu headed by former Biow Company account executive Edward H. Feldman.

Desilu's boom prompted Arnaz and Leeds to consider a move to bigger quarters in the summer of 1953. With General Service having an insufficient number of soundstages (each requiring access to a public street), Desilu, with a $1 million infusion from CBS, took a ten-year lease on the Motion Picture Center, a seven-acre lot located at 846 North Cahuenga Boulevard in Hollywood that featured nine soundstages, six of them readily usable as "Desilu Playhouse" soundstages for the several three-camera situation comedies to be filmed by the production company. Four Motion Picture Center soundstages were transformed into filming sites (to hold live studio audiences), processed concrete floors (the idea inspired from a department-store loading dock) were poured to facilitate smooth dolly movement. Hundreds of offices were created for Desilu employees. Arnaz estimated that, by the end of 1953, Desilu would do a gross business of $6 million. *Our Miss Brooks* would be housed on Stage 8, with Stage 9 the new *I Love Lucy* home, each claiming a studio audience capacity of three hundred. The move to MPC also gave Lucy a four-room apartment very close to the *Lucy* soundstage, including two sizable dressing rooms, a living and dining area, and a fully equipped kitchen. Desi promoted assistant director James Paisley to assistant production manager and brought in Jerry Thorpe (who had been Vincente Minnelli's assistant on *Long, Long Trailer*) to replace Paisley as first assistant director on *I Love Lucy.*

The lengthy daily commute to Hollywood from remote Chatsworth forced the Arnazes to rent a home in Beverly Hills during that summer's production on *Long, Long Trailer.* "As it is, we have to get up at six A.M. to be here at seven," complained Lucille on the movie's set, "and then we get home at eight P.M. If we lived in the Valley, we'd never see the children. After we're through with the picture, we'll vacation at Del Mar and then return home." The comparatively slow pace of feature film production was so evident that Lucy mused on the *Trailer* set, "I never realized how much tension I was under making TV shows."

As the new *I Love Lucy* season commenced, Lucille's mental state certainly was not calmed when she was contacted by the House Un-

American Activities Committee and told to appear for secret, "closed-door" testimony in Hollywood on Friday, September 4. Cutting her Labor Day vacation short, she left the Arnazes's Del Mar, California, retreat to return to Los Angeles. She was told by an aide of Representative Donald L. Jackson, chairman of the committee, that the organization only wanted to review statements she had made on April 3, 1952, at another confidential meeting in which she was queried about her intentions to vote as a member of the Communist party in 1936. On both occasions, Lucille testified that while she (along with other family members) did register as a voting member of the Communist party ticket at that time, it was a gesture made to her aging, increasingly "eccentric" grandpa, Fred Hunt, who had died in 1942.

At the September 4 hearing, it was disclosed that an Emil Freed, an elected delegate to the meeting of the Communist State Central Committee, appointed several delegates as party members, among them Lucille and her grandfather, Fred Hunt. The Committee held a document purportedly signed by Lucille Ball registering in 1936 as a voting member of the Communist party. Lucille, however, discounted the authenticity of the 1936 registration, stating, "I haven't signed it. I don't know where it came from, or what. And my name is misspelled."

She was questioned by investigator William A. Wheeler in room 215 at 7046 Hollywood Boulevard. Excerpts from her September 4, 1953, testimony:

LB: It was our grandfather, Fred Hunt. He just wanted us to [register Communist], and we just did something to please him. I didn't intend to vote that way. As I recall, I didn't. My grandfather... was a Socialist as long as I can remember. He is the only father we ever knew, my grandfather. My father died when I was tiny, before my brother was born. He was my brother's only father.... [Fred Hunt] was in sympathy with the working man as long as I have known and he took the *Daily Worker*.... As a dad, and he got into his seventies, and it became so vital to him that the world must be right 24 hours a day... he was trying to do the best he could for everybody and especially the working man; that is, from the garbage man, the maid in the kitchen, the studio worker, the factory worker. He never lost a chance to do what he considered bettering their position. That was fine and we went along with it wherever we could. Sometimes it got a little ridiculous because my position in the so-called capitalist world was pretty good and it was a little hard to reconcile the two. We didn't argue with him very much because he had a couple of strokes and if he got overly excited, why, he would have another one.

Lucille concluded:

> I am not a Communist now. I never have been. I never wanted to be. Nothing in the world could ever change my mind. At no time in my life have I ever been in sympathy with anything that even faintly resembled it. . . . It sounds a little weak and corny now, but at the time, it was very important because we knew we weren't going to have Daddy with us very long. If it made him happy, it was important at the time. . . . In those days, it was not a terrible thing to do. It was almost as terrible to be a Republican in those days.

Lucille's grueling two-hour testimony finally ended when Wheeler told her, "I have no further questions. Thank you for your cooperation." She was told that she had been completely cleared of any suspicion of Communist party affiliation and further assured that her testimony would remain sealed.

Lucille returned to the Chatsworth ranch while Desi remained in Del Mar for a poker game at producer Irving Briskin's home. Two days after her secret testimony, however, she was reading a *Lucy* script at the Desilu ranch while listening to Walter Winchell's Sunday evening broadcast. During the program, Winchell offered listeners the "blind" item that "the top television comedienne has been confronted with her membership in the Communist party."

"I knew that she was not guilty of anything," said Desi, "but in those days the climate was bad for even the smallest innuendoes. Joe McCarthy and his Senate hearings were like witch-hunts." Careers had been tainted, or destroyed, by even a hint of Communist associations, including such prominent names as Dalton Trumbo, Lillian Hellman, John Garfield, Sterling Hayden, Larry Parks, Dorothy Parker, Dashiell Hammett, Donald Ogden Stewart, Judy Holliday, José Ferrer, Gale Sondergaard, Clifford Odets, Budd Schulberg, and dozens of others. Recounts writer Dan Jenkins, "I was over at NBC. Jimmy Durante was sitting in the dressing room being made up. He said, 'Gee, isn't that awful about Lucy?' Winchell said that she was card-carrying Communist. Winchell never bothered to check it out, to call Lucy and say, 'Hey, what about this?' Of course, she would have denied the whole thing, and he wouldn't have had a story. He was vile. Lucy was completely apolitical. She knew nothing about politics."

Upon hearing the broadcast, Kenny Morgan immediately phoned Desi in Del Mar. Desi told him to locate MGM publicity head Howard Strickling and both meet him at the Desilu ranch. At breakneck speed, Desi drove the 130 miles from Del Mar to Chatsworth. Although Arnaz,

Strickling, and Morgan were in a panic, Lucille was merely puzzled, not yet absorbing the fact that Winchell had been referring to her. She had scanned her mind for other TV comediennes, at first inconclusively deciding upon, and then rejecting, either Imogene Coca or Eve Arden as Winchell's target. When Strickling, however, suggested to Lucy that Winchell might well have meant Imogene Coca, Lucy cracked, "I resent that, Howard. Everyone knows that *I'm* the top comedienne!"

Strickling advised the Arnazes to not respond in any way to Winchell's item, believing that the entire matter would "blow over." (Desi later lamented, "I've known Walter since I was seventeen—I wish to God he would have called.") However, on Monday, September 7, Winchell's nationally syndicated newspaper column carried the same bombshell accusation he had spoken on the air. The following day, New York *Journal-American* columnist Jack O'Brian ominously wrote, "Lucille Ball plans to retire in four years. She will retire a lot sooner than she thinks."

On Friday, September 11—the filming day for the first episode of the new *I Love Lucy* season—Lucy awakened to find two strange men in hats and overcoats among the orange trees on the Desilu ranch. She quickly woke up Desi, who, still in pajamas, bolted to the front door to demand what the men wanted. They told him they were police reporters from the *Los Angeles Times* on a mission to "talk to Miss Ball about her Communist activities." Desi told them Lucy had no statement for the press. The Arnazes dressed quickly and left through the back door to start the twenty-five-mile drive to Desilu Productions in Hollywood.

Following Desi's instructions, she saw no reporters during the day, and she, along with everyone else, maintained the facade that it was a normal working day. Lucille had her hair set in the morning and spent the afternoon in rehearsals. The Los Angeles *Herald-Express* (Winchell's Los Angeles outlet) bannered the headline: LUCILLE BALL NAMED RED, page one featuring a photostat copy of her purported 1936 Communist party registration card. The newspaper fanned the flames by reproducing only a portion of the document—purposely omitting a CANCELED notation— and quoting "fiery Latin actor" Desi as "snapping" to reporters, "What are you going to do—spread it all over the country?"

"I was terrified," Lucille recalled years later. "That first day I was in a panic. I was absolutely bewildered. I didn't know what was going to happen. I had no answers for them. I really couldn't figure out why they were so interested in me. It was a terrible experience."

Desi spent the early morning in tense meetings with "grim-faced" CBS and MGM executives, all offering the Arnazes total support. The future of *I Love Lucy* rested, however, on word from Philip Morris. As writer Eleanor Harris noted, "If the sponsor canceled the contract, Lucille Ball's career as an actress would come to an instant stop; as a suspected Communist sympathizer, she would be employed no more by any sponsor nor by any network. Behind her, both Desilu corporations would collapse like houses of cards, carrying down with them thousands of people and millions of dollars involved."

The call Desi had been waiting for came at ten o'clock. "Our sponsor called when the thing first broke," said Lucille. "He was Al Lyons of Philip Morris. He asked Desi is there was anything to it, and he said no, then he said I could have a half hour the next Monday to tell my side if I needed to. Luckily, I didn't need to."

Hanging up the phone, Desi bolted out of his office to find Lucy rehearsing on a soundstage. "Honey, I just got a call—Mr. Lyons is standing by us." Desi burst into tears. Lucy, somehow maintaining her composure, said, "Well, that's fine. I'll get back to work." Holding herself in check, she returned to the set and continued the rehearsal for that evening's show, "The Girls Go Into Business."

At six o'clock that evening—two hours before Lucy was to go before the cameras—prompted by an urgent call from Desi, Representative Donald L. Jackson, chairman of the House Un-American Activities Committee, held a press conference at the Statler Hotel where he said that she "had never had a role in the Communist party." At seven-thirty, Desi paced back and forth in his office. He was flanked by Harry Ackerman and Martin Leeds, along with Dan Jenkins and his wife, who happened to be wearing a red cashmere seater. "Pat," said Desi, "for godsakes, did you have to wear a sweater that color?"

A few minutes after eight, Desi took the stage and faced three hundred people seated in the audience bleachers. "Welcome to the first *I Love Lucy* show of the season. We are glad to have you back, and we are glad to be back ourselves. But before we go on, I want to talk to you about something serious. Something very serious. You all know what it is. The papers have been full of it all day." Desi paused for a moment and his lower hip began to quiver. "Lucille is no Communist," he said. "We both despise the Communists and everythin' they stand for." His eyes, according to Jenkins, were filled with tears, and his voice was shaking, his hesitation now replaced by anger. "Lucille is one hundred percent an American. Tomorrow mornin' the complete transcript of Lucille's testimony will be released to the papers, and you can read it for yourself. Then you will know this is all a pack of lies."

The audience roared in approval, one man shouting, "We're with you, boy!," to which Desi replied a sincere "Thank you." Desi then introduced Vivian and Bill, steeling himself for the moment when he had to introduce Lucille. "And now," he said calmly, "I want you to meet my favorite wife—my favorite redhead—in fact, that's the only thing red about her, and even that's not legitimate—Lucille Ball!"

Jenkins recalled, "Lucy stepped quietly out from behind a door at the rear of the set. The heavy makeup for the show concealed the lines of worry and strain. She had been in seclusion most of the afternoon and had spoken to no one but Desi and a few close friends. She was smiling, but it was a set smile. She got her answer in short order—an ovation. Still smiling, she punched the air lightly, with both hands, as though to say, 'We'll fight this thing out,' bowed easily, and went through the door. When it was over, the two of them came out arm in arm and asked each of the supporting players to take a bow. Then Lucy stood alone with Desi for a moment, looked into the audience, and said, 'Good night, God bless—and thank you.' It was a long walk offstage, clear across the width of the studio. She received an ovation every step of the way. When she got back to her dressing room, she broke down and cried her eyes out."

The following day, Lucy—casually attired in a pink hair ribbon, white blouse with an embroidered "Lucille" on it, and pink linen toreador slacks—with Desi in close proximity, held an informal press conference at the Desilu ranch, conducted by the Arnazes's neighbor, Bill Henry of the *Los Angeles Times*. Complete transcripts of Lucille's testimony were available, along with a statement from Emil Freed duly noting that he had "never met Miss Ball."

Although Lucille was criticized by some for appearing in photographs during the press conference smiling, holding a highball in one hand and a cigarette in the other, the meeting with the press was successful. Amid beer and ham-and-cheese sandwiches provided the reporters, the Arnazes were covered by four press agents, one from CBS, one from MGM, another from Philip Morris, and Desilu's Kenny Morgan. Lucille told reporters, "I asked Congressman Jackson if I should make a public statement, and he said he saw no reason, that since I had never been a Communist, there was nothing to tell, and if someone had not broken the story on the radio, it probably would never have been printed." She quickly added, "But I'm not criticizing anyone in the newspaper or radio field, because they have a job to do." Lucille thanked her fans for support. "I'm overjoyed and humbled that thousands of people have written and telegraphed that they are behind me."

Desi told reporters, "You know Lucy, and you know she has never

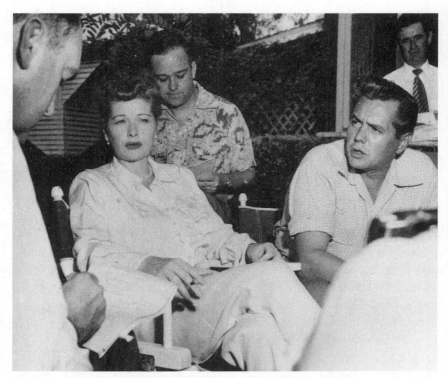

The Arnazes face the press at their Chatsworth ranch. Behind Lucille is
Desi's assistant, Johny Aitchison.
SECURITY PACIFIC COLLECTION/LOS ANGELES PUBLIC LIBRARY

been a Communist. After thirteen years of happy marriage, I think I
know her better than anyone else, and I know she hates everything
Communistic as much as I do—and I have reason to hate them for
what they did to my family. I was kicked out of Cuba by the Communists when the revolution hit there. She merely wanted to please
a fanatical old man, her grandfather, and to sign a paper the way he
wished. Today she is older and wouldn't sign such a paper, even to
please her grandfather. In 1936, it was a kind of a joke, a kind of
very light thing. If Grandpa was alive today, we might have to lock
him in a back room."

"The city desk people were getting pretty damned nasty," recounts
Jenkins of the press conference. "And Lucy was like a piece of ice. She
told the story of what happened; they asked all the questions they could
ask. All of a sudden, there was this silence. I don't know what the hell
got into me, but I got up and said, 'Well, I think we all owe Lucy a vote
of thanks, and I think a lot of us owe her an apology.' There was applause.
Desi threw his arms around me, crying. It was very emotional. Lucy
threw her arms around me and didn't say anything. She never said

anything unless she had to. From that time on, we were very good friends."

To the Arnazes, the most important statement came from reporter Walter Winchell—who had started the entire fiasco—when he stated on Sunday, September 13, "During the past week, Donald Jackson, chairman of the House Un-American Activities Committee, and all its members, cleared Lucy a hundred percent, and so did J. Edgar Hoover and the FBI, plus every newspaper in America, and tonight, Mr. Lincoln is drying his eyes for making her go through this."

Harry Ackerman stated, "We've had very few phone calls, and virtually all were favorable. The people seem to think this thing is silly, not serious, and they all love Lucy." *Variety* noted that the Jackson press conference "at which he gave Miss Ball a clean bill of health was comprehensively shown on KNXT, CBS-TV station here Friday night in an astute piece of public relations by the web." The trade paper added, "Save for the potential seriousness of the situation, the rapid-fire events of the weekend assumed an opera bouffe quality that might have been taken right out of an *I Love Lucy* script."

Some members of the press and public remained unswayed. Syndicated columnist Westbrook Pegler wrote, "I would not forgive her anyway because she did not come clean, but had to be tracked down and exposed." The Huntington *Herald-Dispatch* offered, "Despite the almost frenzied efforts of the very best press agents and public advisors those capitalist dollars can buy, most thoughtful Americans are going to find it difficult to 'love' Lucy with the same old abandon."

Lucille, recalls Robert Osborne, keenly remembered that harrowing weekend long after it faded from the headlines. "On the way home one night, Lucy made some kind of remark about liking Gordon MacRae all right, but not having a lot of faith in Sheila. 'Because they were part of a dinner party I gave one night when that red scare came up about me. I'll never forget that night. We were on top of the world. There were six couples coming. Then the Communist thing broke. Every one of them called and made excuses—they had colds, or they were not well.' She said Gordon and Sheila were the first to cancel. Everyone was so afraid they would become tainted with it. She told me, 'When all these people canceled, I was so destroyed, because I was afraid this would seriously hurt my career but also put a lot of people out of work at Desilu. The next day, when I got up, it was such a grim day for me. We didn't know how people were going to take it.'

"Lucille looked out in the garden, and there was a man sitting out there. She went out and it was Lou Costello. She said, 'I'd known him a little bit, but I didn't really know him. I had done his radio show a couple of times. I went out there and said, 'Lou, what are you doing here?' He said, 'You just go about your business. I'm just hanging out here for the day. I just thought you might need a friend about now.' "

Chapter Five

"Desi and Lucy always loved the people around them. We were family and we felt it and the company was our life."

—Dann Cahn, 1991

*L*ucille Ball, I guess as we all now know, hit the headlines this fall as a girl who once registered as a Communist," noted critic John Crosby in the New York *Daily News* on October 13, 1953. "It was my private guess made long before the headlines broke that Lucy was in for a slide in popular esteem. The *Lucy* shows—let's face it—are beginning to sound an awful lot alike. Miss Ball is always trying to bust out of the house; Arnaz is trying to keep her in apron strings. The variations on the theme are infinite but it's the same theme and I'm a mite tired of it."

Desilu Productions continued to flourish and was becoming an increasingly powerful and prolific company, so much so that *The Hollywood Reporter* announced on February 8 that "CBS tried to buy Desilu but Desilu won't sell." In early 1954, William Morris Agency representatives for producer Parke Levy—mindful of Desilu's successful adaptation of *Our Miss Brooks* from radio to TV—approached Martin Leeds about transferring the long-running CBS radio comedy series *December Bride* to the small screen. On their first meeting, Levy's reps told Leeds that the network's option on converting the property to television was about to expire and that he was furthermore unhappy with CBS's refusal to allow Spring Byington to re-create her role for the TV version. Explains Leeds, "Harry Ackerman wanted to do *December Bride* as a TV show with Spring but, for some reason, Hubbell Robinson said no. Then their time for first refusal ran out. William Morris called me and said, 'Do you want the show?' I said, 'Yes, Desilu will make a pilot.' So about five days later I get a call from Ackerman, saying, 'New York's reversed itself on *December Bride,* but I know you've exercised your right to pick up the option.' 'What do you want me to do?' He said, 'Let us pay for the network time [to air the program], and we'll split ownership with you [and Levy].' I said, 'You've got yourself a deal.' "

Jerry Thorpe was chosen by Arnaz to direct the pilot in late February, starring sixty-one-year-old Spring Byington as live-in widowed mother-in-law to daughter Frances Rafferty and husband Dean Miller with veteran character actors Verna Felton and Harry Morgan as the neighbors. After the filming, Arnaz felt so confident of *December Bride*'s quality and marketability, he remarked, "If I don't sell this one, I'll quit making pilots."

According to Arnaz, CBS founder and chairman William S. Paley was unaware that his network had dropped the *December Bride* option—and had also opposed the Byington casting—during a March screening of the pilot episode. When Paley and General Foods both expressed interest in airing the show on CBS, Leeds firmed up his deal with Ackerman and traded 50 percent of Desilu's half-ownership in the property on the added condition that *Bride* be scheduled to air immediately following *Lucy* on Monday nights; *Lucy*'s enormous lead-in virtually guaranteed *December Bride* certain success. Remaining in the Top Ten for four of its five seasons, *December Bride* was later deemed by Arnaz Desilu's "second most successful series."

Desilu proved to be a four-time winner in the Emmy Awards of the 1953–54 season. At the sixth annual Academy of Television Arts and Sciences honors held on February 11 at the Hollywood Palladium, *Make Room for Daddy* was named "Best New Program" (tied with *U.S. Steel Hour*). Although nominee Lucy lost "Best Female Star of a Regular Series," the winner was Eve Arden for Desilu's *Our Miss Brooks*. While William Frawley was defeated by Art Carney as "Best Supporting Actor," Vivian Vance won her first Emmy as "Best Supporting Actress." Vivian thanked Jess, Madelyn, and Bob for creating Ethel Mertz, then jokingly thanked "the greatest straight woman in show business, Lucille Ball." Lucille and Desi accepted for the series award, Lucille saying, "It wouldn't be right to call our writers up here and give it to them, would it? But I wish we could. . . . We're awful proud to be a part of this industry, really we are. We're trying real hard and we're going to keep it up." Desi stressed, "I hope that next year the Academy does not forget the writers." Frawley—who would lose five consecutive Emmy bids during the run of *I Love Lucy*—reportedly did not take his loss and Vance's gain in gentlemanly fashion, grumbling within her earshot, "It goes to prove that the whole vote is rigged."

Vance's Emmy honor further strained her already unstable marriage to marginally successful actor Philip Ober. Vance would claim that Ober—almost pathologically jealous of his wife's fame and success—deliberately hid her prized Emmy award away from view at home and furthermore told her that her demonstrative on-screen camaraderie with

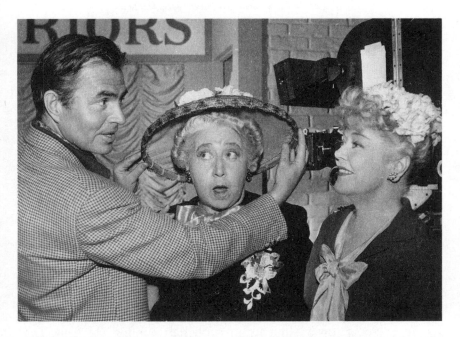

James Mason visits Verna Felton (*center*) and Spring Byington on the set
of *December Bride.*
THOMAS J. WATSON COLLECTION

Lucy had prompted rumors around Hollywood that the two were having
a passionate lesbian affair. "You ought to be more careful about the
hugging and kissing you do on the show," he told her. "You behave like
a couple of dykes in heat." Vivian—still suffering some effects of her
nervous breakdown a few years earlier—was tormented by his wild
accusations.

For some time, Desi and Lucille contemplated retiring from the
weekly-series grind while still at the top, Arnaz alternately hinting to
the press that *I Love Lucy* might cease production upon the expiration
of the Philip Morris contract in April 1955 or, conversely, revitalize the
program by expanding to a new big-budget one-hour format. And, with
MGM's *The Long, Long Trailer*'s early 1954 release expected to launch
for the Arnazes a major new film career, Desi was also scouting motion-
picture properties as well as eyeing Ball-Arnaz Broadway show possibilities. The Arnazes found themselves in the enviable position of having
Metro, Twentieth Century–Fox, and Universal-International furiously
bidding for Lucy and Desi's next feature film, U-I having already submitted Edmond Chevie's tailor-made script *The General and the Redhead*
to them; Lucy and Desi also were seriously considering film properties
not calling for them to appear as a team. In addition, Arnaz was discussing with MGM head Dore Schary the possibility of filming a Technicolor, full-scale motion picture version of *I Love Lucy.*

In March, CBS successfully wooed Arnaz for another two years of original episodes of *I Love Lucy*. In what *Variety* called a "precedential double spread," the deal additionally called for reruns to air concurrently on Sunday afternoons, allowing "added moppet exposure" for children unable to view the prime-time broadcasts. Such reruns would also be seen by millions who were not yet regular television viewers in *Lucy's* earlier seasons—in 1952 only 15 million television sets were in American homes compared to nearly 28 million in January 1955, with an actual audience count several times that amount. Lysol products sponsors Lehn & Fink picked up the option to rerun early episodes of *Lucy* at thirty thousand dollars each—far exceeding the original $1.25 million initially invested to produce those same episodes; weekly 1955–61 network repeats would air under a variety of titles, including *The Sunday Lucy Show, The Top Ten Lucy Shows, The Lucy Show,* and *Lucy in Connecticut*.

Rumors questioning the durability of the Arnaz marriage, however, began to circulate in Hollywood. Directly before the Arnazes were preparing to depart on a multicity promotional tour for *The Long, Long Trailer*, Desi stunned Lucy with a surprise thirteenth wedding anniversary party at Hollywood's Mocambo nightclub. She had expected a quiet dinner with friends Vincente Minnelli and his companion, Georgette, but was flabbergasted when she was serenaded by more than forty guests. Lucy told Desi, "This is the first time in my life I've ever *really* been surprised." Kissing her husband, she told him, "Honey, I just *love* the way you did this." Column items dutifully provided happy anecdotes of the Arnazes's New York visit for Radio City Music Hall's premiere of *Long, Long Trailer*. At one charity gala, Lucy was good-naturedly ribbed "as always wanting to become an actress—and still does"; and when the Arnazes went to see the Broadway production of *Edward, My Son,* Desi was so befuddled by Robert Morley's rapid-fire clipped British accent, he turned to Lucy and quipped, "It took me twenty years to learn to speak English, and I can't understand a goddamned word he's saying!"

Yet only a few weeks later the happy facade began to openly crack when the Arnazes were observed publicly feuding while vacationing in Palm Springs and, according to one report, "Desi didn't love Lucy so Lucy flew back to Hollywood." According to Jess Oppenheimer, "The signs of the eventual bust-up of their marriage were visible even on the early days of *I Love Lucy*. It was clear something was wrong. He'd take off after filming the show on a Thursday night and spend the weekend on his boat at Corona del Mar with his drinking and card-playing buddies, and Lucy would go home alone. Two or three times during the five years of Lucy, she would come storming in and say, 'To hell with

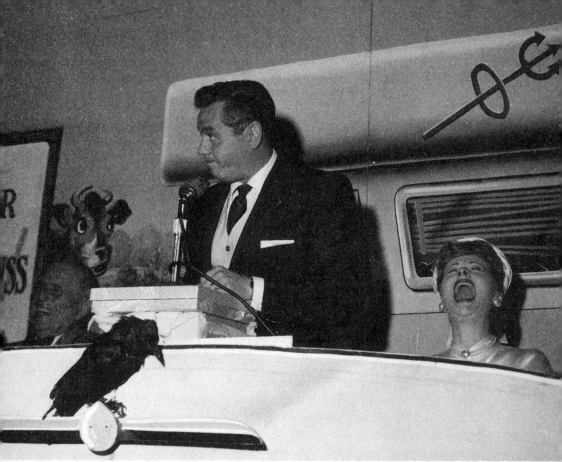

At the Saints and Sinners testimonial dinner while in New York promoting
The Long, Long Trailer
THOMAS J. WATSON COLLECTION

it. That's it. The series is *over*. I'm *not* going to work with him anymore.'
We were always able to calm her down, though." Sometimes the marital
battles were on the lighter side. As Hal King remembers, "Desi used to
bring his mother to the studio. One day, his mother walked in wearing
a sable coat. Lucille says, 'Where the hell did your mother get that sable
coat?' Desi says, 'I bought it for her.' 'Why, you son of a bitch!' Lucille
went right out and bought a sable coat for *her* mother."

Martin Leeds was astounded at Lucille's parsimony, even exhibited
toward her own husband with whom she was, by all accounts, madly
in love. "When I joined the company, I learned that Desi owed Lucy
eighty thousand dollars or ninety thousand dollars of his share of household expenses. That'll tell you something, if nothing else will. When I
found that out, I said, 'How do you want me to handle this?' I was told,
'Well, Desi will pay for what he owes to Lucy. They keep separate
accounts.'" Leeds also discovered that Lucille had stockpiled $425,000
to $475,000 in government bonds by that time.

"When they would fight," recalls Cleo Morgan of the couple's pre-Desilu days, "she would remind him that it was *her* 'goddamned money.' Desi said to me once, 'She just destroys me with the words she uses, the things she says.' "

"Lucy's concept of money and spending had been severely affected by the early days of her childhood," Leeds explains, noting that about eighteen months after joining the company he was approached by an assistant who told him, " 'I don't know what she does with them, but every week we buy a gross of pencils for the program, and after the last rehearsal, even though they have only used about ten or twelve of them, Lucy takes the balance home.' " A week later, at the Arnazes's house for dinner, Leeds confronted Lucille about the pencils. "She took me by the hand and led me over to a closet, opening the door and showing me about ninety gross of pencils. 'Why are you taking them?' I asked. 'You are only stealing from yourself. You own them.' She replied, 'Martin, when I was a little girl, we were poor and couldn't afford pencils. We used pieces of charcoal. Pencils are a symbol of having enough to eat.' She later told me I had unintentionally ruined a symbol."

And, according to Robert Osborne, the successful star often viewed her wealth as a source of power over men in sharp contrast to her early, difficult days in New York. "She had to go out pounding the pavements for work, doing modeling. She used to tell me about how, a lot of times, she used to go to these parties, where she'd go in and there'd be this huge, long table. She said the girls would sit at every other seat. 'The first thing you did,' she'd say, 'is reach under your plate and get your hundred-dollar bill.' I don't know if they had to end up going to bed with them, or were just there as dinner companions while these mobsters were having a meeting, but it was survival, just trying to survive."

Leeds also contends that her frugality stemmed in part from Lucy's own fears of getting older and being victimized by men. "There are some tough, true stores about Lucy with men prior to Desi. When she met Desi, he was six years younger. Desi was a great lover and she married him, but she was always still protecting herself. And it was around 1954 or 1955 when Desi really started to drink. He started to realize he was not the star of the show and was not given enough credit. But he was very knowledgeable about what could or could not hurt her. And he also could read a script once and walk through it."

Adds Desilu business affairs vice-president Bernie Weitzman, "Desi was fantastic. He had total recall. He had a brilliant mind for recall. You had to be very careful about what you said to him, because his philosophy was truth. You could do anything, but don't lie to him. He could handle anything but a lie. That was his philosophy. He said, 'We all make mistakes. I make a lot of them. But don't lie to me. I can handle the truth.' "

Lucille and Desi occasionally exhibited bouts of temperament. As Madelyn Pugh notes, "She would get impatient when things weren't working or impatient that people were phony or weren't doing their jobs. But she didn't know how to put it, didn't know how to articulate it. She was usually right, but she scared everybody. I finally got over being frightened and I could talk to her. What was really valuable with Desi, if he really wanted to know what we thought, he would ask, and we would say, 'We don't think it's any good.' Other people wouldn't say that. They were afraid, but we weren't afraid we would get fired or anything. He had a terrible temper, but he never got mad at us." She adds, "The focal point of Desilu was Desi, but he knew that Lucy was the burning talent. I'm sure he had his ego, but he never once said about the show, 'I don't have enough to do.' "

While she would adamantly—almost defensively—insist she was never in need of therapy, Lucille was victim to a number of strange, severe phobias. "I can't stand pictures of birds on wallpaper or plates or in paintings—anywhere. Whenever I check into a hotel room with bird lamps and pictures in it, I have them all taken away at once. Why? I haven't the faintest idea—particularly since I love real birds." She also was said to have a "compulsive rejection of Indians in native costumes, though not of Indians dressed in regular clothes." According to her friend, writer Katherine Albert, "She told me she could never see *Annie Get Your Gun* because she couldn't stand the idea of all those Indians in it. It's some sort of fear that dates back to her childhood." The phobia that tormented her the most—and was most noticeable on the *Lucy* set—was her inordinate fear of being too close to people, of being touched. "I get numb. The first day I went to Metro-Goldwyn-Mayer in 1942, I wasn't really aware of this phobia. But a new hairdresser spent forty-five minutes working on the bangs on my forehead, leaning against me, breathing on me. At the end of that time, I had tears streaming down my face. My makeup was ruined, and I was paralyzed." (Vivian Vance, aware of this peculiarity, quickly learned to work with Lucy a bit of a distance away from her.) "I have the same feeling away from work, at parties. I can't bear the idea of dancing with some man I don't know and like well. Desi knows this, so he's always ready to help me explain that I'm too tired to dance. Or else he cuts in after a minute or two."

Factors contributing to any strain in their relationship were certainly plentiful. By most accounts, Desi was unable to abandon his voracious appetites for women, gambling, spending, and drinking, and only increased such excesses—perhaps as a form of rebellion and release—as the enormous pressures put upon him as a performer, serving as his wife's supporting player, and Desilu president increased. Despite her devotion to Desi and their two children, it was equally true that Lucille's career to her was, and would always remain, her first priority. The older, more conservative, and controlling Lucille could not tolerate her husband's increasingly embarrassing and self-destructive behavior as their fame and the Desilu empire grew. Ironically, it became increasingly clear that the very reason *I Love Lucy* came into fruition—allowing the Arnazes unparalleled domestic and professional intimacy—now threatened to destroy the marriage of America's favorite couple.

Although it is uncertain whether induced by a tangible problem or by alcohol and self-pity, a poignant indication of such deep-seated problems in their marriage is nevertheless revealed in a note Desi wrote to himself on April 20, 1954, in which he lamented Lucille's inability to forgive him his—unspecified—misconduct, concluding, "I have come to the terrible realization that my wife doesn't love me."

Perhaps attempting to blunt problems in their marriage, Arnaz seemed to focus his attentions on Desilu Productions more than ever before. Desi and Harry Ackerman discussed plans for the Arnazes to appear in a big-budget one-hour Desilu musical spectacular sponsored by Chrysler for the 1955 television season. And with the successful launching of *Our Miss Brooks* and *December Bride,* Arnaz, Leeds, business director Andrew Hickox, and production head Argyle Nelson aggressively pursued other viable television properties. Veteran producer-writer Sam Marx briefly joined Desilu and during his tenure optioned rights to A. J. Cronin's *Country Doctor* book series to star Charles Coburn. When Marx departed Desilu for Universal-International, Arnaz brought in producer-director-writer Bill Spier as his replacement. Another project envisioned but ultimately never executed (and perhaps inspired somewhat by Desi's own beginnings) centered around an impoverished European nobleman who relocates to the United States.

Desilu filmed *Mr. Tutt,* a comedy pilot derived from Arthur Train's *Saturday Evening Post* stories directed by Bill Spier with Walter Brennan and Vera Miles. Also filmed was a comedy-drama pilot starring Spier's wife, June Havoc, as a young attorney (with then-actor Aaron Spelling in a supporting role), and directed by Bill Asher. Also set for the 1954–55 Desilu slate was the revamping of a faltering Ray Bolger ABC series called *Where's Raymond?*; Desilu was brought in to salvage the show in its second season, retitling the program *The Ray Bolger Show* and changing both the cast and premise of the situation comedy. Although *Variety* praised Desilu by offering, "They've done things to the show after a wobbly first season and all to the good," the new version failed to click sufficiently with audiences and finally disappeared altogether by June 1955.

In June, Martin Leeds took the pilots to network executives and advertising agencies. While in Manhattan, Leeds finalized the CBS–General Foods *December Bride* deal and sold the Havoc show to ABC; *Mr. Tutt* and *Country Doctor,* however, failed to attract either network or sponsor interest. Returning, of course, were the non-Desilu-owned series *Make Room for Daddy* and *Our Miss Brooks.*

A Desilu Productions latecomer was *Lineup,* a semidocumentary-style San Francisco–based law-enforcement drama starring Warner Anderson and Tom Tully. *Lineup*—inspired by NBC's successful *Dragnet* series— was very profitable for Desilu in its five-year CBS run, its demise triggered as the result of ill-advised network tinkering when series regulars were recast and the show then expanded to a one-hour format in 1959; it was off the air by January 1960.

The June Havoc show was a chaotic venture from the start. The working title was first *Miss Bachelor at Law* and was alternately known as *The Artful Miss Dodger, My Aunt Willy* and *Willy.* In August, General Foods suddenly removed *The Artful Miss Dodger* from the ABC Friday night 7:30 P.M. schedule, relocating the now-retitled *Willy* to Saturday nights on CBS; midseason, the format shifted as well, with attorney Havoc suddenly leaving her law practice in New Hampshire to work for a vaudeville organization in New York. Blasted *The Hollywood Reporter,* "This alleged comedy series can easily take its proper place as the loudest and unfunniest show of the new season. Odds are against this Desilu production being around very long." *Willy* was indeed off the ABC airwaves by July 1955.

The summer of 1954 found CBS confidently announcing that *I Love Lucy* would be telecast in color, but at the same time rather hazily predicting such broadcasts would begin at the opening of the 1954 season, early 1955, or perhaps starting in the fall of 1956. Several Philip Morris commercials had, in fact, already been filmed in color for inclusion in the series as a test, said the *Reporter,* before "going all the way." While color-television sets in 1954 were in very limited distribution, industry experts predicted a boom of fifty thousand receivers—at a hefty twelve-hundred-dollar price tag—in use by 1955. CBS also proclaimed (incorrectly) that color broadcasts would also begin for seventy-six more "tinted shows" in 1954–55, including Jack Benny, Burns and Allen, *The*

Jackie Gleason Show, Our Miss Brooks, and a new TV version of *My Favorite Husband* with Joan Caulfield and Barry Nelson, which would quickly flop in a live-show format and as a subsequent filmed Desilu series.

The decision to abandon color filming of *Lucy* was the apparent edict of Jess Oppenheimer. Although Oppenheimer conceded in November 1954, "Color is here, at least, it's almost here," he also rather shortsightedly predicted, "I don't feel that color is going to take over TV the way 'talkies' took over silent pictures or the way television itself took the play away from radio." In January 1955, he flatly declared, "We'll never use color for *I Love Lucy.* Color isn't for comedy unless it's just to get humor out of one situation."

At the same time, a minor storm erupted when Lucille gave an interview stating she planned on retiring at the close of the 1955–56 *I Love Lucy* season, perhaps focusing her attentions on directing "an hour-long show, in color, every three months or so" while also spending more time with her children. Seeking to clear the air, Desi remarked shortly thereafter, "Lucy can't quit even it she wanted to, which she doesn't. Our contract with Philip Morris runs until the end of the 1955–56 season. After that CBS has the right to ask us to do two more years of the show, which would carry us through the end of the 1957–58 season." He added, "When you hit the top, as we've been fortunate enough to do, all sorts of crazy things happen. People say we can't last, that they're getting tired of the same old faces. Well, frankly, we're not interested in staying on top forever. All we want to do is put on as good a show as we are capable of putting on, and we hope that the American people will continue to enjoy it."

With Desilu operating out of nine rented soundstages at Motion Picture Center, a chain of events caused Arnaz to contemplate buying the facility. MPC owner Joe Justman had told Desi from the outset that he and his partners were quite willing to sell him the studio outright or a portion of controlling stock and industry talk had long suggested Desilu would assume eventual ownership of MPC. In 1953, though, Desi was not interested in taking on the responsibilities of buying a studio, and through the first half of 1954 Arnaz and Martin Leeds both vigorously denied constant speculation that Desilu—then renting all but two MPC soundstages—was either contributing to the refinancing of the facility or planning on acquiring a controlling interest. The turning point came in June of 1954 when Desi learned that Columbia Studios mogul Harry Cohn was near finalizing a deal to buy Motion Picture Center, triggering his decision to somehow halt the Cohn negotiations and purchase the facility himself, perhaps with CBS brought aboard as a coinvestor. As

Arnaz said of the ruthless Cohn, "If Desilu was dependent on him for its life, it could be a short one. I was certain that if he at any time needed our stages, we would be out in the street looking for another place."

To secure expansion funding from CBS, Desi was required to sell the network a 24 percent interest in the production company. In June, CBS executive Edwin E. Holly joined Desilu as financial vice president at the insistence of the network—which reserved the right to appoint its own chief financial officer—to, in essence, protect the CBS investment.

As closed-door negotiations were continuing, Desi told *The Hollywood Reporter* on July 2, 1954, "We're building three new theaters at Motion Picture Center for audience shows, at a cost of $35,000 each. Altogether we'll have six audience shows next season. I can't understand why we're the only telefilm company to make the pictures with audiences. Our contract has a clause that says we must have an audience. We've found it works out very well and we'd be lost without an audience in front of us." He further added, "A lot of nonsense, that talk that Lucy and I netted $1,500,000 last year. To do that, you would have to gross $15,000,000 in these days of high taxes. Actually, Lucy and I each drew $35,000 salary for all of last season."

An eight-hour meeting at the Chatsworth ranchito between Arnaz, Justman, and Desi's tax attorney, Art Manella, was held, with Justman and his partners ultimately offering controlling interest in Motion Picture Center to Desilu. *Variety* on July 28 announced Justman retained 20 percent of MPC, with Desilu and CBS sharing equally the remaining 80 percent ownership of the facility. The final piece of the MPC puzzle came together on January 17, 1955, when it was announced that the Arnazes, as individuals, assumed voting control of Motion Picture Center for an "undisclosed amount"—actually $750,000, due in monthly $6,250 payments—with Joe Justman continuing as president; board members were Lucille, Desi, Justman, Martin Leeds, Andrew Hickox, and Al Pracca, representative of the Lutheran Aid Society, which, said the official press statement, "has renewed its mortgage on the property under a refinancing set-up. Desilu continues to rent space for its film properties."

At the same time, plans to bolster the somewhat stagnating *I Love Lucy* were found in Jess Oppenheimer's inspired notion that the show's locale would shift to Hollywood—Ricky Ricardo to star in a motion picture—in the coming season. Such a device would expand plot possibilities in the same manner utilized by Lucy's pregnancy. Using their leverage as stars of television's top-rated show—combined with his argument that such a format change to "filmland" would logically add production costs to the show for motion-picture celebrity guest stars, additional sets, and other added production costs—Arnaz notified CBS that he wanted to "renegotiate" the *Lucy* contract. Network business-affairs vice president Spencer Harrison, CBS president J. J. Van Volkenburg, Desilu press agent Kenny Morgan, and Arnaz met at the Beverly Hills Hotel in August to begin talks. Desi demanded concessions by CBS on forty specific points and would not budge on a single one. Stymied, Paley was notified of the stubborn Arnaz's refusal to negotiate and flew to the West Coast. Harrison recalled, "Paley came to terms with all forty points on which Desi had been unyielding. He very seldom got involved like that."

On September 28, *Variety* announced that the Arnazes were entering into a two-picture deal with MGM, not particularly surprising in light of the great success of MGM's *Long, Long Trailer,* which pulled in $4.5 million in rentals for the year and according to *Variety* ranked as the seventeenth-highest-grossing film of 1954. "When I made the deal for Lucy and Desi to do *The Long, Long Trailer,*" Martin Leeds says, "I managed to get [MGM] to agree to pay another hundred thousand dollars if the picture grossed four million. In those days, that was a lot of money. Nobody thought the picture would do that well. At the end of the year, the accounting statement showed three million, nine hundred seventy thousand dollars. We had thirty thousand dollars to go. The next statement came in showing the same three million, nine hundred seventy thousand dollars. Just three days prior to the next statement, I called [Eddie] Mannix and asked if I could show *Trailer* at my house, and that I would pay for the projectionist. He said no problem. I then said I would like to pay thirty thousand dollars for the privilege. He started to laugh, saying 'Okay, I got it, and you will get it.' When the next statement came, it still showed three million, nine hundred and seventy thousand dollars, but a check for one hundred thousand was attached, accompanied by a note bearing just the initials 'E.M.' "

Variety—along with the Arnazes and MGM—all seemed to reverse themselves on October 26, when the trade paper recanted the previous announcement of the MGM-Arnaz "two-pix deal" and stated that Warner Brothers and Universal-International "have entered the bidding" in "competition" with Metro for a single Ball-Arnaz film; Warners had recently scored a hit with a feature film version of *Dragnet* with Jack Webb and apparently wanted to strike gold again with TV stars Lucy and Desi. MGM, apparently concerned about losing the Arnazes, now rushed to sweeten the original offer by discussing plans with Arnaz for Desilu Productions to film the Metro picture at Motion Picture Center, which would add enormously to Lucille and Desi's profit participation and establish Desilu as a motion-picture producer. Although no film vehicle had been selected by the time they made their final decision, the Arnazes chose MGM—despite fervent outside bidding for their motion-picture services—with *I Love Lucy* to feature massive MGM plugs throughout its twenty-seven Hollywood-themed episodes; Ricky Ricardo would be transported to the film capital to star in a Metro picture, and initial (unrealized) plans called for a filmed tour of the studio to be featured in one episode, two episodes actually shot on the MGM Culver City lot, and several top Metro stars to appear in various *Lucy* installments. MGM production chief Dore Schary was even set to appear as himself in one episode ("*Don Juan* Is Shelved") but backed out at the last minute due to an acute kidney infection, although other reports suggest he was simply camera-shy; he was replaced by Vivian Vance's husband, Phil Ober, causing Schary to quip, "Phil will do a better job playing me."

Despite the earlier announcement and plans to tie-in MGM and *I Love Lucy,* the actual Arnaz-Metro deal was not finalized until Friday, November 26, with a multipicture contract. Still, no film property had actually been selected, but the new announcement confirmed previous reports that the Arnaz picture would be shot at Desilu's Motion Picture Center. "I went over to MGM with Andrew Hickox to meet with Eddie Mannix and Bennie Thau," Martin Leeds recalls. "Mr. Mannix looked down his nose at me, saying, 'What makes you people think you can make a motion picture with the fine quality of the MGM tradition?' 'Simple,' I said to him. 'Of the twenty-three hundred employees we have, twenty-two hundred are ex-MGM employees.' This was true. TV had come on so fast that the studios were hurting, and since we could pay people year-round, we were able to get the best."

Ironically, MGM inadvertently triggered its own demise as a dominant film studio by granting Desilu profit-percentage participation and the unparalleled right to film the production at its own facility. The Metro-Arnaz deal was clinched when Desi had successfully argued to MGM chief Dore Schary that Desilu's filming the picture would result in saving a million and a half dollars from the production budget; Desilu was not burdened by Metro's huge overhead and not locked in to previously negotiated, long-standing contracts with various labor unions.

Desilu also began considering a new television-pilot possibilities for the upcoming 1955–56 season. Arnaz was particularly hopeful for a network sale of *Desilu Playhouse,* an ambitious filmed one-hour anthology series; also unrealized were plans for Desi Arnaz to headline his own musical series sans his wife as the 1955 summer replacement for *I Love*

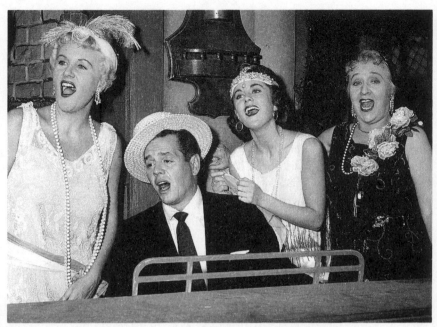

Margaret Whiting (*left*) and sister Barbara Whiting (*center*) along with on-screen mother, Mabel Albertson, on the set of *Those Whiting Girls* with Desi

THOMAS J. WATSON COLLECTION

Lucy. Desi was concerned as well with launching *Those Whiting Girls,* a comedy-with-music series starring singing sisters Margaret and Barbara Whiting, with Mabel Albertson cast as their mother. While the Pugh-Carroll series would debut as *I Love Lucy*'s summer replacement, the high-budget musical situation comedy put Desilu in debt more than ten thousand dollars per episode, and Desi plainly hoped the Whiting series would be picked up as a bona fide fall entry.

Margaret Whiting remembers Desi being heavily involved with *Those Whiting Girls.* "Desi was wonderful—and brilliant. He would come in every day when we rehearsed. When he sat with us while we read the script, he'd change lines and offer great suggestions. He had already read the script and had worked on it with the writers. When we were on our feet blocking the show for the cameras, both Desi and Lucille would come in and offer suggestions."

Despite good reviews, the series was not picked up as a fall entry; *Those Whiting Girls* did return—curiously not in 1956 but in 1957—again as *I Love Lucy*'s summer replacement. Still, with *Those Whiting Girls* not picked up as a fall series, it represented another Desilu disappointment. Another failed endeavor was the musical-comedy series *Just Off Broadway*—with former child stars Rose Marie, Peggy Ryan, and Ray MacDonald. Rose Marie recalls the Arnazes occasionally visiting her

98

and husband Bobby Guy following *Long, Long Trailer* filming: "Lucy and Desi would come to the house for dinner, Desi carrying a bottle of wine. After dinner, we sat on the couch and watched Lucy and Desi do the scene they had done that day at rehearsal. After the scene, Lucy would turn to us and say, 'Wasn't he wonderful? Wasn't he brilliant—pronouncing all those big words!' "

Industry insiders were surprised in November 1954, when Philip Morris announced that it was slicing its *I Love Lucy* sponsorship in half beginning in January, the move, speculated *Variety,* perhaps caused by "the cancer scare [that] may have cut into Morris sales and forced a tightening of the TV budget." Procter & Gamble "will take Morris off the hook for around half the time and talent costs of $2,500,000 for the 39-week season . . . it comes as a surprising move that it will share half of the sponsorship of a show that has topped every rating list almost from the outset. Despite the vast audience attracted by *Lucy,* Morris sales have never risen above fourth place. At one time, Alfred Lyons, topper of Morris, made an appeal to televiewers to buy more of the cigarettes to support the expensive *Lucy.*" Added concern came in December, when *I Love Lucy* slipped to third, then sixth, place in Trendex ratings. The end of the year found Philip Morris and P&G (both represented by the Biow Agency) singing for a two-year extension on their *I Love Lucy* sponsorship pact.

As the Hollywood-themed episodes got under way, Lucille and Desi made a decision which had far more impact, mostly negative, upon their marriage than they could have anticipated at the time. With the multiple demands put upon them—television and film performing, the running of the Desilu empire, and the raising of their two children—the Arnazes found the twenty-five mile Chatsworth-Hollywood round-trip commute needlessly time consuming. An unconsummated but still horrifying kidnapping threat aimed at their children while the Arnazes were at the studio and Lucie and Desi back at the remote ranch location apparently clinched the decision to sell the Desilu ranch and purchase a home in Los Angeles.

Lucille harbored deep reservations at having to give up the Desilu ranchito: "Now we really have a problem. Desi thinks that perhaps we should sell the ranch in the valley and move closer to town. We would have more time with the children, and the schools we want to send the children to are in town. But our roots are in the ranch Desi and I found thirteen years ago in a cloudburst. The furniture is in the same place we put it in. The walls are hung with family pictures. The cupboards are filled with things we have bought. Outside, the trees we planted are now full grown. We have laughed together and cried together in this house. I walk around wondering. I look up and ask God to give me the answer. I firmly believe He will."

In December 1954, through a broker's tip, Lucille happened to look at a house on Roxbury Drive in Beverly Hills. She noticed the home across the street at 1000 North Roxbury—next door to Jack Benny and wife Mary Livingston—favored that one all the more, and rang the doorbell. Opening the door was a Mrs. Bang, who told Lucy that she and her husband had just discussed the possibility of selling their home; it held too many memories of their son who had recently been killed while in the army. Lucy called Desi at the studio, who was too busy to break away and view the house. He told her to use her own judgment and buy the house if she wanted. Mrs. Bang wanted her husband to discuss any deal, so upon his return Lucille made an offer of $75,000; Bang insisted upon $85,000. Lucille agreed, knowing they were saving brokerage commissions anyway, shook hands on the deal, and the Arnazes took immediate possession. "Lucy and I had to say good-bye to our ranch in Chatsworth," Desi later wrote with lingering sadness at the memory. "It was not a happy moment. A whole new era began when we sold the Desilu ranchito. From now on we had to be practical. I hate the word and its meaning."

In his autobiography, Arnaz recounted a conversation with Lucille at this juncture where he posed two directions for their future—ending *I Love Lucy,* investing its expected income of $3–$4 million, living comfortably on $150,000 yearly "without touching the capital" and working, when they so chose, together or separately, at a more leisurely pace. The other option, Desi told his wife, was expanding Desilu Productions even more. "I hate to even consider it," he said. "We must get to be as big as MGM, Twentieth Century–Fox, Warner Brothers, Paramount, Columbia, or any of the other big studios. That means hiring a lot more people, top creative people, if I can get them, to help carry the load, and rent or buy a bigger studio. Motion Picture Center doesn't even have a back lot or the facilities we would need to compete, on an equal footing, with the big giants. They are all coming to television now, and I'm beginning to feel the pressure when I go to Madison Avenue to try and sell a show." Without hesitation, Lucille replied, "I don't want to quit." The decision, in retrospect, was perhaps the very moment where she traded her marriage for continuation of her career.

According to Ed Holly, however, both Lucille and Desi were amazingly adept at juggling their myriad performing and business responsibilities: "Desi was very strongly involved in everything. He would delegate and let you operate, but he expected you to know how far to go without clueing him in. They both had rather the uncommon ability to blend their show-business and business careers. I didn't spend a lot of time on the soundstages, but when I would go to them with major problems, things that couldn't wait until after production to discuss, we would have to make a major decision, right there on the spot. They could make the decision, turn right around, and go back to rehearsal or shooting a scene. This was a very unusual ability that both Desi and Lucy had. And they did it with concentration."

The Hollywood episodes catapulted *Lucy* back into critical favor and, by April 1955, back at the top of the ratings heap. Lucy so crushed its NBC hospital drama *Medic* competition that Vivian Vance quipped when the now-classic William Holden "burnt-putty nose" episode was about to air, "When the public sees this one, the only thing left for *Medic* to do is to redo [transsexual] Christine Jorgensen!" The Holden half hour prompted Lucille to create a bit of mythology in later years, claiming that the putty nose catching on fire was not planned and was, in fact, saved by her ad-libbing for the remainder of the scene. However, as writer Madelyn Pugh counters, "She began to believe it. But her nose was rigged [with a wick at the end of the putty nose designed by Hal King] so that the flame would only go so far. We had to ask her if she'd do it, so I know that it was planned. What was not planned was that she put her nose in the cup of coffee. That she ad-libbed, I think, during rehearsal." Pugh adds, "Every move was choreographed."

Still, the *I Love Lucy* phenomenon showed signs of faltering. At the March 7, 1955, seventh annual Emmy Awards ceremony, for the first time *I Love Lucy* was completely shut out of the winners' circle. The series lost to *Make Room for Daddy,* Loretta Young (*The Loretta Young Show*) was selected over Lucille Ball, Vivian Vance and William Frawley lost to Audrey Meadows and Art Carney in *The Honeymooners*, and *Lucy* scripters Oppenheimer, Pugh, and Carroll were trounced by George Gobel's NBC writing staff.

The following day, Philip Morris dropped another bombshell when it announced it was canceling its *Lucy* sponsorship after the June 27, 1955, telecast "to try new concepts in program patterns at lesser cost." The sudden move stunned industry insiders, *Variety* incredulously noting, "for the first time in TV's history, a sponsor is walking away from the medium's number-one show." Although General Foods immediately jumped in to assume Morris's half-sponsorship (shared with P&G), industry insiders were still mystified at the sudden move, even though it had been long argued that a cigarette company sponsoring a family-oriented program such as *I Love Lucy*—with a considerable "moppet" audience—was not as cost-efficient as would be a more suitable association with home-based products, such as those offered by Procter & Gamble. *Variety,* however, cited the actual reason for the Morris-Desilu split the result of an unspecified "conflict" and "difference of opinion" between the two entities.

The Desilu pact with MGM—despite the obvious benefits of profit participation, the *I Love Lucy* tie-in, and shooting the feature at Motion Picture Center—perhaps only added to the increasing burdens placed upon Desi and Lucille. With a May 2 starting date set for the Metro release—a "Zanra" ("Arnaz" spelled backward) Production—a script or concept still had not been found suitable by the first week of February, and Desi was becoming increasingly concerned, as he and his wife were only available to shoot the film during the relatively limited summer-hiatus period away from *Lucy.* Arnaz, of course, while in front of the cameras still had to serve as full-time Desilu president.

Finally, on March 7, it was announced that the Arnazes had dug up from the MGM story archive a twelve-year-old comedy script by Helen Deutsch (*I'll Cry Tomorrow* and *King Solomon's Mines*) titled *Guardian Angel,* which, under that title, was an intended vehicle for Katharine Hepburn and Spencer Tracy; an even earlier incarnation called *The Woman Who Was Scared* was written for William Powell and Myrna Loy. (MGM later attempted to claim, rather transparently, that Deutsch had written the $100,000 script for Lucy and Desi back in 1942.) The premise of the film hardly seemed to fit the couple, Arnaz playing a research chemist who ignores his wife in favor of his various scientific experiments; their marriage is saved by a guardian angel who has a hand in reuniting the squabbling couple during a camping trip designed to test his new insect repellent. The role of the "angel" was originally written for William Powell in the Tracy-Hepburn draft; Lucille and Desi wanted the high-priced Cary Grant for their remake titled *Forever, Darling* but settled instead for James Mason—ironically, exactly as Judy Garland and producer-husband Sid Luft had done several months earlier for their Warner Bros. musical-drama remake of *A Star Is Born.*

While *Long, Long Trailer* paired Lucille with an ex-lover (producer Pandro S. Berman), Lucille engaged another old flame, Alexander Hall, to direct *Forever, Darling.* "They hired Al Hall, then they wouldn't let him direct," Martin Leeds recalls. The resulting static and uninspired direction further undermined any chances for the film's already dubious chances for box-office success. Bernie Weitzman notes, "She had a lot of sentiment about people. Al Hall was an old-time director who couldn't get a job with anybody else. She made him the director because she liked him and he was nice to her when she was a nobody. She had great sentimental feeling about people who were good to her when she was down. Desi did, too. She surrounded herself with people who knew her for years and years who were really through in this industry, but for her they were very important. She had tremendous loyalty—even if it worked against her."

With the film property hastily selected, and Desilu jumping into motion-picture production for the first time, efforts seemed more centered on cost-cutting than excellence seen in the final product. Leeds remembers, "At the end of the first day [of production], I got a call from Ben [Thau], asking how we were doing. 'We are ahead two days,' I replied. 'What is with you,' he said. 'Are you drunk?' I explained that when we started our color tests, we shot script at the same time, and the two days of tests came out first quality, great. MGM had never thought of that, but we television people knew that you should never waste anything."

Desi immensely enjoyed his new role as film mogul, boasting to the press when his picture was days ahead of schedule, viewing the rushes of *Forever, Darling* on a CinemaScope screen at the Arnazes's new Beverly Hills home. While the film often has an artificial, confined quality far removed from the expansive—and by comparison, big-budget—MGM production of *The Long, Long Trailer,* its ultimate downfall is the script. Apparently, from the start, Desi recognized the weakness of the vehicle, even bringing in Madelyn Pugh and Bob Carroll to salvage what they could of it—concocting a *I Love Lucy*-esque broad physical-comedy outdoor-camping sequence tacked on in the final twenty minutes of footage and having little relation to the film that came before it. (Arnaz acknowledged Pugh and Carroll in trade-paper advertisements for their uncredited contribution to the film.)

Forever, Darling was deemed "substandard" by Radio City Music Hall—the site of *The Long, Long Trailer*'s spectacular New York premiere—and instead opened at the less prestigious Loew's State. The film proved to be a massive flop and barely recouped its initial $1.4 million cost. As one critic blasted, "The script is heavy and the jokes are bad. This is quite a switch on the entertainment pattern of the day—the two stars devote their best energies to television and toss off a quickie for the movies. Movie fans deserve a better break." *Variety* added, "In several studio close-ups of Miss Ball, both camera and lighting are notably unkind."

Forever, Darling effectively ended the Arnazes's joint motion-picture

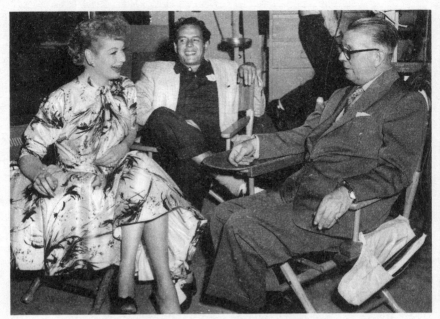

With director Alexander Hall on the set of *Forever, Darling*
RICK CARL COLLECTION

career as well as the ambitious Desilu-MGM "two-pix deal." It also squelched Desilu's plans to form its own independent feature-film unit with a four-picture yearly output; Arnaz at one time had sought either James Stewart or Gregory Peck to star in a "navy story," Desilu's first feature effort. Arnaz also dropped plans to film a theatrical version of the failed TV series *Country Doctor* and a European-based big-budget release, *Journey to a Star* with Dan Dailey. Scuttled as well were plans for Mickey Rooney to star in a Desilu feature based on the life of racehorse-jockey Johnny Longden.

And while *The Long, Long Trailer* had Lucy and Desi portraying happy newlyweds, *Forever, Darling* presented the Arnazes as a disagreeable, unsympathetic couple—directly ignoring the cardinal rules that made *I Love Lucy* and *The Long, Long Trailer* enormously popular hits. Lucy and Desi were perhaps unconsciously reflecting on-screen the increasing friction and coldness in their own marriage. Ironically, during the filming of *Forever, Darling*, Desi told Louella Parsons that the key to the "success" of his marriage was "a sense of humor and the ability to laugh. Often when we've had words, one of us sees the absurdity of it and starts laughing. If people would laugh more, marriages would last longer."

"As corny as it sounds," Lucille admitted years later, "that movie was more than just a dumb fantasy. I kept hoping *something* would come along and save my marriage."

104

Chapter Six

★

"I'm sometimes scared of everything that has happened to us. We didn't think Desilu Productions would grow so big. We merely wanted to be together and have two children."

—Lucille Ball, 1955

★

*T*he rapid expansion of the Desilu empire began to gradually erode the intimate "family" atmosphere of Motion Picture Center, and with it came the inevitable departures of several *Lucy* staff members. Although under Desilu contract, Bill Asher—who had directed more than seventy-five episodes—wanted to expand into feature-film directing and obtained his release from Arnaz in April 1955 to direct two "programmers" for Columbia Pictures. Although Desi had considered directing *Lucy* himself, he ultimately appointed James V. Kern; after training under Asher, Kern directed the 1955 summer run of *Those Whiting Girls*. And, after photographing more than four hundred "telepix" for Desilu, Karl Freund relinquished his position as *Lucy* director of photography at the close of the season, replaced briefly by Robert deGrasse and ultimately by Sid Hickox.

The most significant Desilu departure came on September 26, 1955, when Jess Oppenheimer announced he would be leaving *Lucy,* having signed a lucrative five-year contract with NBC, where, said *Variety*, he would "create shows which he will produce" and have a "percentage ownership of the properties." Oppenheimer signed with NBC only after "several months" of negotiations with both CBS and Desilu proved unsuccessful; although his seven-year CBS contract was to terminate in November, he agreed to remain on *I Love Lucy* until the close of the season.

Oppenheimer's leaving *Lucy* was so significant, *Variety* noted that while CBS had an option for one more year beyond the current 1955–56 season, "exiting from the show of the producer-writer is believed a strong indication that Arnaz may decide to end the video run of *Lucy* after this season." Desi immediately attempted to squelch such rumors by insisting, "I hate to see Jess go, but his leaving won't interfere in the slightest with whatever plans we made for the show. Personally, I would like to expand *Lucy* to a full hour every week, maybe even in color, using big-name guest stars—say, three weeks out of four—to help Lucy and me carry the load. But we'd still appear in every show. Of course, this is just my own plan and will have to be concurred by both CBS and the sponsors. We are working on that right now." He added, "Sure, we'll miss Jess, but who knows? By next spring, Desilu might buy NBC, and we'd be back together again!"

Maintaining the high quality of America's top-rated show and creating fresh story lines had begun to take its toll on the writers who had toiled on well over one hundred *I Love Lucy* scripts. "People say, 'Did you know you were connected with a legend?'" muses Madelyn Pugh of writing *I Love Lucy*. "We were just trying to get a script out and hope to *heaven* we could have a day off. We learned a lot from Jess. We learned discipline. We wrote a script a week. Sometimes we put it in his mailbox at four in the morning, but we did it. He wouldn't let us leave until we had a story line, which was great training." Pugh, Carroll, and Oppenheimer had, by the close of the 1954–55 season, decided that additional writers were needed to lighten their tremendous workload, and, to that end, the team of Robert Schiller and Robert Weiskopf was brought in by Oppenheimer in the summer of 1955.

Schiller and Weiskopf had to their credit one episode of *Make Room for Daddy,* several installments of the short-lived 1954–55 *That's My Boy!* series produced by George Burns's production company, *Professional Father,* and the first six episodes of a short-lived Janis Paige series, *It's Always Jan,* filmed by Desilu at Motion Picture Center. Weiskopf recalls that during one production meeting "on a hot day in August with no air-conditioning," the writers opened the second-floor window of the *Jan* offices, and down on the sidewalk below was Jess Oppenheimer. Schiller adds that Jess yelled up to them, "I just read in *Variety* that you guys were just signed for *Jan.* I was looking for a team to put on *I Love Lucy.*" Already unhappy with the Paige program, Schiller and Weiskopf managed to break their *Jan* contract. Thrilled with the prospect of working on television's top-rated program, the writers were nevertheless concerned. "We were warned not to take the job," recalls Schiller of their William Morris agent. "He said, 'If the show continues as a success, we wouldn't get any credit, and if it's a failure, you'll get all the blame.'"

"The first week we were on the show," says Schiller, "Oppenheimer called us and said, 'Come down and watch the run-through. When you see Lucy performing your script, she'll make you think you're writers.'

We would spend one day working out the story, then we would write the draft, and the other team would polish it. It was that simple. And we never had an outside script."

The writers learned that plans for the *I Love Lucy* 1955–56 season called for several Hollywood shows, the Ricardos and Mertzes then returning to New York before embarking on a seventeen-episode tour of Europe—Ricky's London, Paris, and Rome Latin-band bookings serving as yet another device to expand *Lucy* plotlines. As Schiller and Weiskopf began work on their first *Lucy* script—a two-part "Lucy Visits Grauman's" story line with guest John Wayne—the new writing team was quickly exposed to Lucille and Desi's off-camera demeanor. "Lucy was the mother hen around the studio," says Schiller. "She would get into everybody's lives if she could. Controlling. That's why maybe she didn't like us. I don't recall her saying she didn't like us, but she didn't like us as much as she liked Bob and Madelyn. And Desi—we went to their house in Palm Springs, a Paul Williams home, the famous architect. I said to Desi, 'Wonderful house, who designed this place?' And his answer was, 'Oh, me and Paul.' "

Weiskopf reveals some rivalry between the dual Pugh-Carroll and Schiller-Weiskopf writing teams: "We did the first draft, and then Bob and Madelyn got it. The third week, to get caught up, we wrote two shows," each team writing its own episode. Weiskopf further recalls, "Jess assigned one show to Bob and Madelyn. Desi got ahold of that script and [thinking we wrote it] said, 'Jesus, I don't know if you chose the right ones, these two guys.' But Bob and Madelyn had written it. That really saved our necks."

Oppenheimer's exit from *Lucy* certainly was not altogether unexpected to studio insiders. Desilu newcomer Bob Schiller notes, "Jess and Lucy got along fine, but Jess and Desi had a big ego fight." A truce—albeit temporary—between Arnaz and Oppenheimer was effected soon after Schiller and Weiskopf joined the *Lucy* staff: "Jess called for a peace conference between him and Desi. They set a deal that majority rules. Desi said, 'If you and Lucy feel about one thing one way and I feel the other, majority wins. If Lucy and I feel one way, we win.' Jess was about to leave the room and says, 'Wait a minute. What if you and I happen to feel one way and Lucy feels the other. Who wins?' " Without missing a beat, Desi said, "The majority wins—*Lucy*." Then, at Jess Oppenheimer's farewell party held at the Arnazes's Beverly Hills home, Desi reportedly quipped, "We're not losing a producer—we're gaining a parking space."

Although his CBS-Desilu pact had been severed, his ties to *Lucy* clearly

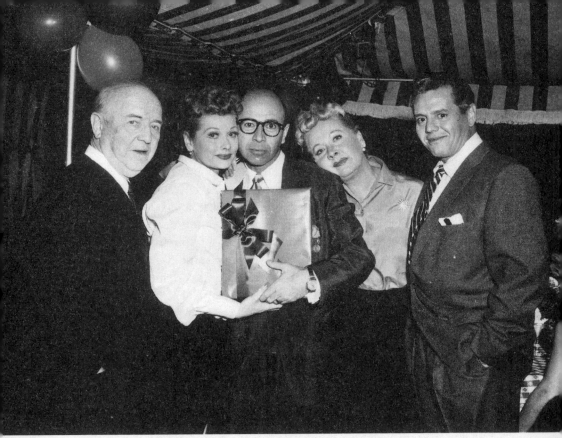

Wistful *I Love Lucy* principals say good-bye to Jess Oppenheimer at his farewell party held in the backyard of the Arnazes's Beverly Hills home.
MAURY THOMPSON COLLECTION

were not. Oppenheimer's original contract stipulated that he had "created" Lucy Ricardo, and he received substantial royalties whenever the redhead portrayed the character in subsequent years; he added to his royalties—amounting to more than "seven figures"—when he became the only individual not to sell his percentage in 1956 when CBS purchased from Desilu all 180 *I Love Lucy* episodes. As Bob Schiller notes, "Jess had real mixed emotions [about leaving the show]. He was hoping it would fall flat on its ass, and yet he stood to make a lot of money if it didn't."

Soon after joining the network, he announced ambitious—but ultimately abandoned—plans to form an NBC "stock company" to appear in sixty-minute variety-format broadcasts titled *A Company of Players,* the first half consisting of a "straight" rendering of a teleplay, the second portion presenting in contrast a "broad satire" of the same script; he also envisioned a series of one-hour "modern" dramas based on the Ten Commandments. Oppenheimer did not fare well in his bid to capture his past *I Love Lucy* magic—he departed NBC when not a single Oppenheimer-produced series won a time slot on the network.

Weathering multiple staff defections, Desilu continued its policy of aggressive expansion. In September, Arnaz snared rights to film Bing Crosby's ninety-minute CBS special based on Maxwell Anderson's *High Tor,* to be revised into musical form for *Ford Star Jubilee* by producer-composer Arthur Schwartz. Desilu also announced plans to film a pilot of *Fast Freight,* a projected (but unsold) on-location ABC series with Keenan Wynn conceived by Martin Leeds detailing the varied adventures of long-distance truck drivers. Also for ABC, Bill Spier developed *Tales of Allan Pinkerton,* based on real-life case histories of the famed detective, the series dropped when Pinkerton's estate refused to grant clearance. Two additional failed series attempts were *Anthology of Suspense* and *Father Duffy of Hell's Kitchen* with Lloyd Nolan; *Duffy* was abandoned when Arnaz and Nolan became enraged by advertising-agency demands that the character be rewritten from priest to social worker to allow "romantic possibilities" in the story line.

One project that did get off the ground was *Whirlybirds*—presenting the exploits of helicopter pilots Ken Tobey and Craig Hill—originally created for CBS prime time, instead sold as a syndicated series by CBS Films due to its particularly strong juvenile appeal. *Whirlybirds* became a substantial hit for Desilu upon its January 1957 premiere; 111 first-run episodes were produced from 1956 to 1959.

Despite poor critical and box-office response to *Forever, Darling*— "release is an inauspicious start for Arnaz as a theatrical film producer" said *Variety*—Desi announced revised plans to film *Journey to a Star;* he would now direct as well as produce the film. Dan Dailey was dropped in favor of Gene Kelly and Leslie Caron. Desi wanted his wife to star solo in a theatrical version of *Fallen Angel,* assuming the Nancy Walker role. He also announced ambitious (but ultimately aborted) plans to "telefilm" in March 1956 a ninety-minute Lazslo Vadnay adaptation of *Don Quixote* with a score by Rodgers and Hammerstein and starring Dan Dailey and (perhaps remembering his kindness to Lucille during the "Red Scare") with Lou Costello as Sancho Panza.

As the 1955–56 season was about to be launched, Desi flew to New York to meet with CBS chairman Paley. Arnaz insisted to Paley that *Lucy* be dropped as a weekly half-hour series for the 1956–57 season and instead air as a monthly, big-budget color offering with top guest stars. While deep in negotiations with New York–based CBS executives— including Paley, Frank Stanton, Hubbell Robinson, and network president Jack Van Volkenburg—it appeared that Arnaz in October 1955 suffered setbacks in launching his new hourlong version of *Lucy.* Arnaz conceded that discussions with the CBS brass concerning the residual values of a filmed hourlong show led to the conclusion that "it will be difficult to clear time for such a show in the rerun market. The half-hour telefilm show is still the big thing, it was agreed. The half-hour show, such as *I Love Lucy,* has its own special appeal, while the hour dramas don't." Desperately wanting to convince CBS of the merits of a one-hour *Lucy,* Arnaz abruptly—and confusingly—reversed himself in November, declaring then to the press that the half-hour series was "slowly but definitely" being replaced in popularity by sixty- and ninety-minute programs.

Ironically, the 1955 premiere of the half-hour *Lucy* indicated that—although its freshness had somewhat evaporated—the series nonetheless had considerable durability and diluted Arnaz's arguments to CBS for scrapping the current format for a one-hour version. Said the *Reporter,* "*Lucy,* well produced by Jess Oppenheimer for Desilu, has some of those same qualities that have sustained Jack Benny down the ages, though in less refined terms . . . with even a little luck, the *Lucy* show should be buoyant for a long time."

I Love Lucy, however, was no longer guaranteed first, or even second, place in the ratings sweepstakes; by the end of November, *Lucy* was mired in third place, beaten by *The $64,000 Question* and Ed Sullivan. Lucille was unable to contain her irritation over constant speculation by the press that *I Love Lucy* had peaked, grumbling, "I don't understand all the ruckus. On your way up to the top, you're a hero. After you're up there, sooner or later, they start taking potshots at you. Slip two tenths of a point and you're a bum. I don't get it." Jack Benny offered little comfort when he warned her, "Being number one is the loneliest spot in the world. There is only one direction in which you can go—down!"

Mid-December, however, found *Lucy* close to again being television's number-one program, only two ratings points separating it from the top-rated *$64,000 Question.* Jess Oppenheimer attempted to explain Lucy's ratings comeback as well as the key to the show's longevity by noting, "Too many shows go all out for the boff laugh, line after line. The straight man sets it up, and the comic knocks it down. There's no time given over to character development. We'll go a whole ten minutes on a *Lucy* episode without a laugh, just to build a situation. Moreover, good characterization is vital. Lucy and Desi are popular because people love them, not just because they're funny." Added Desi, "Comedy needs heart and warmth, even a tear or two, not just a lot of slapstick laughs."

As *Variety* noted, Arnaz "who a couple of months ago said he wants to see *I Love Lucy* go on a monthly, hourlong basis next season admits his prepared arguments with CBS have been thoroughly dissipated by the rapid comeback of *Lucy* in the ratings. *Lucy* is just a couple of points out of first; its second-runs are in tenth, so Desi has this pleasant dilemma: How can he talk Hub Robinson into a *Lucy* change when the longtimer is doing so well?"

With *I Love Lucy* and *December Bride* the only comedies in the Nielsen Top Ten at the close of 1955, Desi confidently predicted, "The situation comedy situation is leveling off. Everybody jumped on the *Lucy* bandwagon at first. It was the natural thing to do. Sponsors kept demanding, 'Get us another *Lucy*.' But you can't do that forever." Desilu Productions, however, showed no signs of slowing down. Rumors shot through Hollywood that Arnaz was about to sell the operation. "I know nothing of such offers," Desi countered. "No one has come to me with them. I don't know if I want to sell my company, for that matter. I have never considered it." He also said, "I'm a young man, and I think *Lucy* will go on a long time. But even if it doesn't, I want to build up a business." Said Martin Leeds at the time, "He is a very bright man with a fabulous memory and a knack for understanding what he's learned. He's learned plenty, too. I can spend a couple of days working on a cost sheet, and he'll read and understand it in one minute flat. Six months later, if the cost of something has gone up, he'll quote that first cost sheet and will want to know what happened. He doesn't miss a thing."

The Arnazes's plans for an idyllic family Christmas at their Palm Springs retreat were somewhat marred when Lucille, running barefoot through the house, impulsively stood on a red-hot floor heater for warmth, and as a result she was bedridden for a good portion of the holiday. Maury Thompson recalls another Palm Springs occasion that following spring: "The kids wanted to go swimming. She said, 'No, you can't go swimming until your father gets home. He's over at the country club.' I said, 'Well, I can take them.' 'No, no,' she said. 'I want him to come home and do it. He *never* does *anything* with them. They want to play with *him*.' She says to the maid, 'Watch the kids while I'm gone. We're going to go on a golf cart.' She loves to hurt a man. She's kicked Desi in the nuts several times. Just bowled him over. She laughed about it. If he's stooped over, she'll kick him in the butt, and she'll aim low and she'll hit him right in the balls. I've seen her. So we get in the golf cart and she puts it into high gear, and the cart has tin, flat seats. I said, 'Holy shit!' She screamed and hollered and laughed so loud. Because she was hurting me and she loved it.

"We got to the country club, and she said, 'Don't you leave me. Stay right here.' We were in the back row, and there's Desi—with about eight or ten beautiful gals around. But there was nothing going on, just kidding around. All the women turned at one time and saw her. So now, she's leaning on me, putting her arm around my shoulder. Finally, Desi looked. 'Oh, honey! Come on down. There's plenty of room. We'll watch the race.' It was Kentucky Derby day, and they had it on a big huge screen. She said, 'No, I want you to come home. The kids want to go swimming.' 'Honey, I'll be home right after the race.' 'No, I want you to come now.' I said, 'Lucille, come on, everybody's looking.' The yelling went back and forth. She turned and got in the golf cart and away we went. We went home, and I put on my trunks. I was in the pool with the kids. They were just little tykes. I was spinning them around in the water. She got into her suit and said, 'You're the only one in the world I would *ever* show myself to in a swimming suit.' I said, 'Well, you look marvelous.' And she did. She was tight, thin, no stomach, long legs, just freckles on her legs. She got in the water, and she swam the breaststroke, always keeping her head above water. I treasure that moment, because she was thoroughly relaxed and enjoying it. Then Desi got home, and she got mad again. There were only those few moments that there was no one to worry about."

Her dark mood triggered upon Desi's return was not improved when her husband insisted that the family spend the upcoming summer *Lucy* hiatus in Del Mar—presumably to be closer to his Desilu burgeoning business empire—instead of a long-anticipated and much-needed romantic trip throughout Europe. Intimacy at the Arnaz home was already

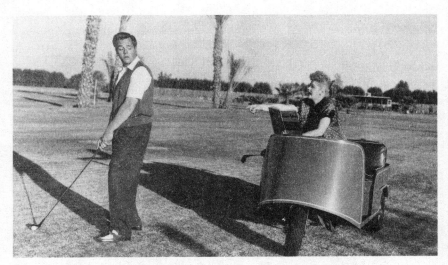

Desi warily eyes Lucille and her golf cart in Palm Springs.
MICHAEL McCLAY COLLECTION

strained, the Beverly Hills Roxbury house now fully staffed with a domestic couple handling cooking and cleaning chores, two nurses for the children, chauffeur Joe Fagan, and a gardener. "Lucie Desiree's nurse was so devoted to her," said Lucille, "that it created a problem. She seemed to resent the baby in the house, and she became overprotective with Lucie Desiree. The nurse became sick, because of it, and it became so difficult for us that we had to let her go, even though we liked her, and she was a wonderful nurse." She added, "Until we found a new nurse, I had to take care of Lucie *myself.*"

Lucille also said at the time, "I never had religion, but I didn't think it was right to deprive my children of religion. That's why I agreed, first, to allow them to be brought up as Catholics, in their father's religion, and that's why I began to look into the entire subject and why I've made up my mind about religion. I will go into Desi's church, and I will start soon to take instruction to prepare myself for becoming a Catholic." By all accounts, however, child-rearing and religious upbringing of Lucie and Desi IV were largely assumed by grandmother DeDe, who herself took instruction in the Catholic Church—although she never did actually convert—so that the busy Lucille would not have to do so in order for the two children to be raised as Roman Catholics.

As DeDe recounted in 1975, "When the kids were old enough to go to church, I went with them. But the minute I found Desi, Jr., sitting up in the choir loft and Lucie sitting with her girlfriends down somewhere else, and my driver sitting in another pew, and I'm sitting all by myself, I figured, 'They don't need me anymore.' I quit goin'. I live my life for me, what I like. I don't have to go to church to cover up anything. Both Lucille and I took instruction, but I never actually became a Catholic." As longtime friend Robert Osborne offers, "DeDe was the real linchpin that held that family together."

Lucie Arnaz explains, "DeDe was great. DeDe raised me basically, and Willie Mae [the maid], and my mother, at night. It sounds so vengeful to say that my mother didn't raise me, but the truth of the matter is that she did very little of it. She did it on weekends, sort of. Willie Mae was there with the hands-on stuff, showing us how to do things, reprimanding us for doing them wrong, reminding us to brush your teeth, giving us the baths, feeding us the dinners, watching our diet, taking us to the doctors. And then DeDe took us all the other places: to buy the clothes, [to do] our Christmas shopping, helping us save our money. And anytime my mother needed to leave, my grandmother would come and stay for the weekend [or] for weeks at a time.

"My mom was like the matriarch who came in now and then and laid

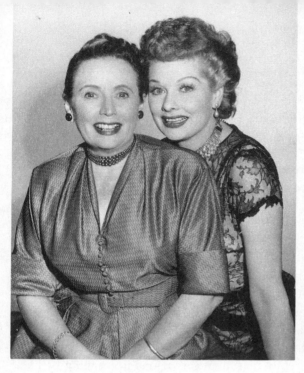

With her mother,
DeDe
RICK CARL COLLECTION

down the rules we had to follow. She had no choice, in a way, my mother. I can't really blame her for any of it. She didn't have that connection because she wasn't given it by her own mother. DeDe ended up being a better grandmother in a hands-on way than she was a mother—unfortunately they were poor and DeDe had to work a lot, so my mother didn't see a lot of love as a child on a day-to-day basis, either.

"I think it hurt my mother a lot that she had to make a choice between this career thing and this child thing. She was trying very hard to make her life happier, so she had a baby, finally, and there was great joy in that. Who knew twenty seconds later she was going to have a hit TV series? And there goes that. Deal with the baby later."

As his marriage began to falter and the Desilu pressures continued to build, Arnaz's alcoholism took an irrevocable turn. Martin Leeds recalls, "When he started to drink, around 1955 or 1956, Ed Holly asked me, 'Why don't you let me talk to Desi?' I said, 'You can talk to Desi anytime you want, but don't come crying to me. If I can warn you of one thing, if you see Desi, see him between nine and ten o'clock in the morning. You're not to see him after ten o'clock.' Desi would take one daiquiri at ten. His alcohol blood-sugar level was so high he'd be drunk by noon. It was so sad—his anger, the womanizing, the drinking. The question was whether he would be drunk at any given time. Ninety percent of the time, I never had to talk to him about what we were doing. The other ten percent I felt I had to, because I was taking some chances and he was entitled to his input."

Bernie Weitzman offers another viewpoint: "The driving force behind the company was really Desi Arnaz. Desi was really the business genius of the company and ran it with a lot of courage. He took chances at a period which were way beyond anybody's expectations. He was a rare individual, and both he and Lucy were truly in love with each other."

As the problems in their marriage surfaced, Lucille focused her attentions—to an almost obsessive degree—on *I Love Lucy*. Recalled Desilu sound engineer Cam McCulloch, "Lucy ran a tight ship and she seemed fair, but if you goofed, she let you know it. She didn't pull any punches. There was a coldness there that you didn't find with Desi. Maybe she was afraid people would take advantage. The only time I ever saw her get really annoyed was when Desi would have a few beers during the day and then start burping. You'd hear her yell, 'Desiiiiiiii. . . .' all the way from her dressing room." On other occasions, "Desi would show up for rehearsal on time, and when he did, he'd be weaving a little. It was clear alcohol was affecting his speech, his walk. That's when it was obvious there were deep problems in their marriage. Until then, they both presented a united front, and there had never been any serious bickering between the two by them publicly." She would often call old friend Ann Sothern. "When Desi was drinking a lot, she'd call me in the middle of the night and say, 'Get the priest. Do something, Ann, do *something.*'"

"When Desi got drunk," says Martin Leeds, "he didn't know what he was doing."

Of her father's alcohol problem, Lucie Arnaz notes, "He always drank—I think from a young guy on the beach, from all the stories he told, it was part of his upbringing. But like any disease, it takes a while to take its toll with your body, to where your tolerance is less and less, and you show the effects of drinking. Under pressure, he drank more, obviously, and the worse their relationship was, the more he would drink, just to show her. 'You're going to tell me I can't get drunk? Well, I'll show you. I'll get drunker than you've ever seen.' It was just awful."

Arnaz's womanizing—which had subsided somewhat over the past few years, and what relatively few incidents occurred were publicly quelled by CBS or Desilu press man Kenny Morgan (derisively referred to by many insiders as Desi's "pimp")—increased along with his drinking. "This is not to say that Lucy was not good in bed," theorizes Leeds, "but Desi's mind was the mind that everyone that he went to bed with would be different and therefore better—not realizing that that's probably the basic fallacy of all sexual relationships." Desi seemed unable to understand Lucille's inability to forgive—or at least ignore—his numerous and apparently escalating extramarital transgressions; Bob Schiller recalls him

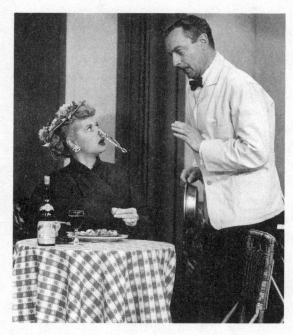

Lucy and waiter
Maurice Marsac in the
1955–56 season episode
"Paris at Last"
THOMAS J. WATSON COLLECTION

reasoning, "What's she upset about? I don't take out other broads. I just take out *hookers*."

"He was like Jekyll and Hyde," Lucille bitterly recalled later. "He drank and he gambled, and he went around with other women. It was always the same—booze and broads. I had seen it all coming. I was always hoping things would change. But Desi's nature is destructive. When he builds something, the bigger he builds it, the more he wants to break it down. That is the scenario of his life."

Arnaz freely bet huge amounts among an assorted network of bookies around town including "Jake" Jaco, who sidelined a bookmaking business out of his shoeshine stand at Desilu. When Desi won eighteen thousand dollars in an all-night session of card-playing, he accepted the loser's two adjacent Palm Springs lots (at the Thunderbird Golf Course) worth $9,000 each as payment—ultimately spending $150,000 to erect the Paul Williams–designed "California-Hawaiian" vacation ranch home on the site. The inordinately frugal Lucille, however, not surprisingly disdained such high-stakes gambling. "She was quite conservative," says Bernie Weitzman. "She saved her money, and she didn't squander it. When Lucy went gambling in Vegas, she would spend a few bucks, comparatively speaking—five or ten thousand. That is good money to most, but to a superstar, not a huge amount. And she handled it very carefully. Desi would go out and blow forty thousand in a night. And that's the way he ran his business, too."

Although Lucille had possibly—perhaps willfully—tried to match Desi's own numerous infidelities during the earliest years of their mar-

116

riage, it is a certainty in the second decade of their marriage, having weathered motherhood and worldwide celebrity, she was unable even to consider indulging in an extramarital affair, and was horrified at the notion. And with Desi now thirty-nine and Lucille forty-five, she became increasingly insecure about her fading beauty as well as the six-year age difference between them—her television makeup becoming heavier season after season as facial lines became increasingly noticeable and her puffy upper eyelids (usually camouflaged on *I Love Lucy* by oversized, upward-turned false eyelashes) became more pronounced; Desi's ever-increasing predilection for young, amply endowed blondes only fueled Lucille's self-doubts about her looks and the security of her marriage.

Her intense fears even began to spill over onto *I Love Lucy*. Bob Schiller remembers of one casting session: "After one meeting, Lucy said, 'Would the writers please stay?' She said, 'I can't work with that woman. Her eyes go in different directions. You can't look her in the eye.'" Bob Weiskopf adds, "She was also pretty, young, and blonde." "That's exactly what she meant," confirms Schiller. "She learned very fast and very well from Ginger Rogers and Carole Lombard, you don't have anybody around who's younger and prettier than you are."

The Arnazes had already weathered a mortifying *Confidential* magazine cover story—"Does Desi Really Love Lucy?"—which deemed Desi a "duck-out daddy" who had already "proved himself an artist at philandering as well as acting." *Confidential*—the prime example of 1950s "rag journalism" at its zenith with a circulation of 4 million readers—painted Arnaz as someone who had "sprinkled his affections all over Los Angeles for a number of years and quite a bit of it has been bestowed on vice dollies who were paid handsomely for loving Desi briefly but, presumably, as effectively as Lucy."

The article further detailed a recent "mixing business with pleasure" night in August at the Beverly Hills Hotel where Desi and a "male relative"—presumably Kenny Morgan—called "one of Hollywood's best door-to-door dame services" for a pair of "cuddle-for-cash babes." Upon arrival at the hotel, according to writer Brad Shortell, one "play-for-pay squab" took ill and left. The other "was given about thirty seconds to admire the mirrored living room and its twin couches when Desi took her off to inspect another room. Twenty minutes later, she was back, and Arnaz's play pal took over. The cash register rang again, and Mindy went home, considerably richer, at about three-forty-five that morning."

Confidential also included another incident—army sergeant Desi allegedly having "swept one siren off her feet in Palm Springs on a sultry night in October 1944, not only without showing folding money but also after telling her that he was still in love with Lucy," even after his wife had impulsively filed for divorce while he was stationed at Birmingham Hospital in Van Nuys. "This marrying for love is the bunk," a hungover, red-eyed Desi purportedly told "dark-eyed temptress" Sally. "Hours later," claimed *Confidential,* "Sally limped back to her own hotel and her weekend pal. To her, Sally sighed one rapturous comment: 'Who ever said Latins are lousy lovers?' she asked drowsily."

Confidential quoted a cocky, wildly out-of-control Desi boasting, "A real man should have as many girls as he has hair on the head."

Desi attempted to discount the widely circulated report of his 1944 extramarital affair with admitted prostitute Ronnie Quillan—described as "a veteran of Hollywood nightlife who marketed love" by newspapers—by deeming it "a lot of baloney." Arnaz heatedly added, "I don't ever remember meeting the lady, and I guess I'm being kind by calling her a lady. I was in the army in 1944, and I think I was somewhere up north. I don't remember being in Palm Springs. From the pictures I've seen of her, I don't think I could have done anything like that."

Lucille attempted to handle the intensely embarrassing situation as lightly as possible and with even a touch of uncharacteristic humor. Arnaz's personal assistant, Johny Aitchison, vividly recalls, "Desi grabbed a copy of it and went on the set and showed it to everybody, saying, 'Look at what these sons of bitches have said now.' I remember Lucy wanted to get a copy. She said, 'Christ, I can't go out and buy that *myself*—somebody go out and *get* one for me!'"

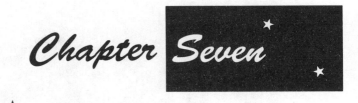

Chapter Seven

"I think they were the happiest when they were working together on *I Love Lucy* or dealing with business at Desilu."

—Lucie Arnaz, 1990

*D*uring Lucy and Desi's January and February cross-country *Forever, Darling* (billed as "the first big comedy of 1956") promotional tour—traveling via a special Santa Fe railroad car to Chicago, Detroit, Dallas, Cleveland, Pittsburgh, Philadelphia, and Lucille's Jamestown, New York, birthplace—Arnaz marveled, "There's something to say for TV. When you tour as a picture star, people look at you as some sort of a curiosity. This time there was a wholly different feeling. The people act as if they were your personal friends." He added, "Perhaps the most amazing thing is the friendlier attitude of the press."

Arnaz's fiery temper prompted some less-than-favorable trade-paper coverage, however, during a Philadelphia *Forever, Darling* promotional stop, the tour designed not only to hype the picture but also Arnaz's MGM recording of the film's romantic theme; the Ames Brothers had concurrently recorded the song for rival RCA Victor. Desi, said *Variety*, went into a "spin of rage" when eleven thousand persons materialized at a personal appearance at a local retail outlet, and he discovered that MGM Records had shipped to the store a scant hundred copies of his recording of the *Darling* theme; his anger further ignited when he discovered no other copies of his recording existed in the entire city as thousands of people had to be turned away. "From here on," stormed Desi, "I'll make sure that there are enough copies of the record when we get into a town. If there aren't, I'll start plugging the Ames Brothers record and tell people to buy that instead of mine!"

February 1956 found Desi Arnaz proclaiming to the industry trade papers that his company—now with eight hundred employees translating to a weekly payroll of $125,000—had mushroomed into a $12 million operation after being launched only five years before on a "$12,000 shoestring." While he tempered his previously optimistic hopes to continue a feature-film division following the flop of *Forever, Darling*—

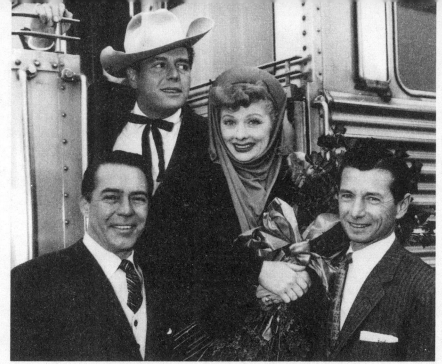

Desilu publicity director Ken Morgan (*left*) and Lucille's brother Fred meet the Arnazes at the conclusion of the *Forever, Darling* cross-country promotional tour.
COURTESY OF FRED BALL

"We'll make a theatrical picture when we have a good one"—he countered with (ultimately abandoned) plans to produce *Mother Cabrini,* a teleplay based on the life of the sainted Roman Catholic nun; at the other end of the spectrum, however, was Desilu's pilot production of a *Mystery Theatre* anthology television series and a western program, *Sheriff of Cochise*, with John Bromfield.

On March 1, the Arnazes became embroiled in a heated controversy surrounding Emmy Awards nomination structuring that many voting members felt did not reflect the rapidly metamorphosing television industry. Although William Frawley was once again nominated for his "Fred Mertz" role and *Lucy* writers for their "L.A. At Last!" teleplay, and Lucille herself in two categories ("Best Actress—Continuing Performance" and "Best Comedienne"), for the first time since its premiere, *I Love Lucy* failed to be nominated. An apparently disgruntled Ball told the Academy of Television Arts and Sciences that she planned on "being out of town" the night of the March 17 ceremony. Although Frawley and the *Lucy* writers lost their Emmy bids, Lucille's absence was particularly conspicuous when she was announced as the winner in the continuing performance "Best Actress" category (losing "Best Comedienne" to *Caesar's Hour*'s Nanette Fabray). Madelyn Pugh accepted the Emmy

120

on Ball's behalf—Pugh, noted *The Reporter,* "was attractive enough not to have rushed off so hurriedly."

Madelyn Pugh offers another perspective: "She really didn't like speaking in public. She had the character fine, but to be herself, she was very nervous. I sat with her quite often at a table when they were going to be presenting something, and she would be so nervous. She felt she ought to say something funny. One time she was at some table, and Carol Burnett spoke. She said to me, 'I guess after Carol Burnett, I'm not funny.' " Of Lucille's inability to express feelings and emotions, she adds, "She didn't want to say how she felt. She used to walk up to me, hug me, and almost crush me. But I knew what she meant."

Desi attempted to diffuse the volatile situation with humor, good-naturedly reminding *The Reporter* that he had himself had never managed to win a *Lucy* Emmy nomination, quipping, "I'm waiting for them to put in a category of bongo drummer—and if they have one and don't nominate me, *then* I'll squawk." Attempting to put the Emmy controversy behind them, Lucy and Desi focused upon their marriage and studio. Arnaz continued juggling his roles as Desilu president and *I Love Lucy* star. "They'll wait for me for about ten minutes," he said, "and then our director will come over and stick his head in the office door and say, 'I hope you're making money in here, because you're sure losing it out on the set.' "

That same month, Desi seemed to court disaster when he announced a partnership with the brilliant but often erratic Orson Welles. As the deal was consummated and a pilot production under way, Welles took residence at the guesthouse of the Arnazes on Roxbury Drive, transforming a three-week visit into an interminable three months, leaving behind innumerable telephone and grocery bills.

Martin Leeds had a luncheon date at fashionable Romanoff's with Welles, having the unenviable task of informing the imposing director of the network's firm refusal to consider an hourlong anthology program, insisting instead upon a half-hour version. After the meals arrived (Welles consumed his entire lunch—three balls of cottage cheese—while Leeds's meat was being sliced), Leeds finally broke the news. *"Why?"* Welles boomed. "Because an hour is not commercial—you can't sell it in syndication," Leeds explained. Welles rose from the table and bellowed, "How dare you talk to me about crass *commercialism!"* Welles then turned on his heels and stormed out of the restaurant, leaving red-faced Leeds alone to fend off the stares of the entire room.

According to editor Bud Molin, the deal was further undercut when an imperious Welles refused to bow to the Desilu corporate structure or keep his production on any semblance of a budget. "Martin Leeds and Orson Welles did not see eye-to-eye. One day Leeds sent word down to Orson via [editing department head] Dann Cahn. Dann says, 'Uh, I have a message from Martin Leeds.' Orson says, 'I do not *believe* in Martin Leeds. Therefore, you can have *no* message from him.' *That* was the end of it." The final straw came, according to Ball, when Welles expanded a five-day shooting schedule into a six-week production and then spent ten thousand dollars on a wrap party, charging the event to Desilu Studios.

Although Welles did appear on an *I Love Lucy* episode, the highly touted Desilu-Welles anthology series was abandoned after the filming of an ambitious fantasy-drama based on the John Collier short story *Youth from Vienna* titled *The Fountain of Youth;* the series failed to sell, according to Leeds, because while Welles was committed under contract to host or appear in every episode, Leeds knew he could not trust Welles to do so. Ironically, the program aired several years later as part of NBC's *Colgate Theatre* and became the only unsold pilot in television history to win a Peabody Award.

Undeterred by the Welles debacle, Arnaz announced "major expansion" for Desilu for the upcoming 1956–57 season, at the same time reporting that he had recently declined a bid for "outright purchase" of Desilu of $12 million by an unnamed prospective buyer. Desilu projected a total production of more than two hundred hours of television shows for the upcoming season, yet despite dispatching thirty models to top New York advertising agencies—armed with scripts, glamour shots, and film reels of a sixty-thousand-dollar highly publicized *Adventures of a Model* comedy pilot written by Sidney Sheldon—Desilu failed to sell the projected series starring Joanne Dru.

Such rapid studio expansion came with a high price tag, and Desi approached tax attorney Art Manella about exploring an outright sale of the *I Love Lucy* series to CBS. Manella recounts, "I remember drawing up very detailed schedules at Desi's request, pointing out to him how much money would be left over after taxes if Desilu could sell the films at a capital-gain rate, versus how much would be realized from reshowing the films and paying a regular tax on rental income. He decided to sell to CBS for what was then an excellent price. We received a capital gain because I got a ruling out of the Treasury Department, the first time it ever happened that such a sale would produce capital gains to the seller."

The sale of the entire *I Love Lucy* program inventory to CBS—which at the close of the 1956–57 season would amount to 180 episodes, "came at a time when we needed more money in which to operate," says Martin Leeds, "because we were growing and we were feeding on ourselves and we needed more money to keep growing. We were the biggest television operation in the world."

CBS business affairs executive Salvatore Iannucci provides another interesting perspective on the *I Love Lucy* sale: "We bought the negatives in part really as an accommodation to Lucy and Desi. No one had the clairvoyance—in hindsight, my God, what a deal it was for CBS. I remember having dinner with Desi and some other Desilu executives talking about the deal at an old Spanish restaurant where they had flamenco dancers. Desi really loved to enjoy his good times—drinking and partying. He was a very charming guy, very open. When he walked into a room, you knew that he was there. He was a very gregarious guy."

The deal, formally commencing October 1, 1956, called for Desilu Productions to sell "all right, title and interest in the literary and artistic property" to Columbia Broadcasting System, Inc., "for a consideration of $4,300,000 payable over a period of years"; the final two CBS payments of $500,000 each, in fact, were not paid Desilu until May and October 1961. As creator-producer-head-writer Parke Levy had done in mid-1956, Desilu would also sell to CBS its 25 percent residual and rerun ownership of *December Bride* for $500,000 to raise additional operating capital; Desilu also (at least partially) benefited from a $1 million payment to Lucille and Desi in order to ensure their "performing exclusivity" with the network until 1970; little wonder, then, that Vivian Vance and Bill Frawley reportedly balked at their low $3,500 per-episode stipend as *Lucy* costars.

The chain of events saw CBS later relinquishing its invested percentage share in Desilu. As Ed Holly notes, "A million dollars of the share money for *I Love Lucy* went to buy back the 24 percent of the company." CBS executive Oscar Katz, however, reveals that Desi's increasingly out-of-control conduct also had a hand in influencing the network's decision to divest itself of the undeniably profitable Desilu: "Paley didn't like the idea of being partners with somebody—particular somebody as wild as Desi in an operation where the other guy owns seventy-six percent and Paley only controls twenty-four percent. So CBS said to him, 'Tell you what—we'll give you the twenty-four percent back. And we'll give you a few million dollars above that, but give us *I Love Lucy*.' And *that's* how CBS acquired *I Love Lucy*."

May 23 brought the announcement that Desi Arnaz had capitulated to network demands and would return *I Love Lucy* to the network for the 1956–57 season in its original half-hour format—now budgeted at sixty thousand dollars per episode—sponsored by General Foods and Procter & Gamble; even Lucille seemed momentarily unhappy with the decision and the sameness of *I Love Lucy*, remarking, "I kept turning to the writers and saying, 'Hey! I've done this before!' And they would come right back and say, 'And now you are going to do it again!' " With Jack Aldworth promoted from assistant director to associate producer, Desi assumed the role of producer; Pugh and Carroll were now *I Love Lucy* head writers, assisted by Schiller and Weiskopf. The problem of recasting the role of "Little Ricky" for the upcoming year was solved (the current set of twins no longer suitable after it was determined to age the Ricardo offspring to expand plot possibilities) when the Arnazes saw orchestra leader Horace Heidt's NBC *Show Wagon* variety series and discovered Keith Thibodeaux; the five-year-old was billed as "the World's Tiniest Professional Drummer." Uncannily resembling a miniature Desi, the boy (renamed "Richard Keith") was immediately signed by Arnaz at $461 per week, and Desi arranged for him to take Spanish lessons; Keith's father was hired by Desilu to work part of each year in the publicity department under Kenny Morgan and subsequently divorced his wife to marry a Desilu secretary.

"Richard was almost two years older than Desi [Jr.], but didn't look it," said Arnaz. "One of the reasons Desi [Jr.] got interested in music and playing the drums was that he wanted to do everything Little Ricky did in the show, and they became really good friends." Keith, he said, "stayed at our house all the time. During the weekends and our summer hiatus he'd come to Palm Springs or Del Mar with us. Desi and Keith got to be like brothers. They grew up together. I taught Lucie, Keith, and Desi how to swim, ride horses, handle boats, and fish expertly. Lucy became Keith's acting coach and looked after his appearance, wardrobe, schooling, etc. It was as if we had three children instead of two."

Recalled Thibodeaux, "I can see why their marriage didn't make it. Desi was really a great guy when he wasn't drinking, but as kids, we'd definitely stay away from him when he was drunk. Once I was sleeping over when he heard that the tutor had called Desi, Jr., spoiled. We were awakened by a fistfight. That night Desi came down and caught the guy talking to a girl in the living room and just beat him badly. Desi, Jr., and I hid in the maid's quarters."

Of Lucille he said, "You had to walk softly around her sometimes, if she wasn't feeling well that day or something. There would be a tenseness in the air. She had a temper. She would slam doors. Lucy had a big heart and could be a joy to be around. But I was always pretty much in awe or scared of the lady, really. My dad worked at Desilu, so Lucy was his boss. She would call and say, 'I want Keith to come over and play with Desi, Jr., this weekend.' Sometimes I'd cry, but my dad worked for Lucy, and that was that. Even so, there was a time when I was basically Desi, Jr.'s only genuine friend, or at least one of the very few."

For his part, Desi Arnaz, Jr., once admitted, "I can still remember watching the show when I was about three and wondering who was the baby with Mommy and Daddy. When my parents said it was me, I was confused, because I knew it wasn't. So I had this identity problem, and it wasn't helped by people calling me Little Ricky, a name I learned to despise. I remember wanting rather desperately to be better at something—anything—than the boy who played Little Ricky. For a while, it seemed as if everything in *my* life was connected to Little Ricky's."

Although the Arnaz family planned on relaxing during the family's impending summer break from *Lucy* in Del Mar, Arnaz became alarmed at his deteriorating physical condition. "I was working much too hard," he recalled. "I knew something would have to give." The year before, Desi had seen his old friend Marc Rabwin, chief surgeon at Cedars of Lebanon Hospital; the Arnazes had known Rabwin and his wife, Marcella, for many years, Lucille having first met Marcella when she served as David O. Selznick's executive assistant. "I'm at the studio at seven or seven-thirty A.M., don't get home until after dinner, then I have a lot of paper work to take care of," Desi told Rabwin. "I hardly ever see my children unless it's just before they go to school and, if I'm lucky, during some weekends." He further admitted with some understatement, "I'm all tied up in a knot most of the time, and in order to untie it and keep going, I'm beginning to drink too much at times." Rabwin advised Arnaz to cut down on his workload and warned him that his colon was "full of diverticula, and continuous pressure and tension would make it worse." Desi was further advised that he would have to undergo a colostomy if his pace was not slackened.

Bob Hope signed to guest on the premiere episode of the season with rehearsals to begin the last week of May, Desi noting, "We are working hard to film shows ahead so we can spend a month in Del Mar with the children as we do every year"; making an effort to break away from Desilu for the summer, Arnaz finally left for Del Mar the end of June and firmly told his staff, "See you September tenth." The Del Mar retreat was far from harmonious for the Arnazes as their marital battles only intensified under the summer sun. As Marcella Rabwin recounts, "Lucy was quick to anger. And when she was mad, *goddamn* was she mad. I've been there when she and Desi had horrible fights, the name-calling.

They were very unrestrained with Marc and me because we had known them for so long. And we had been so understanding of their problems whenever they came to us with them." Marcella was aware of Desi's escalating problems with alcohol. "When he drank, there wasn't a personality change, but an intensification of all the worst things about him— the swearing got much worse. His language was always offensive. He used the worst language I've ever heard. It would get even worse when he was drunk. He was not terribly steady on his feet, and he was a little abusive, a little belligerent. But it took a lot of liquor to make him drunk—he drank all evening long. He'd start at my house, drink all through dinner."

The initial decision for the Arnazes to vacation in Del Mar came as a suggestion from Marc and Marcella Rabwin during happier days in 1949. According to Marcella, Desi came for a visit with his friend Pepito the clown, while Lucy was toiling away on a picture at Paramount. "Desi called me around seven o'clock in the morning and said, 'Look, we're coming down there, and we don't go fishing until midnight. It's the opening day of the races. How about taking me to the races?' Desi won about three or four thousand dollars. He couldn't stand it. He couldn't possibly go fishing. He had to go back the next day and lose it. They spent the night at our house. The next day he went to the races and won again, six or seven hundred dollars. He said, 'This is quite a racket, better than Vegas!'

"Every night Lucy would call Desi. She was doing a picture [*Fancy Pants*] with Bob Hope. Bob fell off a phony horse. I don't think he had hit the floor before Lucille was out of there. Desi had been telling her about his wonderful time there, and she was so jealous. She got in the car and drove straight to Del Mar. They stayed the whole time Bob Hope was incapacitated, which was four or five weeks. And they just loved it. So the next year they decided to rent a house of their own." Marcella adds, "Desi was a wonderful friend. He'd do anything in the world for you, if he liked you. He was full of love. And he was a highly sexed man, no doubt about that. Lucille was always telling me that he was just the greatest, a wonderful lover." In subsequent years, "they always had a birthday party for little Lucie in Del Mar. And Desi—not Lucille— was always the host of those parties for the kids, entertaining them, playing the guitar for them, the whole gang on the little beach. And Lucie, who was so shy on this occasion, locked herself in the bathroom and wouldn't come out for her own party. Desi loved his children." To Marcella, however, Lucille viewed her young children as "possessions" and became increasingly misdirected in her parental responsibilities as

Lucie and Desi, Jr., grew and exhibited self-willed behavior and often differing viewpoints from her own.

And although she credits the Arnazes's longtime and devoted maid, Willie Mae, and DeDe with bearing the brunt of child-bearing duties, Marcella sometimes clashed with Lucille's mother. "DeDe was devoted to her daughter, and Lucille was wildly in love with her mother. I could never understand it. DeDe would boss her around—she would boss me around. I tried very hard not to be disrespectful, for Lucille's sake, because she loved her mother so much. But DeDe was dogmatic. She was dictatorial. She cheated at cards. We used to play canasta, and she cheated all the time. DeDe had to have the last word. She was a bigot. She called Desi 'that spic' behind his back. And she didn't like Jews. Each time I had a disagreement with DeDe, she was so nasty and snotty with me afterward, barely acknowledging me if I came into a room. She was a very vengeful kind of woman. Lucille adored her mother. I never heard her call her mother down for any of the things she did."

DeDe's role in Lucille and Desi's relationship had often been one of mediator, according to Lucille's cousin Cleo Morgan Smith: "In the middle of the typical argument in which Lucille accused Desi of cheating, Lucy would call DeDe. 'Mother, I want you over here right now.' Desi would be saying, 'Jesus, she's crazy. If she accuses me of that, she's crazy.' It really bothered Lucy for him to say she was 'crazy.' DeDe knew that he had pushed a button somewhere, and would say to Desi, 'Now look. Say what you want to say, just stop saying that she's crazy.' That really bothered Lucille, but to him it was just an expression."

Cleo adds, "DeDe was very fair, she didn't take sides. DeDe was very fond of Desi. She was not a mother-in-law problem." For her part, DeDe once said, "Lucy married late, because she was always movin' around too much. I never worried about her during those years because she's always been a good, straight gal, and that's all I had to ask, but when she met Desi, that was it. My reaction was—nothing. That was her life. I had no qualms about it at all. I hardly knew him. I had met him a few times. I've never interfered with my children."

Through the years, Lucille valued the support of family members at the studio. "I'm a great believer in nepotism," she once said. "If they can cut the mustard, they're in." Both her brother, Fred, and Kenny Morgan, cousin Cleo's husband, were longtime employees of the studio. Kenny, in fact, was one of the first people Desi turned to when he was forming Desilu. After serving in the army during World War II, Kenny, a Hollywood publicist, found himself jobless. Cleo recalls, "Suddenly, we had hard times. We had adopted our son, Scott. Ken was unemployed for a period of almost a year. Ken's mother and DeDe were bringing us food in sacks. Out of nowhere Kenny's friend Roy Wilson, who had married into an enormously wealthy family in South Africa, came out to California and said, 'Buddy, you've gotta go to South Africa. It is glorious. You can make a million.' He had already gotten a franchise for some fluorescent lighting, and was in the States looking for more franchises to take back. We said, 'Why not? We're dying on the vine here.' We packed up bag and baggage—car and everything—on a cargo freighter, and off we went to Johannesburg and stayed one year. Ken said of Roy, 'He is the worst son of a bitch. I must even call him "Mr. Wilson" in the office.' I said, 'How do we get back? We had a one-way ticket.' In those days, it cost thousands of dollars to fly back, never mind the furniture, the car, everything else. I wrote to Lucille of this sad, sad tale, no way to get home. I asked her for money for plane tickets to come back. That was a funny side of Lucy. She wrote back: DON'T WORRY. YOU'LL FIND A WAY."

"We did find a way. We sold everything and bought two one-way tickets to California. That's when Lucille and Desi had signed the deal to do TV. Desi said, 'What are you going to do?' Ken said he was going to try to get back in the army [to do public-relations work in Washington, D.C.]. Desi said, 'How about helping me? I'll give you a hundred-fifty dollars a week. We'll start scouting studio space, scout a cast—do everything together.' That's how he ended up doing their publicity. In the meantime, the Washington deal came through. Ken said to me, 'I would rather go with Desilu than accept the Washington offer.' I said, 'It is your choice, but you will live to regret it.' I didn't think he should work for Desi. They wouldn't pay him anything and they would take advantage, because you don't respect people unless they've got something you want and you've hired them for a lot of money."

Cleo's instincts proved correct: "He was always under pressure, never got any money, and it was a very stressful job. A lot of that stress helped to dissolve our marriage." Lucille was extremely loyal to her immediate family, including her great-uncle Ned. Marcella Rabwin recalls, "Uncle Ned was her mother's uncle. Lucille took care of him his whole life. She was so good to him. He never opened his mouth, never spoke, never came to any of the functions that were given." However, Lucille was not always as accommodating of her brother's spouses. Strangely enough, Fred's first wife, from whom he was divorced in 1947, was also a redhead, also named Lucille and an actress—albeit struggling and unknown— and thus became the family's second "Lucille Ball" upon their marriage. The relationship of the two tempestuous women quickly deteriorated when Fred's wife turned to the then-MGM star and with a straight face said, "Isn't it funny—we're both named 'Lucille Ball.' Well, I guess one of us will have to change her name!" And, in 1956, when Fred married third wife Zo, an employee in Desilu's accounting department, the new Mrs. Ball was forced to "retire" from Desilu, since, ironically, the husband-and-wife-run organization had a policy against employing married couples.

The Arnazes returned from Del Mar to continue filming *Lucy* and face reviews for the season premiere with guest Bob Hope. Reaction to *I Love Lucy,* though still favorable, was also somewhat pallid. Said the *Reporter,* "We thought the show no better and no worse than former shows, but somehow didn't get the reaction we once got. Lucy has been on a long time doing the same things." *Lucy,* however, was the highest-rated program of the week.

Arnaz announced at the end of the year that Desilu in 1957 would hit a total production-output peak of $21,420,000. The company's burgeoning roster of programs included current network and syndication properties, a possible Bob Hope filmed series ("I'm thinking about my estate," quipped the comedian), and comedies starring Eve Arden, Zsa Zsa Gabor, and a syndicated domestic comedy about a young girl, *This Is Alice.* Arnaz sufficiently charmed Claudette Colbert to take the television-series plunge and starred in the situation comedy (ultimately unsold) pilot titled *Mrs. Harper Goes to Congress.* Although Lucille vehemently opposed the idea after the "Red Scare" incident, Desi made a "handshake deal" with Walter Winchell to discuss plans for Desilu to film a dramatic series based on the purported real-life adventures of the controversial newspaper columnist. Desilu also signed a lucrative six-to-ten title "about fifty-fifty" deal with syndication giant NTA for several action-adventure series. Arnaz also announced plans to film a theatrical version on the life of "famed singer" Gene Austin ("My Blue Heaven") deemed by *Variety* as the "Elvis Presley of his day."

I Love Lucy experienced some midseason changes. Bill Asher returned and replaced director James V. Kern. "Lucy came on a bit too strong with Jim, and he couldn't take it," said Asher, Ball exhibiting some of her old habits during rehearsals upon his return. "Lucy started in again, saying, 'Okay, Vivian, you come over here and you say so-and-so.' I said, 'Hey, Lucy, let's not start this again.' But we never really had any problems. The troubles that Lucy and Desi were having as husband and wife never got into the 'Lucy-Ricky' relationship. There might have been moments, but nothing considered tension on the set or trouble."

The writers—reflecting the move of much of urban America's flight to the more serene suburbs—relocated the Ricardos and the Mertzes to Connecticut to once again expand plot possibilities. Says Madelyn Pugh, "The [original] sets were awfully tiny. We got so sick of those. That's one reason why we moved them to the country. And *they* were tired of them—the furniture wasn't very good. We had a beautiful Connecticut farm with a front door and an entryway into the living room. But we found, you'd come in the front door, and now you had to make a long cross into the living room. You have to have dialogue, jokes, before you would get in there and see anybody. To remedy that, we thought of a lot of things. We had a guest door and kept them coming and going over to the Mertzes and vice versa. We put in a wood closet. We figured you could hide in it. We put in a stairway that you could make entrances from up above and talk from the landing."

I Love Lucy won its longest laugh (sixty-five seconds) on the "Lucy Does the Tango" episode—Lucy attempting to hide from her chicken-farming husband dozens of store-bought eggs in her blouse and an unknowing Ricky smashing against her during a tango dance. Bob Carroll, Jr., gives much of the credit to the success of the routine to Vivian Vance: "Viv had all that presence. When Lucy danced with three dozen eggs in her blouse and did the tango, Viv's face tells you that someone is doing the tango with three dozen eggs in her blouse—'My God, she's not really going to do that, is she? Uh-oh!' You watch her face. She was magnificent. On the other hand, dear Frawley didn't know *where* he was."

Desi Arnaz hosted the ninth annual Emmy Awards ceremony (telecast on NBC and held at the network's Burbank studios) on Saturday, March 16, 1957. The top-rated *I Love Lucy* failed to win a nomination, Ball, Vance, and Frawley all lost Emmy bids, and host Arnaz won decidedly mixed reviews. "It was clear watching the Emmy show if the emcee isn't top drawer in that department you're in trouble," said the *Reporter; Variety,* however, said Arnaz was "in fine comedic form."

In February 1957, high-stakes gambler Arnaz held firm on his CBS pledge that—despite its top-rated position—if *I Love Lucy* returned to the network, it would be in a new one-hour format or not at all. "It will be like an hour movie once a month," he insisted, "and we'll give it theatrical quality." The projected budget was announced at a record high of $250,000 per hour production. Desi so strongly envisioned *Lucy* airing as eight color "specials" during the upcoming 1957–58 season (with "stronger guest stars") that he even turned down CBS's offer of a whopping eighty thousand dollars per original episode—half that amount for same-season, prime-time reruns—if Arnaz bowed to network demands and continued the series in its original half-hour format. He stunned advertising-agency representatives and current *Lucy* sponsors, General Foods and Procter & Gamble, in announcing in March 1957 that the cost for a sixty-minute *Lucy* was a revised-upward—and staggering—$350,000 per hour, translating to an unprecedented $4 million sponsor outlay.

During Palm Springs meetings, Arnaz was advised in short order that his current sponsors were "not interested" at that price and admen even queried him, said *Variety,* whether the "$350,000 price tag was for 'publicity' or for real." The paper added, "Both P&G and GF are pulling out after this season because of two factors: the price is too high and both demand weekly exposure." When GF and P&G hinted that they might go along with the once-monthly *Lucy* program if they agreed on the programs designated to air the other weeks, Arnaz suggested that CBS fill Lucy's current Monday night time slot with *December Bride* and the still-unsold *Adventures of a Model* the weeks the eight Lucy-Desi hours did not air; CBS, though, insisted on filling the vacant hour with network-owned product, and as a result, both P&G and GF soon dropped out of *Lucy* sponsorship for the 1957–58 season altogether.

CBS's Hubbell Robinson advised unhappy network affiliates not to look for *I Love Lucy* in its traditional Monday night position: "We go along with Desi on his plan to do eight or ten hourlong shows in the fall, but at the moment nothing is definite, nothing has been resolved in terms of placing them on the schedule." The CBS vice president pointedly stated that Lucy and Desi might remain off the air entirely during the 1957–58 season if details could not be "ironed out." He could not resist leaving the Arnazes with a parting shot: "They deserve a rest if they want it—and when you have their kind of money, you can afford to stay off TV." Indeed, Desilu at the same time sold its new series, *The Walter Winchell File,* to ABC after a heated bidding war with rival NBC.

As Desi's negotiations alternately heated and stalled for the new hour programs, Lucille escaped to Palm Springs with *Hollywood Reporter* columnist Radie Harris, who wrote on April 11, "I only spent three days as Lucille and Desi's houseguest but when I left Lucille said she had seen more of Palm Springs and the floating population in those three days than in the two years she and Desi had lived there! . . . Lucille doesn't budge from their beautiful Californian-Hawaiian ranch house, set ker-plunk in the middle of the Thunderbird golf course, but devotes her entire weekend to her two youngsters [and] never missed a meal with them. . . . After family lunch with 'Mom' Ball and the Kenny Morgans, we had a divine visit with Kay and Clark Gable in their private bungalow at the Tennis Club and then stopped for more laughs with Mary and Jack Benny and Gracie Allen. Mary scolded Lucille for neglecting her until my arrival, so as soon as we reached home, Lucille phoned Mary and deadpanned, 'I just called to see how you are feeling!' "

However, although CBS did not yet have a time slot or name for the new Ball-Arnaz program (the *I Love Lucy* title was now owned by CBS), Ford Motor Company, via the J. Walter Thompson Agency, expressed strong interest—despite the high price tag—in sponsoring the show to introduce its "new Edsel model." At the same time, to further entice sponsors concerned with the high cost, Desi was considering dropping the number of "eight to ten" hour shows to only five per season, and in short order the per-hour *Lucy* cost dropped as well from $350,000 to $250,000 and finally to $200,000, proving, quipped *Variety,* "that the law of gravity works in TV too." Finally, on May 1, Ford—uniquely bypassing CBS and dealing directly with the Arnazes and J. Walter Thompson—decided against sponsoring the new CBS *Perry Mason* crime series and signed to sponsor five *Lucy* hour programs; the sponsorship would be timed to the unveiling of Ford's 1958 models; the deal also called for Lucy and Desi to film a Ford nonbroadcast industrial film.

On May 9, *Variety* leaked that Desilu was "near closing deal for purchase of RKO-Pathé Studio from General Teleradio. Desilu, because of mounting production of 'vidpix,' both under own aegis and for other firms, long has been looking for more space, in addition to present perch at Motion Picture Center. Desilu reps were on the RKO-Pathé stages yesterday, measuring and surveying facilities." On May 13, however, an RKO-Pathé spokesman declared that negotiations "were off" despite a "firm bid" which had been declined by RKO. During the RKO negotiations, Lucy, Desi, and the children escaped to Hawaii. Lucille sent to columnist Radie Harris a giant color postcard of the "Eruption of Mauna Loa" inscribed with the following message: I TOOK ONE CUP OF SUGAR, ONE CUP OF FLOUR, JUST A PINCH OF BAKING SODA—AND LOOK WHAT HAPPENED. LOVE, LUCY.

The month of June suggested trouble when the Arnazes vacationed separately, Lucille catching current Broadway shows in New York and Desi fishing in Mexico. While in Manhattan, Lucy phoned New York–based Radie Harris and told her that "the Paleys" were escorting her to *My Fair Lady*. "The Sam Paleys?" deadpanned Radie. The humorless Lucille countered in dead earnest, "No, the *Bill* Paleys!" prompting Harris to write, "It was the first time I had ever heard that oft-quoted gag work!"

Lucille's old friends Hedda Hopper and Ann Sothern—for a record

$25,000—were signed to guest on the initial hour *Lucy* episode. *December Bride* director Jerry Thorpe was assigned to the first hour episode, upon the completion of the pilot episode of *The Walter Winchell File*. The Ball-Sothern teaming was such a happy experience for the two that they soon after were "talking" about costarring in a feature film; at the same time, Arnaz negotiated with the star—who had recently exited her *Private Secretary* hit comedy following a bitter contractual dispute with producers over residuals—to star in a new series called *Career Girl*.

A month before the first hourlong *Lucille Ball–Desi Arnaz Show* was to premiere, Arnaz rejected an offer from Texas oilman Clint Murchison to buy Desilu, saying, "I don't want to sell my freedom." The deal would have made Arnaz executive producer under Murchison, but Desi was "skeptical" at the actual power such a title would have given him after the contracts were signed. "We give our employees bonuses totaling from one hundred fifty thousand to two hundred thousand around Christmas. I asked him if we could still do this if the company changed hands, and the reply was 'Yes, I think so, but of course that would have to be taken up by the board of directors.' I value my freedom too much to sell—that's why I wouldn't sell my company to Metro three years ago." During the first half hour of talks with Murchison, Desi kept calling the tycoon "Mr. Murchison," while the oilman called him "Desi." Finally, Murchison told him, "Call me Clint" which prompted Arnaz to quip, "I can't help it—with this much money involved, I *have* to call you Mr. Murchison."

The "Lucy Takes a Cruise to Havana" flashback story recounted the first meeting of Lucy and Ricky twenty years earlier—man-chasing best friends Lucy and Susie on a cruise to Cuba, where they meet crooner Rudy Vallee, suitors Desi and Cuban cohort Cesar Romero, along with newlyweds Fred and Ethel Mertz. Ironically, while Desi Arnaz had pressed CBS to allow his one-hour *Lucy*, his first effort delivered to the network what *Variety* deemed a "precedential 75-minute segment." Desi recalled, "When I showed the sponsor and agency the picture, they said fine, they liked it, but to cut fifteen minutes. I told them it was impossible, it would ruin the show. Why louse it up when it was just right, I asked? The reply was it had to be an hour. So I said—why? Who's looking at their watch? So we called in CBS and J. Walter Thompson, I explained the situation, and they said it's never been done before, but it made sense. So they got U.S. Steel to relinquish fifteen minutes of its show, which follows our November 6 special. I call it *Playhouse Seventy-five*."

Although it posted an outstanding 57.5 first-place Nielsen rating for the month of November, *The Lucille Ball–Desi Arnaz Show* largely failed to enchant the critics. Said the *Reporter,* "Maybe we were expecting too much but this is still painfully thin situation comedy with much studio laughter made over thin jokes and fancy mugging." *Variety* called it a "cornball yarn" with "thin charm."

For the second hour installment, the Arnazes signed Bette Davis to be "The Celebrity Next Door" to the Westport, Connecticut, home of the Ricardos and the Mertzes. Davis—once a classmate of Lucille's when both attended John Murray Anderson's dramatic school in New York— demanded a twenty-thousand-dollar salary, a twelve-day rehearsal and shooting period, along with equal billing with Lucille and Desi. She further insisted that Desilu pay return airplane fare to Maine if she left within ten days after completing the production. Although Desilu ac- quiesced to her demands, Bette Davis was replaced by Tallulah Bankhead when Davis, in June, fell down a stairless basement entrance at a rented Los Angeles home and cracked her vertebrae.

Bankhead seemed scarcely impressed by the *Lucy* operation: "They had this plot. They were living in Connecticut, or *somewhere,* and re- hearsing a play for the PTA, *whatever* that is. In one scene, I was supposed to sit down in wet paint. In another, I said to Lucy, 'Remove yourself before I pull out that pink hair and expose the black roots underneath.' Then I locked her inside an iron maiden [suit of armor] while she was smoking a cigarette. When they wanted to paint a mustache on me, I drew the line." She also insisted, "I *did* have pneumonia at the time. And someone nearly *blinded* me one day at rehearsals with hair spray. But Lucy! She's *divine* to work with! And Desi! He's *brilliant.* He *has* a temper, however. But that's because he's *fat.* It worries him."

Desi countered, "Tallulah would arrive at the set at nine-thirty in the morning. But she wouldn't really wake up until eleven. Between eleven and twelve she was fine. But at one P.M., right after lunch, we'd lose her again." Arnaz conceded that Miss Bankhead did refuse to wear a painted mustache. "So I finally had to drop the good manners and lay it on the line to her. I told her we were paying her good money, and we expected her to do her best. The night we did the actual filming, I was terrified. I kissed her quickly, wished her luck, and walked away, hoping against hope—so what happened? She was magnificent."

Lucille's bid for perfection was indeed challenged by Bankhead's ap- parently half-inebriated condition. "Tallulah was a little squirrelly, tough in rehearsals," Ball later recalled. "She'd never finish a scene, and that got me worried, so I planned all sorts of things to cover for her when we actually shot the show. Well, when we did the show, Tallulah sailed through every scene magnificently—but I didn't." Ball, according to

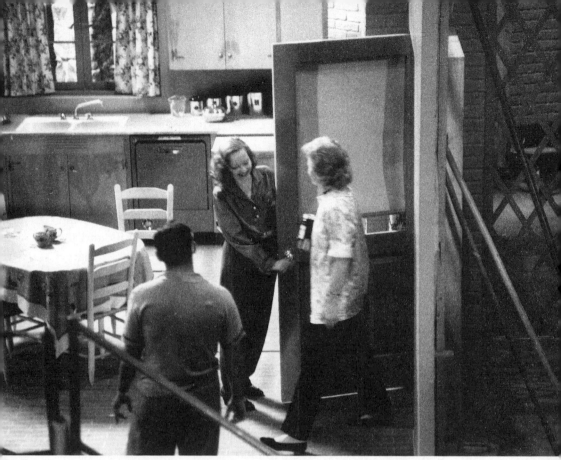

Tallulah and Lucille rehearse "The Celebrity Next Door" with
director Jerry Thorpe
LEONARD NADEL

director friend Herbert Kenwith, was not at all intimidated by Bankhead's legendary status: "Lucy was giving Tallulah line readings. Lucy had a habit of snapping her fingers in front of your face. She'd say, 'Read it this way' right in front of Tallulah's face. Tallulah grabbed her hand and said, 'Don't ever do that to me!' Lucy said, 'Well, I want you to read the lines right.' Bankhead said, 'I have been acting for a long time. I know how to read my lines. Don't give me readings.' Finally, Tallulah walked off the set and wouldn't continue working. But of course she came back."

Maury Thompson recalls, "Tallulah was a little tiny thing. Short and small. At first Lucille was afraid the studio audience wasn't going to recognize her. We all guffawed at that, but she was right in a way, because Tallulah was a New York stage star, and the audience there at Desilu were all local people practically. When she made her entrance, Lucille said, 'Open the door real wide, Desi, be sure they see her.' So when he opened the door, there she was, leaning on the doorjamb, and my God, the place went wild. We had to cut a lot of it out because they just went on and went on and went on. After the show, we said to

Lucille, 'And you thought they wouldn't know her, huh?' "

Tallulah apparently took pleasure in unnerving not only Lucille, but anyone in proximity. Thompson relates, "The night before the show, we had notes in Desi's office, Tallulah, Lucille and Desi, Vivian and Bill, the four writers, [script supervisor] Adele [Sliff], and myself. Desi made us a drink, and we sat around the office, like a living room, in a circle. It was a family affair, very comfortable, nothing austere or businesslike. Tallulah had a crocheted sweater over her shoulders, and Lucille said, 'I *love* that sweater.' Tallulah said, 'My God, dahling, take it!' and just took it and threw it at Lucille. Lucille said, 'I don't *want* it, I can get one,' but Tallulah said, 'No I want you to have it, I've got dozens of them, so don't worry about it.' Then there's a couple of beats, and Viv says, 'Well, for me the slacks. I love the slacks.' Off came the slacks. And there she stood in her teddy with the crotch that hangs down to about the knee. Lucille shouted, 'Desi, get her a robe! Get her a robe!' Adele went right under the coffee table. Of course, Madelyn, who is so ladylike, covered her eyes. Tallulah was all set to sit there with her legs crossed on the floor for the rest of the evening. Here came Desi with a dressing gown and put it on her, and she condescended." Cowriter Bob Weiskopf was so taken aback that he bolted up off the couch and out the side door of the office when Tallulah started to peel off her slacks.

"I sent Lucille flowers," said Bankhead after filming was completed. "She called me on the phone. 'It was *your* show, Tallulah,' she said. 'Yours, yours, yours!' She couldn't have been more generous." And, noted, *Variety,* "Lucy and Tallu are an irresistible combination and they had a ball. . . . *Lucy,* let's face it, ain't cerebral, but it sure is physical and it ain't what they do but the way they do it that seems to count." The Bankhead hour was the highest-rated show of the week.

On November 20, 1957, *Variety* bannered that RKO was "near sale" of its Gower Street and Culver City Studios to Desilu; RKO board chairman Thomas F. O'Neil and Arnaz expected to complete negotiations "within days"; Daniel T. O'Shea represented RKO in the talks, with Martin Leeds protecting Desilu's interests. According to Ed Holly, Martin Leeds was out of town on Desilu business when O'Shea first alerted him—along with Argyle Nelson, whom O'Shea had known at RKO— and "told us privately that he had been instructed to find a buyer for the RKO studio properties, not the film inventory, just the physical studio. And since we were the major tenants of RKO at the time and because of his relationship with the two of us, he felt that if we could make a deal—a very quick deal—we could do it. We worked for several hours and brought Desi in. We were in heavy production on the [Bank-

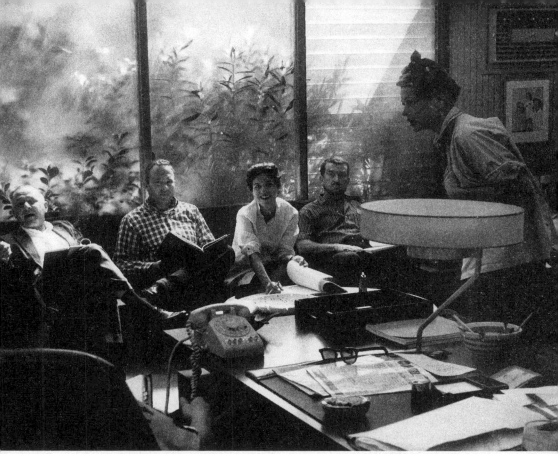

"The Celebrity Next Door" story conference in Desi's Motion Picture Center office: Desi (*back to camera*), and (*from left*) writers Weiskopf, Schiller, Martin, and Carroll observe as Lucille makes a heated point to (*not seen*) director Thorpe.
LEONARD NADEL

head] Lucy-Desi special. Desi came into his office because it was too important to have any news leaks on the stage. We briefed him. It was a six-million-dollar acquisition—a lot of money at the time, especially for a company that didn't have six million dollars. And there was to be a million dollars paid within twenty-four hours.

"It took maybe half an hour talking to Desi, but he was so up-to-speed on everything we were doing in the studio operation area that he understood everything we were saying and approved the deal. Then he turned to me and said, 'You have to go sell it to Lucy.' He wasn't going to go out and tell Lucy she was going to have to mortgage the house, the ranch, the kids, and everything else. This was, in effect, putting everything they and the company had on the line. I went out, stood on the side until Lucy and Vivian finished. I suggested we go into her dressing room because I had something important to discuss. I went through it, not in as much detail as with Desi because she at that point was primarily interested in her own show and leaving the rest of the

137

business to us. But she understood everything, asked a lot of the right questions. She finally said, 'Is this your recommendation?' I said yes. She said, 'Then go do it.' She walked out of the dressing room right onstage with Vivian—she had just made the biggest decision she'd ever make in her lifetime from a business standpoint, and went right back into the routine they had been doing. It was just incredible working with someone who could deal on that basis and could handle it. But dealing with them that quickly, with all that authority, we were able to close the deal. Then we waited until the end of the day to take some champagne to Lucy and celebrate, toast the new owner of RKO where she had worked for seventy-five dollars a week not that many years ago."

Leeds remembers, "I called Desi from New York. I said, 'If we don't do it, three years from now we'll be out of business. You're paying eight hundred thousand dollars a year in rent anyway.' As the final papers were drawn, I received a call from O'Shea that there was one clinker: they had a tax problem, and we would not be able to refinance the studio during the payoff period. This could have been a serious problem for us, because if things got bad, and we needed to borrow money on the studio, what could we do? I told Shea that was okay, but that the down payment would have to be broken up into two payments of four hundred fifteen thousand over two years. He was furious, realizing that we could, under California law, walk away at the end of each of the first two years if the deal didn't work for us, and with no liability on our part. He had no choice and agreed. He did not talk to me for three years after that."

On November 26, *Variety* announced that "final papers, whereby the RKO studios will become the property of the Desi Arnaz–Lucille Ball company for a sum over $6,000,000 will be signed in two or three weeks." RKO would be purchased from General Tire and Rubber Company, which bought RKO in July 1955 from Howard Hughes for $25 million; the studio, once a giant in the industry, had become erratic under Hughes's control; as *The New York Times* concluded, "In recent months, the producing facilities on the West Coast have come to a virtual standstill." Leeds said the sale would result in a "haven for indies" and added there were no "immediate plans" for the disposal of Motion Picture Center. Between the two RKO Studios (Hollywood and Culver City) and Motion Picture Center, Desilu would have a total of thirty-five available soundstages for its own use or rental.

The deal was concluded on Wednesday, December 11, for a "bargain" $6,150,000. The deal, said *The Reporter,* included "all physical assets of

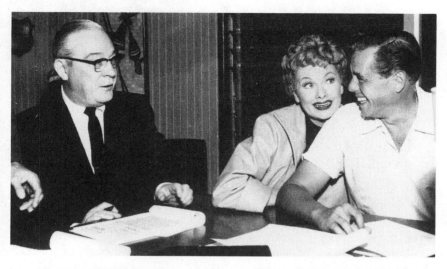

RKO's Dan O'Shea and the Arnazes complete the Desilu acquisition of the motion picture studios, December 11, 1957.
ARNAZ FAMILY ARCHIVES

RKO's Gower Street and RKO-Pathe's Culver City lots, including 26 soundstages and 457 furnished and equipped offices." Mary Wickes remembers Lucy telling her of visiting the vast RKO wardrobe department soon after the purchase. "She said, '*God!*' It took her back to when she was a contract player, and to see all those furs and things that suddenly were hers. She couldn't believe it. God knows, she didn't need them anymore, but it was a giant look backward."

Arnaz also apparently always had in mind the firm belief that, despite his business acumen, it was wife Lucille who represented the cornerstone of Desilu's success story. Shortly after the RKO buy, Lucille tripped over some tangled cables during a rehearsal and fell to the ground. Desi immediately rushed to her side and helped her up. Looking at his writers and other staff members gathering around, he dusted off the unharmed Lucille and cracked, "Amigos, if anything happens to her, we're all in the shrimp business."

Chapter Eight

★

> "Desi protected Lucy and knew how to promote her. He was a large part of her talent—I'd say it was a forty-sixty situation. She knew it. You can't explain it—love is a funny thing."
>
> —Fred Ball, 1992

★

"*I* keep rememberin' that right here I first met this crazy character," mused Desi Arnaz shortly after the RKO Studios purchase. "Six months later, we was married. What a woman! It's been sometimes up and down like an elevator—but every day, I say, 'Desi, you are a *very* locky guy.' "

Arnaz was also fortunate that the long-established television viewing habit of watching Lucy and Desi's antics continued despite the critical pummeling of the new hourlong episodes. The Bankhead program—despite largely lukewarm notices—was ranked the fourth-highest-rated program of December 1957; topping it were *Gunsmoke,* Perry Como, and *Lassie.* The third hour installment, a Las Vegas–set romp with guests Fred MacMurray and wife June Haver, fared no better with critics. (Summed up *Variety,* "Thin for the 60-minute course.") A Ball-Arnaz comedy hour, despite the reviews, again proved to be a strong ratings performer, ranking as the second-highest-rated show of the week, following *Gunsmoke.*

The Vegas location filming indicated Arnaz continued to play as hard as he worked. Vivian Vance recalled, "Desi risked some of the Arnaz bankroll on the gambling tables. We worried enough about that to hire a private plane so that he could be pried away and flown home to Los Angeles. Up in the wild blue yonder, Desi changed his mind and bribed the pilot to turn around and bring him back again. Before he was through, another forty-five thousand dollars had to be kissed good-bye."

As Desilu prepared to move administration headquarters from Motion Picture Center to new RKO headquarters—while the Gower Street lot's famous water tower and on-site signs were hurriedly changed from "RKO Studios" to "Desilu Studios"—Arnaz continued to juggle his dual roles as performer and business executive in a lavish oak-and-leather office occupied at various times by David O. Selznick and Dore Schary. (Lucille promptly took over the former dressing room once occupied by Ginger Rogers.) Soon after the RKO purchase, Martin Leeds locked up a new syndicated series, *Grand Jury,* and *The Texan,* a Rory Calhoun western series, which enjoyed a two-season prime-time run on CBS.

Despite Desilu's vigorous attempts to acquire viable television properties and the recent RKO purchase, Arnaz was no doubt alarmed when he read in *Variety,* "A year ago, Desilu was the unquestioned leader in TV film production but in the span since then Revue has grown tremendously, outdistancing Desilu in the process." MCA's Revue television subsidiary claimed such series as *Wagon Train, Bachelor Father, Alfred Hitchcock Presents, The Jack Benny Show, General Electric Theatre,* and *Schlitz Playhouse;* Desilu had the CBS network Lucy-Desi hours, ABC's *Walter Winchell File,* as well as such less-prestigious syndicated programs as *Whirlybirds, Sheriff of Cochise, Official Detective,* and *This Is Alice.* It was equally true, however, that Desilu and Revue for the 1957–58 season monopolized nearly half of all Hollywood-based filmed television production.

Desilu planned to dramatically reduce its expenditure in funding pilots in contrast to previous years, announcing in late 1957 that the company would produce only a cluster of pilots for the upcoming season—*The Texan,* Ann Sothern's comedy series *Career Girl* (later renamed *The Ann Sothern Show*), an (abandoned and untitled) "air-force drama," and an (eventually unsold) trio of pilots starring Marie Wilson, Joan Blondell, and George Jessel.

At the same time, *The Walter Winchell File* was creating monumental headaches for Desilu. As producer Bert Granet recalls, "He was getting about seven thousand dollars a show. It turned out that he really had no stories to provide for us, that all he was going to do was come in as a narrator." Despite internal Desilu troubles with Winchell, reviews of the program were outstanding, although ratings did not match the critical accolades; further undermining of the fledgling program's chances of survival came early in the season when Winchell and Desilu found themselves in the perplexing situation of suddenly being competitors when CBS pitted a *Lucille Ball–Desi Arnaz Show* against ABC's *Walter Winchell File.* Upon ABC's cancellation, and not willing to dismiss the program as a complete loss, Arnaz produced a cluster of additional episodes (above the initial first-season ABC broadcasts) for syndication, but *The Walter Winchell File* soon vanished.

Lucy's luster continued to diminish among critics. The February 1958 airing of the fourth *Lucille Ball–Desi Arnaz Show* (with Betty Grable and trumpeter-bandleader husband Harry James) met with even more critical

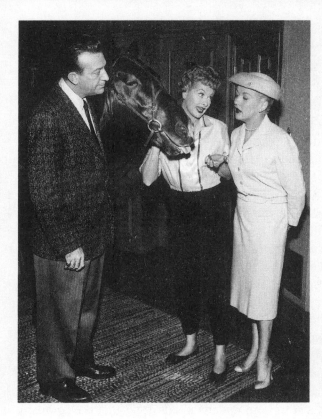

Harry James, Betty
Grable, and Lucy in
"Lucy Wins a
Racehorse"

disfavor than the previous MacMurray hour. Noted *The Hollywood Reporter* of "Lucy Wins a Racehorse," "Might it not be better to first write a solid comedy script punching up the Ball-Arnaz talents and *then* hire star guests (if needed) for added impact?"

Television audience numbers once again belied such critical drubbing, and *The Lucille Ball–Desi Arnaz Show* ranked as the second-highest-rated show of the month. "At the beginning of the season, they said Ford was crazy to sponsor our hourlong shows at such cost, but look at the ratings," boasted Arnaz. He continued to defend his decision to abandon the half-hour *I Love Lucy:* "You've got to change in this business. You can't afford to sit still. I would rather make a big change while we are still ahead. It would be ridiculous for us to wait until people got sick and tired of the regular half hour every Monday night. We have been the luckiest show on the air, but we've worked for it. I have never worked so hard in my life." He added, "I can honestly say we have never done a really bad show in six years and one hundred eighty shows. We threw out only two scripts that whole time and started again. What other program ever had writers with a record like that?" And when asked by *TV Guide* what *I Love Lucy* had "done for him in six years," Desi grinned and replied, "That's a silly question—I would ask another question and say what *hasn't* it?"

Desi's loyalty in crediting those who had helped him in the past again manifested itself when he learned that George Murphy's long MGM association—as actor and then as the studio's publicity director under Howard Strickling—dissolved in the wake of the studio's drastic cost-cutting moves. Recalled Murphy, "Desi called me up and said, 'Hey, amigo, what are you going to do?' I had been with MGM for twenty-two, twenty-three years. He said, 'I just bought a studio—why don't you come over and help me run it?' The next day I went over and looked at the place—the dusty stages, the inactivity—and went to work for him."

George Murphy had the unique distinction of having worked separately in films with both Lucille and Desi—costarring at RKO with Ball in 1941's *A Girl, a Guy, and a Gob* and two years later top-billed in MGM's *Bataan* with Arnaz as a supporting player. Murphy's friendship with Lucille began in 1933 upon her arrival in Hollywood as a Goldwyn Girl; during her early days in Hollywood their relationship blossomed to the point where they knew each other, according to Murphy, "quite well." Years later, when a suitable leading lady could not be found for leading-man Murphy by *A Girl, a Guy, and a Gob* director Richard Wallace or producer Harold Lloyd, Murphy immediately suggested Ball. Never forgetting his kindness, "Lucille always said that if I was ever out of work and she *was* working, I had a job. She was a great, great gal. I was very fond of her."

Despite his personal devotion to the Arnazes, George Murphy—who departed Desilu after three years and later briefly became a California senator—was immediately placed in an adversarial relationship with another powerful Desilu executive: "I felt then that Martin Leeds was a little jealous of me. I knew things that he didn't know, and he knew things about television that I didn't care about. I wasn't challenging anybody, I wasn't challenging Martin Leeds—I was doing what I thought I had to do to help my friend Desi."

Although Leeds was criticized by some loyal Arnaz supporters for being increasingly—and inappropriately—vocal to outsiders about Desi's escalating drinking problem as well as claiming for himself a bit too much of the company's success (deservedly or not) at the expense of company founder and president Arnaz, he still managed to maintain a close relationship with Lucy and Desi. "We decided that Christmas was getting out of hand with all the present buying," recalled Leeds. "So Lucy, Desi, and I decided not to get each other presents. Came Christmastime and Lucy held her 'present time' for her crew and personal assistants, as did Desi. We all met on one of the stages, where there were bleacher seats for an audience, and we were all assembled. Me there, as I thought and as they thought, as a spectator. At the very end of giving out some hundred presents, she commented, 'There is one person here for whom there is supposed to be no present. Martin, get your body down here!' When I got down, I said to Lucy and Desi, 'This is not fair play.' She handed me two wrapped packages. They were oil paintings of my two sons. How much planning—the two of them, and I'm sure mostly Lucy—had to do, months and months. It was inestimable. While the tears actually rolled down my face, I reached into my pocket and handed Desi a little packet, saying at the same time to Lucy, 'Your present is at your home.' I had for Desi there a set of cuff links and a tie pin made from his coat of arms from Cuba that had taken four months to get and for Lucy—who seemed to have everything—a sterling champagne bucket, appropriately engraved."

To Vivian Vance, Lucille displayed infrequent but sometimes remarkable acts of friendship. Vivian recalls, "One Christmas, Lucille presented me with a scrapbook, embossed on the cover with *This Is Your Life—Vivian Roberta Jones*. She'd put it together herself, with baby pictures, photographs of Mom and Dad and the family, including uncles and aunts. It had taken weeks of telephoning them—as well as my psychiatrists along the route—before she got together all the souvenirs to sort and paste in. Then she threw a party at the studio and had everyone at Desilu attend. At the climax, she handed over the scrapbook."

At least initially, remembers Bert Granet, Desilu "inherited the character virtue of RKO—it was a very small studio, very personal," despite its vastly expanded headquarters and hundreds of employees. To that end, Lucille reportedly took an interest in overseeing the menu of Desilu's new eating facilities (hating "bad studio food") at the former RKO sites, bringing in a new catering company to redesign the menu along with a remodeled dining room and coffee shop. Lucille also delighted in organizing company picnics and soundstage wrap parties. Desi's longtime assistant Johny Aitchison recalls one such event held in Palm Springs. "They rented buses. It was really a big thing. Eddie Stevenson, the designer at that particular time, commented he loved the way Lucy was dressed—very simply. He said, 'Now that is so nice.' She could have really gussied up and been the star. But she dressed down. I always thought that was wonderful of her."

"Desilu Productions became a family," once recalled Vivian Vance, "and it stayed like that all the way through, two hundred people working for a common cause. Lucy spent a lot of her time like a little girl planning the fun, while she gradually learned the ins and outs of business from Desi. Every year, she'd hire a whole park out in the Valley for Desilu

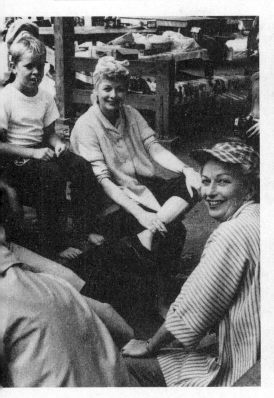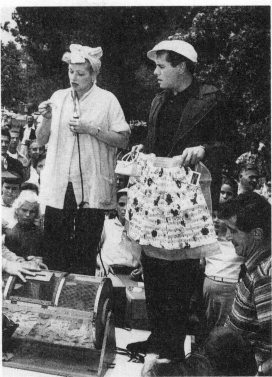

The 1955 annual Desilu picnic: (*left*) Lucille relaxes with employees and
their children; (*right*) the Arnazes announce raffle winners.
MAURY THOMPSON COLLECTION
RICK CARL COLLECTION

picnic day, which was her great joy. When that season came along, we
could scarcely keep up with the schedule of the show—she was so busy
ordering the carousel, the rides, telephoning the caterers, setting the
timetable for the gunnysack race and all the other events. What a kick
she used to get from running a picnic!"

Bud Molin recalls, "After he bought RKO [renamed Desilu-Gower],
we had to go from Desilu Cahuenga [Motion Picture Center] to Desilu-
Gower. We get to the gate. The guard says, 'What do you want?' He
says 'I want to get on the lot.' 'Who are you?' 'I'm Desi Arnaz.' 'Have
you got a pass?' 'No, I own the studio. It's mine.' 'I'm sorry, you have
to have a pass.' I forgot who he called, but we got on. So I said to Desi,
'He's not long for that job.' Desi said, 'Of course he's going to stay here,
he's doing his job.' In the early days, Lucy had a great attitude about
that also. I was on the set. The script supervisor was a nice guy. He
comes over to Desi and says, 'You weren't in that position.' Desi said,
'Yes, I was.' Lucy turns around and says, 'Look, you hired him to do

what he's doing. Either do what he says or fire him.' "

On one occasion, Desi prepared for his young son a bowl of "Arnaz rice," which he set in a bowl in front of little Desi. The boy clamped his lips shut and refused to eat. Desi attempted to coax him with a colorful tale about the three generations of Arnazes who had grown "big and strong" on rice.

"Did Great-grandfather Arnaz eat it?" asked Desi IV.

"Yes, he did."

"Did Grandfather Arnaz eat it?"

"Of course," said Desi.

"Did you eat it?"

"You know I do."

"Well," said little Desi, "here's one Arnaz who isn't going to."

Lucille's brother, Fred, who joined Desilu in 1954 to help organize the physical operations of Motion Picture Center, found his responsibilities expanding exponentially with the acquisition of RKO. "We were really cramped at Motion Picture Center—which we were still trying to whip into shape and make work from a physical standpoint—and all of a sudden we pick up RKO, which involves two studios. There's a lot of work to be done, because Desilu was growing by way of taking on companies who wanted studio space. And we were providing not only studio space but a service—a budgeting service, a management service, and so forth. The offices at RKO were a disaster. Every office needed refurbishing—every stairway, every parking lot, everything in the studio needed work." As Desi remarked, "Those cubbyholes were no good. These are creative people, and creative people gotta have room to think."

According to Fred Ball, the growing success of Desilu further exacerbated Desi's self-destructive patterns of drinking, gambling, and womanizing—which ultimately resulted in increasingly frequent absences from corporate duties. "Over a period of time, he assumed he didn't have to work hard to keep it together. As a result of that, his life deteriorated. His relationship with Lucy deteriorated, his relationship with the studio deteriorated—and the studio itself deteriorated. He figured he had other interests that were more important than keeping a tight rein on the studio. That began to manifest in 1956. It was a continual deterioration. It was catastrophic. Desi was a great talent—he had many talents. He was too good to all of his employees. He paid well. That was his problem—he gave them too much responsibility. He never followed through and kept a tight rein. And therefore, with studio politics, everybody had their own ax to grind."

"I just keep my eye on things," said Desi. "If I had to make a choice,

I would stick with the creative end of the business. But I can't. The toughest part of my job is to find the right people for the right job. But when I do, I leave them alone. I love to see people do their work well, and we got a lot of them there that do."

"They were generous—although Desi more than Lucy—and in all the years I was with them, I never had to ask for a raise," recalls Bernie Weitzman. "They would improve the money two or three times a year. They would always give you more than you anticipated. They never asked for anything except for you to be honest and straight-shooting. I was really spoiled by these people. I thought the rest of the world was like that. Desi never had a political bone in his body. He never looked at people as other than what they were. If they were good, decent, and fair to him, that's all he cared about."

Cleo Morgan recalls that it was one of Lucille's primary concerns that Desi be respected by the studio's employees. "I was at Desilu helping out one time, and Lucy came to me and said, 'Do they respect Desi [behind his back]?' I told her, 'Yes, they do. They all think very highly of him.' " Arnaz seemingly did not allow his vast Desilu success to inhibit his enthusiasm or open amazement at his new role of studio mogul. A few days after completing extensive location shooting in Idaho for "Lucy Goes to Sun Valley" (with guest Fernando Lamas), Desi exclaimed, "When we were shooting our current picture in Sun Valley, I was standing on top of a mountain, surrounded by a cast and crew of eighty people, and as I saw all kinds of Desilu equipment being transported on the ski lift, I thought, What a long ways TV has come since those early days—only about six years ago."

Despite work pressures, late hours, and increasing reliance on alcohol, Desi managed to retain his often uncanny ability for recall. "Desi was a great editor and a great showman. He had a photographic memory, and we wanted to kill him," said Lucille. "We didn't use cards at that time, and he would come down with reams of dialogue, having gone through the script a couple of times, and he knew *every* word. He was *never* there. He was up in his office making business deals—he'd come down, do the run-through while we were stumbling over words that he *knew*." Adds Bert Granet, "Desi was a very, very bright man. His image was sorely tarnished by the role he played on *I Love Lucy*. He had a photographic memory. You couldn't shoot the breeze with him without him quoting you six months from now. He could write. He could read a script and knew everyone's part on one reading. And he was a very respectable boss, because when things went wrong, Desi would say, 'Well, amigo, I guess *we* blew it'—instead of 'Well, amigo, *you* blew it.' "

"Desi was a delight when he bought RKO," recounted Vivian Vance. "He behaved like a child who'd been given a playhouse overflowing with toys. 'It's a treasure trove, Veev!' he gasped as he explored every inch of the place. He came bursting in one day after he'd put his nose into another warehouse. 'Pianos!' he cried. 'You never saw so many. Dozens of 'em. You want a piano, Veev?' He made a new discovery before the week was out. 'I opened this door and there was wallpaper. Millions of rolls! We'll never have to buy wallpaper for the rest of our lives! Can you use some wallpaper, Veev?' "

The Lamas episode (the fifth and last of the season) won more consistently good notices than any other Lucy-Desi hour program to date. Said *Variety,* "Good fun for the whole brood . . . Lamas is taking his ease at the lodge and to steam up Arnaz's 'yealousy' [Lucy] makes a big play for the Latin lover boy. . . . For the big yoks there are a brace of physical situations that Miss Ball tosses off like a chef's salad. . . . If Ford is of a mind to return for next year, this closer should have a stimulating influence."

Rumors had, in fact, been widely circulating in Hollywood that, despite initial assurances that the Ford-Desilu relationship would be a lasting one, Ford would likely cancel sponsorship of the high-ticketed Lucy-Desi programs at the end of the current season—the per-episode sponsorship cost, according to *The Reporter,* not sufficient to "match the slow movement of new car sales." An industrywide recession had afflicted the auto maker in the 1958 model year, one of the circumstances that led to the notorious failure of its Edsel line.

Still wanting to preserve the personal "family" atmosphere of his company, Desi Arnaz was also zealously determined to reestablish Desilu as the undisputed leader of television filmed production. Arnaz, Leeds, and their battery of top-ranked executives spent the first months of 1958 in closed-door negotiations with CBS. On February 20, a long-standing dream of Desi Arnaz's finally came to fruition and, in what *Variety* deemed "telefilm's most ambitious series to date" *Desilu Playhouse* was announced as a CBS 1958–59 season entry. The deal called for a "group of 37 hour-long films establishing a production outlay of approximately $7,500,000"; when Westinghouse the following month signed to sponsor the new Desilu series, the revised package called for forty-eight episodes (forty-two originals and six repeats, four of them Lucy-Desi hours) totaling a $12 million production-cost outlay—regular installments were each budgeted at $125,000–$150,000, with seven new Lucy-Desi hours estimated at $300,000–$350,000 each. CBS planned to position *Desilu Playhouse* in the Monday nighttime slot formerly occupied by the Westinghouse-sponsored *Studio One* anthology series; as part of the new pact, Ball and Arnaz would occasionally appear in Westinghouse commercials.

In a highly unusual move departing from then-standard network practices, CBS bought *Desilu Playhouse* without benefit of a sponsor signed to bankroll the high-budget series. "This time I decided to go with the show first," explained Arnaz. "There are so many problems and elements usually involved in a series. When you deal with a sponsor, an ad agency, and network while preparing it, by the time you go ahead on production, you're apt to forget the show you started with. I told a top agency exec my feelings about this, and he agreed it might be best to concentrate on the show first for a change."

The success of *Desilu Playhouse* was largely dependent on its ability— and ultimately was substantially undermined by its failure—to attract superstar guests. "When we started out, the sponsor dreamt of Katharine Hepburn and all these things," recalls producer Granet. "That's how all shows start out. We didn't quite realize at the time that on *Playhouse 90* and the others, those great names were only being kinescoped, which didn't affect their motion-picture salaries. We were putting our shows on *film,* which, if we had important stars, would have affected their motion-picture salaries." Granet further notes, "The truth of it is that I don't think we ever sold it on the basis of the anthology series. It did sell on the basis of getting the *Lucy-Desi* show every four weeks." Concurs Bernie Weitzman, "We couldn't get a dramatic series, the one thing that Desi wanted, which Desilu never had before. CBS, in return for the jumbo *Lucy* shows, let him have the dramatic programs."

Eager to launch *Playhouse* with a guaranteed ratings winner, Desilu set "Lucy Goes to Mexico" with guest Maurice Chevalier as the first show in the series. Although it was not announced at the time, Desilu suffered a major setback at the close of the 1957–58 season when writers Bob Carroll, Jr., and Madelyn Pugh Martin (recently wed to Desilu sound-cutter Quinn Martin and mother to an infant son, Michael) tendered their resignations. Although signed to a 1956 three-year renewal pact, the writers felt unable to create fresh *Lucy* material; an understanding Desi released them from their contractual obligations, which allowed Madelyn to be a full-time mother and Bob his long-standing dream of relocating to Europe. Arnaz then brought aboard Everett Freeman to assist Bob Schiller and Bob Weiskopf in writing the Ball-Arnaz *Desilu Playhouse* premiere.

"When Desi was head of the company, everything had to be first class," recalls Hollywood publicist John Strauss, whose firm was retained to augment Desilu's internal public-relations efforts after the RKO pur-

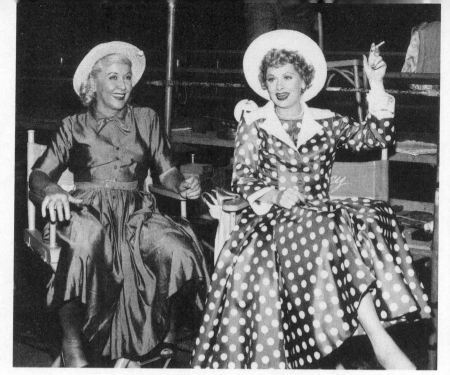
Lucille and Vivian between takes on the set of "Lucy Goes to Mexico"
MAURY THOMPSON COLLECTION

chase. "I designed a poster for the *Westinghouse Desilu Playhouse*—a bullfight poster with Lucy as the matador for 'Lucy Goes to Mexico.' The first version looked exactly like the bull had his horns right up Lucy's *buttocks*. Desi said, 'I *love* it, but we just *can't* do that.' We had to redo the whole poster. It cost a fortune. And when she left the Desilu lot, that's all she took with her."

Desilu Playhouse represented to Arnaz no less than the stunning apex of his company's phenomenal—and phenomenally rapid—success story. The extraordinary financial aspects of the *Playhouse* deal were matched by his ambitious plans for the program itself. The CBS deal called for "five or six" Lucy-Desi hour episodes as part of the *Playhouse;* six installments of the anthology series would air as special ninety-minute presentations of original musicals budgeted in excess of $500,000 each. Arnaz would serve as both series host and executive producer, assisted by director Jerry Thorpe and (Lucy-Desi hour episode producer) Bert Granet, along with Paul Monash (*The Helen Morgan Story*) and the team of Don Sharpe and Warren Lewis. The ambitious Quinn Martin was promoted by Arnaz from sound cutter to production consultant as well as producer of three *Playhouse* programs.

Both Lucille and Desi planned to appear separately in a few comedies or dramas throughout the year. In discussing plans for the Arnazes to appear separately on the *Playhouse,* Lucille was no doubt stung by Desi's pointed—and rather unkind—remark: "Maybe Lucy herself would play opposite somebody else in a one-shot. Maybe I would play opposite some *young blonde* or somethin'—I don' know." *Playhouse* programs, said Arnaz, would consist of "melodramas, westerns, adventures, family drama" but "no stories of violence or psychopaths"; indeed, Arnaz's first *Playhouse* story purchase was Margaret Blanton's "The Song of Bernadette."

A particularly distinguished *Playhouse* entry was Rod Serling's "The Time Element"—the genesis for the subsequent series *The Twilight Zone.* Recalls Bert Granet, "Robert Parrish, the director, introduced me to Rod Serling. I asked Rod if he had anything worthwhile. Rod said, 'I haven't written anything in a helluva long time. But I sold something to CBS, which they shelved.' I said, 'Could I see a copy of it?' I liked it and bought it from CBS for ten thousand dollars. Westinghouse had the privilege of reading the scripts I was doing. They read it and said they didn't want to do it. They didn't want to do it so bad they sent out three vice presidents who told me why they didn't want to do it. I went to Desi. Desi backed me up. They said all right. They had offered to buy it back for ten thousand dollars. But they agreed to do it provided I did no more unfinished stories. We made the thing and it got big critical acclaim, enough to get Rod and his agent a series on CBS."

For the special ninety-minute musicals, *Playhouse* unsuccessfully attempted to lure Frank Loesser and Garson Kanin. Arnaz did snare former MGM musical chief Johnny Green to score episodes of the show and write two original full scores, including Arnaz's pet project, *Don Quixote;* Desi also brought aboard noted producer-director Bill Colleran, who had won a Peabody Award for *Your Hit Parade* and critical acclaim for his string of sophisticated, stylish musical specials with Frank Sinatra, Bing Crosby, and Peggy Lee. In the end—such ambitious original musical productions never aired on *Desilu Playhouse*—neither Green nor Colleran remained long with Desilu. The East Coast–based Colleran saw an often-inebriated Desi directly after several domestic battles with Lucille, while both men were temporarily living at Hollywood's Château Marmont Hotel. "I was with Desilu very briefly," says Colleran, "and left when it became quite clear that Desi, Lucy, and I had very different ideas of musical-show concepts. I wanted Harold Arlen, Cole Porter, Gershwin. They, on the other hand, had absolutely no class at all."

Lucille's stormy battles with her husband escalated as his behavior grew more erratic. Desi's assistant Johny Aitchison recalls one such incident: "Desi slammed the car door, and it almost hit her hand. It was an argument about something or other. He had been drinking. She went to her dressing room, and he went to his office. I went in and saw she was upset. I asked, 'Can I put a Miltown in your coffee?' 'What for?' I said, 'Because you're upset.' Later in the afternoon, I hear, 'The queen wants you on the set.' She handed me a watch. It said *With Appreciation, Love, Lucy & Desi.* It was a wrist alarm. She said, 'Now you can take your fucking pills on time!' This was her way of saying thank you."

Looking beyond *Desilu Playhouse,* the company pursued other television properties but still managed to pick more losers than winners. Arnaz signed sultry Marilyn Maxwell for an unsold pilot titled *Private Eyeful* and also targeted redhead Rhonda Fleming for a never-produced series. Desilu failed to sell several action-adventure pilots and fared no better with a Revolutionary War drama, an anthology series, a Vincent Price vehicle, or *The Bandwagon,* detailing the 1880s exploits of a band of traveling entertainers. Quinn Martin—rapidly climbing the Desilu corporate ladder—created *Don't Blame Jane,* the unsold series casting Jane Russell as a onetime showgirl adjusting to her new life as wife of a college professor. Desilu managed to launch *U.S. Marshal,* a spin-off from *The Sheriff of Cochise.*

Although Joan Blondell and Melvyn Douglas were envisioned to star in a Desilu-produced situation comedy about a "Serutan Set" modern-day grandmother titled *You're Only Young Twice,* George Murphy and Martha Scott were eventually cast in the pilot. Offers Martin Leeds, "You know how I got rid of Murphy after he became head of public relations? I tried to get him a series—*You're Only Young Twice*—but we couldn't sell it. He really wanted that." Bob Schiller amusingly recalls, "[Murphy] never gave up. Wherever he would go—he went all around the country often on trips—he would carry the pilot around and show it to his friends. We got a call every now and then. 'Hey, Bob, I'm in Akron, Ohio, and my friend Biff Jones, the head of U.S. Tire, is interested in the pilot.' I said, 'Murph, forget it, it's dead. We don't have Martha. We don't have a director. We're working on *Lucy.*' So when he got elected senator, I sent him a telegram saying, 'Nice try, but I don't think it will sell the pilot.' "

Immediately following the news of the *Playhouse* pact, *Variety* bannered an announcement that Desilu—in another attempt to supplant Revue as industry television-film-production leader—had begun "exploratory" discussions "relative to an amalgamation" of Desilu, Four Star Productions (*Dick Powell's Zane Grey Theatre; Alcoa Theatre; Richard Diamond, Private Detective*), Danny Thomas's Marterto "vidfilmery" (*The Danny Thomas Show, The Real McCoys*) and Louis Edelman's (*Wyatt Earp, Adventures of Jim Bowie*) production company; the projected merger would make the new entity the clearly dominant force in the TV film field with more than nearly three dozen series housed under the new company's banner. The ambitious idea was soon abandoned, although Desilu would discuss possible mergers with Danny Thomas several more times in future years.

With only a handful of Lucy-Desi comedy hours on the horizon for the upcoming season, Desi formulated plans for a "Fred and Ethel Mertz" spin-off until he was unexpectedly stymied by Vivian Vance who flatly refused his fifty-thousand-dollar offer—or any dollar amount—to appear with nemesis Bill Frawley on a weekly basis sans Lucy and Desi. When CBS dropped its option for a situation comedy called *Guestward Ho!*, Arnaz immediately purchased it as a starring vehicle for Vance, cast with Leif Erickson—in a role unsuccessfully and hotly pursued by Vivian's real-life husband Phil Ober—as a New York couple who purchase a sight-unseen New Mexico dude ranch. Ralph Levy—director of the *I Love Lucy* pilot—was brought in to supervise the production and direct the pilot. Recalled Levy, "On the first take, I yelled 'action,' and Vivian just stood there frozen. On the second take, the same thing happened. And again with the third. I went up to her to find out if she was all right, and Viv said, 'This is the first time in eight years I've been in my own light,' meaning, of course, that after being in the shadow of Lucille all that time, she was finding it a little difficult going it alone. It was a big change for her." When the pilot was rejected by potential buyer ABC, a loyal Desi Arnaz wanted to reshoot a different version with Vance; the network, however, insisted that the lead role be recast. Starring Joanne Dru and Mark Miller, *Guestward Ho!* finally premiered on ABC on September 1961 and lasted only a single season.

Despite its impressive growth, the Lucy-Desi combination clearly remained the company cornerstone—a March 1958 Nielsen tally revealed the first 4 one-hour *Lucille Ball–Desi Arnaz Show* episodes ranked as the four highest-rated specials of the season. In June 1958, CBS's Oscar Katz planned on airing *I Love Lucy* reruns weekdays beginning that summer until General Foods—sponsor of *Lucy* prime-time summer repeats—reminded the network of its contractual exclusivity. Weekly prime-time repeats of *I Love Lucy* from 1957 through 1959 were consistently top-rated, and summer 1958 repeats under the banner *The Top Ten Lucy Shows* (actually *thirteen* episodes) performed better than did same time-slot, first-run installments of *The Danny Thomas Show*—which had inherited *I Love Lucy*'s old Monday night CBS berth.

Underscoring *I Love Lucy*'s unparalleled popularity, when Lucille was the recipient of a Genii Award from the Radio and TV Women of Southern California shortly after the *Playhouse* deal was revealed, Art

Linkletter turned to Desi and quipped, "Save your money and be happy while you're waiting to buy MGM." Lucille took the podium and, displaying a flash of humor, cracked, "Since a genie usually comes out of a bottle, you should be giving this award to my hair!"

She then turned to Desi and assured the audience, "I'm not the one who bought RKO—*I'm* the one trying to get it *dusted!*"

"I think Lucy's objective is to buy every studio she's ever worked at," topped Desi, "and every night when we go home, she starts looking at Paramount!"

Chapter Nine

"Desi was a very, very bright man. And a wonderful boss. But he would sometimes go away for two or three weeks at a time. He loved to play. Desi was really a silent-picture star at heart."
—Bert Granet, 1991

*B*y July, rapidly filling network schedules for the 1958–59 season positioned Desilu as the industry's television-film-production leader, followed by Revue (*G.E. Theatre, Wagon Train, Bachelor Father, Alfred Hitchcock Presents*) and Screen Gems (*Naked City* and *The Donna Reed Show*). Desilu claimed *The Ann Sothern Show, The Texan,* and *Westinghouse Desilu Playhouse*—Desilu's actual count jumped from three to four series if accepting the widely held industry notion that the Lucy-Desi hours constituted, in effect, an occasional series totally separate from *Desilu Playhouse.* Tipping the scales in its favor was revenue derived from the many shows filmed, but not owned, by Desilu: *The Danny Thomas Show, Wyatt Earp, The Real McCoys, The Californians, The Millionaire, Man with a Camera, December Bride,* and *Derringer,* representing a record $32 million production slate. Further expanding its profit centers, Desilu appointed George Murphy to preside over its "newly expanded" commercial-film division (complete with animation and special-effects departments), targeted also to produce industrial and documentary films. With western programs fast becoming television's most popular genre, Desilu, at a cost of $200,000, built Old West exteriors for its own series (*The Texan*) and other rental-basis-only productions.

That summer, Arnaz gave nineteen veteran executives generous amounts of company stock; at the same time, other employees were "being asked" to purchase shares—industry insiders predicted the move as the first step of the privately held corporation's plan to eventually offer Desilu stock on the open market to infuse the company with additional operating capital and fund further expansion. On November 11, Desilu announced it had filed a regulation statement with the Securities and Exchange Commission for a public offering of 525,000 shares of common stock; although market price of the issue had not yet been set, Desilu estimated the total value of the offering would be in excess of $5 million. "The offering," stated *The Wall Street Journal*, "would include 250,000 shares to be sold by the company for 'new money' and 275,000 shares by the Arnazes—all the Desilu common [stock] now held by them. . . . Desilu would use most of the proceeds from its 250,000-share part of the proposed public offering to pay off a portion on the old RKO Studio properties purchased in January." Desilu announced it expected the stock sale to generate $6 million for the company, with present stockholders still retaining company control by virtue of owning more than 50 percent of the stock.

Lucille remarked years later, "Don't make any mistake—they talk about my business acumen. They're wrong. It was all Desi. He built Desilu into an empire." Intimates, however, suggested that as far as the personal fortunes of the Arnazes were concerned, Desi was in distant second place. According to one Desilu insider, "Lucille has the stocks and annuities, but all this character has is holes in his pocket—and one other thing. He knows how to make TV films that keep earning money."

Martin Leeds suggests, however, that Arnaz's problem with alcohol was already common knowledge and had begun to impact negatively Desilu's image: "When it came time for the president of the company to go to New York to speak in front of the security houses, Desi wouldn't go. He said, 'You go.' I suspect he was scared. I went. One of the questions asked me by the securities people was, 'Is Desi not here because he's drunk again?' I said, 'If he *is* drunk again, he still smart enough to have somebody like me.' Got a round of applause for that. I covered up a lot for him. But you reach a point sometimes where you just can't cover it."

Maury Thompson recalls that Desi often spiked his tomato soup with vodka. "We knew if he asked for tomato soup in the *morning,* we were in trouble." Desi's assistant, Johny Aitchison, had long since developed a secret code during business hours for cocktail requests: "If he wanted a Seven-Up, that meant he wanted a *vodka* and Seven—we got so used to the drinking, we almost didn't notice it anymore." He adds, "Desi was a screamer, but then I found out the way to handle it was to scream back at him, and we got along very well. He was not disciplined the way Lucille was. It had taken her longer to arrive at a certain point in her career than it did him. She was a worker. He could play all night and then go to work. But you can only do that for so long."

"Many times Lucy would try and get very close to me," recalls Bert Granet. "We had a boat. Lucy would bring the kids down. She'd work on my wife, Charlotte, to work on me to talk to Desi about the drinking. Long associations with actresses like Merle Oberon and Paulette Goddard have taught me to be careful about dispensing advice and playing God. My wife and I had a very practical way of avoiding these situations. We'd say to Lucy, 'You're so smart. You've had so much more experience than us.' And put it off.

"She was older than he was. He was an absolute Cuban and lived under different morals than most Americans. She was very straitlaced. It was just a difference in their personalities. We'd be down at Del Mar at their little house on the beach. Late in the afternoon, Desi would be looking at the ocean, and she'd say, 'What are you looking at?' 'The ocean. It's beautiful, with the sunset and all.' She'd say to him, 'Why do you want to waste your time? C'mon, there's a gin game down the street.' But she loved him very much. Desi, like many Latins, was very permissive, that it was fine to have a wife and do a little cheating on the side without it breaking up their marriage. Their fights became more open in front of guests. That became embarrassing. Then he moved to the Château Marmont. She stayed at the house. That was sort of the end."

Former *TV Guide* writer Dan Jenkins recalls, "Desi could be the most charming individual who ever lived—he could charm needles off a pine tree. At the same time, he was chasing women all over town and drinking too much. I faced him once at a press party. I said, 'Desi, you're drinking too damned much.' He said, 'I never drink when I'm working, you know that.' I said, 'Desi, you're working right now. This party *is* work.' He was almost teary."

The Arnazes and Desilu Productions might well have also regretted its recent sale of *I Love Lucy* to CBS for a relatively low $4 million when the network finally was able to jump sponsor-conflict hurdles and schedule the series to air on its weekday daytime schedule beginning January 5, 1959. As *Variety* observed, "There's a whole new career shaped out for *I Love Lucy,* which already enjoys the distinction of being probably the all-time high billings bonanza for CBS-TV, what with its multiple rerun schedules, etc. For a while, it looked like *Lucy,* with approximately a 200-episode backlog on hand, would be tossed into the CBS Films syndication hopper, with a multi-million dollar potential on tap in that area. But there's method in CBS's apparent madness in passing up such syndication loot and channelling *Lucy* into the across-the-board-daytime network arena. Even forsaking *Lucy*'s potential as a syndication entry, CBS estimates a $6,000,000 annual bonanza in sales of quarter-hour network segments across-the-board. Within 24 hours after the Columbia boys let its strategy be known around the agencies, the orders were coming in."

Adding considerably to the company's coffers, though, was a 50–50 ownership deal of *The Ann Sothern Show;* Desilu owned half and Sothern's production company, Anso Productions, the remaining percentage. "My company did all the work," recalls Sothern. "We flew the scenery [up and down] like they do in the theater. I put in new air-conditioning for the actors, did my dressing room and office over—everything was like MGM at Desilu. It got to the point where I'd ask for something, and they'd say, 'What does Miss MGM want *now?*' But we ran my show quite independently, made a lot of money—and saved a lot of money."

"Before we decided to do the program, William Morris had offered us Ann Sothern but did not have a program idea for her," says Martin Leeds. "We called for a meeting with Schiller and Weiskopf. Desi, the writers, and myself were kicking ideas around. At one point, I remarked, 'Since Ann has done *Private Secretary,* why not now make her an assistant hotel manager?' It was pooh-pooed by Desi and Weiskopf. Three hours later, Desi said, 'Why don' we make her an assistant manager in a hotel?' We all agreed that was it. As we were walking out, Schiller said, 'Boy, are *you* in trouble.' I asked why. 'If the show is a hit,' he replied, 'Desi will take the credit, and if it's a flop, he'll remember to blame you.' "

Sothern herself assesses Desi as "a very good businessman—very generous, very honest, had great integrity. The only thing Desi had was a hell of a drinking problem." She and Lucille "were great personal friends." Their success in working together, she notes, came from disparate comedic styles. "She [was] an active comedienne, and my work is reactive, so we just complemented each other."

Sothern was perhaps unaware of the later turmoil caused by her series at Desilu, sparked by her friendship with the fiercely devoted Lucille. According to Leeds, "During the nearly eight years that I was at Desilu, Lucy and I had only one fight. We were doing *The Ann Sothern Show,* on which the William Morris Agency had a commission, despite the fact that I had sold the program without their assistance. Two years into the show, it was decided to do a spin-off [ultimately abandoned] of the program. When her agents came to me about it, they wanted Desilu to take only ten percent of the program. I told them, without mincing any words, that we started with half, financed the original pilot, sold it, and there was no way we would take ten percent. We wanted our fifty percent. I was adamant and told them it was either fifty-fifty or nothing

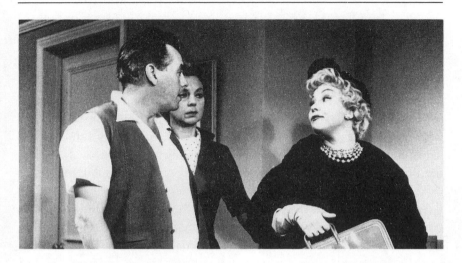

Desi directs Ann Sothern (*right*) and her co-star Ann Tyrrell, in the pilot episode of *The Ann Sothern Show*.
ARNAZ FAMILY ARCHIVES

would be spun off. The next day Lucy stormed into my office, saying, 'If you don't want my friend Ann Sothern on this lot, tell me and I'll make sure she leaves.' I tried to explain to Lucy that what had been asked for was untenable and not fair and that of course I didn't want her off the lot. She just wouldn't listen and stormed out. The next morning, she walked in and quietly said, 'I talked to [attorney] Mickey Rudin, and he said that you are the general, and I should go along with you.' "

Martin Leeds recalls another problem: "The producers and the writers commented that it was getting very difficult to keep shooting Ann from behind desks, credenzas and plants, because Ann, who always had the most beautiful face in the world, had put on weight everywhere else." Not helping matters was her penchant for sweets. As Maury Thompson recalls, "About three in the afternoon, she'd call to her maid, 'Hazel?' 'Yes, Miss Sothern?' She was standing right *beside* her. 'Do we have anything in the fridge?' 'Yes, Miss Sothern, you know we have it in the fridge when you're ready.' She'd say, 'Oh, let me have the *chocolate* today. And six Oreos. Oh, and don't forget the *diet soda,* darling.' We'd have to wait until she ate six *scoops* of ice cream *and* six Oreos and her Diet Coke. Then she'd say, 'Oh, I feel so much better with a little bit of *sugar!* ' "

"Although we first met at Columbia, it was when we met again at RKO that we became—and have remained—best friends," Lucille once said of Sothern. "Always, from the beginning, Annie has been a big-sister helpful kind of friend. I used to worry about Ann when she wasn't worrying about me."

Shedding a key vestige of the vintage 1950s Lucy Ricardo, Lucille had adopted a new tousled, "bubble-cut" hairstyle, which was introduced in the MacMurray hour. During the 1958–59 season, she had begun wearing a wig, and from this point on, she would largely refrain from displaying her own henna-tinted hair on television unless it was so required by a strenuous physical-comedy routine; sometimes she switched back and forth within the same episode.

As Lucille harbored deep concern about her age—now forty-seven—and the way she now photographed, Ann Sothern presented her with a temporary cosmetic solution that Lucille initially disdained but neverthe-less would adopt in some variation for most subsequent personal and TV appearances. Recounts Maury Thompson, "Ann put on that [Gene Hibbs] makeup—painting her chin dark, putting on all those face-lifting adhesive tapes that strap on and affix to the top of her head. And, as the tapes dry, everything on the face pulls up. Then they put the blond wig on, and out she comes. Lucille did a guest spot on Ann's show, and Ann said, 'Now, Lucy, I want you to try this.' Lucy said, 'I'm *not* putting on any makeup like that.' Ann said, 'Just try it—it's *marvelous*.' Lucille finally gave in. Of course, Lucy likes her face mobile . . . And here she comes out of the makeup room, her face all taped and pulled up. She said, 'What do you think, Maury—does my mouth look like an *asshole* to you?' "

Bert Granet contends that the Arnazes's intense, constant working relationship—and Lucille's often haphazard appearance—contributed to the demise of their marriage. "If you're married, you see your wife in many, many stages. You see her dressed up nicely, you also see her when she gets up in the morning. But here you also have to get up and work together for an eight-hour day or ten-hour day or twelve-hour day on a set. Well, Lucy hasn't put any makeup on, and she has on a pair of pajamas that looks like she got at Pic 'n Save, arguing about every point. As husband and wife, something has got to give—if you're going home and you're going to get romantic later, it's going to have its effect."

"Lucy Goes to Mexico" followed the pattern as Ball-Arnaz hours of the past season—excellent ratings (although it managed to appear as only the sixth-highest-ranked show of the month) but decidedly mixed critical response. While *Daily Variety* said, "The situation isn't strong enough to sustain an hour and the pace of the farce isn't quite as headlong as in the past," *Weekly Variety* countered, "Tossed off with beltline

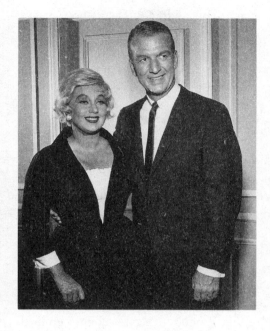

**Ann Sothern and co-star,
Don Porter**

precision. It's formula stuff, keyed to a new situation each time, but brought off with such skill, polish and unerring awareness of what tickles the risibilities of the average viewer that the results are frequently explosive."

It appeared that the Arnaz marriage was itself still volatile—Lucille was noticeably absent from Desi's party launching the *Westinghouse Desilu Playhouse;* she was "too busy" rehearsing her solo *Playhouse* program (as manager of hapless prizefighter Aldo Ray in the comedy "K.O. Kitty") to attend. At the bash, Desi screened the upcoming "Song of Bernadette" episode with Pier Angeli and invited "Lucy Goes to Mexico" guest Maurice Chevalier to sing and join him in a duet. "I have always wanted to sing with Desi," quipped the Frenchman, "someone who has a worse accent than me." Arnaz revealed his plans to film his long-delayed *Don Quixote* but was undecided whether it would be for the *Playhouse* or theatrical release. And, the *Reporter* noted rather tellingly, "If it'll make Desilu studio workers happy, he's decided not to buy any more race horses."

The column squib was perhaps prompted by a late-night incident with Martin Leeds: "I was fast asleep in my own bed. It was one in the morning when the phone rang. It was Desi. 'Hey, sport, we bought a horse.' 'We bought a horse?' 'Yup, for eighty thousand dollars.' '*You* bought a horse, not me.' My deal with Desi was that I had the right to share ten percent in any investment that he made if I so desired. So my response was in order. I asked, 'Have you told Lucy?' 'No.' 'Boy,' I said, 'are *you* in trouble.' He said, 'She will love it.' I asked, 'Where are you going to get that kind of money?' 'Will you call Ed Holly?' I said, 'No, you call Ed Holly. I don't know where he will get the money.' He got the horse, called King Harrah, a gelding that ran twelve races and never came into the money. They put him in a claiming [selling] race for fourteen thousand dollars, the horse was claimed, and the next time out was a winner."

Arnaz apparently had more success with writers than horses. Determined to bring Madelyn Pugh Martin and Bob Carroll, Jr., back to the Desilu fold, he cannily decided as his first move to promote Madelyn's ambitious new husband from sound cutter to *Desilu Playhouse* writer-producer. According to Bert Granet, "Desi came to me and said, 'I want to re-sign Madelyn, and I think it will be a lot easier if I get her husband a job.' And that's how Quinn got on the show. And he turned out to be a very talented producer."

Adds Madelyn, "My son was born, and I decided I would stay home. I stayed home about six months, and I thought, Maybe I better go back to work. Bob was gone [to Europe]. I went in to see Desi. I was sitting by his desk in the big office he had at RKO. He talked about my coming back. He didn't know I was thinking of it. We talked more, and he said, 'You know I'm conning you.' I said, 'Yes, I know.' He said, 'But I really want you to come home.' He told Bob he would pay his way back to work, and if he didn't want to stay would pay his way back to Rome. And Bob didn't go back—somehow living in Rome for about a month wasn't quite as glamorous as being a tourist there. And Desi had the propmen fix up the middle of Desilu like an Italian garden, so that Bob would feel welcome. He knew he could persuade me to do things." (In an innovative corporate move for the times, Arnaz installed a built-in nursery for Madelyn's baby on the former RKO lot.)

In previous *I Love Lucy* seasons, she recalls, "We were always saying, 'We've *got* to quit.' It was such a grind. We worked all night. It was a lot of fun, but very grueling. Desi said, 'I want you to have lunch with me.' Phil Harris was coming, and then Phil had a big contract with NBC. Desi said, 'I want you to have lunch with Phil, and we're going to talk about a show idea.' So Bob and I said, 'Whatever we do, we're not going to promise to write a pilot. We're on vacation.' We only had four or six weeks. We met with Desi and Phil Harris. We talked about stories. Two and a half hours later, we had promised Desi to write a pilot for Phil Harris, a pilot for somebody else, and a rewrite on a movie."

Although writer Ludi Claire's "Song of Bernadette" on *Desilu Playhouse* failed to win its time slot, it won generally good notices—*Variety* deeming it "Desilu's most ambitious project to date—superbly produced." The subsequent week's dramatic episode followed the same pattern of respectable critical reviews but an alarming ratings defeat—the Desilu hour crushed by NBC's regular competition, *Arthur Murray's Dance Party,* in what *Variety* deemed "the major upset of the new season." Future *Playhouse* entries were a mixed bag—shows and performances ranging from very good to mediocre—and while the series often performed well, it was hardly a ratings blockbuster despite appearances by such well-known if not top-ranked personalities as Eddie Albert, Jean Hagen, Steve Forrest, Janis Paige, Harry Guardino, Eli Wallach, Susan Strasberg, Franchot Tone, Jo Van Fleet, Tony Randall, Ernie Kovacs, Carl Reiner, Gilbert Roland, Jane Russell, and Rhonda Fleming. By mid-November, *Variety* noted that, although not a complete failure, *Playhouse* was still "in trouble in terms of its cost with a 20.0."

Lucille found it increasingly difficult to continue to uphold the Arnazes's facade of a happy marriage. The last week of October and the first week of November found Desi in Las Vegas with Lucy for a golf tournament and embroiled in two separate highly embarrassing incidents at the Riviera Hotel—both without Lucille present. On October 31, Arnaz threw a drink at a pit boss during a 4:00 A.M. gambling argument. Witnesses said that Desi got into a heated discussion with a female player and was asked to "calm down" by Sid Wyman, part-owner of the Riviera, who was working at the table; Arnaz responded by throwing a drink in Wyman's face. Further suggesting he was under the influence, Desi vaguely denied tossing a drink at Wyman—"at least I don't *think* I threw a drink in anybody's face." On November 5, Arnaz was ejected from the casino after becoming "noisy" at a gaming table; he returned to Hollywood after the incident was made public by national wire services.

"Desi was really not a great gambler since he always thought he would continue winning," observes Leeds. "One evening, he was playing craps and had quite a winning streak. Since I was placing his bets for him, and he was shooting the dice, I kept siphoning off some of his winnings and hiding them. He refused to quit, and naturally he soon lost what was in front of me. The next morning, he said, 'Well, I guess I blew that money. I should have quit while I was ahead.' I had made a bundle of his winnings and said, 'All was not lost—I put aside some for a rainy day,' and handed him the money. He lost, that night, all of it—eighteen thousand dollars. A few weeks later, we were sitting in his den when the phone rang. We were told Jim Bacon of the Associated Press was on the phone. Desi told me to take it, which I did. Bacon said,

'What is all this noise about Desi tossing a drink at a croupier at the Riviera Hotel in Las Vegas last night?' I said, 'I don't know what you are talking about. Desi is sitting right here with me, and there is no way he was in Las Vegas last night. Where did you get that story?' He said his source was usually correct, and I said, 'No way.' I hung up the phone. Desi was hysterical with laughter. 'Hey, sport, I *was* in Vegas last night. Flew up at seven and came home on the four o'clock plane.' I said, 'But you made me lie.' He said, 'No, I didn't. You lied on your own.' "

Compounding his personal embarrassment was a tragic incident that occurred on November 23 when more than one thousand guests honored Lucy and Desi at the Friars' tenth anniversary dinner for "their continuing philanthropic activities and the esteem in which they are held by the trade and the public"—ironically not long after Desi's Riviera Hotel escapades had become the talk of Hollywood. Dais entertainment was to be provided by Milton Berle, George Burns, Eddie Cantor, Sammy Davis, Jr., Dean Martin, Tony Martin, George Murphy, Danny Thomas, and Harry Einstein—better known as "Parkyakarkus" of old-time radio fame; Art Linkletter was the emcee. The $50–$200-a-plate dinner evening began well enough. George Murphy delivered the night's only serious speech praising Lucy and Desi; Berle (referring to the honored couple as "the Cuban Leopold and Loeb") cracked, "We may laugh, but someday he will buy the whole country, and *we'll* be talking funny." Entertainment from Tony Martin, Dean Martin, and George Burns came next, followed by "Parkyakarkus"—quipping in his monologue that the Friars' roster included many prominent figures—"several fine judges and quite a few defendants." When he finished to an ovation, Linkletter asked the audience, "Why isn't this man on TV in prime time?" The comic reached his seat and replied, "Yeah, why aren't I?" He then turned to event producer Barry Mirkin and asked, "Was everything all right?"

At that very moment, the comic was seized by a fatal heart seizure in full view of nearly twelve hundred persons in the International Ballroom of the Beverly Hilton Hotel. "He had for a moment lurched forward," said *Variety*, "mortally stricken with a heart attack with the crowd's applause and laughter still ringing in his ears."

Linkletter took the microphone and called out for a physician, and the stunned audience began almost hysterically shouting for doctors. Ed Wynn, seated nearby, ran to the dais, shouting, "Put his head down!" Einstein's wife, actress Thelma Leeds, rushed up from the audience and pushed nitroglycerin pills into her ashen-faced husband's mouth. Five physicians converged from all corners of the room and were at his side in seconds but could detect no pulse or respiration and, after carrying him to a narrow vestibule in back of the dais, vainly applied artificial respiration for about twenty minutes without noticeable results. In a grisly scene, City of Hope chief surgeon Alfred Goldman sliced open Einstein's chest with a pocket scalpel and with a trio of doctors took turns at massaging his heart. "Electric shocks, effected by makeshift means from a lamp's wire cord were also applied directly to the heart," continued *Variety,* "but life's spark was gone from Einstein." He was pronounced dead at 1:10 A.M., an hour and twenty minutes after first being stricken.

"No play ever held the dramatic impact of the backstage tragedy," wrote *Variety's* Army Archerd, "when five top medics, in black tie, performed battlefield surgery to try and save the life of Harry Einstein. The scene could never be used in a film—no one would believe it! Actor John Bromfield, hobbling painfully because of torn ligaments in his leg, aided by a coupla newsmen in assembling an electric line for the medics to use in a last ditch fight; waiters rushing towels from the men's room to be used in the gory emergency surgery; the 'waiting room' onstage, with the top names in show biz hoping against hope for a happy ending; the suddenly saddened faces of friends who had minutes before been laughing hysterically at 'Parky's' great lines."

Adding to the macabre sight, the stunned and horrified audience— in full view of the frantic lifesaving attempts of Einstein by a battery of doctors—were entertained by George Burns, Dean Martin, Tony Martin, and Milton Berle in a misguided attempt to divert audience attention from the tragedy. "It didn't work," said the trade paper of their efforts. "A great and funny dinner had become veiled with the pall of a mortuary."

Understandably, Lucille begged off from saying even a few words. A shaken Desi could barely speak when he was finally introduced by Linkletter and took the podium. "This was an evening that comes to you once in a lifetime," he said, his voice shaking with emotion. "It meant so much, then all at once, it doesn't mean a damn thing."

Chapter Ten

★

"They had one of those historical marriages, like
Napoleon and Josephine, Richard and Liz—destined to be trouble but destined for them to never
find anyone as passionate or as fabulous."

—Lucie Arnaz, 1991

★

"We had everything, Desi and I," Lucille Ball once said, "two beautiful children, our own show, even our own studio. That's when everything *really* began to come apart. My dream had always been to have a home, one home. Instead, we had three houses—the ranch, the house in Beverly Hills, a house in Palm Springs. And how do you make a home, or put down roots, in three houses? Everything was on the same scale—we used to go to beach parties, just the four of us, plus one lunch hamper, in one car. Our outings became weekend safaris consisting of two or sometimes three cars loaded with paraphernalia, and with one or two of the household staff to handle it."

She further reflected, "As Desilu built and continued to build, we had everything money can buy—and in excess. I dislike anything that is excessive. It confuses me. It makes for indecision. I was happier when I had two dresses, both black, and two coats—one black and the other beige—to my name."

Increasing Desilu pressures and marital discord did not erode the Arnazes's onscreen facade as a happily married couple. Danny Thomas, along with television wife Marjorie Lord and on-camera offspring Rusty Hamer and Angela Cartwright, appeared on a December 1958 Ball-Arnaz *Desilu Playhouse*. Arguably the strongest of all thirteen 1957–60 Lucy-Desi hours, the program won excellent reviews—*Variety* called it "a top comedy effort" and *The Reporter* said it was "one of the funniest shows ever on television—this *Lucy* show is a TV classic."

"Lucy Makes Room for Danny" served as a professional reunion for Marjorie Lord and Vivian Vance, onetime roommates and costars during their years as struggling Broadway actresses before relocating together to California to appear in the Edward Everett Horton play *Springtime for Henry*. "Funny things just came out of her," recalls Marjorie Lord of

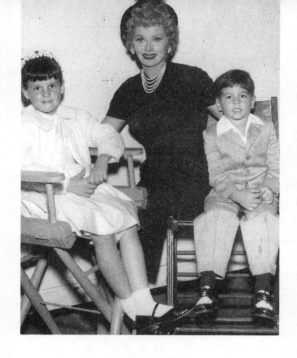

Lucie and Desi IV visit the set of "Lucy Makes Room for Danny."
THOMAS J. WATSON COLLECTION

Vivian. "Deep down, she was a very sensitive woman and a romantic. She loved to play romantic parts. I was with her when she fell in love with Philip Ober. She was madly in love with him. It was difficult for him later because Phil had been an important New York actor and was an unknown in Hollywood. I don't think she loved being Ethel Mertz. In the beginning, she loved the success—but who knew it would go on forever? And she certainly didn't like being 'married' to William Frawley—she saw herself a little differently."

Although she had been on the Desilu lot for some time, the experience of actually working with Ball and Arnaz gave Lord a new perspective: "Desi was the real moving force of it all. He knew what was good for her, he fought for her and protected her. Desi's memory was phenomenal. We'd have him for ten minutes at a time at a rehearsal. He'd leave to make a deal on the phone, and he'd come back, jump in, and know the entire script. And then leave again and make more deals."

Lucille, recalls Marjorie, "was very moody. We used to see each other at makeup. Some days she'd be very warm and friendly, ask about my children, and I'd ask her about her children. Other days, she would come in, be very quiet, and not say a single word to me. Perhaps it was a reflection of what was going on at home." As her marriage crumbled, Lucille took refuge in her work with a fiercer determination than she ever had before. "It was difficult for her to leave the studio. She was so intent on rehearsing, rehearsing, rehearsing. Danny and I were used to a more spontaneous approach to comedy, but not Lucy. It finally got to the point where I'd say, 'Oh, here she comes!'—I was tempted to go the other direction!"

Lucille proved equally difficult when she and Desi, in an exchange agreement, later appeared as the Ricardos on *The Danny Thomas Show*. Director Sheldon Leonard recalls, "Lucy and I had a very ambivalent, many-sided relationship. I had the greatest respect for her talent. She had a magnificent sense of how to manipulate an audience. At the same time, she was a very strong lady. I had worked with her as an actor on *My Favorite Husband* and played a vacuum-cleaner salesman on *I Love Lucy*. But this was the first time when I was directing her. She and Desi came on the set for the first day's work. I said, 'Okay, we'll start on this set'—the set represented a department store—'Lucy, you and Maggie [Lord] please make an entrance from stage right and cross over to the perfume counter saying your dialogue as you go across, and we'll pick up the balance of the scene there.' Lucy said, 'Why should I come in from *that* side?' I said, 'Because I want to take you all the way across and reveal the set. The camera will pan.' She said, 'Well, it would be *easier* for me to make an entrance upstage. It's a much shorter walk.' I said, 'Lucy, I don't *want* the shorter walk. I want the *longer* walk.' She said, 'I *still* don't understand why I have to make that long walk.' 'You *have* to make it because I *told* you to do it. *I'm* the director, and *that's* the way I'm directing it.' She said, 'Okay.' And she did it. Desi came over to me and said, 'You did that just right. You did the right thing. She was testing you.' "

On December 3, Desilu placed 525,000 common-stock shares on the market at ten dollars per share, proceeds, noted *Variety*, to be utilized for "corporate purposes including payments to RKO Teleradio for the two studios purchased from it by Desilu"; of the 525,000 shares offered the public, 250,000 were from the corporate account and 275,000 from the holdings of president Arnaz and vice president Ball. All 525,000 shares—in over-the-counter bids quickly rising to fifteen dollars—were sold the first day of offering, and the total sales filled only a scant 5 percent of orders received during the unparalleled stampede for Desilu stock. Further enhancing the company's strength was Westinghouse's somewhat surprising full-season renewal of the struggling *Desilu Playhouse* for the 1959–60 season; at the close of 1958, the program ranked only twenty-fourth in Nielsen ratings with an average 26.9 audience share. As *Variety* noted, "One of the disappointments of the season to date has been *Westinghouse Desilu Playhouse*. Other than the Lucille Ball–Desi Arnaz specials and other numbered outings, the *Desilu Playhouse*, many concur, hasn't lived up to the high expectations."

The new $12 million deal called for 42 one-hour *Playhouse* installments, including seven Ball-Arnaz comedy hours, at least one single-billed Desi Arnaz installment, as well as two solo Lucille Ball musical-comedy specials. As *The Hollywood Reporter* noted, "Desi Arnaz's announcement of the Westinghouse renewal stressed his gratification at the early timing of the deal. Insiders maintain that the trouble with this year's *Playhouse* was Desilu's lateness in getting started on the series, with only seven properties locked in by the initial airdate. This hurt all season long, and fact is, that Westinghouse's renewal was inspired not so much by its pleasure with the quality of the series as with the fact that Desi and Lucy are moving those Westinghouse goods as they've never moved before"—of more than the seventy specials aired during the 1958–59 season, three Ball-Arnaz *Playhouse* 1958–59 entries ranked within the top five rated shows.

Desi displayed typical largess to writers Bob Schiller and Bob Weiskopf in conjuring up a unique device to involve Lucille—per Westinghouse's demand—in *Desilu Playhouse*. "Desi called us. We were on vacation," recalls Weiskopf. "George Jessel used to do an act, and a big part of it was talking to his mother on the telephone. So we figured, let Lucy call Desi after the show. She's at home, and she asks him, 'How was the show tonight? What's on next week?' He didn't jump for joy over the idea. He said, 'Well, maybe.' He had to call the sponsor that afternoon. We were in the office. He told them the idea. He hung up the phone and says, 'Boys, you've saved my life. They bought it. They liked it. What do you guys want? Stock in the company, a car?'"—Weiskopf opted for a new Cadillac, and Schiller chose a Jaguar Mark IX.

Yet despite the Westinghouse multimillion-dollar *Playhouse* renewal, Desilu by the close of the year had alarmingly not only slipped from first place in network "vidpix" production but had been vastly outdistanced by Revue, Screen Gems, Four Star, and Warner Bros. Desilu continued to search for television product for the upcoming 1959–60 season. Arnaz discussed a pair of situation-comedy ideas with film-star bombshells Arlene Dahl and Zsa Zsa Gabor. Bert Granet discussed series possibilities for the new comedy team of Mike Nichols and Elaine May— the project abruptly abandoned when Nichols told him, "What you have is very good, but we're just beginning. If we fail in television now, we're dead." Mort Briskin created one of several failed Desilu Fernando Lamas pilots; also unsold was an adventure series, *Where There's Smokey,* a Gale Gordon–Soupy Sales comedy, a Marie Wilson vehicle, and *Caballero* with Cesar Romero. Another ultimately unsold Desilu series was *All About Barbara,* a Quinn Martin–produced comedy series—written by wife Madelyn Pugh Martin and Bob Carroll, Jr.—designed as vehicle for overripe platinum-blond film starlet Barbara Nichols.

As the 1958 holiday season approached, a lonely and desperately unhappy Lucille found herself grasping a tottering marriage and an increasingly absent husband who chose to lavish his attentions on corporate—and extramarital—affairs. Attempting to somehow fill the void, Lucy hit upon the idea to create a "Desilu Workshop" stock company of resident contract players under her personal supervision. It would be modeled on the RKO New Talent School, run by Ginger Rogers's mother, Lela, which Lucille had attended during her early RKO days. In late 1958, Lucy ordered construction and renovation of RKO's two-hundred-seat Studio Club Little Theatre at a cost of ninety thousand dollars; rehearsals were set to begin in January 1959 for the first production. Two large offices were installed for directors, and the blue-and-gray burlap walls had contrasting red seats, movable to allow cameras to occupy the auditorium space. To promote her new project and display the newly furbished Desilu Workshop Theatre, Lucille invited Hollywood gossip columnist and close friend Hedda Hopper to Desilu-Gower. "Our workshop will cull from about two thousand," Lucy told her. "It might go to five thousand the way it's going. It started to snowball so, it's frightening. People will come from colleges. Besides actors, there'll be directors, writers, teachers. But it's not a drama class. When I was a beginner at RKO, it was wonderful having Lela Rogers give us a stage and scripts to get our teeth into. I know how much that experience meant to me, besides all the little things Lela taught us. The most important, however, is playing before an audience and learning how to project yourself."

She also told Hedda, "We have nineteen or twenty independent producers on the lot. We have three separate types of operations here, films we make on our own, those we film for other producers, and those to whom we rent studio space. These kids will be considered for casting and be first in line for these producers."

Ultimately, Lucille signed less than two dozen performers and envisioned television stardom for each of them: Paul Kent, Mary Welles, Patricia Huston, Chuck Hicks, Steven Marlo, Roger Perry, Majel Barrett, Rogero Romor, Nicholas Georriade, Louise Glenn, and—none of them related—Janice Carroll, Laurie Carroll, and Ann Carroll. Subsequent additions to the group were Johnny O'Neill, Mark Tobin, Jerry Antes, Dick Kallman, Robert Osborne, and Carole (née Mildred) Cook.

Recalls Cook, "I'm in Warren, Ohio, doing *Kismet,* and they call me on the loudspeaker during rehearsals. They said, 'Mildred Cook, come to the phone'—there was excitement in the voice—'*Lucille Ball* is calling from Los Angeles!' I said, 'No *shit?*' Dick Kallman, an acquaintance, was on the phone. He said, 'I'm in Los Angeles now with Lucille Ball. She has a group together called the Desilu Workshop. She couldn't find a comedienne that suited her, so I told her about you. She would like to meet you.' She got on the phone and said 'Hello, Mildred.' I knew that voice. And I got so flustered, I said, 'Yes, ma'am, your holiness!' I went out to Los Angeles. All my clothes were packed into a cardboard box. I was trying to be chic, and it wasn't working. I told her about my grandmother from hell, about my religious background, and I talked the way I talk. She loved that. To this day, I think that's what made her like me. She had told me on the phone, 'I want you to think about something. I know people are protective about their names, and I know you've been Mildred Cook all your life, but I wonder if you would think about changing your name?' We all went out to dinner at an Italian restaurant that first night. She wrote on the tablecloth the name she wanted for me and said, 'I'd like you to change your name to Carole— for Carole Lombard.' I said, 'Right, perfect, Miss Ball, *wonderful!*' I was lucky she didn't say Rin Tin Tin. She told me, 'You have the same healthy disrespect for everything in general that Carole did.' She worshipped Carole Lombard. She also said, 'I want you to have an 'A-R' in your name.' I said, 'A-R?' She said, 'Yes, that's my good luck.' I said, 'You haven't done badly with Lucille Ball.' She said, 'I didn't hit it big until I changed it to *Arnaz*.' " (Lucille's Lucy Ricardo character, and all of her subsequent series characters, had the 'A-R' combination in their names as well.)

"They had a lengthy trial casting period where she would see people and have them audition," recalls Robert Osborne. "She absolutely loved that, because I always thought she was a frustrated song-and-dance girl. But Lucy looked just like a showgirl. She always used to say to me, 'You know, I look like a cigarette girl at the Mocambo'—when she wanted to look like Carole Lombard and behave like Kay Kendall. I had done a show on the Desilu lot. I had gone back to the lot to thank the people for casting me in the show, and Milt Lewis, the great casting director at Paramount, said, 'Have you met Lucille Ball? She's looking for people for her Desilu contract-player group. Let me call upstairs and see if she's there.' She was there and told him, 'Bring him over.' It all happened so fast. I had done a test with Diane Baker, so Lucy called over to Fox and asked them to send it over. We had about half an hour to wait before the film arrived. I had a wonderful time talking to her. I asked, 'Who's the most impressive person you've ever worked with?' And she said, 'It's not any of the stars—it's the character people. *They* are the great ones.' She got fascinated by me because I had this great knowledge of movie

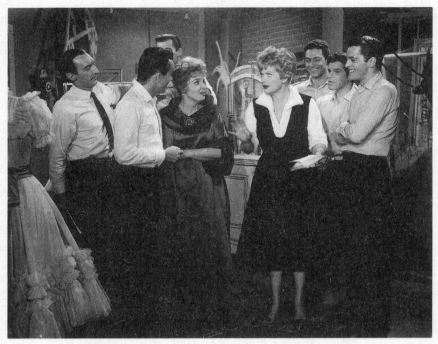

Lucille and the Desilu Workshop players in a scene from the televised version of *The Desilu Revue:* (*left to right*) Al Kramer, Jerry Antes, Bob Trevis (*hidden*), Carole Cook, Lucille, Mark Tobin, Dick Kallman, and Robert Osborne
COURTESY OF ROBERT OSBORNE

history, which was not a common thing then. We watched the test. She didn't make any comments. I thought I had blown it.

"A couple of days later, I got a call from Lucy's secretary, asking me to Lucy's house for dinner that night. She said, 'She wants you to meet Desi.' So I went. Desi was not there, but Cleo and Kenny Morgan were, and Kay Thompson, Roger Edens, and Chuck Walters. We had dinner, and Lucy screened *Funny Face.* As I left that night, when Lucy said good night at the door she asked me, 'Have you signed your contracts yet?' And I said, 'What contracts?' She said, 'I want you in my group. Do you want to be in my group?' I said, 'Well, yes, I would love to be.' She said, 'Well, then they will get the contracts for you to sign. They'll be sending them to you.' I think she took me under her wing because I had been to college, which had always impressed her because she had never been to college and thought of herself as a dumb person. She was so impressed by anybody that had an education. And she also liked that I wasn't 'show biz'—and although she loved show biz—she liked the fact that I wasn't really like that."

Lucille took a break from taxing revue rehearsals—and escalating marital turmoil—by escaping briefly to Manhattan, where she told *Hollywood Reporter* "Broadway Ballyhoo" columnist Radie Harris that she hoped to snare Alan Jay Lerner and Fritz Loewe to write the score for one of her Desilu Workshop revues. She also revealed plans to star in a Broadway play: "You started it all," Lucille told Radie, "by introducing me to Morton ["Tec"] DaCosta. Now, he's got me so stagestruck that he's even convinced me I can act on Broadway. Desi says it's okay for me to take a vacation from our show in 1960, so Tec is going ahead and whipping up a play for me. I'm not even asking what it's all about, because he's warned me that he's writing what he knows I can do—not what I think I *can't* do!"

However, so focused was she on developing her workshop, and without Desi's assistance, Lucille rejected MGM's offer to either appear as a nun in *Girls' Town* or star in the musical *By the Beautiful Sea*—in 1962 briefly envisioned as a Judy Garland–Bing Crosby vehicle. Lucy was, however, actively scouting for a "period-piece musical" for a solo stint on *Desilu Playhouse,* a *Playhouse* "dramatic show" with Jackie Gleason, and a film project teaming her with Billy Wilder. At the same time, she began rehearsals for a *Lucy-Desi* hour with guest Red Skelton. During a run-through for their tramp-costumed pantomime routine, Red, on his knees for the beginning of the number, quipped, "While I'm down here, I'll just say the rosary." After attempting several takes of the same steps, Lucille looked at Red and cracked, "I don't think the old man is going to make it."

Although *Variety* deemed it "an altogether delightful and hilarious outing," the Skelton *Lucy-Desi* episode managed to rank only as the fourth-highest-rated show of the month—trampled by *Gunsmoke, Wagon Train,* and *Have Gun, Will Travel.* Losing to the trio of horse operas prompted Lucille to grouse to *Variety,* "Kids dominate that dial. I don't think they should have so damn many westerns. But this is the problem with networks. And why do the networks have two good programs opposite each other? Comedy is a victim of the western trend."

Upon the dissolution of an option held by producer Ray Stark, in the spring of 1959, Desilu announced it had obtained dramatic rights to the Eliot Ness–Oscar Fraley book *The Untouchables,* the tome derived from government-agent Ness's real-life anticrime Prohibition-era exploits. Recalls Martin Leeds, "Desi had read the book and asked me to read it, which I did. I suggested that we buy the motion-picture and television rights. Little did I know that his plan was for him to do a feature picture with *him* playing the part of Eliot Ness. Desi sprung that idea on me.

I asked him, 'Des, do you really believe that the world is waiting for Ricky Ricardo to pull the plug on Al Capone?' He started to laugh and said, 'Okay, not such a good idea, sport. Put it in the library and let's wait for an opportunity to do it.' A year later we were doing the *Desilu Playhouse*. Somebody said, why don't we use *The Untouchables?*"

The Desilu purchase of *The Untouchables* took Hollywood by surprise in view of Arnaz's firm stance against violence-laden television productions. "Our policy has been never to do shows of violence of a psychopathic nature, of adultery, or such things," Desi vowed a few months earlier. "These may be fine on a stage or in a movie theater, but they should not be put on a TV screen in a person's home."

The Untouchables was immediately targeted to be *Desilu Playhouse's* first two-part episode, produced by Quinn Martin and narration provided by Walter Winchell. The Paul Monash script adaptation dramatized the fierce battle of federal Prohibition agent Ness and his handpicked collection of uncorruptible—and therefore "untouchable"—agents determined to dismantle the Chicago-based Al Capone bootlegging syndicate. The supporting cast included Keenan Wynn, Neville Brand (as Al Capone), and Barbara Nichols. At a record $300,000 per-hour production cost, filming was scheduled to begin March 16. Rumored to play Ness were Alan Ladd, Jim Arness, Fred MacMurray, Van Heflin, or Van Johnson.

"I wanted Van Heflin to play the lead," recalls Bert Granet. "He was a good friend of mine. He said, 'Bert, I love you, but fuck off. I don't want to be on television every week.' I called Bob Blumofe at United Artists because of the show's cost—it had to be sold in Europe as a feature. I said, 'Who do I get, if it's between Van Johnson and Bob Stack?' He said, 'You're crazy. Nobody knows who the hell Stack is. Take Van Johnson.' So I signed Van Johnson. [Van's wife and agent] Evie calls me up on Friday night and says, 'Bert, he's not coming in.' The top of the show then was $10,000 for the star of *Desilu Playhouse*. It was two parts, and he was getting $10,000 [total]. Evie claimed he thought he was going to get $10,000 for each one. It comes Friday night with shooting to begin Monday, and I call Bernie Weitzman, who finds Desi in Las Vegas. The three of us had a triple phone conversation, and that's how Bob Stack got the part. I really didn't think Stack was [appropriate] because he always struck me as a still camera—never blinks. Yet he turned out to be just the right guy for the show. He sold a dummy corporation to Desilu, which made him a partner."

With shooting to start Monday morning, on Saturday evening Arnaz began his frantic search for Bob Stack—finally locating him Sunday morning at 2:00 A.M. at Chasen's. "For the two hours you'll get ten thousand dollars," Desi told him, "and if goes to a series, seventy-five hundred per episode, plus fifteen percent of the profits, which I will give you in Desilu stock." He advised Stack to return home, where he would find two *Untouchables* scripts waiting for his perusal; he accepted the role when Desi phoned him a few hours later but was taken aback when told filming was to commence Monday morning. "Now go back to bed," Desi said. "At six tonight, I'll have the wardrobe man over at your house to fit everything to your satisfaction, and tomorrow, Monday, report to Desilu-Culver makeup department at eight A.M."

The first half of the semidocumentary, violence-laden *Untouchables* saga blasted the competition with 31.8 Trendex rating; generally excellent reviews boosted the ratings of the second part to 37.6. The New York *Herald-Tribune* said "the script and production glittered" and the Los Angeles *Herald-Express* deemed it "rousing good drama." So successful was the two-part showing that Desilu quickly mounted an expanded theatrical version—retitled *The Scarface Mob*—for domestic and international release at a reported cost of $100,000. The extraordinary critical and popular response immediately led to overtures from CBS—as well as third-place fledging network ABC—for Desilu to produce a weekly one-hour series based on *The Untouchables*.

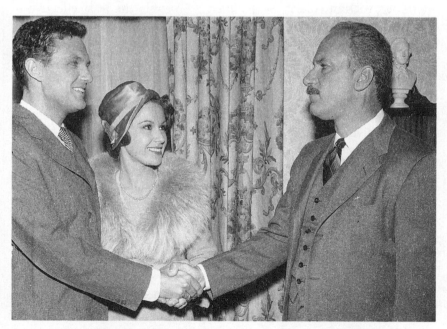

Robert Stack (*left*), Patricia Crowley, and Keenan Wynn in the *Desilu Playhouse* production of *The Untouchables*

Desilu stunned the industry—and ignited fireworks—when it was announced in May that *The Untouchables* had been sold not to CBS but to ABC—at a cost of $110,000 per episode. As *Variety* revealed, "Purchase created hard feeling between Desilu and CBS-TV, on which *Playhouse* appears. CBS called Desilu on the carpet hours after ABC locked up the deal. CBS's contention that it was unfair for the production company to sell off a program to a rival network which was nurtured and presented by CBS. Although ABC made the first bid for a regular *Untouchables* series on telefilm, CBS quickly got into the bidding but on Friday last, ABC firmed up with Desilu sales official Martin Leeds. Another CBS gripe is that the *Untouchables* sale really twists the knife in the wound in light of the fact that CBS already has a similar series on the boards for next season. The CBS show in question is *The Lawbreakers,* at the moment unsold."

The Untouchables ABC weekly series—with Quinn Martin as executive producer—called for the network to bankroll a minimum of 26 one-hour episodes; ABC and Desilu each owned 35 percent of the show and star Robert Stack's Langford Productions held 25 percent, while and certain "outside interests" held 5 percent.

The April 1959 Ball-Arnaz hour—"Lucy Wants a Career"—featured guest star Paul Douglas, who regrettably hires Lucy as his television morning-program cohost. Said *Variety,* "Probably the least effective of the scripts Weiskopf and Schiller have turned out for the comedy team this year. Yet Schiller and Weiskopf, along with script consultants Madelyn Martin and Bob Carroll, Jr., do provide some hilarious bits for Miss Ball. She has emerged from an accomplished slapstick comedienne to a peerless clown in the classic tradition of the great mimes."

Lucy appeared rather defensive about the drubbing the hour episodes had been given by critics, complaining to television writer Hal Humphrey, "How can they label a show as a slapstick when there may only be one or two scenes in it which are slapstick? Do they know what that word means in comedy? It doesn't bother me, but I guess it does Desi. I don't read the reviews," she concluded, the TV critic adding, "exercising her woman's prerogative to be slightly contradictory."

"Lucy's Summer Vacation," the final *Lucy-Desi* hour of the season, which aired in June, was a strained, belabored affair—the Ricardos and the Duffs inadvertently sharing a lodge when the wives instead hope for second honeymoons—marked by a behind-the-scenes uproar among Lucy, Desi, director Jerry Thorpe, and guests Howard Duff and real-life wife Ida Lupino. Ball reportedly became incensed when Arnaz, according to observers, brazenly flirted with Lupino in the presence of both Ball and Howard Duff. The volatile situation exploded when Lucy learned that Thorpe had advised Lupino of Lucy's confidential comment to him that she hadn't wanted her on the show, believing Lupino was unable to meet the comedic demands of the script. "They used to have open fights on the set," recalls Granet. "Lucy got jealous. She first accused Thorpe of throwing the shows to the guests, then Desi took over the direction." (Several observers recall that Lucille was so enraged that she actually walked off her own show until Thorpe was replaced.) *Variety* called the hour "the least rewarding" of the *Lucy* specials, adding, "this one falls flat most of the way"; it ranked as the lowest-rated *Lucy-Desi* hour to date.

Lucille's quest to salvage her marriage became increasingly frantic. "She had gotten very close to Dr. Norman Vincent Peale. She had developed a friendship with him while she was at the Palm Springs Thunderbird house around 1958," says Cleo. "He had come to the area to speak. She had followed his readings, his work. She was desperate, and yet she had to be very careful. She didn't want her marital problems known. It occurred to her that a man like this would be a man she could confide in. So she invites Dr. Peale and his wife to dinner, telling me, 'Maybe I can get him alone for a little bit to talk to him.' He said, 'Would you mind if my brother was also here?' She said, 'Oh, no, fine.' The brother is an alcoholic. So there she is—looking to try and save her marriage. Then Peale says to her, 'If only you knew what a role model you two are—a marriage with love.' This is the whole evening. She told me—laughing, with tears running down her face. Her desperation became worse and worse. She wrote to [Dr. Peale] in heartbreaking terms, and so he invited her to come to New York. Smiley Blanton was Dr. Peale's right-hand man. Norman wanted it known that she could talk to Smiley—whose wife just 'happened' to have a script for her to read.

"That's when she called me and said, 'Cleo, come to New York.' I could never say no to Lucille. When I got there, Lucille said to me, 'Why can't I be happy?' " Cleo then asked her, "What is it that you want more than anything in the world?" and was startled when Lucille unhesitatingly replied, "My *career*."

Lucille's startling response was perhaps not altogether unexpected. In speaking of breaking off her string of earlier romances before meeting Desi, she once frankly admitted, "Somehow marriage ties never loomed as important as making a name for myself—a name that had a lot of respect behind it."

New York had also provided Lucille with a perhaps uncomfortable glimpse of what she might face if she could not save her marriage.

"Claudette Colbert was doing *Marriage Go-Round* on Broadway, and Greer Garson was in *Auntie Mame*," recounts Robert Osborne. "Claudette was a great friend of Lucy's. Lucy had gone backstage after seeing *Marriage Go-Round,* and Claudette said to Lucy, 'What are you doing now—right now?' Lucy said, 'I have no plans.' She said, 'Let's go up to my apartment and cook some scrambled eggs or something.' Lucy said to me later, 'I was surprised because I had always thought in New York theater, there should be mobs of people backstage, and I was the *only* person who went back to see Claudette.' Pretty soon there was a knock on the door, and Lucy opened it. And there was Greer Garson. Greer said, 'Lucy, what are *you* doing in town?' Lucy said, 'For some meetings.' She said, 'Oh, I came over here because nobody came backstage after my show, and I thought maybe Claudette wanted to get a bite of food.' Claudette said, 'Well, we're going up to my house and make some scrambled eggs. Would you like to join us?' She said, 'Oh, yes—I have no one *else* to do anything with!' Lucy said to me, 'So here we were—Claudette Colbert, Greer Garson, and Lucille Ball—three old *broads* making scrambled eggs two o'clock in the morning and bored to *tears* with each other!' "

Lucille's distraught mental state likely contributed to an unfortunate

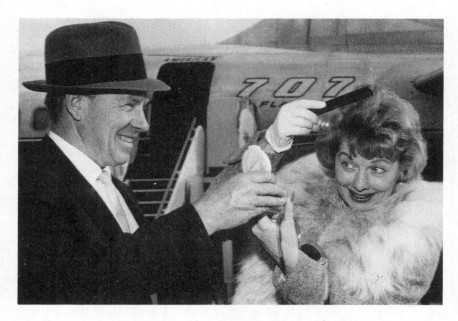

Desilu executive George Murphy sees Lucy off on one of her solo trips to New York.
THOMAS J. WATSON COLLECTION

incident that created national headlines early in May 1959. Lucille stormed out of an Oklahoma City youth rally after refusing to perform because of what she deemed a "small crowd." The Associated Press lambasted Ball: "The high-priced performer had agreed to appear at a Kiwanis Club Youth Rally combating juvenile delinquency in Taft Stadium. It seats 12,000. Some 2,000 persons showed up. So did Miss Ball, with three entertainers. But with the program under way, she refused to leave her air-conditioned Cadillac for a scheduled comedy routine and a talk on delinquency. The show went on without her." Lucille further fanned the controversy by snapping to a reporter at the airport on her return to Hollywood, "I didn't go on because of the small crowd. I believe in the youth rallies, but there weren't enough there today to do any good." She defensively added, "I've played to thirteen people in a dugout. It doesn't matter to me how many there are. But when they don't care enough to publicize the affair, it's high time they stopped asking people to go thousands of miles to perform."

A week after the incident, in a last-ditch attempt to patch up the marriage, the Arnazes embarked on a multicontinent, one-month European vacation. Perhaps to quell growing rumors of divorce, Desilu claimed that Lucy and Desi would "shoot a picture with French guest stars for next season's Westinghouse series" while on a stopover in Paris. Gossip columns were quick to mention that the Arnazes—installed in six *Liberté* staterooms—were to set sail on the "Unlucky 13th" of May. Curiously, while the trip was designed to salvage their marriage, Lucille insisted that the couple be accompanied by young Lucie and Desi, Jr., along with Lucy's cousin Cleo and her husband, Kenny Morgan.

No doubt concerned with the rumors, Lucille launched a one-woman public-relations campaign from shipboard, dashing off letters to her pals in the press detailing the idyllic Arnaz vacation. On Sunday, May 24, she sent similar notes to both Hedda Hopper and Radie Harris:

Radie dear—

I don't know if Paris is ready, but we sure are . . . Cleo, Kenny, Desi IV, Lucie, Daddy and me—40 bags, two trunks and look out . . . here we come—Capri, Rome, Paris, London. Have had a delightful crossing. Weather perfect, food divine—eating ourselves out of shape—won't be able to get into my new chiffons. Flying home June 14—over the North Pole directly to Calif. Have to work on the 15th—so

Bye til later,
Lucy & Desi

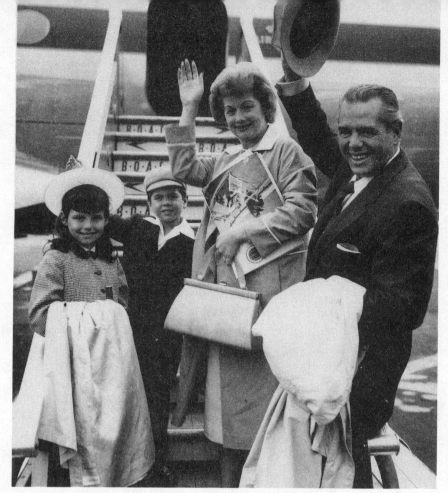

The Arnaz family departs London at the end of their ill-fated European vacation.
RICK CARL COLLECTION

In addition, Lucille's letter to Hopper noted, "Everyone loves our kids—that makes us happy."

The real story was far from pleasant. "It was just a nightmare," reveals Cleo Morgan Smith. "Desi was falling-down drunk everywhere. He wasn't too bad on the ship, though he kept disappearing down on the other levels, wandering off to steerage, folk-dancing with the folks down there. We hit London first. The press was all over them. Then we hit countries where they didn't have *I Love Lucy* yet, but they knew her. France hadn't yet had the show, only England. In France, Desi became 'Mister Ball' and 'the Cuban.' He'd always wanted to see Spain, so he went off by himself. He didn't stay long, because they didn't know him. He'd been wanting to get away from it all, but when they didn't know him at all, it didn't sit too well. An overcoat or something had been left at a hotel in France, and they sent it to our next stop in Rome. The package arrived for him, and it was addressed to 'Mister Ball.' So from there on, it was

180

all downhill. We went to Capri. Desi did not draw a sober breath. He chased everything in heels. He fell down and hit his face on an old cobblestone street. He face turned purple and looked like a pomegranate. We had been invited to this magnificent house, and here he is with this great purple face. Lucie couldn't go to Europe for years—she never wanted to go. It was such a traumatic experience. The kids were crying all the time, 'Poor Daddy.' From there on, it was all downhill."

Chapter Eleven

"I don't think Desi Arnaz was ever any happier than when he was sitting there, singing and playing the bongos. I think he absolutely loved building an empire—but he also had absolutely no stomach for maintaining an empire."

—Carole Cook, 1991

"When I look back on our marriage now and ask myself went wrong," Desi once reflected, "I think that one of the problems was that we were both working too hard and were together too much—all day and all night. Little arguments became big arguments. There was really no chance to be away from each other and let things cool off. It was really ironic. For the first ten years of our married life we had both worked like hell trying to solve the problem of being separated too much." Arnaz attempted to deflect his escalating alcohol dependency by defensively noting, "I had always been a drinking man. Lucy knew that. That first night after we went out after that rehearsal of *Too Many Girls* at RKO, we both got bombed and had a ball. But now she was resenting it. As president of three studios and all that bullshit, I should be more dignified."

Upon returning home from their disastrous trip abroad, Lucille threw herself into her work with even more fierce determination. She attempted to obtain television rights to the Rodgers and Hart musical *By Jupiter!*—envisioning the two male roles being rewritten for herself and Vivian Vance as a special *Playhouse* presentation. Lucille began taking singing lessons from Judy Garland's onetime accompanist Buddy Pepper, having been approached to star in an upcoming Broadway musical titled *The Unsinkable Molly Brown* upon the signing of Meredith Willson to write the show's score. She dropped out of *Molly Brown* consideration when *Diary of Anne Frank* writers Frances Goodrich and Albert Hackett offered to create a Broadway-bound Ball vehicle under the aegis of producer-director Morton DaCosta.

By this point, Arnaz was a semipermanent resident at the Château Marmont; when he did spend the night to be near his children at his

Roxbury Drive home, he resided in the guesthouse on the property. "It is a horrifying experience to watch someone you love, someone you think you know, turning into a stranger," Lucille said later. "We saw it happen. Then we hardly saw him anymore."

Lucy increasingly relied on the companionship of her workshop players in an attempt to fill the void left by her shattered marriage, often taking several members of the group for Las Vegas jaunts or weekend trips to her Del Mar and Palm Springs residences. Robert Osborne recalls one incident: "Jane Kean, Dick Kallman, and I were down in Palm Springs, supposedly guests of Lucy and Desi, but Desi was never around much. She wanted to go see Nat 'King' Cole at the Chi Chi Club and had made reservations. Desi, all of a sudden, showed up for dinner. Instead of being in a noncommunicative mood, he was feeling very sentimental about Lucy and the family. He started talking about family and family things. She was not much in the mood at this particular point. This was not melting her—this was past the point of no return. She said to us, 'Just follow my lead.' The more he talked, the more awake he got. She said, 'Don't worry. He'll want to go to bed at about nine. We'll still be able to get to Chi Chi by nine-thirty and see the show.'

"After dinner, instead of going off to bed, he wanted to sit in the living room and talk more about those stories. I remember Lucy starting to yawn. But he'd keep talking. It was like watching a 'Lucy' sketch. She finally got him so drowsy, she said, 'I'm going off to bed.' She went off to her room. He went off to his room. We'd been given instructions to keep the motor running and wait outside. Pretty soon, out through a window she snuck. She had obviously gotten undressed because she was buttoning her blouse and throwing her coat on. They sat us down in front, and all we could see were the fillings in his teeth. After the show, we got some champagne and went out to the middle of the desert and opened the champagne. She was laughing and in a frisky mood."

On another occasion, recalls Osborne, "Lucy thought it was very important that we all go see *The Gold Rush* because of Chaplin. Some theater had brought it back, and we were at the house planning to go, when Desi came in. He was a little drunk. She thought there was going to be trouble, so she says, 'Go outside.' So Carole, Dick Kallman, and I zipped outside. She said, 'Wait outside for me.' Pretty soon, she came out, jumped into the car, and off we went to see *The Gold Rush*."

Maintaining their public facade as a united couple, the Arnazes made a joint appearance at Desilu's first annual stockholders' meeting held July 20 on a Desilu-Gower soundstage. To the audience—comprised of

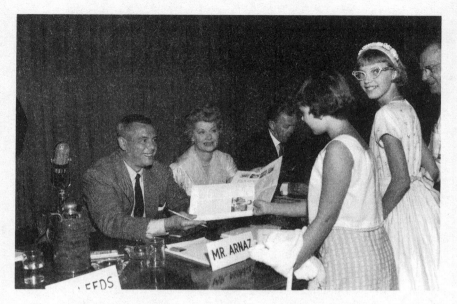

Desi and Lucille sign autographs after the first annual Desilu stockholders'
meeting, July 20, 1959.
ARNAZ FAMILY ARCHIVES

stockholders, several children, and a voluptuous blonde actress looking
for a part in a Desilu production—Desi boasted, "We now estimate that
our gross income during the current television season will be not less
than twenty-three-point-five million dollars. This is an increase of three
million dollars or fifteen percent over the last fiscal year."

George Murphy recalls an amusing incident that also underscored the
strain in the Arnaz marriage: "For the first stockholders' meeting I wrote
a statement for Desi. He was concerned about all the hotshots out from
New York. It was quite important that it went well. Desi read what I
wrote. When he finished, there was silence. Lucille turned to him
and said, 'Would you mind repeating that—I didn't understand a *word*
you said!' "

Despite Desi's attempt to put a positive spin on corporate earnings
to the stockholders, he later wrote, "The company had realized a profit
of only $250,000 for the year. That is about one and one-quarter percent
of the gross. We could have done better by putting our money in a
savings account. And sometimes people wonder why I got fed up with
the whole business." He added, "I wanted to sell. I wanted to sell then
more than ever. Our book value was even better than the price of our
shares indicated at the time. If we'd sold at 14 or 15, which we could
have gotten, everybody who wanted to get out would have gotten out

in fine shape. Most of our stockholders had bought at 10, the price at which our shares went on the market." Desi concluded, "I am sorry to say my partner did not want to sell." Talks of a Desilu buyout had surfaced again that March, when *The Wall Street Journal* reported that National Theatres & Television—operators of 250 motion picture the-atres and owners of 45 percent of them—had held "preliminary dis-cussions" about acquiring "a controlling interest" in the company. The overture was not altogether unexpected—Desilu and an NT&T subsid-iary, National Telefilm Associates, shared ownership in a number of syndicated series including *U.S. Marshal* and *Grand Jury*. However, as one columnist offered, "The rumor that the impending sale is due to matrimonial difficulties is quashed by both Mr. and Mrs. Arnaz, both of whom have firmly denied that there will be a divorce."

Although it appeared by the end of November that the NT&T buyout deal was near acceptance by Desilu, Lucille's unwillingness to sell the studio apparently prompted the Arnazes to abruptly reject a firm buyout offer at the end of December. Renewed negotiations with Four Star Productions—unpublicized at the time—to merge with Desilu were also abandoned after talks with Four Star's president, actor Dick Powell, fell apart. Per Martin Leeds, "You had two egos—Dick Powell and Desi Arnaz—who wanted to be chairman of the board. It just wouldn't work."

Attempting to underscore corporate growth, Motion Picture Center was renamed Desilu-Cahuenga. Desilu formulated a batch of new tele-vision-pilot possibilities for the 1960–61 season. First on the slate was *Homicide Squad,* a Joseph Cotten western series, a contemporary action-adventure series for *Texan* star Rory Calhoun. *My Friend Irma* and *Life with Luigi* creator Cy Howard was signed to a five-year pact to create, develop, and produce "telefilms" for Desilu. Quinn Martin was set to produce a one-hour series titled *Secret Service Man;* by March 1960, however, Martin had departed Desilu to launch his own independent company. In the end, Desilu sold only two new series—*Harrigan and Son* (with Pat O'Brien) and the recast version of *Guestward Ho!* with Joanne Dru.

Milton Berle appeared on the 1959–60 *Lucille Ball–Desi Arnaz Show* premiere episode ("Milton Berle Hides Out at the Ricardos' ") directed by Desi Arnaz. Said *Variety* of the Schiller-Weiskopf effort: "It was a classic example of how the masters of their craft can make a limp script jump for joy"; *Lucy* continued its ratings decline, ranking only seventh for the week. Rumors of the Arnazes's marital discord again circulated the day the Berle episode aired, Desi's appearing at Bob Stack's *Untouch-ables* premiere party without his wife—Lucille purportedly "too busy" with her upcoming Desilu Workshop revue to attend.

Lucille stirred up more rumors that she and Desi were headed for divorce when she announced that she and her husband would "take time off" from the small screen in 1960 to star in "separate" Broadway shows; while she declined to offer specifics about her stage property, Lucille stated it looked "very good" she would appear in a Kermit Bloomgarten–produced play. Lucy pointedly noted that her Broadway debut would be solely under Bloomgarten's direction and without Desi's involvement; she also expected to produce a Broadway version of *Desilu Revue*.

A lonely Lucy often turned rehearsals into social occasions. Workshop stage manager Al Morley recounts, "We had all gone to dinner. We did that many times. On the way back from dinner, I reminded Lucy that I met her when she and Maureen O'Hara had crossed the country in 1940 to promote *Dance, Girl, Dance*. All of us kids went to the stage door for autographs. Maureen O'Hara was so nice, gave everybody pictures. Finally, a limousine drives up, the driver gets out and opens the back door. The stage door opens, Lucy runs from the stage door into the limo and closes the door, rolls the window down, and says, 'You may hand your autograph books through the window.' As she left, the stage-door manager we called Pops said, 'Well, that Maureen O'Hara is going to be a big star, but that Lucille Ball, with *that* attitude, is never going *anywhere*.' When I told Lucy, she said, 'Oh, really—and where is *Pops* today?' "

Lucy's protégée Carole Cook moved into the Arnaz guesthouse. "Desi would come by, seeing the kids, having dinner some nights. We were sitting there having dinner one night when the kitchen door opened and in came Jack Benny playing the violin. He never said a word—just walked all around the dining-room table, walked out the kitchen door, and went to his house next door.

"I saw the emotion that nobody else saw. I saw her cry. I tried to make her laugh. I knew I had that ability to make her laugh. We'd go out in the back garage. She had a little beauty shop set up there. She used to set my hair. I'd tell her, 'Lucy, my hair looks like *shit*—you're a better *star* than you are a *hairdresser!*' Bob Osborne, Lucy, and I played Monopoly a lot when I lived with her. She'd say, 'Why don't you play word games? You're a college graduate.' I said, 'I don't play those dumb games.' That would make her furious—I did talk back to her because I loved her."

Making Lucille laugh was no easy task, even when she was not emotionally distraught. Osborne notes about her serious mien, "I don't think she had any humor at all, strangely enough, for someone that funny. She could laugh, and she liked a good laugh, but she didn't *think* funny, although she knew what was funny and could make a situation funny. I don't think of her as a 'light' person at all. I think of Lucy as 'heavy'—serious about comedy, serious about having *fun*."

Despite their warm friendship, Carole quickly discovered that Lucille was also a stern taskmaster. "One of the first things I did was play a dance-hall girl," recalls Cook. "Many times, for our rehearsals, there were people sitting in the grandstands watching. She was tough—but I learned to love that. I did my speech, and she stopped me and said, 'Just hold it.' Everybody stopped. Two hundred people stared at me. She said, 'I don't want to hear any letting down in the middle of that speech.' She just read me the riot act. I was quite embarrassed and shaken up by it. She said, 'Now go out and do it again.' Everybody was quiet. I turned around and said, 'Someday I'm going to own all of this!' I walked out, and I didn't hear one sound. Then I heard Lucy, dying laughing. *Then* everybody joined in laughing. Where were they when I needed them?"

Lucy's ambitious Broadway-bound plans for her workshop production were discarded when the Walter Kent–Walton Farrar–scored *Desilu Revue* won decidedly mixed notices. Said *Variety,* "Exquisitely mounted and strikingly staged, the show lacks the expected punch—its reliance on ambitious production rather than unpretentious satire does not always pay off." While Osborne, Dick Kallman, Roger Perry, and Jerry Antes won special mentions, Carole Cook was singled out by trade reviews as "the hit of the show, just about the funniest comedienne to come along since Lucille Ball herself. She alone could make the show worthwhile, making bad material look good and good material look great."

The Arnazes took the entire workshop troupe across the street after the performance to Lucey's Mexican restaurant where, said *The Reporter,* "Desi relaxed, led the band and sang up a storm to celebrate." That night, Lucille announced plans to move the revue, if business warranted, to larger quarters after its initial four-week run; highlights would air on a special 1959 Christmas Eve edition of *Desilu Playhouse.*

"She enjoyed having all of us around her because she was having trouble in her marriage," says Osborne. "But one time, we had a screening at her house. She had always made everyone feel very welcome. She always had food. There were a couple of people in the crowd that went, without being invited, into her liquor cabinet and started pouring their own drinks. She never said anything at the time. When the evening was over, she said to me, 'I'm never going to have them back at the house again.' That's when she thought, 'I'm paying these kids a salary, but I don't care about them personally anymore.' That's when she started spending more time with Carole and me, which kind of sealed us off from everybody else.

"Lucille once said to me, 'I always think of my life as a chest of drawers. When I get up in the morning, I open one drawer only. And that drawer is to shower, get dressed, and have breakfast with the kids. I don't think about what I have to do at noon or at five that afternoon. When that drawer is closed, I open up the next drawer. That means getting my hair set, getting my makeup on and my script lines finalized in my mind. Then I open my drawer about my noon meeting with my stockholders.' She was full of wonderful, sensible ideas like that.

"She used to have notes to herself on the dashboard of her car. And then when they were done, they'd be thrown down in a basket. Once, I was at her house, and we were reminiscing about *The Desilu Revue.* I said, 'I'd really love to see that show again sometime,' and then we talked about something else. When I got home that afternoon, the phone was ringing. It was Lucy's secretary, Wanda Clark. She said, 'Where do you want the film sent?' I said, 'What film?' She said, *'The Desilu Revue.'* That fast she had done it. It was sent over to me, and when I tried to return it, it was given to me. She was so great about that. When one needed something, she'd say yes or no—there was never a maybe. Lucy was very loyal—she'd really be there for you. But she would be the last person you would want to go to because she'd be so disappointed that you weren't able to solve your problem because she had always solved hers."

The second half of 1959 found Desi embroiled in some highly publicized and unsavory incidents. He was sued by character actor David O. McCall for $100,000 charging a "grossly intoxicated" Desi on the studio lot struck him "without provocation" and "with great force," resulting in back injuries and bruises.

On September 19, Arnaz made headlines when booked by Hollywood police on a "common drunk" complaint after an argument with a plain-clothes police officer who reported seeing Desi "staggering down Vista Street"—the notorious site of numerous West Hollywood bordellos—at 1:00 A.M. Behind-the-scenes maneuvering by Martin Leeds to minimize public-relations damage resulted in news accounts reporting only Arnaz's "plain drunk" charge, although the "Vista Street" reference was a some-what euphemistic indication that he had, in fact, been arrested while patronizing a house of prostitution. Desi only worsened the situation when police asked for identification, and he angrily retorted, "It's none of your business." Desi was taken into custody, released on twenty-one dollars cash bail after spending a half hour in a jail cell. At one point, a nearly incoherent Desi shouted to vice investigators, "I got friends who can identify me—get me *J. Edgar Hoover.*"

Desi's drunken escapade triggered a Desilu crisis averted at the last moment by Martin Leeds. "He was picked up for being 'plain drunk,'" recalls Leeds, "outside a whorehouse and booked. He was downtown when I found out about it at one in the morning. I covered up a lot—but you reach a point sometimes where you just can't cover it. He could have been booked *in* the whorehouse. I got a call at eleven-thirty from his chauffeur. He said, 'Martin, he's in the whorehouse, and I think the house is on a stakeout.' I said, 'You go inside and get [Desilu art director] Claudio Guzman, and tell him if he doesn't get Desi out of there in five minutes, he'll never work in Hollywood again.' He got him out. The cops had been alerted to him. They met him outside. He's drunk. I got a call the next morning from Bob Healey, the head of McCann-Erickson, representing Westinghouse. He said, 'Westinghouse doesn't like its host. I think you'd better come down.'

"Desi hated being the host of *Playhouse.* Healey says, 'We want to drop him.' I said, 'You can't. I've got thirty-seven shows, two prepping, and three more after that. Let me finish the forty-two. Let's make a deal—you let me do the remaining shows. I have thirteen one-hour Lucy-Desi hours. Put them on as thirteen specials, pay me only one hundred thousand dollars each. He says, 'CBS won't agree to it.' They did agree to it. I made Desilu one million, three hundred thousand dollars for thirteen shows. I called Desi on the phone and said, 'Desi, you're gonna absolutely love me. I got you out of hosting the *Playhouse.*' But he never knew *really* why."

"Desi hadn't been around for a couple of days," Robert Osborne says of the sordid incident. "Lucy and I went to see something at the Huntington Hartford. She loved to go out to the theater and do all that stuff. The morning edition of the Los Angeles *Herald-Examiner* was already on the street. When we came out of the theater, we passed a newsbox stand, and there was this story on the front page that Desi had been arrested coming out of a house of prostitution. She just went white, just white. She was a very moral person. Although she wasn't to the manor born, she was a very classy lady. And that was just unacceptable behavior. Particularly public humiliation. And she loved him so much."

"I would go to Vegas with her," recalls Cook. "She went a lot at the time of the breakup. She was in tears a lot of the time and in a lot of rage. I would see reporters come to her all the time and say, 'Well, Desi owes you—you're the one.' It didn't matter how full of rage Lucy was.

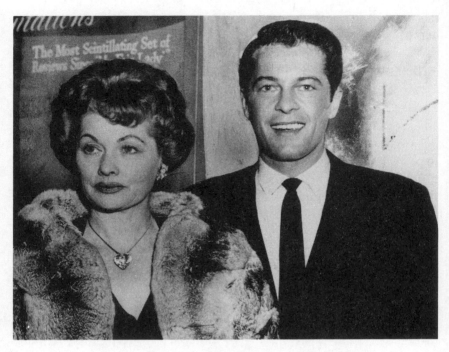

Lucille and Robert Osborne at the Huntington Hartford Theatre
SECURITY PACIFIC COLLECTION/LOS ANGELES PUBLIC LIBRARY

She'd say to them, 'That's where you're wrong. Desi is the one. I'm not at the business end.' "

By late 1959, Lucille, however, had become so greatly alarmed—and highly embarrassed—at Desi's public escapades and erratic professional conduct that she was considering assuming a more active role in Desilu business affairs in order to safeguard the studio—despite often quipping of her lack of business acumen, "All I do is sign a million papers I never read. Someday they'll catch up with me." Leaked *The Reporter* on November 11, "We hear Lucy may align with Martin Leeds so there would no longer be a solid Arnaz family block of stock."

In his autobiography, Desi recounts his version of the events leading up to their divorce: "Sometime during November of that year, 1959, Lucy had just left my office after some other goddamn argument. There was a water fountain on the second floor of the administration building, to the right of my office, just before you go downstairs. I followed her and as she stopped to have a drink, I told her, 'Lucy, I want a divorce.' " He further told her, "I just can't take it anymore. Perhaps if we had just done *I Love Lucy* and we had stayed at Chatsworth and I hadn't gotten involved in so many projects, this wouldn't have happened." Lucille turned on her heels, without saying a word, and left. That night, they had another stormy confrontation. "Her temper got the best of her. 'Why don't you die then? That would be a better solution, better for the children, better for everybody.'"

"She didn't want to admit defeat. She was an ordinary person, and she didn't want to be an ordinary Hollywood person who got married and divorced," offers Osborne. "It was so cold and hostile. A lot of of that was because of the damage Desi had done by running around with other women. They had really a great sexual relationship, and they were really in love with each other. Then he started running around with other women just as she was losing to the age game."

The 1959–60 *Playhouse* run was destined to be as rocky as the Arnaz marriage. In April the series had been shunted from a premium Monday evening slot to a less-prestigious and less-viewed Friday evening berth. And as the big-budget *Lucy-Desi* shows began slipping in the ratings—the public finally weary of the Ricardos' shenanigans or the often-lacking hour-length scripts of past seasons—the cornerstone of the *Desilu Playhouse* deal was suddenly less valuable to the sponsor. As a result, Westinghouse announced in October that it was cutting *Playhouse* sponsorship in half as of January 1960—the series to air only on alternate weeks. Offers Bert Granet, "Desi, while he gave so much to the company, also [contributed] a great deal [to] the demise of the company. He just wasn't putting his mind to it. There were times when Warner Brothers was getting shows like *77 Sunset Strip*—cheap, cheap shows to produce—that we could have easily, readily made. Desi just wasn't around to pick up on these things and say, 'Look, I gave you *The Untouchables*—give me two of these nonsense shows.'"

The uncertain future of the *Lucy-Desi* hours halted bookings of celebrities for the upcoming year; Debbie Reynolds was the only *Lucy* guest set for the 1960–61 season, based on Lucille's commitment to appear on a projected *Debbie Reynolds Show* ABC special in September 1960. Although Bob Schiller and Bob Weiskopf had been the primary *Lucy-Desi* writers of late, another clear signal that the *I Love Lucy* era was indeed ending came when script consultants Madelyn Martin and Bob Carroll, Jr., announced in December they were departing Desilu to write the first season of the CBS situation-comedy series *The Tom Ewell Show*.

Talk predicting an imminent Arnaz split began anew when Lucille was conspicuously absent for Desi's press screening of his first solo *Playhouse* dramatic effort—his "So Tender, So Profane" performance, called "first rate" by *The Hollywood Reporter*. Lucille fled to New York the next morning, while Desi left three days later on October 26 for another

European vacation; the studio attempted once again to scotch rumors of marital discord by claiming that the purpose of Arnaz's trip was to film on-location footage in Italy and South Africa for an extended *Playhouse* "Thunder in the Night" episode, which Desilu purportedly planned to release overseas as a theatrical feature with Desi as its star.

The day Desi departed for Europe on the *Queen Mary,* speculation of divorce circulated throughout Hollywood. He denied to reporters any possibility of a split-up. "We're working too hard, that's the only trouble," Desi maintained. "Probably someone heard we had an argument, but we have lots of arguments. When a redhead and a Cuban get together, we argue pretty good." Two weeks later, Lucille was still keeping up the front. "Desi is in Europe on business. When he returns to this country around December first, he will come home and live here with his family as he always has." The Arnazes were not completely successful at their domestic subterfuge; as one column item noted, "When Desi returned in November, he moved back into the family home. But those close to the Arnazes said he was living in a small house behind the main house and predicted an early separation."

Lucille again attempted to deflect rampant rumors of a marital split and Desilu dissolution upon her husband's return from Europe. "I'm not too well informed about the business end of Desilu, but I do know that if the studio were going to be sold, I would have been told about it. And I have been told about no such thing," she insisted. "As for those rumors that my marriage is breaking up—they are cruel and totally false." She had, in fact, been reconciled to an inevitable divorce for months, but hesitated filing for fear Desilu would be sued by Westinghouse for failing to deliver a certain number of *Lucy-Desi* programs.

The Arnazes dutifully continued their on-camera roles as the happily married Ricardos to fulfill their Westinghouse contract—although only two of the projected seven *Lucy-Desi* hours had been filmed for the 1959–60 season by the close of the year. The second Ball-Arnaz entry of the season, "The Ricardos Go to Japan," aired November 27 and featured Robert Cummings and Desi Arnaz as director. *Variety* dismissed it as "overworked. Lucille Ball steamrolled a piece of cockamaymee about Lucy and a set of pearls. Obstensibly about Japan, it was about as Japanese as Desi's accent."

The Desilu Revue aired on the *Playhouse* a month later. Even with guest appearances by "Lucy, Ricky, Fred, and Ethel" along with Ann Sothern, Spring Byington, Hedda Hopper, Rory Calhoun, George Murphy, and Danny Thomas, critical response to the small-screen adaptation was divided. *The Reporter* praised that "seldom has a revue been presented on TV so flawlessly." *Variety,* however, concluded, "This television edition was all wrong from start to finish. It wasn't a revue. For some reason, perhaps for 'insurance,' the basic idea was converted for TV into a situation comedy starring Miss Ball, who also produced. It purported to show how nervous she was on opening night of the stage presentation, and had a one-joke running story line intermittently interrupted by acts from the revue."

Stung by middling reviews for both the stage and television versions of her *Desilu Revue,* Lucille soon forgot her workshop as her marriage collapsed and she, in turn, set her career sights on a new Broadway career to escape Hollywood and husband Desi; the revue ended after its initial four-week run, and no subsequent shows were produced. "Desi started coming in and revamping the orchestrations and so forth," says Robert Osborne. "He was so knowledgeable about music and so good at that. She was smart enough to know that he was an asset, but then it became not her project anymore. It became Desi's. And so then she lost interest."

Lucille later recalled her Desilu Workshop experience with great bitterness, perhaps associating its failure with the simultaneous dissolution of her marriage. In 1962 she remarked, "I had them two years, and I found myself *caring* about each one. They took two years out of my life as a lay psychiatrist. That's over now, because they drained me dry." Lucille in 1977 viewed the experience even more harshly: "It was very difficult. It took eighty-two years out of my life. In class, I would have to take some students apart. I'd hear someone say, 'I want to be like Irene Dunne' and *I'd* say, 'But you look like a *prostitute.* You act like one, and you sound like one.' I'd tell them, 'Let's look at ourselves the way other people see us.' I had students who couldn't pay their rent, and I would get jobs for them that would pay seven hundred fifty dollars for three days' work. And they'd refuse it. They wouldn't even show up. They wouldn't even try. They came out a bunch of ingrates."

Perhaps the most alarming—albeit quickly denied—report of problems in the Arnaz marriage appeared in the December 22 *Reporter:* "Lucille Ball's black-and-bruised eye, cheek and elbow did not come from anything as unexciting as bumping into a glass doorknob imported from Venice by Desi—saying which Lucy lit out for Sun Valley solo"; Lucille, according to other reports, had taken the children to spend the Christmas holidays with Ann Sothern in Idaho while Desi traveled alone to Palm Springs. The trade paper hastily attempted to disclaim the earlier report on December 24, insisting, "We are glad to report that the couple of lines here Monday morning regarding Lucille Ball and Desi Arnaz are wrong. We were fed this 'stiff' by one we thought knew what he was talking about."

Lucille and Desi were faced with the agonizing task of explaining their imminent divorce to their children. As Lucy later recounted, "I drove the children to our house in Palm Springs, where Desi was spending weekends, and together we told them. We said that Mommy and Daddy were not getting along well together, and that when mommies and daddies do not get along well, they are not happy, and neither are the children. By way of easing them into what was ahead, we explained that there was going to be a separation 'as of now' and then, or a little later, there would probably be a divorce. They would be seeing more of Daddy, Desi assured them, than they had been doing, and above all, we said in unison, we loved them very much.

"When we had finished speaking, there was a silence, an aching silence. Finally, Lucie broke the silence by asking in a small voice, 'But you don't have to get a divorce, do you?' Another silence, and then little Desi asked, 'Can't you take it all back—and make up?' After Desi and I had answered both questions as best we could—I had such a lump in my throat I couldn't speak—by saying they were not to worry, everything would be all right, the silence was resumed and continued unbroken during the two hours or more it took to drive from Palm Springs to Beverly Hills."

"She used to come to my house," recalls Bob Osborne. "She would sleep on the couch. And cry. Just cry. She really felt terrible. She didn't want to stay in the house because that was their home, and I think she also didn't want to unburden herself with close friends. Because she didn't want advice. She just wanted to think it through. On the balcony of the house you could see all of Los Angeles and lots of lights. I said to her one time, 'It's a wonderful feeling to know that every one of those lights out there, you just have to say the word 'Lucy'—you don't even have to say a last name—and they know it's you. And she said, 'Oh, God, don't say something like that. That's terrifying.' She was really upset that I said that. That wasn't a pleasing thought to her at all.

"We went to see *Duel of Angels,* a play with Vivien Leigh. We went backstage and met Vivien. Lucy and I went to the Brown Derby across the street. She was very depressed and just sat there and fiddled with her food. She said, 'What I do is so meaningless, so unimportant. She is such a great actress. Look what she can do.' To cheer her up, I said, 'But, Lucy, think of the millions of people you've affected. Could Vivien ever, ever affect that many millions of people like you do?' She turned to me and said, 'Have you ever heard of a little movie called *Gone With the Wind?*' "

In late February, Lucille was reunited with former dramatic-school classmate Bette Davis backstage after a performance in *The World of Carl Sandburg* at the Huntington Hartford Theatre. Davis, according to Lucy's escort, Robert Osborne, apparently still harbored some resentment over being replaced by Tallulah Bankhead in 1957's "Celebrity Next Door" *Lucy-Desi* hour. "We were waiting to go backstage," he recalls. "We could hear Bette screaming to George Seaton and his wife, 'How *dare* you come! They told me *no* celebrities! This is a *preview*. It was a *terrible* show! You should have *waited!*' We hear this, and we're sitting there, getting a little nervous. We went in. Lucy, trying to solve a bad situation, said, 'Bette, don't worry about a thing. It was a wonderful show. We really enjoyed it.' And Bette said, 'What do you *mean,* don't worry about a thing? I thought it was a *great* show tonight!' All of a sudden, there's this thing happening in the room. At this point, Bette's career was really in the toilet, and Lucy was famous. But Bette had been the queen of Warner Brothers while Lucy was a stock player at RKO. So Bette said to her, 'Lucille, the last time I saw you, you were on a *bandstand* doing something with *Kay Kyser* [in the 1939 RKO film *That's Right, You're Wrong*]. But you've done so *wonderfully* well!' This froze the room. Then Bette started talking. Lucille got out her compact and started powdering her face—the rudest thing you can do when someone is talking—and never said another word."

The first week of March was perhaps the most painful in Lucille Ball's life—she would film the final *Lucy-Desi* program and the next day file for divorce. "Lucy Meets the Moustache" teamed the Arnazes with Ernie Kovacs and wife Edie Adams. "When we did the show, we knew there was a rift," Edie recalls. "There was gossip all over town, but we had no idea what we were facing. They literally would not speak to each other. Lucy was a little more than upset. I remember the first reading. She'd say to the writers without a laugh or cracking a smile, 'That's funny' or 'That's *not* funny.' During rehearsals, Desi would roll his eyes and say, 'Would you tell Miss Ball to move over?' 'Would you tell Mr. Arnaz I *can't* move over there because . . .' We'd pretend not to hear it. The daggers were center stage. The show was incidental.

"She had my hairdo redone three times. I was not amused. I came in with my hair sort of in a pageboy. The hairdresser had come to my house. Ernie was at the studio. I wasn't to be there until eleven o'clock. I went in. Everybody says this curt hello. I see Lucy talking to the set

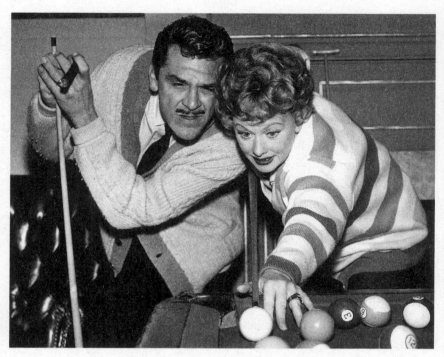

A publicity shot with Ernie Kovacs for the final Ball-Arnaz show, "Lucy Meets the Moustache"
RICK CARL COLLECTION

hairdresser. This hairdresser said to me, 'I have to redo your hair. Lucy doesn't like it that way.' I am fuming. It was a young-looking hairdo, I think. I had to get my head soaked and roll it up in big rollers. They were all going to lunch. I told Ernie, 'I can't go. I have to get my hair done.' He said, 'Oh, swell,' said good-bye, and went to lunch with Lucy. I was furious. I'm getting my hair soaked, and Desi came over and said, 'She's just a little upset.' He was trying to smooth it over. Then she came back after lunch—not to me, but to the hairdresser. Another conference. The hairdresser says to me, 'She doesn't like it.' She had said, 'It looks too much like mine. Put it back the way it was.' Again I had to go soak my head—and for one shot. I wound up having it done the way I came in that morning."

The final *Lucille Ball-Desi Arnaz Show,* filmed on March 2, 1960 (Desi's forty-third birthday), was an inauspicious, if somewhat poignant, ending to a television legend. *Variety* stated, "This is probably the last show Desi Arnaz and Lucille Ball will make together within the framework of that wackiest of all TV families, the Ricardos.... Miss Ball wasn't particularly up to form and Kovacs, apart from a couple of good sight gags, had to play reasonably straight. Even the lesser *Desi-Lucy* hours had at

196

least one sequence in which Miss Ball turned in a show-stopping clowning routine. This one didn't."

"Those were emotional days for everyone on the show," recalled Vivian Vance in 1976. "I still get misty-eyed when I talk about Lucy and Desi's breakup. After their last show together, a lot of us just stood there and cried. The reason we were all so involved with the split was because we all shared a bond—the cast and crew were straight out of *Our Town*. We had a tight little circle and knew about all the fortunes and misfortunes of everyone's lives. It was like living in a small town and sharing every emotion."

"After Desi and I went into the final clinch and the lights dimmed, there were no laughs, no smiles," Lucille later recalled. "The marriage, after nineteen years, had also ended that day. There is something about an ending—even when it is something you have wanted to end—that hurts inside."

On March 3, the day after the Kovacs show was filmed, Lucille filed for divorce in Santa Monica Superior Court. In her complaint, Arnaz was charged with "extreme cruelty" and subjecting his wife to "grievous mental suffering"; Lucy noted that her marriage had ended in a formal separation as of February 26. She further remarked to Hedda Hopper, "I'm sure our separation will come as no surprise since every columnist in the country has hinted at this for months." Lucille added, "We each own 25 percent of the company and have no intention of selling it." Lucy also stated, "I've tried so hard to be fair and solve our problems, but now I find it impossible to go on."

"When Lucy and Desi decided to divorce, it was friendly," recalls attorney Art Manella. "It certainly was not rancorous or adversarial. I had been the only lawyer in the picture until then. I remember them saying, 'Arthur why can't you handle everything?' I couldn't do that. It was an ethical matter. They each had to have their own representation. They said, 'Well, find a lawyer. It doesn't matter, because we're not going to be fighting about these things.' I got hold of [Milton] Mickey Rudin, an entertainment lawyer who was a friend of mine. Mickey represented Lucy, and I represented Desi."

Despite persistent rumors of marital discord, news of the divorce came as a shock to the country, even to Hollywood insiders. "I received eight thousand letters at the time of the divorce announcement and read most of them," Lucille said later. "I couldn't answer them all, of course. They asked me not to get a divorce. They said, 'Why isn't there something you can do?' They didn't know I had been trying to do it for years. I was painfully aware of the feeling the American public had for Lucy and their need for Lucy and Ricky as a happy family. The awareness held up my decision for a long time, until I couldn't allow it to do so anymore. Lucy solved a lot of marital problems for our viewers, and the idea of finding a laugh in a hopeless situation worked for Desi and me for a long time, too."

Although Lucille requested full custody of eight-year-old Lucie Desiree and six-year-old Desi IV, she stressed in her divorce petition, "We both love the children very much, and Desi can see them as often as he likes." Desi responded by issuing a statement through the studio: "We deeply regret that, after long and serious consideration, we have not been able to work out our problems and have decided to separate. Our divorce will be completely amicable and there will be no contest. Lucy will pursue her career on television and I will continue my work as head of Desilu Productions." While Lucille added, "I hope to do several spectaculars for Desilu and a motion picture before I move to New York to do a play in the fall," she also, however, insisted the Lucy-Desi era had ended. "Even if everything were all right, we'd never work together again. We had six years of a pretty successful series and two years of specials. Why try to top it? That would be foolish. We always knew when the time came to quit, we'd quit. We were lucky. We quit while we were still ahead."

Whatever bravura Lucille affected with regard to "quitting," Bob Weiskopf recalls that she was lost in the wake of losing both her husband and her beloved work arena. "The first week after the show shut down, she came to us crying. She said, could we have lunch? We said we had just had lunch. She said, 'Well, have lunch again.' We went across the street to Lucey's. She was crying. She said, 'What'll I do?' I said, 'Why don't you go home and be a good mother to your kids?' Those kids were raised by servants. She didn't know how to handle that. She said, 'What are you talking about? I'm a good mother.' She didn't know what the hell to do—unless she was working, she didn't know what the hell to do with herself." On other occasions, remembers Bob Schiller, "Lucy used to cry on my shoulder and say what a beautiful man he used to be and how sad it was."

At the May 4 hearing for the final divorce decree, Lucille arrived at the Santa Monica courthouse, noted one Hollywood columnist, "stylishly clad in a form-fitting black and white tweed silk suit, appeared chipper as she alighted from a limousine. She joked with reporters until court convened." Surrounded by newsmen, she recalled her previous October 6, 1944, divorce decree also filed in the Santa Monica Court—but nul-

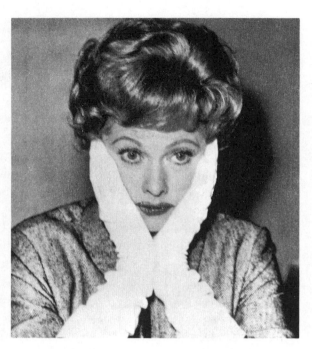

Lucille on the witness
stand at her May 4,
1960, divorce
THOMAS J. WATSON COLLECTION

lified within forty-eight hours due to their cozy reunion. "Will there
be a reconciliation this time?" one reporter queried. "Nope," she flatly
replied.

A tearful Lucille won her divorce after testifying that Desi had made
their marriage "a nightmare for the last three years." She also told Judge
Orlando H. Rhodes, "My husband would frequently have temper out-
bursts in front of the children, and this was very bad. It was so bad I
thought it would be better if we were apart. It was sort of a Jekyll and
Hyde sort of thing. He would have tantrums in front of friends and
relatives, and we could have no social life for the last three to four years.
It could be anything—you never knew. It could happen before friends,
relatives, people in the studio, anyplace we were." Lucille recounted an
incident when water pipes burst in their Beverly Hills home one evening.
"He made himself sick for two days over it. He blamed everybody for
everything. By count there were sixteen people he blamed. He was
hysterical and screamed and raved about it." When attorney Rudin asked
Lucille, "Did you try to work these things out?" she replied, "There's no
discussing anything with him. He doesn't discuss very well."

Lucille later offered, "Having asked for the divorce, Desi did not
contest it, nor did he offer any defense on that charge of 'mental cruelty.'
He did not, in fact, even appear in court." Ball was given custody of
their two children, Desi granted visitation rights with them at "reasonable
times." The property settlement provided her with $450 per month for
each of the children; she did not request alimony. Each retained ap-

199

proximately 25 percent ownership in Desilu. The 120-room Desi Arnaz Indian Wells Hotel revenue would be divided between the two until 1966, at which time Lucille would purchase Desi's interest and proceeds would be placed in a trust fund for Lucie and Desi IV.

As *Time* concluded, "The split: for Lucy, their two children, half of their $20 million Desilu TV interests, the leaky mansion, two station wagons, a cemetery plot at Forest Lawn. For Desi: the other half of the $20 million, a golf cart, a membership in a Palm Springs Country Club, a truck and several horses."

"Desi could win high, high stakes," recalled Lucille with lingering sadness many years later. "He could work very hard. He was brilliant. He was sweet and generous—overly generous. But he had to lose. He had to fail at everything that he built up. Everything he built up, he had to break down."

Only ten days after her divorce, Lucy spoke with old friend Dan Jenkins in her Desilu-Gower dressing room. "She looked over at a framed picture of Desi that stood on a small table. 'Look at him,' she said. 'That's the way he looked ten years ago. He doesn't look like that now. He'll never look like that again.' "

At one point, Jenkins asked Lucy if she had found happiness after finally dissolving her tumultuous and often painful marriage. "Am I happy?" she replied with a cold stare. "No. Not yet. I will be. I've been humiliated. That's not easy for a woman."

Chapter Twelve

"I hate failure and that divorce was a Number One failure in my eyes. It was the worst period of my life. Neither Desi nor I have been the same since, physically or mentally."

—Lucille Ball, 1971

"I've got a whole new life to make and a happy way to do it," insisted Lucille Ball not long after filming her final *Lucy-Desi* program. "I'm overworked and I'm overbooked. I don't have time to see friends. But I love to work and try new things. It's good for me."

Once again calling upon a busy workload to distract herself from personal turmoil, Lucille became immersed in her feature-film return as well as her Broadway debut. To that end, she signed to costar with Bob Hope in the comedy *The Facts of Life,* a Melvin Frank–Norman Panama film to begin shooting in June; the team, formerly based at Paramount, had written such previous Bob Hope motion-picture successes as *My Favorite Blonde, The Road to Utopia,* and *Monsieur Beaucaire.* Frank would direct the adult comedy written by Panama, originally created and discarded in 1951 as a potential film property for Olivia de Havilland and, at various times, James Stewart and William Holden.

In a departure from her television characterization, Ball would portray a married woman tempted to have an ultimately unconsummated affair with an also-married Bob Hope. ("Am I really doing this? Me? Kitty Webster, Pasadena housewife, secretary of the PTA, den mother of the Cub Scouts—have I really come to spend a weekend with the husband of my best friend?") The United Artists release was designed as a joint venture of Desilu, Bob Hope, and the newly formed Panama-Frank independent production company. Desilu would film *The Facts of Life*— to be shot in part on the old *I Love Lucy* soundstage. Don DeFore was cast as Ball's neglectful husband, Ruth Hussey portraying Hope's decidedly unromantic wife.

Lucille also continued to search for a suitable play to launch her new stage career. Although she had made a verbal commitment to star in a vehicle mounted by producer Kermit Bloomgarten and Morton DaCosta, negotiations were halted when Lucille rejected their chosen vehicle based on Dorothy Parker's short story *Big Blonde*. She did, however, have great enthusiasm for another property brought to her—a new libretto for a musical titled *The Wildcatters* and then *Wildcat*—written by N. Richard Nash and reminiscent of his previous nonmusical hit *The Rainmaker*. Lucille Ball would, reported *The New York Times,* portray "a blue-jeaned, hoydenish Annie Oakley of the Oklahoma oilfields."

According to author Nash, however, Lucille Ball was far from his first choice for his play. "I wrote thinking the character which Lucy later played would be an older sister, say, twenty-seven years old. And her younger sister would be nineteen or twenty. Having finished, I gave it to Michael Kidd. I started to do a second draft, and one night Michael called and said, 'What would you think of Lucille Ball for this?' And I said, 'Lucille Ball? My God, she's wonderful, but she's about *twice* as old as the character should be.' He said, 'Well, I've got news for you. I gave it to her, and she's crazy about it.' So I said, 'We're in kind of a jam here. This is *not* for Lucy.'

"A week or so later, we were at Lucy's house, just Lucy, Mike, and myself. She asked me to read two or three speeches aloud for her. One of them was her opening speech, which as yet did not have music. It was a speech that had in it the phrase 'hey, look me over.' It was the first thing I read, and she said, 'I'm going to do it!' That was it. And I went home with a headache because it was a totally different character. She was so smart. She said, 'You know, this is not for me by any means, but I want to do this part—do you think you can rewrite it?' So I went away and did a lot of rewriting. I took out all references to age. About two or three weeks after our first meeting, I had scenes that Michael submitted to her. The next thing I know, Desi was on the phone, saying, '*I love thees thin*'! I want to produce it!' It was all packaged and literally taken out of my hands. The final product had *nothing* to do with what my original intentions had been."

Leading men immediately lined up for the chance to costar with Ball. Kirk Douglas was approached, but his high price tag and multiple-picture commitments ended negotiations. Although Gordon MacRae campaigned for the role, Lucille instead considered the rugged Jock Mahoney and then personally offered the part to Gene Barry, who declined due to concurrent demands of his television series, *Bat Masterson*. Finally, athletic actor-singer Keith Andes—who had played Marilyn Monroe's husband in the Fritz Lang melodrama *Clash by Night*—won the role.

By the close of the 1959–60 season, Desilu continued its decline within the industry as a television-film-production leader, outdistanced by MCA's Revue, Warner Bros., Columbia's Screen Gems, and Four Star. Desilu claimed only one blockbuster series, *The Untouchables,* but held high hopes for its two new ABC situation comedies, *Harrigan and Son* and *Guestward Ho!*—both series, however, were canceled after only one season. The faltering *Ann Sothern Show* was renewed by CBS and General Foods for the 1960–61 season; when, ironically, it was moved midseason opposite ABC's ratings powerhouse *The Untouchables,* ratings plummeted so sharply that the Sothern comedy was dropped before its full thirty-two-episode run. Brightening Desilu's financial picture, though, were filming of commercials, industrial films, and new rental deals for *My Three Sons, The Andy Griffith Show, Miami Undercover, The Hawk, Press Time,* eighteen filmed episodes of *The Jack Benny Show,* and Jess Oppenheimer's new CBS situation comedy, *Angel.* In addition, *The Danny Thomas Show, Wyatt Earp, Lassie, The Real McCoys, Lassie,* and *Barbara Stanwyck Theatre* renewed rental-space contracts with Desilu. Also adding to the company's 1961 revenue would be payment of $1 million from CBS, the remaining sum owed Desilu from the network's 1956 purchase of *I Love Lucy.*

Although the studio's television production of Desilu-owned shows —versus filmed-by-Desilu productions, which did not provide profit participation—was alarmingly low, the company's considerable land holdings, on the other hand, were becoming increasingly valuable. Financier Louis R. Lurie announced he would act as a catalyst for a studio buyout offer from "an unnamed Chicago man well able to make the kind of offer" consistent with the value of Desilu property. Two weeks after the Lurie deal was put on the negotiating table, *The Hollywood Reporter* noted, "The truth of the matter is that Desi *will* and Lucy *won't* sell."

Desi zealously pursued new television properties. He ambitiously— but fruitlessly—pursued John Wayne, Burt Lancaster, and Tony Curtis to headline a "rotating stars" anthology series, with each actor to star in alternate episodes. Desi began negotiations with Mickey Rooney, Patti Page, Janis Paige, Dan Duryea, Jane Wyman, Eve Arden, Eva Gabor, June Havoc, and Phil Harris with wife Alice Faye to star in various Desilu comedy and dramatic vehicles; none were ultimately sold. Desilu and the McCann-Erickson advertising agency formed a partnership to produce a one-hour (eventually discarded) series titled *Counter-Intelligence Corps.* Anso Productions and Desilu vainly attempted to spin off two *Ann Sothern Show* comedies—aging film star Constance Bennett and Tallulah Bankhead's ex-husband, John Emery, in *Always April;* and Pat Carroll in *Pandora and Friend.*

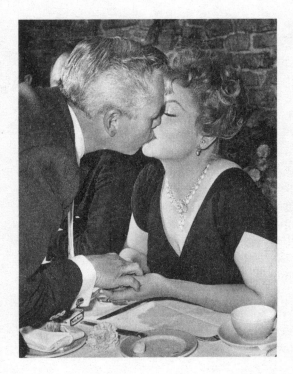

Desi kisses Lucille at the
Facts of Life press
luncheon.
THOMAS J. WATSON COLLECTION

Facts of Life filming commenced with a press luncheon June 2. Making a surprise appearance at the reception was Desi Arnaz, who, said *Variety,* "arrived to wish 'em well, to also plant a kiss on Lucy—who obviously was very happy to see him." At one point, Arnaz noted that he had hired Lucy's divorce attorney, Mickey Rudin, to represent him in a civil suit—"It's just part of my usual pattern," he quipped, "to recognize talent—no matter what was previously done." No longer able to conceal years of personal excess and professional strain, Arnaz's appearance alarmed visiting reporters in contrast to Ball's cosmetically "lifted" countenance; one columnist candidly noted, "Lucy, in a chic black Edith Head gown, looks 35 again. White-haired Desi, in contrast to his ex-wife, is looking his years and more." So cozy were the newly divorced Arnazes at the press party that *Variety* announced, "Lucille Ball and Bob Hope sent a copy of their *Facts of Life* script to Desi Arnaz to try and get him for a guest stint." He quickly declined the offer, explaining that he had "no time" for any feature-film work.

The Facts of Life was a problem-laden production from the start. Production was shut down for one week after Lucille was knocked unconscious during filming—attempting to leap aboard the deck of a power cruiser for a scene, she instead plunged into a three-foot water tank. She was rushed to Cedars of Lebanon, treated, and discharged, then escaped to the Del Mar retreat to recuperate—with ex-husband Desi constantly by her side nursing her various bruises, contusions, and an egg-sized lump on her forehead. While Lucille maintained that there had been "no talk of a reconciliation," friends described the reunion as "very significant."

Arnaz good-naturedly wired Bob Hope a telegram when he first learned of Lucy's accident: I PLAYED STRAIGHT MAN TO HER FOR NINE YEARS AND NEVER PUSHED HER—WHY COULDN'T YOU CONTROL YOURSELF?

Then, only a day after Lucy's mishap, director Melvin Frank broke his ankle at a Saturday golf tournament and was hobbling about the set on crutches. Don DeFore suffered a back injury, was rushed to the hospital, and put in traction after filming a scene while Desilu *Facts of Life* publicist Dave Golding at the same time was temporarily taken off the picture after being stricken with a two-week bout of the mumps. With Ball and Hope to appear together in most of the scenes to be filmed, the producers deemed it "impossible" to shoot around her during her absence and announced a one-week hiatus. Lucille's face and forehead, however, were still so bruised when she reported for work that filming was postponed for another full week; when shooting began anew, seven men were closely positioned off-camera to grab the star if she should take another tumble off the power cruiser. The *Facts of Life* jinx even extended to outsiders—the first day shooting resumed, a drugstore messenger arrived on the set to deliver a prescription to Lucille; he tripped and also fell into the huge tank of water housing the prop boat.

Strange occurrences continued to haunt production. Ball at one point peered around a crowded *Facts of Life* Desilu-Gower soundstage and cracked, "How do you get out of this firetrap?"—eerily, the set caught fire a few nights later and was partially destroyed. After smashing a finger during one take, Bob Hope quipped, "This film should have been shot at Cedars of Lebanon Hospital."

The Arnazes were again briefly reunited—Lucille taking a break from the first day of renewed *Facts of Life* filming—for the company's July 19 second annual report to stockholders. Desilu enjoyed a net profit of $811,559—a jump of 225 percent over the $249,566 net profit of 1959. Arnaz announced the company would invest $360,000 in *Wildcat*—set to open in December—in exchange for 36 percent of the profits after recoupment of the original investment. The deal also gave Desilu full original-cast album rights and television rights for *Wildcat* musical numbers to be featured in a projected television "spectacular" starring Ball—titled *Lucy Goes to Broadway*. To fulfill her Desilu commitment to headline two solo programs during the 1960–61 season, Lucille also announced (unrealized) plans to star with Art Carney in "two or three specials."

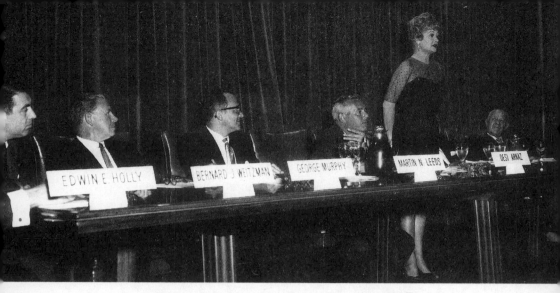

At the July 19, 1960, stockholders' meeting: (*left to right*) Bernard
Weitzman, George Murphy, Martin Leeds, Arnaz, Ball, Charles Schwartz
Arnaz Family Archives

Wildcat, announced Desilu, would premiere in New York in December
1960 as an N. Richard Nash–Michael Kidd production, with a book by
Nash, lyrics by Carolyn Leigh, and music by Cy Coleman; Kidd would
choreograph and direct.

Lucille explained Desilu serving as the sole financier of the stage
production by noting, "I just didn't like the idea, once I'd made up my
mind to do this show, of having to be responsible to a number of
individual backers, including many friends, who were all too willing to
invest in it. Also, the Desilu stockholders weren't too happy about my
stepping out of the TV picture after eight very profitable years. But, by
making Desilu the backer of the show, there is a continuing relationship,
and I am still working for them with the possibility of bringing in more
profits." After Desi gave his report to the stockholders, he said to Lucille,
"You are excused by the chair," prompting her to deadpan, "Where's
the chair?" Arnaz then quipped, "Every minute you're here is costing us
money." Lucille then had difficulty in finding the Desilu-Gower Workshop Theatre exit. "How do you get outta here?" she called to Desi, who
shot back, "You oughta know—you built it!"

While wrapping up *Facts of Life* filming in August, Lucille bubbled
over with enthusiasm over plans for her new life as a stage star. "The
Broadway stage has always been my first love," she insisted. "I never
made it, and I want to prove something to myself. Years ago before I
came to Hollywood I was a showgirl. But just before a new revue or
musical would start, I'd always get fired. I was shy and had no personality—I don't blame them. *Wildcat* is a story about a female wildcatter in 1912. It's sort of a tomboy sort of role. She wants to link up

with the top male wildcatter in the territory and spends the show chasing him."

She admitted, "I'm *terrified* of the musical end of it. But I have some good people who know I'm not a singer and will write accordingly. I'll be doing a lot of cavorting around while I'm singing—and maybe that will keep people from paying too much attention to the quality of my *voice!*" Lucille further stated, "If it's a hit, I'll stay with it a year and a half. I'll take the children and put them in parochial school back there. I'd like to devote about five years to Broadway."

Simmering bad blood between Desi Arnaz and Martin Leeds—aggravated by Desi's drinking escapades and Martin's assuming greater autonomy—publicly erupted a few weeks after Lucille left for the East Coast when *Variety* announced that the two Desilu executives had "a falling out." Arnaz prepared to purchase Leeds's thirty-five thousand shares of Desilu stock—valued at $367,500—and settle his $135,019 yearly salary employment contract, which had several years to run.

Bernie Weitzman, however, says the conflict stemmed from Leeds's "talking to the general public about Desi's drunkenness, which is not a great thing to say to advertising agencies and buyers. It got back to Desi. Martin was running the company on a day-to-day basis, and so he felt that Desi was hurting the company. And Lucy was telling that to Martin, saying, 'We've gotta do something about it.' But, unfortunately, Martin was talking about this to certain people who were also friends of Desi's, so it got back to Desi. Desi finally said to Martin, 'I don't think you should be talking to people about me, the outside people, because it makes the company look bad. You're working for me—I'm not working for you.' He did a lot of things without discussing them with Desi. That's what pissed Desi off. It finally got down to, 'It's either me or you.' And Martin was no longer excited about being under the control of this guy who he no longer respected because of his drunkenness."

Leeds offers, "He phoned me at three o'clock in the morning, dead drunk. I could have turned it around. I always had whenever we had a fight. My wife had died two months before, and I was physically, as well as mentally, exhausted. He said, 'Why did you reverse me?' I said, 'Because you were wrong.' Then he said, 'You're fired.' And I said, 'Thank you very much.' My contract had four more years to go. I settled for half, I could have gotten all. I couldn't hurt this man."

CBS executive Mike Dann notes, "The loss of Martin Leeds was serious for Desilu because he was such a good businessman. He had show-business savvy, was highly professional, and was a great part of the team."

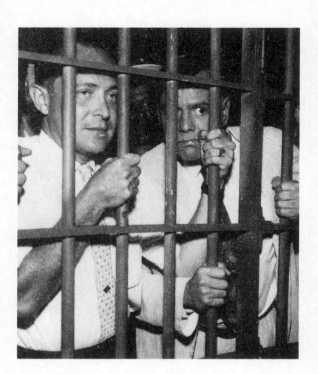

A gag shot of Desilu
executive Martin
Leeds and Desi on
the set of *Desilu
Playhouse*
Courtesy of Bert Granet

Days before Lucille left Manhattan for her six-week Philadelphia *Wildcat* tryout, she dined with *Hollywood Reporter* columnist Radie Harris: "Here in her new surroundings—her beautiful New York apartment at Imperial House—a new Lucy seemed more content and happy than I've seen her in Hollywood the past five years. 'There's an electric excitement in this town that makes you want to get up and do things. Even little Desi and Lucie feel it. On the Coast, they were used to a big house and separate bedrooms. Here they share a room, ride in the subway, ice skate in the park—and you know something? They are happy, adjusted kids, and so is their Mom. I'm mad for everyone in the company of *Wildcat*. Have you ever heard of a cast without a single backstage argument to repeat, all during rehearsals? Well, that's us!' beamed Lucy. 'Give us time. Remember, we have six weeks to go in Philly!' spoke up Lucy's leading man, Keith Andes, as he winked at us across the table. Keith, too, has recently separated from his wife after a longtime marriage. Lucy, realizing his loneliness, often invited him for dinner between rehearsals and this camaraderie has been good for her morale, too."

"She was interested in Keith Andes," confirms Nash. "I don't know how deeply their relationship went, but it was there."

Armed with DeDe and a battalion of domestic help—her own two maids, the children's nurse, driver Frank Gorey, and two automobiles, including a limousine—Lucille settled into her new East Coast home. "I know this sounds like an awful lot of help," she said defensively,

208

"especially when you're going to live in an apartment. But I knew I was going to be very busy and that we would need all the help we could get. Desi, Jr., has been watching the firemen and he's decided he'll be one. And Lucie's going to be a nurse—she's got a pair of binoculars, and she knows every time one of the children in the hospital cries."

Lucie Arnaz, however, recalls her mother's *Wildcat* days with a different perspective. "It was very traumatic, leaving my friends, being ripped away from my father. I only remember those New York months as gray. The trees were gray, the sky was gray, the buildings were gray. I had this thing about limousines. They always smelled. I made it up in my mind that they were slowly trying to poison you. Because I must have gotten a whiff of some dirty leather, or something, and I carried this memory with me forever of this horrible stuff. I look back on it now, and it was just embarrassment. I didn't want to be dropped off at school, or picked up from school, in a limousine. I used to make them meet me way down at the other side of the street. I don't remember getting any other way to drive around, so I guess my mother just ignored it—and I just had to ride in the limousine, kicking and screaming." She adds of those difficult childhood days, "I always wanted to be normal. I didn't want to ride in the limo or grow up with flashbulbs in my face. No one could be more famous than my parents. I didn't dream about being a star—I dreamed about being ordinary, having peace in my life."

Wildcat opened in Philadelphia on October 29, and *Variety* gave the new musical a glowing review. "Surefire for Broadway," predicted the trade paper. "Miss Ball sings acceptably, dances with spirit, shines as a comedienne and even does a couple of dramatic scenes with ease and polish."

"Lucy was very concerned with details," learned Michael Kidd early in the *Wildcat* run. "She had an amazing ability to know exactly what was going on onstage at all times. In the midst of the big production number, she'd come offstage and say, 'Why is Marcia wearing the wrong shoes for this scene? She's wearing the *white* ones instead of the *pink* ones.' We were amazed."

Back in Los Angeles, Arnaz's own contributions to show business were honored by the Masquers at a November 4 testimonial dinner. Guests and dais members included Bob Hope, Red Skelton, Milton Berle, Ann Sothern, Danny Thomas, Fred MacMurray, Ed and Keenan Wynn, Robert Stack, Hugh O'Brien, Barbara Stanwyck, Walter Brennan, William Frawley, Vivian Vance, Andy Griffith, Joanne Dru, Pat Buttram, and Pat O'Brien as toastmaster. At the time, Carole Cook had recently signed to star in a Cy Howard–produced Desilu series pilot, *My Wife's Brother,*

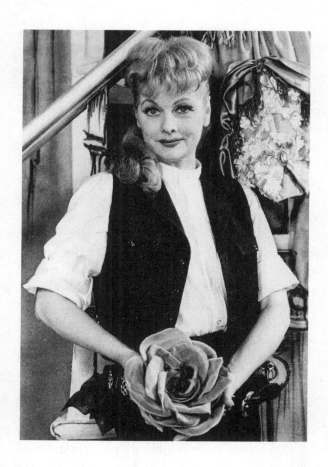

Lucille as Wildcat
Jackson
THOMAS J. WATSON
COLLECTION

with the comedy team of Dan Rowan and Dick Martin. She recalled, "Desi takes such a personal interest—at the testimonial dinner for him, he came over and started talking to me about my series. Imagine—here it was, a dinner for him, and he's talking and getting very excited about *my* series."

At the beginning of *Wildcat* rehearsals, an enthusiastic Lucille revealed, "Professionally, I exchanged Desi for Michael. I needed someone strong—someone I could depend on. I love people who know their business. I bow down to talent." Kidd says of Lucille, "She was a very hard worker. I had the utmost admiration for her work ethics. She never gave less than a full-out performance, all stops out."

"My father produced *Wildcat,*" counters Lucie Arnaz. "He was there and directed them out-of-town for some material and helped her with the scenes and came to the openings. He was there a lot, and they were friendly." Concurs N. Richard Nash, "We had to fight off David Merrick, who wanted to produce it. I told him, 'Well, David, we already have a producer,' and he said, 'Well, what does *Desi* know about it?' In fact, Desi knew quite a hell of a lot about it. He had very good dramatic instincts and was very bright about entertainment and the theater. And he adored her. He would do anything for her, even after they separated."

Despite their divorce, it was clear that Lucille and Desi maintained a strong personal bond. When she discussed her Broadway plans with actor Peter Lind Hayes while dining at "21," she remarked to him, "Desi and I were never happier than when we were working together." She added, nostalgically, "I wouldn't mind doing some more. But Desi wanted to quit." From her table, Lucille telephoned Desi in California to ask his advice whether she should appear on an NBC *TV Guide Awards* special while under exclusive contract to CBS.

Arnaz flew to Philadelphia on November 18 to catch *Wildcat* and spend Thanksgiving with Lucille and the children. As Lucy took her curtain-call bows at the capacity-filled Erlanger Theatre, he tossed an orchid to her, prompting her to quip, "The least you could have done was to take the pins out!" Desi later enthused, "When she is on that stage, buddy, there ain't nobody can touch her."

"My father had very strict rules about what he would let my mother do, and what he wouldn't let her do," reveals Lucie. "He used to tell me, 'When your mother and I were married, I never let her go on a talk show.' Because she was so completely different from what the public thought Lucy Ricardo was like that he didn't want to shock them. He was always protective of her, saying, 'Look, don't tell people that—they *don't* want to know about this part of you.' "

Despite her grueling workload, Desi remained often in Lucille's thoughts. When she took up residence with DeDe, Lucie, and Desi, Jr., in her New York apartment, she immediately put photographs of Desi in the living room, her bedroom, and the children's rooms, where she mused, "Our marriage lasted through innumerable separations, one world war, several private wars, a divorce decree, a reconciliation, two wonderful children, many homes, ranches, not enough money, lots of money"—before, she sadly added, "it all ended in a cold and soggy mess." Lucille's melancholy over her failed marriage as Christmas season approached was somewhat displaced by the box-office success and excellent reviews for *The Facts of Life*. *Time* deemed it "a quick, slick, slyly satirical and sometimes wonderfully nutty comedy of middle-aged manners and middle-aged morals."

Perhaps an omen of trouble ahead, *Wildcat* missed its scheduled Thursday, December 15, Broadway opening. The day after the final Philadelphia performance, three trucks carrying *Wildcat* sets, costumes, and props departed for Manhattan. On Sunday night, a fierce blizzard raged and closed the New Jersey Turnpike, stranding the caravan there until Tuesday afternoon. Joe Harris, general manager of the production, and master carpenter Jim Brennan frantically drove to New Brunswick to locate the missing vehicles after devising a plan to transport the trunks to New York by helicopter—they, too, were lost for several hours during the snowstorm, further creating backstage chaos, until the pair located the stranded vehicles on the turnpike, the drivers sound asleep.

"Look, I'm just a slob—I have no desire to play heavy drama," said Lucille the week of her Broadway opening. "I want to do things with heart in them, yes. That's as much drama as I care about. The technique of getting a laugh fascinates me. I love feeling out an audience every night. What strikes them funny? Why do they remain silent when I expect them to break up?"

Although her *Wildcat* contract would run for only eighteen months, Lucille had nevertheless signed a five-year lease on her seven-room Sixty-ninth and Lexington apartment. "Five years would be too much in *one* show. How long can you have a ball saying the same things and dancing the same steps?"

New York critics indicated she perhaps need not concern herself with a long run—*Wildcat*'s Friday, December 16, opening was not greeted by critics with particular enthusiasm. "Is it simply the unsmiling libretto of N. Richard Nash that makes her seem to be performing by proxy?" wrote *Herald-Tribune* critic Walter Kerr. "The general temperature is mild for a big Broadway fandango, and the rueful silences are many," concluding with, "It's the time, it's the place, where's the girl?" The *Journal-American* offered, "This mishmash could have been conceived on any TV-Western assembly line." The *New York Post* added, "It is good to see the handsome, talented and vital Lucille Ball on the Broadway stage. It would be even better to see her in a good show."

"It was a very tough musical to do," offers Nash. "Lucy worked like a dog. She was really wonderful about it, but she got mad at me a great deal because I couldn't revise enough of it to make it believable that a woman in her fifties was going through these kinds of shenanigans. So we had to pretend that she was in her late twenties. That was the pretense that I think the musical fell apart on."

"Hey, Look Me Over!" proved to be the single smash-hit tune of the show and was eventually inserted into curtain calls at the finale. When Lucille initially signed her *Wildcat* contract, she approached Nash, as he recalls, "and asked if we would consider Sammy Cahn and Jimmy Van Heusen to do the score. I like them and was all for saying yes. Mike wanted some different kind of voice in it. And he said he knew this new team: Carolyn Leigh and Cy Coleman. A script was sent to them, and they flipped over it. Cy and Carolyn played some tunes for Lucy, and she liked it, and so we made the deal, and we were never regretful about that at all. That was their first Broadway show. I think their work was far better than any of the rest of us. If we hadn't had that good score, the musical would not have worked at all." (RCA Victor released a *Wildcat* original-cast recording; only six months after its January 1961 release, the LP brought Desilu sixty thousand dollars in initial royalties.)

However lukewarm were reviews—three favorable notices and four pans in all—virtually no Broadway critic underestimated Lucille Ball's onstage magnetism. "The ovation greeting the frisky lady threatened to reach into next month," wrote *World-Telegram* critic Frank Aston. "And all evening affection ran so high that the last words and notes of specialties were drowned in applause."

Michael Kidd maintains praise for his star: "The thing that impressed me about her was the audience's complete adoration of Lucille Ball. It was their 'Lucy.' At the end of curtain calls, they would shout, 'We love you, Lucy!' as if they knew she was having a hard time and were sympathizing with her. At the end, when she would come out of the stage door, there'd be an enormous crowd waiting, and she would sign countless autographs, and you would hear, over and over, 'We love you, Lucy!' It was their 'Lucy,' it wasn't just an actress named Lucille Ball. I'd never seen that particular kind of unquestioned adoration before. The only other person I can compare her to is Judy Garland."

Lucille vividly recalled the tremendous audience response greeting her, fondly later remarking, "It was one of the biggest thrills of my life— the attendance of thousands of *I Love Lucy* fans was my greatest pleasure. I found myself wishing I had more and better things for them." Adds Ed Holly, "It was a rainy, cold New York night. I waited backstage for Lucy for forty-five minutes after the play ended. The lobby was full of people. I said to Lucy, 'Look, I'll get the manager and clear the lobby out so we can get to the car.' She gave me a dirty look. 'What, and put my fans outside?' She expected them to be there and would have been crestfallen had these hundreds of people not waited to see her. As tired as she was doing the show, she was not going to pass up the chance to be among her fans."

"The show ran on Broadway really on the strength of Lucy's fame and skill," Valerie Harper told *TV Collector* magazine. "When we were on tour, she was kind, she always cared about the whole team, she was wonderful to all of us in the chorus. She got to know everybody's name. When we arrived in New York, even before we opened, Lucy came downstairs to see how we were doing. And she said, 'Oh, my God, what a dungeon! This is terrible! We gotta fix up the chorus dressing room.' And she made it a real point. With unions, it gets painted only so many times. But she said, 'Well, forget it—we'll come in on a Sunday with buckets of our own. Who cares? The paint's falling down, it's dingy, it's a horrible green.' And she had the place painted. She fought it through. She was very direct, very warm, very giving."

"There'd be parties where we'd sing songs and have some fun, and she was one of the group," remembers Joe Harris. "She was exceedingly popular with everybody in that company. They liked her. She was not the big boss, Lucille Ball. She was an amateur. She was at the mercy of the skills of many, many people around her, and she understood it and paid deference to it."

The star quickly discovered that ticket buyers expected to see not her stage characterization but rather an in-person replication of her television persona. Lucille gradually acquiesced to audience demands. "They wanted 'Lucy,' the TV Lucy," she stated. "I came in playing Wildy Jackson in *Wildcat*. But they wanted Lucy. So, after a while, I gave 'em Lucy. It's fine with me. I love Lucy, love doing her. Love the mugging. Saying to a character onstage, 'Say, you know a fellow named Fred Mertz?' They eat it up. I have a ball. Do what I like. Little Mousie, the Yorkshire terrier we use in the show, made a mess onstage one night. I stopped the show, grabbed a mop and pail, and cleaned it up. Told 'em, 'I read the small print of my contract.' They loved it."

"She was desperate for laughs, and so she would ad-lib on stage," concurs Nash. "Sometimes her laughs came off, sometimes they didn't. She would ask me to write laugh lines for her—I was not a gag man by any means. She wanted gags right at the beginning of the show. She was right because audiences came to see her doing those things. Finally, Desi called me and said, 'Do you mind if I bring in Madelyn and Bob?' And I said, 'Look, anything to keep Lucy happy. I know she is up there suffering.' So they came in and wrote about ten or twelve opening gags. She had the most appalling experience—not one of the lines got a laugh. Michael and I went backstage and said, 'It's a different medium, Lucy. It's early in the show, they can hardly hear you, they haven't accustomed themselves to the acoustics of the theater, to your voice coming over the orchestra.' She took all the lines out instantly. That was a bad shock for her. In television, those lines had worked."

During *Wildcat*'s run, Lucille had an unexpected—and bittersweet— encounter. Previously, on yet another trip designed to salvage their marriage during their last months together as man and wife, Lucille, Desi, and the children went to Hawaii. After a heated verbal exchange on the beach, Desi retreated to swim in the ocean. A huge wave engulfed him and ripped off a gold neck chain that held his wedding ring and a Saint Christopher medal. "It was kind of symbolic," she later mused. "Our marriage was gone—so why shouldn't his ring be, too?

"I shouldn't have had time to think about romance, but I missed Desi," she related to Jim Brochu in *Lucy in the Afternoon*. "I even missed the fighting. It was something. I had the kids and I had my work, but I didn't have a rock. I didn't have that one person I could lean on. A very strange thing happened one night after a performance of *Wildcat*. I had been thinking about calling Desi and asking him to come to New York, but I didn't do it." At that precise time, a married couple visited Lucille backstage after a *Wildcat* performance. They told her that they had just returned from a Hawaiian vacation. "The lady opened her purse and pulled out a gold chain with a Saint Christopher medal and a wedding ring. I looked at the ring and it read, 'To Desi, with love from Lucy.' . . . I thanked them, kissed them both, and then closed the door and wept. Just sat there and wept. It's funny, but it was then that I knew it was really over. Having that ring in my hands didn't bring the good times back to me, it brought the terrible times back, and I knew it was right. I knew Desi and I could be friends, but that we shouldn't be married."

"Their relationship with each other was very intense," explains Lucie. "He knew her in a way that I don't think anyone else ever could. And because of that, and because they both didn't have any help in handling their emotions, they could wound each other deeper than anyone else ever could."

Offers Nash, "I'm quite sure she still loved him quite a lot and that he loved her. But she desperately wanted to get away from Hollywood and get away from him. So for her, this musical was a period of major escape. When she got to New York, she went a little wild. Come Wednesday matinee, you'd think she would stay in the theater and have her dinner brought to her and rest. Not Lucy. She would run out and have a dinner date. She'd race back to the theater, run through the evening performance, go out to dinner and then a party. She would frequently not get to bed before four or five in the morning. She was on a treadmill escape. She was deeply, deeply unhappy. Her health began to fail. She came into the production weighing one hundred thirty-five pounds— she left weighing ninety-six pounds."

A vulnerable, lonely Lucille could not have known that a chance December meeting would profoundly change the course of her life. While on a dinner date with MCA agent Danny Welkes at Danny's Hideaway,

Welkes introduced her to his boyhood friend, comedian Gary Morton. "The gentleman didn't register. I didn't even catch his name," Lucille later said. "Paula Stewart, who played my younger sister in *Wildcat,* called me about three weeks after I had first met Gary, to ask me to have dinner with her and her fiancé, Jack Carter, at the Half Moon Pizza Palace. 'There'll be four,' Paula said. 'You and I, Jack, and a friend we'd like to have you meet, name of Gary Morton. You'll like him. He's a great guy.' My first reaction was, thanks but no thanks. 'I'm bone tired,' I told her. 'I feel like a wet mop.' Nevertheless, off I went."

"The first thing I noticed about Lucy was her warmth," said Gary Morton not long after. "The second was her carriage. I mean, she's like a thoroughbred. When she walks into a room, you know she's there." For her part, Lucille said, "Besides liking his looks, I also liked his sense of humor. Before I met Gary, I hadn't laughed in years. I'd made other people laugh, but I hadn't laughed."

After their initial meetings, she recounted, "Gary took off to play a two-week engagement in some godforsaken hamlet in Ohio. While Gary was away, he called me on the phone, or wired me, every day, and when he got back to New York, he continued to call every day. He also called for me at the theater every evening after the show and took me home or somewhere for supper. As a date, Gary was quiet and relaxed, comfortable to be with." Two months later, "when striking a serious note for the first time, but trying to give it the light touch, he asked, 'Would you like to go steady with me, be my girl?' but my instantaneous reaction was, 'Oh, no, I don't think so. I'm not ready yet.' When I fell in love with Desi, it was at first sight—my love for Gary was slow growth. I liked him before I loved him."

Despite their budding romance, Lucille was not above offering suggestions to improve Morton's stand-up comedy act. "I heard him do his act one night at the Concord," she recalled. "One word bothered me. I didn't say anything for weeks. Then he did it again, and I said, 'Guess I'll tell him about the one word he's dropping.' " Gary welcomed her clinical evaluation of his performance. "Criticism of that kind is like coming from the queen. And it worked. I wasn't pronouncing one word clearly. When I corrected it, what was a snicker became a scream."

Ball's close friend Robert Osborne observes, "Gary made her feel like a woman. He made her laugh. It was somebody for her to be with. It's very hard for a woman in that star category—like it was for Judy Garland and Bette Davis—to find acceptable men to be with, because they need somebody around them all the time. If it's somebody of their equal stature in business or career, those men don't have the time to be with them all the time. They need keepers, in a certain way." He adds, "Although Gary was just what the doctor ordered, I don't think the love affair between Lucy and Desi ever ended. She was really a one-man woman."

Further notes Carole Cook, "The pickings were going to be slim for a woman in that position—famous and rich. And, in some areas, certainly, she had gained balls, also. It wasn't like she was a shrinking violet." Or, as Lucille once told her cousin Cleo, she clearly dreaded approaching fifty—"loaded and lonely."

Fueled by Lucille's undeniable star power, *Wildcat* did tremendous, near-capacity to capacity business—despite the critical pummeling. *Wildcat* was a virtual sellout every week—until an exhausted Lucille announced a one-week layoff for the entire production beginning March 27. "She was forever hurting her legs, spraining her ankles," recalls dancer Swen Swenson. "They put her in Levis. She did not look good. I told her about this famous husband-and-wife costume team in New York, specialists for dancers. They were miraculous. They constructed marvelous black jeans, which looked terrific. Then I noticed her feet were not strong. They were almost rounded on the bottom. So I started giving her exercises. Before she'd go on, I'd warm her up—bring her out onstage and give her very simple ballet to strengthen her feet and the legs to get the blood flowing. I'd go down to her dressing room. She'd be hanging over a table saying, 'Swen, I can't go on. I'm *shot*.' I said, 'Oh, *shut up,* Lucy—get your makeup on!' I'd get her out onstage, and then I'd make her do the warm-ups. The curtain would open, and I was literally pushing her out. And she'd work until she dropped."

Close friend Hedda Hopper became alarmed at Lucy's failing health during the run of the show. One performance was attended by "Vivian Vance and Bill Frawley—the night he was in the audience of *Wildcat,* he created a minor sensation. 'It's Fred Mertz!' they all said. I went backstage to see Lucille when Bill came in. When he saw how thin Lucy was there were tears in his eyes."

The announced suspension came about earlier than planned. On February 8 *Variety* reported, "*Wildcat* began an abrupt fortnight's layoff last Monday to permit star Lucille Ball to take a Florida rest on the advice of her doctor. Miss Ball has been suffering from a virus and chronic fatigue"; the musical was scheduled to resume Monday, February 20. Bolstering *Wildcat*'s interrupted momentum with an appearance on *The Ed Sullivan Show* (performing "Hey, Look Me Over!") the night before,

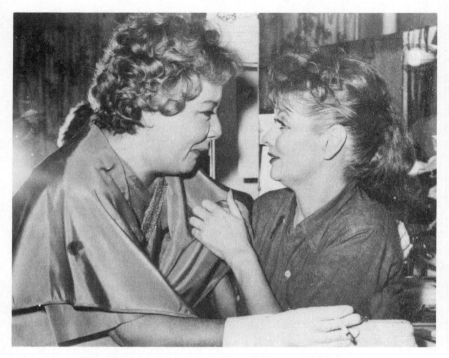

A tearful Vivian visits Lucille backstage after a *Wildcat* performance.
HOWARD FRANK ARCHIVES

Lucille returned to the show on the promised date, and did SRO business but soon announced she would temporarily shut down the entire production beginning the last week of May.

"We became a joke," notes Broadway producer Ronald Lee, who was in the *Wildcat* chorus. "It was the only show that played two out of every three weeks. We never could really get angry at her because we knew she was sick. Exhausted. This was a great, great lady who was a huge star in another medium, and she didn't know what eight performances a week, week after week after week was. She found herself there, with her name above the title, and she was sorry. Perhaps if she had been in an artistic success, she might have felt differently." Further recounts general manager Joe Harris, "She would continually ask, 'What would happen, Joe, if we did less than eight shows?' Of course, if we did less than eight shows in those days, there would not be a profit, which was explained to her. But she did have trouble doing the Broadway routine. She was only forty-nine at the time, so it surprised me that she wasn't strong. We used to have oxygen on the side. She was out of breath doing the show."

Her health further deteriorating, on April 22 Lucille collapsed onstage during her second Saturday performance. Shortly after the beginning of the second act during a song-and-dance routine, Lucille lost her breath and fainted. Her dance partner, Edith King, attempted to break Lucy's fall as she crumpled to the floor but was pulled down and in the process broke her own wrist; assistant choreographer Shelah Hackett assumed the role for the remainder of the night. By the final curtain call, Lucille recovered sufficiently to make a brief speech to the audience. She later announced that she was once again suffering from a "virus infection"— curiously, Desi had been hospitalized in Hollywood, also stricken with a severe virus infection.

Ball's understudy, Betty Jane Watson, took over the role for the remainder of the week, and predictably, ticket sales plummeted. "The musical will lay off following the evening performance next Saturday," advised *Variety*, "so that Miss Ball may rest up for the next nine weeks, prior to the show's resumption August 7." Lucy promised to resume the show in summer and promised to continue *Wildcat* through the end of January. "I can't shake the virus," she said while preparing to depart for Capri. "I need sun. I've got to get out and bake in the sun."

Despite her assurances that she would resume the show in August, Lucy's final *Wildcat* performance was the evening of Wednesday, May 24. "When I went into *Wildcat,* I still had a bad leg from a movie fall," offered Lucille. "We opened in Philadelphia, and I fell again, breaking a finger and pulling a tendon in my leg." With some exaggeration, she added, "They put my leg in a cast for six weeks, which threw my back out of kilter. When the show finally opened in New York, I felt like somebody had stabbed me with a red-hot knife. And the accidents *really* began. First, I fell into the footlights, then off a chair. I blacked out twice—once falling off a derrick and the second time taking another woman down with me and breaking her arm. For months, I spent every Sunday at the doctor's. Then the doc said he wouldn't be responsible anymore, and I was forced to quit." She added, "I gave back a hundred and fifty-five grand at the box office when I closed. And I closed because I had lost twenty-two pounds, and the doctor refused to be responsible anymore with the insurance company. I was very, very ill."

According to Nash's assistant at the time, Ashton Springer, "She was very concerned about everyone else in the company. She didn't want to put anyone out of work. She spoke to the cast and tried to explain, apologize, actually, to the company for leaving." And, adds Nash, "It was plain that she was ill. Though we were all very disappointed, there was no resentment. When she left the show, we had a bigger advance than we had before opening night. We approached Mitzi Gaynor, Ginger

Rogers, Gwen Verdon, and they all said the identical thing: 'Follow *Lucille Ball?* Are you *crazy?*' "

"We really got mad at the musicians' union because when we were on the verge of making a deal with one of the actresses, the union would not allow us to lay off for eight weeks to rerehearse the show. They wanted us to pay full salaries to the musicians. I said to [a union representative], 'We'll have to close the show,' and he said, 'You're not going to close the show, it's a gold mine.' Gold mine or no gold mine, Desi was not going to pay all those salaries and the rental for the theater without a nickel coming in."

Despite the debilitating and disappointing *Wildcat* experience, Lucille did, briefly consider another play—ultimately never produced—based on James Kirkwood's semiautobiographical novel, *There Must Be a Pony,* the script submitted to her by the show's anticipated director, Josh Logan. At the same time, Bob Hope and Vivian Vance signed to appear on her *Lucy Goes to Broadway* television special to be written by Madelyn Martin and Bob Carroll, Jr., directed by Bill Asher, and set to air December 3, 1961; an exhausted Ball, however, abruptly canceled the special in late May, the same week she exited *Wildcat.* The box-office success of *The Facts of Life* having rejuvenated her film career, Lucille began negotiations in April for a three-picture deal with Twentieth Century–Fox. The projected properties were a film version of *Wildcat* and two Jerry Wald productions, *Pink Tights* (also envisioned for Marilyn Monroe) and *Mr. Hobbs Takes a Vacation,* teaming her with James Stewart; redhead Maureen O'Hara eventually was cast in *Hobbs,* the only one of the three films ultimately produced.

By summer, Lucille planned a permanent move to Switzerland, where she and her children would live far way from the ghosts of her failed marriage and *Wildcat* disaster. When Louella Parsons asked her, "Are you going to marry Gary Morton?" Lucille shot back, "Oh, don't talk marriage to me. I've had it." An embittered Lucy said, "Desi never loved me. It took me a long time to realize this," but tenderly added, "He's taken hold of himself and I'm proud of the way he's straightened out his life. Our children are a bond which will always come first." As Lucy planned her departure, Parsons queried, "Are you ever coming back to California?" Lucille flatly replied, "Only if my movie career takes me there."

With Desilu vice president Ball preparing to leave the country, company president Arnaz had to bear the brunt of negative press surrounding his studio's most popular series. As *The Untouchables* grew in popularity, so did the controversy surrounding it. Director of U.S. Bureau of Prisons James V. Bennett objected to an episode depicting corrupt prison officers "toadying to a character like Al Capone," which Bennett deemed "an unforgivable public disservice." Hours before the conclusion to the two-part Capone saga was to air, Bennett warned ten ABC stations—each scheduled for impending Federal Communications Commission license review—that he would launch a nationwide FCC protest and challenge each station's renewal if the program should run. ABC, however, refused to cancel the broadcast, and fury over the crime drama continued.

New York congressman Alfred E. Santangelo accused *The Untouchables* of "seriously injuring the good character and reputation of the greater majority of American citizens of Italian origin" by depicting an inordinate number of Italian gangsters, which, he stated, "greatly distorts history." ABC executives Thomas W. Moore and Alfred R. Schneider promised the series "would not portray a disproportionate number of Italian characters or any other ethnic groups" in a manner defaming those nationalities. After *The Untouchables* production office had closed one night at the height of the negative ethnic-stereotyping controversy, the telephone rang. A stagehand picked up the receiver and was greeted by the voice of a woman with a marked Italian accent who admonished, "If you don't stop showing Italian people as bad people and start showing us as good, peace-loving people, some night, someone is going to throw a bomb and blow up your damn studio."

According to Robert Stack, mobsters "turned their wrath upon the sponsors and Desi Arnaz. Desi received an anonymous phone call threatening to 'blow his brains out' if the program wasn't withdrawn. One of our sponsors, Liggett and Myers Tobacco Company, also had its problems. They discovered that their cigarettes were left on docks all over the country. The head of the longshoremans' union in New York was one of the Anastasia brothers, also numbered among our archcritics. Rumor had it that Liggett and Myers would continue to have shipping problems until they dropped *The Untouchables*. But we were so hot by then that other sponsors jumped in, and we kept right on going."

Underworld assassin Aladena "Jimmy the Weasel" Fratianno later revealed that Desi at one point during the 1959–63 network run of *The Untouchables* became the target of a Mafia "hit" ordered by Sam "Momo" Giancana resulting from "bad publicity" given to gangsters Al Capone and Frank Nitti. Fratianno claimed the order to murder Arnaz was canceled because the hired guns couldn't get close enough. "I don't know how the hell they couldn't get me," said Desi, attempting to dismiss the incident. "I always drove to the studio myself and never had a bodyguard in my life."

Arnaz met with members of the Italian-American League to Combat

Defamation. He promised to no longer use fictional characters with Italian names in future *Untouchables* episodes; he also agreed to more prominently feature government-agent character Nick Rossi. Congressman Santangelo was not satisfied, however, demanding that the program no longer feature real-life gangsters—such as Frank Nitti—in fictionalized situations. Although Arnaz and ABC hedged in making such a commitment, Santangelo abruptly dropped his boycott plans.

Despite the truce between Italian-American groups and ABC and Desilu, an enraged Frank Sinatra abruptly moved his production company off the Desilu-Gower lot to Samuel Goldwyn Studios. "What started as a discussion about Italians on Desilu's TV series, *The Untouchables,* ended up close to fisticuffs," said one observer, who noted that Arnaz inflamed the altercation by calling Sinatra a "television failure." *Variety* reported, "Frank Sinatra and Desi Arnaz almost came to blows at Desi's Indian Wells Hotel when Frank looked him up after midnight to discuss the depicting of Italians as ruthless mobsters on the *Untouchables* programs." To make peace with the volatile singer, Desi made Sinatra a standing offer of $1 million to produce any film of his choice at Desilu. "That's what I think of Frank's talent and ability to draw at the box office," stated a conciliatory Arnaz.

A Senate probe on television violence prompted ABC's Cleveland affiliate station to drop the series; nationwide summer repeats depicting violence were edited to eliminate objectionable scenes. "How dare they tell us how to run our business?" retorted Robert Stack. "How would they have us tell the story of this violent era?"

The Untouchables won four 1959–60 Emmys (including an "Outstanding Performance" award to Robert Stack) and became Desilu's most valuable domestic and international property and was quickly sold to West Germany, Japan, and Australia. Despite the financial windfall derived from the series, Desilu suffered a sharp profit decline—posting a net 1961 profit of $319,146 versus $811,559 in 1960. (Arnaz might well have regretted his sale of *I Love Lucy* to CBS for only $4 million; CBS had recently announced that *Lucy* currently ranked as its top-grossing series in foreign markets—sold in twenty-six countries and dubbed in Spanish, Portuguese, Italian, Japanese, and Swedish—all *prior* to eventual syndication sales.)

Her romance with Gary Morton and a desire to maintain career momentum prompted Lucille to abandon her idyllic—if not implausible— plans to live indefinitely in a Swiss chalet. "I thought I was finished in Hollywood," she revealed. "I came back after the show closed to sell the houses and take the children and move to Switzerland—I even had their schools picked out. I had fallen in love with Gary in New York, and I was thinking about a new life somewhere else."

Instead, Lucille returned to Los Angeles—with Gary Morton—but was nevertheless noticeably absent from the Desilu stockholders meeting, prompting *The Hollywood Reporter* to query, "Why hasn't Lucy Ball called any of the old guard Desilu mob?" Desi advised his ex-wife that he wanted her to star in Desilu film and television productions. "I've finally learned how to rest," she countered. "I haven't gone near the office. I still have to take things easy. When I go out, I have to rest the next day." Rumors of an impending marriage shot through Hollywood. In October *The Reporter* noted, "Lucille Ball and Gary Morton give every indication they are building up to settling down here as Mister and Mrs."

Lucille later revealed, "Prior to meeting Gary—and for some while after meeting him—I had no intention of marrying again, ever. I saw no reason for doing so, nor did I suppose, being at low ebb emotionally, that I would be capable of falling in love again. I doubted that I would allow any attachment to become serious enough for marriage. There would be too many problems—the one looming largest being how the children, who adore their father, would react to, and be affected by, a stepfather."

Despite such reservations, on Monday, November 13, Lucille Ball and Gary Morton announced plans to be married in New York the following Sunday; his previous marriage to actress Jacqueline Inmoor had been annulled in 1957. Lucy visited Hedda Hopper shortly after the wedding details were set. "I like to make someone happy," said Lucy, "and Gary was a likely candidate since he makes me happy."

"Desi has been very sweet and very nice about the whole thing," insisted Lucy. "He certainly has given us his approval."

Accompanied by Jane Kean and Paula Stewart, Lucille and Bronx-born Gary Morton—born Morton Goldapper—obtained their marriage license late Tuesday afternoon at New York's Municipal Building; curiously, Lucy sported the exact salt-and-pepper silk suit and black wool coat she had worn while obtaining her divorce from Desi. On the marriage license, Gary Morton listed his age as forty-four, although he reportedly was ten to fourteen years younger than Lucille. "We talked about being married for several months," Lucy said. "It was after Gary came out to California to visit me that I decided it would be the right thing to do. And certainly the wrong thing to do, just drift along knowing each other when we would all, especially the children, benefit by having a 'great guy' around the house."

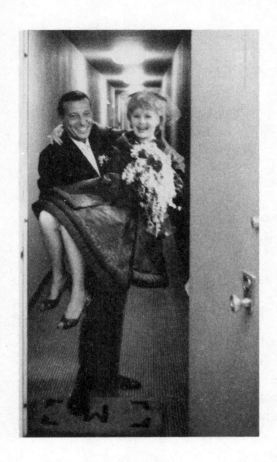

Mr. and Mrs. Gary Morton
THOMAS J. WATSON
COLLECTION

As a crowd of more than three thousand spectators waited outside, Lucy and Gary were married the following Sunday, November 19, by Dr. Norman Vincent Peale in a private ceremony held at Marble Collegiate Church; the dozen attending included her mother, DeDe, and ten-year-old Lucie and eight-year-old Desi IV; Paula Stewart served as matron of honor, and Jack Carter was best man.

There was no honeymoon for the newly married Mortons. The day following the ceremony, Gary jetted to Palm Springs to fulfill an engagement at the Chi Chi Club. His new bride had decided, from this point on, not to attend any of his nightclub performances. "I'll frequently be busy, but even if I weren't busy, I wouldn't go," she said. "Because if you go, people mistake the reason. They don't think you go because you want to be with somebody you like—they think you go to help business." Instead, Lucille climbed into her rehearsal clothes the day after her wedding to work with Henry Fonda for a CBS special titled *The Good Years*.

"Lucy lives in Beverly Hills," Gary told one reporter as they announced their marriage plans, "and we'll lead, like, a suburban life."

"Right, darling," concurred Lucille. "I'm glad you like that."

224

She then looked at her new husband and added, "I'm looking forward to a nice, quiet life."

"She once told me that *the* great love of her life was Desi," recalls N. Richard Nash. "She said she'd known a lot of men and had a lot of men, but the great love of her life was Desi. She said, 'I always thought if I lost Desi, I would die.' I said, 'The word "lost" is a strange word because when you get to a divorced state, frequently it's mutual—you can't really say you "lost" him if you decided to divorce him.' She said, 'It makes no difference.'

"That was a big, big hurt to her. And it embittered her. She loathed the thought of going back to Hollywood. Once she got back into that rat race again, she had to put on a whole new shield—and it was a shield of bitterness. It would affect everything she did from then on."

Chapter Thirteen

"I will never do another TV series. It couldn't top *I
Love Lucy,* and I'd be foolish to try. In this business,
you have to know when to get off."

—Lucille Ball, 1960

*H*er brief honeymoon period over and her dream of Broadway success
suddenly aborted, Lucille Ball concentrated on her film career. Producer
Joe Vogel unsuccessfully sought Lucille and James Cagney for *Here Lies
Ruthie Adams,* a comedy about a psychiatrist who marries a chronic liar.
In December 1961, she signed to costar with Bob Hope in the Warner
Bros. release of *Critic's Choice* based on the moderately successful Ira
Levin play, which, coincidentally, had opened on Broadway the same
week as *Wildcat;* Lucille was also pursued by Columbia to team with
Hope in *The Great Sebastians.* She then planned to return to Desilu in
a domestic-comedy theatrical release titled *Full House* written by Madelyn
Pugh Martin and Bob Carroll, Jr. Based on the real-life Beardsley family,
it concerned a widow with eight children who married a widower with
ten offspring. Desi reportedly purchased theatrical rights in 1961; Lucille,
however, later recalled Desilu Studios first optioning the story in 1959
for a projected Ball-Arnaz film.

On the strength of the announced Ball motion picture—later retitled
The Beardsley Story—Desilu boasted a $2 million production slate for
the first quarter of 1962. Arnaz and programming vice president Jerry
Thorpe announced plans to produce several television pilots for the
upcoming 1962–63 season: a color half-hour comedy series combining
live action and animation; Bobby Rydell in a musical-comedy series titled
Swingin' Together; College Hour, starring Bing Crosby's three sons, Phillip,
Lindsay, and Dennis; and a one-hour domestic comedy, *Fair Exchange*—
based on the premise of two wartime pals and their families, one based
in London and the other in New York City, swapping their two teenage daughters for one year. Arnaz also planned a theatrical feature, *The
Story of Elliot Ness,* with Robert Stack to reprise his *Untouchables* television role.

A pilot episode for a projected *Desilu Comedy Playhouse* anthology program starring Victor Borge was produced as a possible CBS series. Lucille and Gale Gordon appeared in an airplane comedy sketch directed by Arnaz. "She was the one who insisted he direct the program," recalls Gale Gordon. "Because he had a great facility with props. He knew what to do with props. Whenever she had a question about that, she'd ask him. The only person she would have directing her was Desi—even though they were divorced. And he was an excellent director."

At the same time, Desilu entered the syndication market and would also distribute television and motion-picture properties created by other independent producers and series owners. However, the company catalog—without the previously sold *I Love Lucy* or *December Bride*—held only one top-rank title in *The Untouchables;* the other big Desilu draw, *The Lucille Ball–Desi Arnaz Show* comedy hours, were partially owned by CBS and thus could not be included in Desilu's syndicated offerings. Thus, Desilu's inventory was largely comprised of lackluster or aging series such as *Those Whiting Girls, Desilu Playhouse* (minus the *Lucy-Desi* hours), *Guestward Ho!, The Texan, Harrigan and Son,* and *Willy.*

Desilu's real estate holdings were becoming increasingly valuable, and the studio steadfastly refused all offers—including a bid to transform Desilu-Gower into a forty-acre shopping center. "We're not interested in land deals," insisted spokesperson Ken Morgan. "Our assets consist of our land, our studios, and our pictures, and we are not interested in selling off the land piece by piece." Despite Lucille's insistence since her *Wildcat* days that she was not interested in tackling another weekly series, on January 17 *Variety* announced that Desilu and CBS were in negotiations for a new *Lucy* series for the 1962–63 season. The star, however, stymied negotiations when she balked at being given the Sunday slot against the top-rated *Bonanza,* which had that season triggered the demise of Jack Benny's long-running CBS series; she insisted upon the same Monday night berth given *I Love Lucy.* Then, Lever Brothers and General Foods initially hesitated sponsoring the Ball series, said *Variety,* "the deal contingent on the delivery of an okay pilot." Negotiations were completed the first week of March, CBS conceding to give Lucille her prized Monday evening time slot. Lever Brothers and General Foods—without a pilot—signed as alternate-week sponsors.

"Lucy decided to go back to work because the network wanted her," states Gary Morton. "CBS wanted her back. Mr. Paley wanted her back. The network came to her and asked her if she'd like to go back on the air. She only would go back if they held her regular time spot—her spot was the spot that the public was used to seeing her in. That's when they said, okay."

According to Desilu documents, the CBS contract—in addition to her $25,000 yearly salary as company vice president—would provide Ball with "$15,000 to $16,000 per episode and in lieu of any profit participation in *The Lucy Show*." Presumably as a tax shelter, "$10,000 per episode was to be payable to her commencing after the termination of her employment in connection with all episodes of *The Lucy Show* in equal monthly installments over a period of 84 months." Ball's new CBS deal provided her additional compensation for *not* starring in another weekly series on a rival network until September 21, 1970; Desilu financial vice president Ed Holly described the CBS $2.3 million contract for thirty episodes of the Ball series "the highest price ever paid for a half-hour series."

Lucille enthused, "It was a tough decision to make. It took four months to make up my mind. It's a wonderful deal—big, big, the biggest. But it wasn't the deal that prompted the decision. It was the thousands, the tens of thousands of people who wrote asking me to come back to television. Lucy is the character I like playing the most, and that is why I am doing another session of *Lucy*. Lucy has brought me closer to the general public than any role in a movie could ever do. Lucy is understood all over the world—there is no language barrier. This is great for our stockholders, sponsors, and CBS. And that is what they buy."

Ball's return to weekly television was, in fact, triggered by several factors. She was still devastated by her *Wildcat* failure, an ill-suited—but ambitious—attempt to expand beyond her "Lucy" characterization, which she had essayed virtually without respite in various incarnations, from radio's *My Favorite Husband* series until her recent film *The Facts of Life*. Television was the only medium in which Lucille Ball had won unparalleled critical acclaim and worldwide popularity. It was not surprising, therefore, that she would choose to return to weekly television—with Desi Arnaz as executive producer. It was also true that the fortunes of Desilu had peaked with the 1957 purchase of RKO Studios. Indeed, Desilu fully expected to sell CBS the Victor Borge *Comedy Playhouse* series along with the Lucille Ball series, sort of as an unofficial package, knowing how badly the network wanted to secure Lucille's services; after her series negotiations were finalized, however, the network abruptly dropped the Borge series from its projected prime-time schedule.

"They asked me to save the studio," Ball later recalled. "I wondered if there was anything to save. The one salable product we had was *Lucy*."

Despite persistent rumors of network cancellation and sponsor defection resulting from the various negative ethnic-stereotyping and antiviolence controversies surrounding *The Untouchables,* ABC renewed the top-rated series for a fourth season. CBS purchased *Fair Exchange,* starring Eddie Foy, Jr., and Audrey Christie—the one-hour comedy, however, faltered in the ratings, was dropped, and then was briefly revived in a half-hour version for the remainder of the season (due to a letter-writing campaign by loyal viewers) before the series was irrevocably axed.

During the spring and summer, Desilu produced *The Kraft Mystery Theatre* on NBC, a sixteen-week summer replacement for *The Perry Como Show.* Desilu created two game shows, *By the Numbers* and *Zoom.* Programs employing Desilu's production facilities and services included *The Joey Bishop Show; Ben Casey; I'm Dickens, He's Fenster; The Andy Griffith Show; Lassie; My Three Sons; The Real McCoys; The Danny Thomas Show;* and *The Dick Van Dyke Show.* Feature films shot on the Desilu lot included the George Stevens epic *The Greatest Story Ever Told* and *The Caretakers* starring Joan Crawford and Robert Stack.

CBS executive Hubbell Robinson asked Desi to host a prime-time weekly game show for the upcoming television season. Bristling at the demeaning CBS offer, Desilu president Arnaz retorted, "Only if you throw in the Republic lot."

Soon after Lucille signed for her weekly series, Desilu announced that *The Beardsley Story* filming would be postponed until Lucy's 1963 summer hiatus; Lucille campaigned for *My Three Sons* star Fred MacMurray or James Stewart as her leading man. *Critic's Choice* began shooting at Warner Bros. in March, as writers Madelyn Pugh Martin, Bob Carroll, Jr., Bob Schiller, and Bob Weiskopf began writing the first of thirty scripts needed for the new series' first season, production to commence in July following a $65,000 Desilu-Gower soundstage renovation.

Ball's new program was obstensibly based on Irene Kampen's amusing book *Life Without George*—briefly the show's original title—which chronicled the mishaps of two once-married, man-hunting middle-aged mothers. "We have to be without husbands," quipped Lucille. "With so many of our old shows around, we'd look like bigamists!" Desi attempted to discount obvious similarities in the two programs. "We tried to find an area that Lucy had never touched, not in all the years of *I Love Lucy.* And we think this is it—a mother of a teenage girl. Then also the problems of two women with children but without husbands."

Another *I Love Lucy* alumnus, Jess Oppenheimer, surfaced only days following news of the upcoming series. In a story apparently planted by Oppenheimer himself, *Variety* reported on March 6 that Oppenheimer was "reported yesterday returning to the same duties" as Ball's head writer on the new venture. The contradictory *faux* announcement had the writer-producer, however, concede that he had not "been approached directly" for the job. "I'm always interested in what Lucille Ball does," stated Oppenheimer in his rather obvious—albeit unsuccesful—bid for employment on the new series; his ego clashes with executive producer Arnaz during *I Love Lucy* certainly undermined his chances.

Executive producer Arnaz assigned Jack Donohue as director of the series—for a time titled *They Love Lucy,* a reference to her two on-camera children. Subsequently, Elliott Lewis—husband of *I Love Lucy* occasional supporting player Mary Jane Croft—was chosen as Lucille's series producer, following his producing Desilu's *Kraft Mystery Theatre;* Lewis also had worked with Lucy on *My Favorite Husband* and had directed the Arnazes on a *Suspense* radio broadcast.

Ball's new show might well have been designed as a single-season endeavor to significantly bolster the studio's sagging fortunes, Arnaz declaring not long after that he would produce six Ball specials—based also on the *Life Without George* premise and characterizations—for the 1963–64 season. Concurrently, Desilu executive Ed Holly admitted that the studio had experienced recent financial problems: "We tightened our belts and cut four hundred thousand dollars from the overhead." As one example, to cut $20,000 per-episode union penalties and overtime costs resulting from expensive evening filming, *The Untouchables* began shooting nighttime scenes during less-costly daytime hours by placing black muslin over camera lenses.

Not all of *The Untouchables'* problems were so easily solved. The violence-ridden series had sparked hearings by the FCC and congressional committees. Responding to such criticism and forced to tamper with the show's solid success, Arnaz brought aboard *Route 66* producer Leonard Freeman. The new executive producer vowed that *The Untouchables* would be devoid of "violence without motivation." He added, however, "To give gangsters their due, I don't think they went around killing without reason." Robert Stack heatedly objected to the many changes imposed upon his series: "The criticism of *The Untouchables* is a paradox—it's because the show is successful. If it weren't, there'd be no need to criticize." He bitterly noted, "Television is a completely ruthless business. It's a dollars-and-cents biz, and you have no control over your destiny, because you're selling merchandise. You can't please everyone, and if you try, by doing something for a sponsor each week and the network the next, you soon end up with nothing."

The toned-down *Untouchables* perhaps satisfied members of the FCC and an ongoing Senate probe on excessive television violence, but appealed to few viewers. As ratings for the once top-ranked show plummeted, Arnaz moved swiftly and returned the crime drama to its original successful formula. "I don't like violence for violence's sake," Desi insisted. "I don't think *The Untouchables* originally had too much violence, because we are portraying an era of violence. If we do a story on the St. Valentine's Day Massacre, they weren't throwing flowers at each other that day." Answering the charge that the program also displayed excessive erotica, Arnaz countered, "I don't think there is too much sex on TV— I don't think there's *any*." Leonard Freeman exited *The Untouchables* after only thirteen episodes.

While *The Untouchables* controversy continued to swirl, Lucille actively campaigned for Vivian Vance to once again serve as her television sidekick. In January 1962, recalled Vivian, "Lucy came East with a script in her purse for a new series for me. I said, 'Lucy, don't take it out. I won't read it.' And she didn't. And I didn't." Despite Lucille's repeated pleas, Vivian refused to consider resuming her television career and relocate to Hollywood from her new home and new husband in Stamford, Connecticut.

In 1959 she had been sued for divorce by Phil Ober, who charged Vance with "mental cruelty." In his complaint, Ober asked for half of the couple's community property, estimated at $160,000; when asked by the presiding judge whether she thought the split to be equitable, Vance retorted, "No, sir, I think the terms are pretty liberal—after all, I made and saved all this money!" That summer, Vivian met literary agent John Dodds, six years her junior, at a party hosted by *Guestward Ho!* co-author (with Patrick Dennis) Babs Hooten. Dodds proposed soon after, and on January 16, 1961, the two were married on the Hooten ranch.

Following the Arnaz and Vance divorces, Cleo and Ken Morgan divorced, Cleo later wed to Los Angeles *Times* television-critic Cecil Smith. Madelyn and Quinn Martin had also divorced, reportedly due to his extramarital affair with *Untouchables* starlet Barbara Nichols. "You all did it because *I* did it," Lucille often remarked to Cleo, who adds, "and she was *serious!*"

With Vance still vacillating on returning to weekly television, Ann Sothern and Gale Storm were alternately considered for the supporting role. Eventually, Vivian agreed to commute weekly to the West Coast if several conditions were met: Unlike her *I Love Lucy* years, she would no longer be contractually obligated to remain twenty pounds overweight for filming and would furthermore be allowed a more flattering wardrobe in contrast to her frumpy, drab Ethel Mertz garb.

One unresolved issue remained important to Vance before signing her Desilu contract. "Before the contract was signed, I had a talk with Desi," recalled Vivian. " 'I'll come back,' I said, 'but I want a clause that says my name will be Vivian.' 'Okay, Veev, I understand.' He had run up against a similar problem as mine with Ethel. For nine years, he'd been Ricky Ricardo and lost his own identity. [Lucy] was to have a six-year-old son and a teenaged daughter, while 'Vivian Bagley' had a ten-year-old boy. I had some reservations about that, but there was no way around them. I remembered Desi, Jr., as a child having a difficult time seeing another boy play the Ricardos' son. 'Who's that?' he'd ask Desi and Lucille. 'Is he like a brother?' "

Initially, Ball and Vance were to portray divorcées, the roles soon rewritten as a pair of widows. Ultimately, Lucy Carmichael would be a widow with a fourteen-year-old daughter, Chris (Candy Moore), and a seven-year-old son, Jerry; she shares her suburban Westchester County, New York, two-story home with boarders Vivian Bagley, a divorcée, and her twelve-year-old son, Sherman, played by Ralph Hart. Jimmy Garrett vividly recalls his audition for the part of Lucille's wisecracking, pre-cocious son, Jerry: "They held callbacks on Stage Fourteen of the old Desilu-Gower lot. Lucy and Viv were there. Lucy made a point of trying to direct everything and get more out of the kids. She'd say, 'Try it *this* way.' I was directable—she could get me to do things—I had been acting since I was nine months old. All the kids were standing around in a group outside of the lot. Someone came out and read the names of the kids they wanted to stay. Lucy, I don't think, was pleased with the girls that they had picked. They picked Ralph Hart and myself. We didn't know who was going to play her daughter, Chris, until we went in Monday for rehearsal."

Recalls Candy Moore, "Lucy evidently had combed Hollywood for a kid and couldn't find anybody that was right for her. Elliott Lewis, the producer, called me at home and told me to come in and meet her. I had just done a year of *Donna Reed,* playing virtually the same giddy teenager on that show. I met with Lucy and Elliott on a Friday in the producer's office at Desilu. She had me read. I had the upbeat, vivacious, outgoing persona she wanted. She said, 'You've got the part.' That was it. She said, 'Let me meet your mother.' I guess she wanted to see if my mother was going to be a problem. My mother had been a model, very sophisticated, a dynamic person. Lucy liked her right away. She said to her, 'We're interested in your daughter.' My mom said, 'Great.' Lucy said, 'Monday.' "

According to Jimmy Garrett, "Lucy was absolutely lovely to me, as was Vivian. I only remember seeing her mad once that had anything to do with me. The first season the next-door neighbor was Dick Martin. I adored him. He was terrific, the coolest guy I had ever met. On Thursday nights before the filming, we'd all sit in the green room they had at the corner of the stage. I'd sit on Dick's lap, and he'd tell me stories. I was enthralled. One Thursday night, my mom had to go somewhere else, to the dressing room or someplace, and while she was gone, Dick gave me a sip out of his can—which was a beer—and gave me a couple of puffs off his cigar. And I'm seven years old. During this particular episode, I had to come in and give Lucy a good-night kiss. Now after a couple of puffs of cigar and a beer, I come in and give her the kiss. She continued with the scene, but I'll *never* forget the look in her eye. I'm sure I reeked—and she knew why. You heard her through the entire soundstage, yelling, '*DICK—MY DRESSING ROOM!*' That night when we got home, my mom had a talk with me, and Dick *never* gave me any more beer."

Candy Moore was surprised at Ball's acute anxiety directly prior to facing the live studio audience. "She'd be so nervous, you couldn't talk to her," she recalls. "I would talk to her sometimes before the show. It was scary—she'd be looking at me, and she wouldn't hear a word I said. She was tuned in to her own thoughts, and she'd be looking right through me. Vivian was a nervous wreck, too. They were buzzing on adrenaline, they were so scared. I still see Lucy with that glazed look in her eye before the show. I would think, '*What* is this woman so nervous about? Everybody *loves* her.' It never ends—we never get used to being successful."

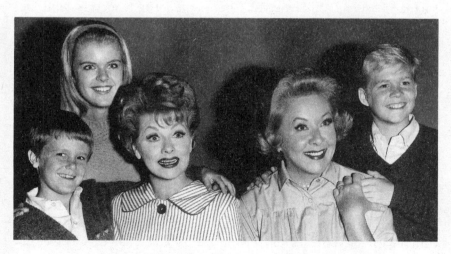

The cast of *The Lucy Show:* (*from left*) Jimmy Garrett, Candy Moore, Lucille, Vivian, and Ralph Hart
THOMAS J. WATSON COLLECTION

The young actress initally was taken aback at Lucille's startling facial transformation from her casual appearance during rehearsals in contrast to her heavy stage makeup and the temporary "face-lift" provided by surgical adhesive tape and nylon netting concealed under her bright orange-red wig. "Lucy was a very lovely looking woman. I never understood her wearing that. I still see her with that netting they would put on her, Scotch-taping her face up, essentially. And then they put the wig on over it. And it stays maybe a few hours."

The on-camera mother and daughter had a pleasant, but not particularly close offstage relationship. "She was warm and tender toward me, but it just didn't go too far. I never could feel like she was my friend or confidante. I never felt she was my surrogate mother—and I'm sure she never thought I was her surrogate daughter. She just didn't have that knack to make people feel relaxed with her. Watching her relate to her own children, I knew, in a sense, that she just didn't know how. She'd say things like, 'I'm not raising you to be a *do-nothing!*' when she wanted little Lucie to put on plays and do things. That was the authoritarian side of her. The other side of her, she adored those children."

When rehearsals for the first episode of *The Lucy Show*—abridged from *The Lucille Ball Show*—commenced on July 12, Desi presented Lucille with a kiss and a good-luck emblem of a tiny four-leaf clover crafted from antique emerald jade. "It was a fabulous piece of jewelry," recalls Candy Moore. "But that wasn't the point. The point was that he adored her to that extent that he was thoughtful enough to give her such a smashing gift. She cried. They had a lot of tenderness and love between them." Desi climbed a soundstage catwalk and watched Lucy rehearse a scene, prompting him to break into tears. Vivian went to him, and the two embraced. "Oh, Desi," she sobbed, "it isn't the same, is it?" As she later observed, "Here we were, starting again, only this time he was on the outside looking in, and it wasn't fun anymore. So much had happened to so many people, but most of all to Desi, leaving him alone and a little sad, although he tried to hide it."

Executive producer Arnaz apparently was affected not only by bittersweet memories of another era but by his increasingly severe alcoholism. "He seemed very grim and distracted in a strange way," observes Candy Moore. "There was a part of him that wasn't there anymore. Maybe his heart wasn't totally in it. He seemed chronically distracted. Although he never really did anything, he seemed like he was seething and almost about to explode. He had a drinking problem. He was hung over." Adds Bob Weiskopf, "When he was drunk, he was a different person. He would often get nasty"; and, as writing partner Bob Schiller further observes, "It was very painful for Desi to have Gary on the set."

As Lucie Arnaz notes, "When my mother came back to television, my father directed and produced *The Lucy Show*—and she was married to Gary Morton, who's doing the warm-up. My God, that's really psycho. There were these three years, that crossover period, where they tried— 'Okay, we *won't* be married. We won't change anything. I can have my women. She can have whoever she *wants*. Fine, maybe it's better this way. Sure, let's try that.' See how long *that* works when the two people are still madly in love with each other."

Aware of his addiction—and anguish—Lucille remained protective of Desi. "He would be on the set and fall asleep during rehearsals," recalls Moore. "And she, rather than wake him up, would send the assistant director over to him and have him *pretend* to trip on his feet, so that Desi would wake up and think he woke up on his own—she was very tactful with certain people and could be very gentle."

On the other hand, Lucille's brother, Fred—who had returned to Desilu at the start of production on *The Lucy Show*—was sacrificed when forced by his sister and other executives into a direct confrontation with Arnaz to alert him that his drinking was increasingly affecting his professional conduct. "They decided someone had to talk to Desi," recalls Bob Schiller. "Fred went over to him and said, 'There's been a lot of talk around the studio, that you're not really running the studio.' Desi says, 'I'll tell you who's running the studio—you're *fired!*' "

The first year of *The Lucy Show*—far superior to its subsequent five seasons and, in essence, largely a continuation of the original half-hour version of *I Love Lucy*—placed particular emphasis on physical-comedy and slapstick routines, centered around a logical premise. The first episode had Lucille bouncing on a trampoline; later shows had her walk on stilts to gain access to the top mattress on a bunk bed; operate a home-kitchen caramel-corn business; run an all-female volunteer fire department, and, with Viv's assistance, attempt to install a television antenna. "She was an absolute kick to work with," recalls Tommy Thompson. "On one occasion, she was putting an aerial up on the roof. She was supposed to stand on the chimney, and it caved in with her. So she said to me, 'Get up on that chimney and let them pull that trap'— they had a trap with springs on the bottom. She said, 'Get up there and do that for me.' I got up, and they pulled the trap. And just in watching someone doing something, she would know what made it funny. I was in terror, but she could see what twist, what body movement and expression, could make it funny."

On a subsequent episode, "We put them in a shower," recalls Madelyn

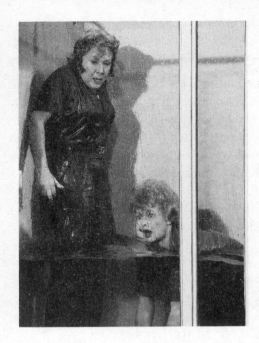

"Lucy and Viv Put in a Shower"
THOMAS J. WATSON COLLECTION

Pugh Martin. "They were fixing the shower, and they got the water on, which then kept the shower door from opening. The water kept rising. That's a pretty good stunt for girls. They did it. Boy, they were sports. It was marvelous. But we could take for granted that the special-effects men would build a shower that would work but wasn't dangerous. It must have cost a fortune. Desi never said, 'That's too expensive.' If he told them he wanted something, they'd find a way. So he was a lot of protection. And we knew that Lucy and Viv would do it. And nobody ever said, 'I'm not doing that.' Lucy would do anything."

"During rehearsals, the writers would sit up in the audience bleachers, and you could hear the four of them laughing," says Jimmy Garrett. "That's how you knew it was working, because you could hear the writers laughing. I was really amazed that they got such a kick out of their own material." The four writers were not always so convivial. "When [Bob Weiskopf and I] signed for *The Lucy Show,* we negotiated a small piece of the profits," reveals Bob Schiller. "One day, I happened to mention it at a story meeting. Bob and Madelyn shut down. They said, 'Will you *excuse* us?' "

"They had the same writers as *I Love Lucy,* and they were so used to a formula," says Garrett, "that I got a lot of the 'Fred Mertz' lines. I was the real grumpy, skinflint kid. One show, I had what Vivian liked to call 'a Fred line.' After the show, she picked me up and gave me a big hug. She said, 'You got a great laugh on that line—and you're a lot cuter than that old *poop!*' " He adds, "It was always sad for me to see William Frawley walking around the lot—he was on *My Three Sons* next door. He was very ill, not as spry as you think of him on *I Love Lucy.*"

236

The redhead grew impatient at constant press reports comparing her new venture to *I Love Lucy*. "They don't seem to understand that I'm not trying to prove anything, and nobody's out to top *I Love Lucy*," she said testily. "I don't mind these TV critics wondering if I can make it a second time on TV, but do they have to do it out loud?" Lucille also revealed how deeply her *Wildcat* failure had impacted her decision to remain firmly anchored to her comfortable and secure television characterization: "Sure, you get tired and decide you want to look around for other things to do. But after a while, you find there aren't so many other things. Most of the movie offers I get are for roles which take me too far away from my Lucy character. The stage keeps me from my kids too much. So here I am, and as long as people want to laugh, I want to be in there punching. I don't want to retire."

At the opening of the annual August Desilu stockholders' meeting—held at the former site of Lucille's Desilu Workshop Theatre—Arnaz greeted the 250 stockholders and then sank into an overstuffed leather chair, quipping, "It's so low, I disappear." Desi painted a bright picture of Desilu's future, prompting one stockholder to remark, "A broker said I'd be a fool to buy Desilu stock, but after today's meeting, I think I'll buy more." Desi cracked, "Let me have his name—he's probably working for Xavier Cugat!"—referring to the long-standing gag feud between Arnaz and the Latin bandleader.

Arnaz proudly proclaimed Desilu's 1961 net income had soared to $611,921, compared to a 1960 figure of $319,146—largely derived from the March 1962 sale of thirteen *Lucille Ball–Desi Arnaz Comedy Hours* to CBS for $750,000 as part of the network's deal to secure Ball for a weekly series. After Lucille made her entrance to applause during Desi's prepared speech—causing him to grumble, "As I was *saying* . . . "—Arnaz then introduced Desilu's new legal counsel, Mickey Rudin, prompting Desi to quip, "He was so good representing Mrs. Arnaz in our divorce, I thought he should be working for both of us." He then turned to Rudin and good-naturedly muttered, "You *bum*." During the meeting, television pioneer Arnaz rather shortsightedly advised stockholders that he opposed the notion of filming Ball's new series in color, despite the boom in sales of color-television sets. "She's just as funny in black-and-white," he insisted.

Desi also deftly deflected suggestions that he team on-camera with his ex-wife for her upcoming series. "I love to work with her," he said, "but I am producing her show, and with my other duties, I don't think I will be able."

Notes attorney Art Manella, "I never felt that I had to make a choice

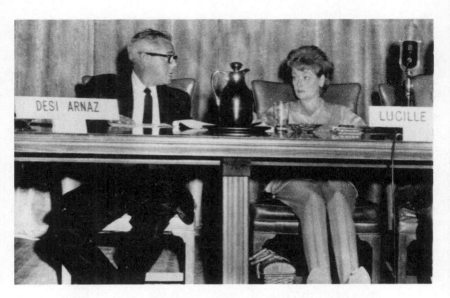

The August 22, 1962, Desilu stockholders' meeting
THOMAS J. WATSON COLLECTION

between Lucy and Desi. In fact, on the contrary. Lucy knew I did work for Desi. Desi knew I continued to represent Lucy. Many times, she would say, 'Well, you've gotta help Desi out—have you talked to Desi about this? I understand he's having a problem with this, why don't you see if you can be of help to him?' Lucy was just that kind of person. She cared about her children, her husband, she cared about the people who worked for her, she cared about her friends. She wasn't effusive, nor was she overly emotional about it. But she really cared about Desi. It was important to Lucy that people that she loved and grew up with were part of her life. Even when they were divorced, I think she still loved Desi. She worried about him. She wanted to do whatever she could to help him."

Lucille, however, often became impatient with Desi in business matters. When he once asked his former wife whether he might suspend nine-hundred-dollar-per-month child-support payments in view of her exceedingly robust financial state, Lucille sweetly replied, "Of course you can—if you're willing to go public about it." Desi dropped the issue.

Friction between the estranged couple over child custody had soon surfaced in the months following their divorce. "Now the children get to enjoy their father for long periods and as often as convenient for him," said Lucille with a trace of resentment. "They love his ranch, his horses, his bunk beds, his racing cars, his beach house, his fishing sprees, his racetrack, his golf tourneys. In fact, life with Desi these days is a bowl of cherries. One good time after another. I'm not complaining. I accept it. But their days with me are the drudgery days—the school-

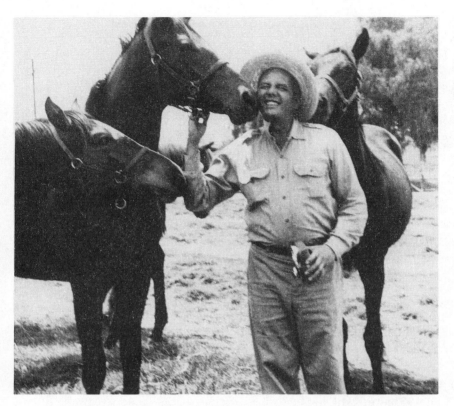

A carefree Desi away from his Desilu responsibilities at his Corona, California, ranch
ARNAZ FAMILY ARCHIVES

days, the doctor, the dentist, the 'Do your homework' and the 'Go to bed early' and 'Take your medicine for the cold you caught at Desi's ranch' days."

Desi, Jr.'s days with his father were not always a positive experience, however. As Johny Aitchison recalls, "At Del Mar, he was teaching little Desi how to shoot a gun. The poor kid wasn't doing it right. His dad just lit into him, yelling, 'You motherfucker, can't you do *anything?*'" Of Desi's personality shift when affected by alcohol, Lucie Arnaz recalls, "He would be very jovial, a terrific host. He would sing, he'd be very outgoing. But he'd also lose his temper. He wouldn't understand things clearly. He would misunderstand situations. He would think people were talking about him. He would hear something and think he heard something else. When it was at its worst, he'd blow up. If the TV was on too late, and it was bedtime, instead of saying, 'It's bedtime,' doors would crash. It was awful. It was terrible. Then he'd be terrifically sorry and feel awful. After I got a little older, I stopped going down there."

Lucille—very briefly—shunted her son to St. John's Military Academy in Northridge, located near the Arnazes's Desilu Chatsworth ranchito.

239

She explained, "He travels about fifty miles every morning, which he fights with all of his little ways, such as running hot water on thermometer to prove he has temperature of one hundred eight degrees." More harshly, she later recalled of the school, "They held him on weekend detentions for eight hours a day—he had to sit bolt upright the whole time. He was having nightmares at night. He couldn't sleep. I said, 'What's the *matter* with you?' He said, 'They gave me detention for tying a shoelace during drill when I was supposed to be at attention.' I said, 'Oh, *come* on!' And he told me that thirteen-year-old 'generals' were giving these bullying orders. I took him out of that school. He went to Beverly Hills High. My God, he'd come home hungry, tired. The poor waif. So I took him out of that school, too." Lucille also was faced with a formidable and strong-willed twelve-year-old daughter. "I must admit that Lucie does intimidate me," she once admitted. "Any kind word from her, I fall down!"

Despite the obvious, and expected, difficult period of adjustment facing her two children, Lucille publicly maintained that, from the start, Desi IV and Lucie were virtually untouched by the tremendous emotional and domestic upheavals in recent months. "For a long time, there wasn't any reaction," she insisted, "because they hadn't seen very much of Desi in the preceding three years. They were used to his being away. Then, in this last year, Lucie saw *The Parent Trap* four times and worked giddily toward a happy ending of her own. Which made me realize, first of all, they certainly didn't know the problems—and there was just so much I could explain—and I am resigned to being the 'heavy' for several years."

"So many years she tried not to get divorced, that once they finally did the official thing, it was just a relief," notes Lucie. "She was exhausted, he was exhausted. She wasn't pleased, but I'm sure she never saw it as a possibility that it could be resurrected. And, of course, she was almost immediately remarried to Gary, which left little hope for a reconciliation. That didn't stop us. We *still* showed her *The Parent Trap*. Gary sat there and watched it every time we showed it to her. 'Don't you love this part, Gary, where they get back together at the end?' 'Oh, yeah, that's my favorite part!' He was a good sport, I must say. He never said a bad thing about my father. Gary was always a great supporter of my father's. I think he secretly wanted my father to teach him the business so that he could try and take his place. And he was always nice to my father, which must have pissed off my dad, because he wanted to hate this man—and he never did anything to incite my father's anger. He let Dad kid him mercilessly—he was great about that.

"It's not easy to be a stepparent. But he didn't have a lot to complain about. He got the best of the deal. He really stepped into a great, great place. My mother was at her absolute bottom socially, apparently from those episodes with my father. They weren't invited to parties anymore. When she married Gary, he was a hero. They were back on the circuit again. They could have friends over. So, everybody appreciated that Mom had somebody who could make her laugh. I don't think anybody thought it was a great love affair. I hope it was. I like to think that it was."

Lucy held tight reins on Gary Morton's outside career. As New York *Daily News* reporter Kay Gardella wrote of one interview session, "Almost too politely, he took a seat opposite Lucy. His manner indicated he did not want to intrude. Frequently, he had to be prompted by his wife to talk. 'Nightclubs are dying,' explained the comedian, who had just finished an engagement at the Copa. He no sooner said this than the phone rang. It was for Morton. After the conversation, he turned to Lucy and said lightly, 'That was an offer for a job in Milwaukee.' 'Forget it,' replied the redheaded tycoon, with a wave of her hand. Morton did."

Despite the convivial facade of Desi working amicably alongside his ex-wife, he loathed Morton's supplanting him as Lucille's husband. "He was extraordinarily jealous of Gary and didn't hide it very well," says Lucie—who also remembers her father invariably referring to Gary Morton as "Barry Norton"—perhaps a reference to an obscure Argentinian-born actor. Johny Aitchison recalls "a golf tournament in Corona. Gary was involved, as was Desi, whose car was on the fritz. I was driving a Volkswagen at the time, and he had never ridden in one, so I said, 'This is your chance.' I took him to the tournament. I'm driving in, and they're all looking at us in this little Volkswagen. He didn't realize Gary was going to be there. He then found out Gary was there and said, 'You better call the ranch manager and tell him to drive me over in *his* car.' He had a bigger car, to take Desi to the tournament—he didn't want Gary to see him in a Volkswagen."

Personal tensions were perhaps somewhat momentarily eased by generally enthusiastic critical reaction to *The Lucy Show*'s premiere episode. Said *Daily Variety*: "Lucille Ball is back and welcome." *The Hollywood Reporter* countered, "It's going to take a lot of getting-used-to-Lucy without Desi. His absence was felt, tribute indeed to any comedian." Critic Edith Efron offered, "To discover a Desi-less Lucy on the screen is like finding a revised edition of *Gone With the Wind* in which Scarlett O'Hara appears without Rhett Butler."

Although future episodes often featured neighbor Dick Martin, pointed criticism from critics, network executives, and agency executives

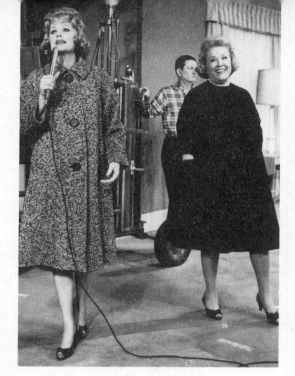

Lucille introduces Vivian
to the studio audience
after filming "Lucy
Becomes a Reporter."
THOMAS J. WATSON COLLECTION

over the series premise of Lucy and Viv—two single, middle-aged women living under the same roof sans men—prompted industry wags to derisively dub the Ball series *The Dyke Sans Dick Show*—patterned after Desilu tenant *The Dick Van Dyke Show*.

Ball's return to weekly television was nevertheless a ratings triumph, her premiere episode the top-rated show of the week. As *Variety* noted, "No one at the agencies or networks can single out one outstanding show unless it's the return of *Lucy*." Desilu placed two-page advertisements in *Variety* and the *Reporter* with selected, highly favorable review quotes and top-ranked Nielsen ratings figures—featuring an *I Love Lucy* stick-figure drawing of Desi Arnaz and the bittersweet caption: HOW DO YOU LIKE THAT—THEY DIDN'T EVEN MISS ME!

On the strength of the new *Lucy* series, Desilu in late October announced "a sum conservatively estimated at $1,000,000" for the production of 1963–64 pilots. Projected series candidates included an Ethel Merman situation comedy with music, and situation comedies featuring Nancy Walker, Glynis Johns, Julie Newmar, and Gale Storm. Arnaz also planned an anthology series dramatizing the adventures of people who immigrated to the United States, "made good, and contributed to the growth of the country." Also in development was a western series, *High Horizons,* and two spin-off series derived from *The Untouchables,* one starring Barbara Stanwyck as a tracer of lost persons, and *The White Knights,* with Dane Clark and Joseph Schildkraut, detailing exploits of the Public Health Service. Desilu would further explore live television, Ralph Andrews and William F. Yagemann creating the game show *You*

Don't Say? and named as heads of a new "live programming" division.

Desilu also acquired rights to film a television series based on the 1952 Paramount circus drama *The Greatest Show on Earth,* which had starred James Stewart, Betty Hutton, Cornel Wilde and—briefly—Lucille Ball. Arnaz negotiated the deal for the pilot, starring Jack Palance, to be a coproduction with ABC; the network purchased the series for the 1963–64 season. Jess Oppenheimer, who had recently produced a Danny Kaye NBC special with Lucille as guest that snared her a record $100,000 guest-star fee, began negotiations with Desilu to create and produce programs under the banner of his own independent production company.

Two weeks after Arnaz announced Desilu's ambitious 1963–64 production slate, industry insiders were stunned when on Friday, November 9, 1962, it was announced that corporate president Desi Arnaz had abruptly departed the studio, with Lucille Ball installed as the new president of Desilu Productions—*Variety* noting it was "the first time in Hollywood history a femme has been prez of a major telefilmery. Only other woman who was prexy of her own company was Mary Pickford, who some years ago formed her own indie for theatrical films."

Reported *Variety,* "Telefilm's oldest partnership ended yesterday when Lucille Ball bought out Desi Arnaz's stock interest in Desilu Productions, Inc., for a sum estimated at $3,000,000. Miss Ball is buying the 300,350 shares of Desilu stock owned by Arnaz, which ups her total holdings to 600,650 shares, or 52% of the total outstanding stock of Desilu. Arnaz also quit as director of the company, and henceforth will have no association with it. He was executive producer of *The Lucy Show* and relinquishes this also. Associates of the pair indicated the break-up was due to a number of factors. Arnaz wanted out for some time, but didn't care to exit last season, when studio fortunes were at a low ebb."

"I quit the business because it got to be a monster," said Arnaz. "At the beginning, it was fun, but when you are in charge of three studios, with three thousand people and thirty-five soundstages working all the time, the fun is long gone." He added, "The funny thing is that I never cared that much about making money just for the sake of making money. I wanted to be able to take care of my family and live well—which I've done."

Lucille maintained, "Desi has wanted to sell out for five years, and I had first refusal on the stock. It's a big and wonderful company—the real estate alone is worth six million—and I didn't want to close up shop and hand over my shares to a stranger. That's why I did what I did. It's not necessarily what I wanted."

The actual reasons prompting Desi's departure, however, were far darker and far less amicable than Lucille and Desilu press releases indicated. "At the time of going public, we worked out between Lucy and Desi an agreement where each one would have a buy or sell option on the other's stock," explains Desilu's Ed Holly. "Meaning that one could buy the other out at the stated price and had a period of time in which to decide whether he or she would sell their stock at that price, or buy the other person's stock at the same price. It was a marvelous legal means of forcing a fair price to be offered. And, although there was a lot of pride and emotion, his leaving the company had nothing to do with Lucy's marriage to Gary Morton."

"That was in Lucy and Desi's agreement," says Gary. "Each had the option to buy the other out, if one of them wanted out, whether it be Lucy or Desi. Desi was the first one to retire. He was being romanced by a lot of people, thinking they would buy his shares, but Lucy had the first option, and she bought out the option."

"Desi's interest in the company and in his own affairs diminished as his depth of alcoholism increased," notes Ed Holly. "Desi's alcoholism was established medically. He had been in the hospital. He had come out three times dealing with it, but each time would come back and just get deeper into it. He became very difficult to deal with, and his accessibility was reduced to the point where we would have to go to Del Mar, Palm Springs—wherever he was—to do business. And unless you did business before noon with him while he was still sober, you just weren't going to have a good result. Desi had gotten himself to that point. Many of us, as friends, had wanted to help, tried to help. It was just a classic case of alcoholism driving a person to the point where they are no longer operative. Mickey Rudin, Art Manella, and myself, basically, along with Lucy, concluded that it was not in anybody's best interest, including hers—most *especially* hers—for him to continue in the company. We decided to invoke the buy-sell agreement. This all happened within a short period of time—within a matter of a week or two weeks."

Bernie Weitzman offers, "Desi was an alcoholic, although he wouldn't admit it. No matter how much you loved him, there was the problem that he did not represent the best qualities for his image, the company's image, Lucy's image, and the kids' image. She'd call him on it. He just wouldn't change his ways. She kept hounding him and hounding him. Although they were divorced, she still kept after him. Finally, he said, 'Lucy, we can't continue to run the company this way. It's either going to be you or me. We can't do this to each other. You're getting in my way. So here is what I propose—either you buy me out or I buy you out, and you've got the first crack.'

"She had a wonderful adviser, Mickey Rudin, a very smart guy who had a connection with City National Bank's Al Hart, the president and chairman of the board—who was also a real gambler. When he felt that his clients were in need of money because they were doing the right thing, he'd come up with it. So Mickey convinced Lucy to buy Desi out, because he felt the investment was a very good one. Mickey convinced Lucy to take over Desilu's stock, which she did."

Of her new role as Desilu president, Lucille quipped, "Signing papers? I've always had to sign papers. Only now, I read 'em first. I used to be vice president in charge of emptying ashtrays. Now I say whether there *are* ashtrays." She added, "If I get in a jam, I can always call up Desi and ask him what he'd do." Desilu announced the studio would continue under the aegis of finance and administration director Ed Holly; programming vice president Jerry Thorpe; and W. Argyle Nelson, head of production and studio operations.

"I think he just saw the writing on the wall, thinking, This is not working—me being here, you being there with the 'Barry Norton' person. You want me out? I think this is a very good idea. But he didn't think it was a very good idea," offers Lucie Arnaz. "He just saw it wasn't going to work anymore like that. I give them credit for actually trying for three years. And the only reason they did that was because of the thousands of employees at Desilu. They were really scared to death that if they broke up their union, the studio would falter, people would lose their jobs. And they really had a tremendous loyalty to employees. But I say, 'Why the employees—why not *yourselves*?' I don't think Dad knew why he was having trouble. I don't think he would admit he had a problem with his drinking—'Yeah, I drink a lot. So what?'—I don't think he was aware of the fact that he was letting the company slip through his fingers because of it. But he certainly sensed things were falling apart."

Desi once poignantly attempted to reflect upon the causes of his exit from his company—the same addictions that, he hinted, triggered his personal demise. "Once you arrive at the plateau of success we were at, you find yourself in a whole new ball game," he observed, "where the players are engaged in fierce competition for more and more success and more and more money and more and more power, and which strains and tensions are such that the only relief they find is in pills, alcohol, and sex, which enables them, for at least a short time, to continue in this seemingly endless contest. A merry-go-round you wonder how you got on and how in hell you can get off! Most people never get off for fear of losing it all."

Despite statements to the contrary issued by Desilu and Lucille Ball over the years, Desi Arnaz, according to Desilu insiders, had, in fact, been effectively removed—and not altogether willingly—from the company he had founded in 1950. "I seemed to always be the messenger who had to carry the bad news. I had to sit with Desi and tell him that Lucy was invoking the buy-sell agreement, and I gave him the papers and told him the price," reveals Ed Holly. "Then I had to put on my hat in representing Desi and talk to him about it from his standpoint. I had to say to him, 'I think you will be better off to be out from under the responsibility and the pressures. Maybe you can get your life back together.' He was hurt. But he rather readily agreed that he had lost the drive or the punch or the interest to continue. Then I had to tell him that, due to his financial condition, which was indebted—I had failed to be able to control his spending and committing money—I did not believe that it was in his best interest to try to borrow the money to buy Lucy's stock. So there was the double-whammy that I had to deliver to him."

"When he left the studio," recalls Johny Aitchison, "all he took from his desk was one of those photo cubes that had pictures of his kids in it. He took just that, and he went out the studio gates. And that was it."

Chapter Fourteen

"Desi once said to me, 'I'll always love Lucy—now *Lucille Ball* is another thin'.' "

—Cleo Smith, 1992

"*I* could have been very happy as an old-fashioned homemaker," insisted new Desilu president Lucille Ball. "I think we'd all be happier if women didn't have careers outside the home. The old-fashioned existence was more beneficial for women, for the family. I could have done all that was required of a woman in the pioneer days, and enjoyed it."

Despite such oddly anachronistic musing by the intensely ambitious star, Ball attempted to adjust to her simultaneous, demanding roles as performer and studio executive—Desilu at the start of 1963 operating at near-capacity studio production with 1,700 employees. In his new Desilu pact, Jess Oppenheimer created and produced a Glynis Johns comedy-mystery series, *Be Careful, My Love,* costarring Lucy's *Wildcat* leading man Keith Andes; sold to CBS as *Glynis,* the British actress cast as a scatterbrained mystery writer solving real-life crimes with her attorney husband attracted poor reviews and few viewers before being axed after only thirteen aired episodes. Desilu's other 1963–64 entry, ABC's *The Greatest Show on Earth,* did not fare much better, and was dropped after its first season.

In February—in what would be a ritual for several years to come—Lucille refused to commit to CBS and series sponsors Lever Brothers and General Foods on a second season of *The Lucy Show,* citing as the cause her increased administrative workload as Desilu president; her network deal uniquely gave Lucille—and not CBS or her sponsors—the option to continue on a yearly basis. The star, several weeks later, firmly announced she would not continue her series despite the concerted efforts of network president Jim Aubrey. Alarmed at the prospect of losing his top-rated female star, CBS founder and chairman William Paley flew in from New York the first week of March and met with Lucille, prompting her to remark shortly after, "I have been asked to reconsider my decision. I am now thinking it over." While *The Lucy Show* cast and crew waited anxiously, her director, Jack Donohue, took a realistic—

and ultimately accurate—approach to her negotiating tactics. "It's the company's biggest money-maker, and as president she wouldn't want to lose all that loot."

Indeed, as she contemplated continuing the weekly-series grind, she received word of the imminent cancellation of ABC's *The Untouchables* and the demise of *Fair Exchange*. The simultaneous release of *Critic's Choice* suddenly put her film career on shaky ground, the strained attempt at sophisticated comedy surrounding the domestic discord between a Broadway critic and his neophyte-playwright wife proving a critical disappointment and a box-office flop; perhaps not concidentally, Lucille's plans to film *The Beardsley Story* during her *Lucy Show* 1963–64 summer hiatus were indefinitely postponed, the star instead opting for a Hawaiian vacation.

As Lucille contemplated her television future, on Sunday, March 2, 1963, Desi Arnaz—on his forty-sixth birthday—and Edith Mack Hirsch were married in Las Vegas. As Desi recalled, "I told Edie, when I asked her to marry me, 'Sweetheart, I don't know what we will find in this new venture we are about to embark on—the only thing I can promise you is that it won't be dull.' " Van Johnson and Jimmy Durante were witnesses, with Marge Durante acting as matron of honor and Dr. Marcus Rabwin serving as best man. The previous evening, the former Mrs. Clement Hirsch had flown to Juárez, Mexico, and divorced her husband,

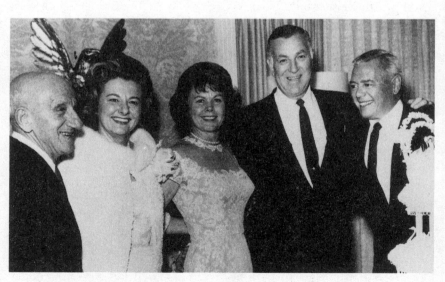

Desi's Las Vegas wedding to Edith Mack Hirsch, March 2, 1963, at the Sands Hotel: (*left to right*) Jimmy and Marge Durante, Edie, Sands Hotel owner Jack Entretter, and Desi
ARNAZ FAMILY ARCHIVES

the Kal-Kan pet-food magnate. As they prepared for a Palm Springs honeymoon, Lucille gallantly sent the couple roses in the shape of a horseshoe. The card said: YOU BOTH PICKED A WINNER.

"I met Edie," recounted Desi, "when she was a cigarette girl at the Santa Anita racetrack, and whom—in spite of my reputation as a successful Lothario in those days—I could not get into the hay until I married her twenty-five years later." The actual facts, however, surrounding their Las Vegas elopement suggested otherwise. "Desi had to marry Edie because there was a big scandal," says Marcella Rabwin. "Hirsch knew about them and had them followed." Confirmed Arnaz, "At one time, he had two private eyes following us, and I had two *others* following the ones that were following *us*—we both decided after a while it was a waste of money." Adds Marcella, "Desi said to her, 'Oh, come on—leave him. You don't need him. I'll take care of you for the rest of your life.' She left him—which was the biggest mistake she ever made, because Hirsch really was a wealthy man and a considerate husband. She just fell for the Arnaz charm. With Desi, she wound up not in need, but very, very limited financially. Desi made the mistake of buying his place in Las Cruces [Mexico] and then used the rest of his money for living on capital, which was insane. Nobody could stop him. He said, 'I'm not going to live so long that I'll outlive the money.' It wound up that they couldn't pay their bills some of the time. Edie always said, 'If worse comes to worst, we'll get out of here and go live in Mexico.' It was so idiotic, because he had been such a smart businessman."

Aware of his still-active predilections for gambling and high living, Arnaz in 1976 ruefully observed, "Why she came aboard and how she has managed to stay afloat for over thirteen years is beyond my comprehension and a tribute to Irish-American womanhood." Indeed, Desi taxed the patience of his new bride soon after the marriage ceremony. "I went to the wedding in Las Vegas," recounts Marcella. "Following the wedding, he won twenty-five thousand dollars. He was hysterical. He kept saying we were trying to pull him away from the tables. And Edie pulled him away. The next morning, he left and went to Florida and bought a yacht with the twenty-five grand. A couple of weeks later, he lost that and more—he was a real addicted gambler. It was impossible to stop him. He would bet incredible amounts of money. He'd take me to the roulette table with him and say, 'Come on, you're good luck.' He'd put a three-inch stack of hundred-dollar chips on one number on the roulette table. I've seen him in his gambling moods when he was so self-destructive—because he was a self-destructive man. He had a definite ego—he had to prove himself constantly."

By the end of March, Desilu announced that Ball would return with *The Lucy Show* for another year—new episodes would be filmed in color, although CBS continued airing the series in black-and-white until the 1965–66 season. As part of her CBS renewal pact, the network purchased several unsold Desilu pilots to air as *The Lucy Show*'s 1963 summer series replacement under the umbrella title *Vacation Playhouse* featuring the Merman pilot, *Maggie Brown,* as well as failed series attempts for Diane Jergens, Ginger Rogers, Don DeFore, Ruth Hussey, Bobby Rydell, Barbara Nichols, Darryl Hickman, and Eva Gabor. Her renegotiated contract also resulted in (ultimately discarded) plans to revive her *Lucy Goes to Broadway* 1961 special, which she envisioned as a ninety-minute original-book musical.

Bolstering the company's financial condition was an anticipated $22 million in billings charged to television and motion-picture productions leasing soundstages and studio-operations facilities in 1963–64, prompting *Variety* to dub Desilu "the largest indie rental studio in the industry." In addition to the feature film *The Greatest Story Ever Told,* and the three Desilu-owned series *Lucy, Greatest Show on Earth,* and *Glynis,* non–Desilu owned programs renting soundstages and operating facilities were *Ben Casey; My Three Sons; Breaking Point; Lassie; The Andy Griffith Show; I'm Dickens, He's Fenster; The Danny Thomas Show; The Joey Bishop Show; My Favorite Martian;. The Bill Dana Show; The Real McCoys;* and *The Dick Van Dyke Show.* For the 1964–65 season, additional Desilu nonowned series included *The Bing Crosby Show; Gomer Pyle, USMC; Kentucky Jones; My Living Doll; Slattery's People;* and *Tycoon.*

A heavy emphasis on comedy-series pilots was planned for the 1964–65 season, including *Letters of a Hoofer to His Ma,* created by *Lucy Show* director Jack Donohue; a Jack Carter comedy series; *Hooray For Hollywood,* a silent-screen-era spoof with Joan Blondell and Herschel Bernardi; a musical series starring Gogi Grant; a Jess Oppenheimer–produced song-and-dance show for Dan Dailey; and a turn-of-the-century vaudeville vehicle starring Donald O'Connor.

In the wake of *The Untouchables'* cancellation, the Desilu president offered her harsh criticism on violence-laden television programming: "Making a hero of psychotics five, six times a night is very dangerous. It's been proved a lot of rape, drug addiction, and strangulation is due to this. The glamour of actors playing those parts puts a stamp of approval on it. We take the abnormal type and depict it as a hero. Everything today is aimed at the teenager. Teenagers rule the world today, and there is too much responsibility on their shoulders. Parents are following their children, and the children are getting more demanding. We are afraid

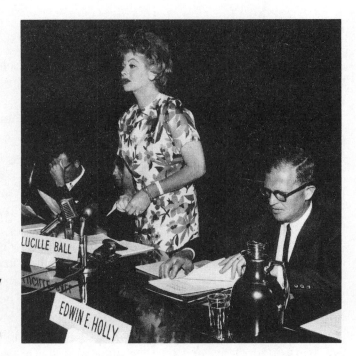

Lucille and Desilu senior vice-president Edwin E. Holly at the 1963 stockholders' meeting
COURTESY OF EDWIN E. HOLLY

to take their rights away. There is a complete lack of respect."

Warned of an impending barrage of television, radio, and newspaper reporters planning to attend her first August stockholders' meeting as studio president, Lucille arrived in full television makeup, a purple-flowered white summer dress, and open-toed sandals and remained stiffly "business-like and terribly formal" according to one news report—likely the result of giving stockholders the sobering news of a 1962 net loss for the company of $655,387 from the previous fiscal year. She was quick to note that in a swift turnaround, however, Desilu posted a gross income of $4.8 million for the first quarter of 1963, against $3.3 million for the same period the prior year as well as a seventy-thousand-dollar rise in net income from the first quarter of 1963 compared to the 1962 period. She revealed that *Lucy Show* sponsors General Foods and Lever Brothers had agreed to back two Desilu pilots each: situation comedies with Red Buttons and Dwayne Hickman, a one-hour suspense series, and a nineteenth-century saga—ultimately, none were sold.

Rarely did Lucille depart from her scripted, formal demeanor during the business proceedings. However, when programming vice president Jerry Thorpe boasted of numerous pilots in development and expansively declared that the production slate represented "a greater number of concrete projects in August than we have ever had before," she admonished him by remarking, "We don't go around blowing our horn about anything we're not sure of—our policy here is conservatism." Then, when a stockholder requested that vice president Ed Holly repeat first-quarter financial results, Lucille pushed the table microphone over to the soft-spoken Holly and advised, "You speak right into that gadget, honey."

At the close of the stockholders' meeting, a shareholder rose and pointedly asked Lucille, "Can Miss Ball give the time necessary to the presidency when she is employed full time as an actress?" The six male board members flanking the president remained silent and fixed their attention on the redhead. Lucy coldly stared down the stockholder for a lingering, hostile moment. "Well," she sharply retorted, "I'm giving it."

"It's like a board of directors meeting," remarked Lucille shortly after the stockholders' session. "When I'm forced to make some comment, I find 'oh' very effective, provided my eyebrows are arched. Sometimes I'm forced to make a more substantial contribution. Then I say, 'Oh, really,' or 'I see.' When things are really looking good, I say with great authority, 'Let's continue in that vein.'" She also candidly admitted, "We're all kind of running on Desi's momentum. Desi learned everybody's job, outside of the accountants' jobs. He spent months at it. Then, when he got the right men, he put them into the jobs and let them alone. That's substantially what I'm trying to do."

"Once Lucy and Desi split up," notes Holly, "we felt more the need to keep her apprised of what was going on, so that when she did step into the control position . . . and started having to make decisions, it was an easy transition, because she was ready for it. She wouldn't have been ready for it five years earlier, but when the time came, she was up to it."

Lucille's keen sense of personal frugality had not diminished upon her assuming the role of studio head; it had, in fact, only worsened. "Even when Lucy was Desilu president," recalls Ed Holly, "and chairman of the board, at the end of our board meetings, she'd walk around and pick up all the pencils. I never could find out what she *did* with all those pencils."

"When she was starting to become a rich woman and own Desilu," according to Hal King, "I went up to her office. I had saved twenty-five thousand dollars. 'Lucy, we're such good friends,' I said. 'And you've got so much money. Couldn't you take my twenty-five thousand dollars and give me stock or invest it in your company, so that one day perhaps I could become rich?' She said, 'I don't need your money.' I said, 'I know you don't. But you'll be helping a friend.' She said, 'Oh, you'll be fine.'" Lucy became a very rich woman, but she wouldn't spend a nickel, she was so stingy."

After a three-month hiatus, *The Lucy Show* resumed filming in September with Jack Donohue elevated to producer-director and Elliott Lewis promoted from producer to executive producer; upon Lucille's insistence, Charles Lane's curmudgeonly banker character, Mr. Barnsdahl, had been replaced by her long-favored supporting player Gale Gordon in the role of bank vice president Theodore J. Mooney, Lane's blustering, pompous counterpart who now managed widow Carmichael's trust fund, to his great chagrin. For his part, Charles Lane recalls, "Lucille was an extraordinary talent, and I was madly in love with her. She was always wonderful to me, and we had a marvelous time." Although legend has it that Lane had been asked to move to *Petticoat Junction* for a more prominent role than offered him on *The Lucy Show* prior to Gordon's casting, Lane reveals some lingering sadness at his departure: "She had me doing this very big character part on a permanent basis—and then Gale Gordon was again available—and she wanted him in the role. I was terribly disappointed, but I could understand perfectly."

Notes Gary Morton, "Gale's [character] was always a 'threat' to her, and that's the way she wanted it. She always had a threat. Desi was the threat on *I Love Lucy*. Gale was the threat in *The Lucy Show*." And, notes Candy Moore, "She adored Gale Gordon. She thought he was the funniest man alive."

No doubt resulting from the absence of guiding-force Desi Arnaz, the series from this point irreversibly declined in both script quality and the level of Ball's performance—the star now visibly relying on cue cards during filming instead of continuing the demanding task of memorizing dialogue. She claimed that she resorted to this shortcut as a result of the time-consuming corporate duties put upon her as Desilu president; also gradually deteriorating were the impeccable comedic timing, subtlety, and beautifully realized split-second reaction "takes" she exhibited during her peak *I Love Lucy* years.

"She started using cue cards," says Madelyn Pugh Martin, "and I don't think her performances were quite as good. It broke the connection with the other actors."

Desi became alarmed at the sharp decline in the quality of scripts following his departure as series executive producer. Of one ultimately unproduced effort, "Lucy Flies a Helicopter," submitted to Desi in September 1963, he astutely critiqued: "The situations seem to be arrived at for the sake of the writers, not for the logic of the story. If you don't start off with a strongly motivated setup scene, then what follows will not be funny, but merely ridiculous. Lucy should never take a chance at looking funny or idiotic. She should always have a strong and logical reason to be able to get away with the outlandish situations in which she becomes involved. The girls like a TV announcer because he looks cute on television, and when they learn his Girl Friday is leaving him, they decide they want to be his next Girl Friday. That's the story in a sentence. Thus, we start out with a premise that is not only weak, but silly. [Many scripts] I have seen seem to indicate a complete lack of directional course for the series—a type of lackadaisical, unenthusiastic approach that almost spells out a type of thinking that says, 'while maybe it's not right, Lucy can get away with it.'

"The property to follow *I Love Lucy* was based on a book that we bought, *Life Without George*. It was very carefully considered for many reasons. We didn't want to copy *Lucy,* and at the same time, we didn't want to go too far away from the Lucy character. We all agreed that the fact of these two women trying to raise children, make a living, face plumbing problems, etc., etc., without a man around the house, offered tremendous possibilities. But when I read a script such as 'Lucy Flies a Helicopter,' it makes me wonder if anybody ever read the book. If they didn't, then perhaps it would be wise to have them re-read it, very carefully."

Her *Lucy Show* return met with a chilly critical reception, the premiere episode capitalizing on the then-current controversy surrounding the multimillion-dollar debacle, *Cleopatra,* starring Elizabeth Taylor and Richard Burton. Blasted *The Reporter,* "A tired retread of all the lampoons of amateur theatricals that ever were. To debut a new season with a seg as trite as this is just coasting on last season's reputation. Also coasting were series writers Bob Carroll, Jr., Madelyn Martin, Bob Schiller and Bob Weiskopf, who stretched one joke beyond humor."

The same might have been said of Gary Morton's appearance in October at Hollywood's Coconut Grove, sharing the bill with singer James Darren. "Business figures to be relatively light," said *Variety*. "Morton gets off some scattered good gags and is an ingratiating, though conventional comic, but too much of his material is creaky and his mannerisms and style of delivery bring other comedians to mind. Most of the topics he kids are overly familiar as comic territory—among them TV doctor shows, TV commercials and golf gags. He also tends to overdo the campy pose—especially when there's a lull in the laughter."

Gary Morton relished his role as warm-up comedian during filming of *The Lucy Show*. And, as Jimmy Garrett recounts, "DeDe Ball would always show up with her cronies. She always had six or eight other pals with her. They'd all sit in the back row, just below the control booth. Every week during the warm-up, Gary would come out and say, 'DeDe, darling, are you comfortable?' And she would say, 'Yes, I'm doing just fine.' I don't remember her missing a show, ever."

"Gary was smart in two places," offers Hal King. "He never, never looked down at her family or her children. He treated her children as though they were his own blood. He never chastised them. He always treated them as adults. And, for all the years that they were married, I never heard them argue. If she started an argument, he would either never answer her, or he would laugh it off. That's where he was clever. So the kids grew up loving him, too."

In December, Desilu and eleven-year Desilu-Cahuenga studio tenant Danny Thomas, along with his partner, Sheldon Leonard, confirmed rumors of a merger. T&L Productions, noted *Variety,* was "the most successful comedy factory in the world," with top-rated series headlined by Thomas, Dick Van Dyke, Andy Griffith, Joey Bishop, and Bill Dana. Although Desilu, and not Danny Thomas, instigated discussions, negotiations were abruptly halted when Ball reportedly became disenchanted upon learning Sheldon Leonard—whom she held in high esteem—would not be involved in the newly formed conglomorate. "When T&L Productions was at its peak," recalls Leonard, "Danny and I decided to go our separate ways; I decided make some shows on my own, *I Spy* and several others. There was no point in proceeding with the merger. I wanted to continue putting shows together—I didn't want to become a real estate manager." And, as Hal King offers, "Danny wanted to buy a part of Desilu, and she wouldn't sell him anything. She said, 'I don't need him—who needs him?' "

Soon after the Desilu-Thomas merger discussions had cooled, CBS and Ball's agent, Don Sharpe, negotiated an expansion of *The Lucy Show* for the 1964–65 season to a one-hour format to assume the half hour vacated by the voluntary exit of *The Danny Thomas Show*—which directly followed *Lucy*—after a highly-rated eleven-year run. As in previous seasons, Lucille hesitated in renewing her CBS deal for another season, in either the half-hour or proposed expanded hour version. Simultaneously, Lucy planned to costar with Carol Burnett for an October CBS special; Burnett's critically acclaimed earlier hour with Julie Andrews, *Julie and Carol at Carnegie Hall,* was the Ball-Burnett blueprint. Lucille also signed to costar in a $300,000 Lever Brothers–sponsored *Lucille Ball Comedy Hour* with Bob Hope to be titled *Mr. and Mrs.,* the redhead cast as a fictionalized version of herself—television star and (non-Desilu) television-studio president. So taken was she with this more sophisticated television characterization, she for a time considered scrapping the existing format of *The Lucy Show* and utilizing the special as her spin-off program—although the revamped one-hour program would again feature Gale Gordon, if not Vivian Vance, who had grown increasingly weary of weekend commutes from Hollywood to her East Coast–based husband, John Dodds.

Although Lucille assigned Jack Donohue to the special, she continued her practice of virtually directing the entire production. Once during rehearsal, Hope wandered near a camera and was gently admonished by director Jack Donohue. Scowling, Ball roughly shoved Hope to his proper position. "Lucy," purred Donohue, "please don't touch the actors—you don't know where they've been."

"On the set, she would embarrass people by yelling or criticizing," says Candy Moore of *The Lucy Show*. "I thought that was unprofessional, for her to yell at people in front of others—particularly the director, Jack Donohue. It undermined his authority. He was a strange character, though. He wasn't funny, either. He hated child actors. He hated me, he hated Jimmy, and I think he hated Ralph. He was not a happy man." She adds, "He was probably scared to death."

Tensions manifested in a variety of ways, according to Moore. "I'd developed a nervous tic on the show when I talked. She said, 'Candy, what are you *doing* this all the time for?' And she said it in front of everyone, which, of course, made me do it *more*. She had no sense of psychology and had no idea that one remark from her and everybody was just paralyzed. I expected the show was going to be warm, funny, festive, really sizzling with laughs. I was not ready for everybody's somber, serious nature." When Lucille did display an occasional flash of humor, it was more often than not at others' expense. "When she did tell jokes," recounts Candy, "they were usually off-color, and I would stand there, blushing. She'd say, 'Look at Candy—she's going beet-red!' whereupon I would turn *purple*. Then she'd say, 'Candy's pretending not to know what we just said.' I wanted to die. She had a *very* raunchy sense of humor."

Lucille's imposed direction—often overriding Jack Donohue's—created problems with many actors. As Moore offers, "I think the show fell apart when we were required to provide a certain attitude, independent of the logic of the situation or the scene—my character might be forlorn or depressed because I've lost a boyfriend, or whatever, but I had to come in peppy and very upbeat nevertheless. Once I decided—I was reading Strasberg—I didn't like the singsong chatterbox tone everybody had for no apparent reason. I came in during a rehearsal and talked the way you really would talk to your mother in a certain situation, and

Lucy said, 'What's the *matter* with you today? Are you *anemic?* Where's your *tempo*—pick up the *tempo!*' "

William Windom guested on one episode and was subjected to Ball's wrath for most of the week's rehearsals and filming. Says Candy Moore, "He started on a Monday, we filmed on Thursday. He had a big part, but he was not getting it, just not clicking. He was a little intimidated or hadn't found his character yet. He knew he was off, but he couldn't quite get it right. She said to him, 'This *isn't* working—you just don't have it. It's not funny. I can't *stand* this. This won't work.' She was ready to fire him. She was screaming for the producer. She thought he was ruining the whole show. On Thursday, he came in and had totally redone his character. He was hilarious. And she was just as appreciative of him as she had been upset with him. She said, 'You're so *wonderful.* This is so *funny*—I *love* you!'

"She was very blunt and direct. She didn't have a sense of how to spare people while you're telling them what you need to tell them. Sometimes she upset people to a point where they just couldn't bounce back. She did it infrequently, but the times she humiliated a director or another actor, of course, it flattened them." Offers Lucie Arnaz, "My mother had a way of testing people. If you were the kind of person who gave it right back to her, she wouldn't do it to you. But if you let her walk on you, she would do it continually. She got off on that power of being able to tell you what to do. The few people in her life who said, 'Excuse me, I'm a human being,' in a nice way, especially if they had a sense of humor, then she had enormous respect for those people.

"There are people I would never hear her criticize. Cleo was a person I never heard her say a bad word against, because Cleo was also the kind of person who would say, 'Oh, you're full of *shit!* You're a fine one to talk!' The other people she'd say things to would either take offense or say something like, 'You don't like this? I don't know why I wore this,' and she'd feed right back into that line. Even if she backed off for the moment, later on, it would be a very easy target. And when you have anger and don't know what to do with it, that's where you send it. She had a ranting, raging sort of personality. She could rage on and on about something until she ran out of steam, mostly about unimportant things. She had fears and angers and hostilities, and she'd take them out wherever she could."

"Sometimes she was abrupt," adds Mary Wickes, "but it was usually because of time. She knew what was right for her. And there was no quarreling with her. I had great respect for her, but I think she scared some people. There was a period where Vivian was handing out insults like it was going out of style. Somebody finally said to her, 'Vivian, don't you think that's *risky?* ' "

Vance was one of the few who was not afraid of confronting the formidable, willful star, and retained Ball's respect in the process. As Carole Cook notes, "Viv was kind of tough, too. They'd been together so long, it was like Leopold and Loeb. They had been through so much together. She trusted Viv. Viv was really the only one who could say on the set, 'Lucy, why don't you move over there? . . . ' Not many other people would say that to her, but she would do it when Viv told her so." "The thing that was amazing about watching the two of them work," adds Garrett, "was when Vivian would say, 'You know, honey, if you do things this way, you might get a bigger laugh.' They were always trying to help each other bring out something extra."

Lucy's beloved Gale Gordon also remained largely exempt from her occasional tirades or harsh criticism. "The funny thing about him," recalls Jimmy Garrett, "is when he wasn't on the set, he was the most quiet, down-to-earth guy. But he'd get on the set and get that blustery thing going—it was amazing, because he wasn't at all like that off-camera. He was a very nice man."

"I learn from my mistakes," Lucille remarked with steely determination. "I don't admire people who beat their heads against the same mistakes over and over again. I don't like people who flounder too long. I don't admire these everyday martyrs, the pitiful drunken messes, the hysterical floundering women—all these people who cling to you, who need your help. You help them up to a point, but after a while, you wish they'd go cry on somebody else's shoulder. Nothing is more important than being able to stand on your own feet."

"I'll tell you about Lucy," said a close friend at the time. "She was a warm, passionate, loving woman years ago. She was crazy in love with Desi. She's been hurt. Hurt for years and years. It's frozen her. There's a lot of kissing and calling people 'darling,' but really underneath, it's cold. The warm part of her is hidden, down where nobody can hurt it again."

"Lucy didn't have Desi," offers Carole Cook. "She was kind of wandering. You couldn't get more famous. You couldn't get more money. That wasn't her driving force. She told me that all she wanted to do was work. But she would not give herself to people, to a director, to anybody. She was a self-made woman. She became very guarded—and she got tougher."

"My mother would have benefited greatly from some sort of basic psychotherapy," says Lucie, "someone she could go to and cry all the time, to give her a handle on where it all was coming from. Instead, it just compounded itself. The worst thing you can do is suppress pain, and she made a career out of suppressing all of her pain. Little pains became big pains because she couldn't ever deal with them. I don't say that she walked around depressed all her life. Thank God she had her comedy to act out all this childhood fantasy. She was really stuck at a young age emotionally, and she probably stopped any sort of serious emotional growth around that five-to-six-year-old stage. My mother would get angry or react emotionally like a child, like a frustrated child in a tantrum. And that adolescent period, too, where you talk back to people. And yet, that's why she was such a great comic. Because she could identify with that childlike humor and youthful craziness and unabashed bravery. An overcoming of that pain in performing, if you're lucky, gives you a gift that you can give to people. It doesn't necessarily make you a happy person. I don't think it helped her all that much— I don't think my mother was ever very happy."

Ball's bravado indeed often shielded an enormous amount of insecurity. *The Lucy Show* cast and crew visited Disneyland, where, recalls Candy Moore, the redhead's appearance sparked a near-riot. "The fans started to congregate and gather, and it got to be absolutely frightening. She had to go to the ladies' room. And they all started to pour into the ladies' room after her. She went into the stall, and they're slipping her autograph pads under the stall." Yet despite such public adoration, Tommy Thompson vividly recalls another incident that same day. "Lucy and I were driving out to Disneyland. We were laughing and telling funny stories. All of a sudden, there was a pause. I was driving, and she was looking at me. She said, 'You know, if I had your sense of humor, I'd really *be* something.' And I about steered off the road. Later I realized what she meant—she didn't have a real sense of humor. She could see what could be funny, but that spontaneity just wasn't there." Hal King remembers evenings acting as Lucille's escort at parties when she would often refuse to socialize with fellow performers such as Katharine Hepburn, telling him, "Oh, they don't want to have anything to do with me."

"She gave us great birthdays," recalls Candy Moore. "We'd be called down to the set and there'd be gifts for all of us, like Christmas morning— bicycles, fabulous presents. She tried very hard to be very sweet to us. It was just hard to get close to her. I don't think she wanted anybody to see her vulnerable side. She worked so hard at acting invincible that she could never quite relax. She felt awkward with intimate exchanges, and she didn't know why or what to do about it." Jimmy Garrett recalls "sneaking around the bleachers, and I'd come up and watch behind the cameras. I don't think Lucy liked it very much. But instead of saying, 'Get out of there,' she'd say, 'Now, you be careful out there—remember, I'm your second mother—I can tell you!' She was very motherly, if anything."

She did, however, seek advice on how to raise her two children. "She was very concerned with being a mother," recalls Garrett. "Many times, she would talk to my mother and say, 'What do *you* do, how do *you* handle it when Jimmy does so-and-so?' Or, 'Desi did this, what do I *do* about it?' She used to want to talk mom-to-mom." Desi IV and, particularly, Lucie appeared several times on *The Lucy Show*. "Lucie was already very gracious and thoughtful," remembers Jimmy Garrett. "She wanted to soak everything up, and she wanted to learn."

Lucille's daughter recalls another strong impetus for her several on-camera appearances: "My brother had a huge crush on Candy Moore, and I was madly in love with Ralph Hart, who played Sherman Bagley. Chris was her daughter's name on the show. When she'd say, 'Do you want to be on the show? There's a part next week where Chris has a friend named Cynthia and the girl's about your age and there are only about four or five lines. Do you want to play Cynthia?' I'd say, 'Is *Ralph* in the show? I just want to be near *Ralph!*' That was the best part, because I'd get all dressed up and go to the reading, and they'd block a scene I

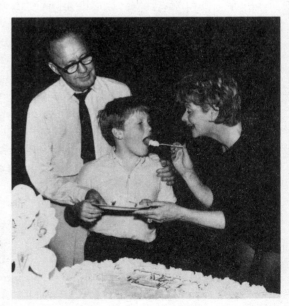

Jack Benny and Jimmy Garrett celebrate Lucille's birthday during rehearsals of *The Lucy Show*.
COURTESY OF JIMMY GARRETT

wasn't in, and Ralph and I would go and learn how to kiss in the dark under the bleachers."

The first week of February found Lucille proclaiming that she would abandon weekly television to "devote more time to the business and program affairs of the company." She announced plans to star in six specials (one with Art Carney) and unsuccessfully offered CBS the option of her appearing in a one-hour format on a rotating basis with Jackie Gleason. Rumors circulated that the star wanted to dissolve her CBS contract and move to NBC, despite the fact that she remained under exclusive contract to the network through 1970.

Only a few days later, *Variety* reported that Lucille had reconsidered and announced her return to the half-hour *Lucy Show* for the 1964–65 season. With Aubrey having rejected five Desilu pilots for the 1964–65 season, her new CBS pact stipulated that the network would finance two Desilu pilots and, in addition, was contractually obligated to place at least one Desilu series on the 1964–65 prime-time schedule. The network continued to woo the star, even reversing Aubrey's previous veto of the one-hour *Lucy Show* format. Although the network juggled the Monday night schedule to allow the expanded version, a petulant Ball continued her firm negotiating posture and refused to return to the CBS fold, although insiders reported she was proceeding with her plans

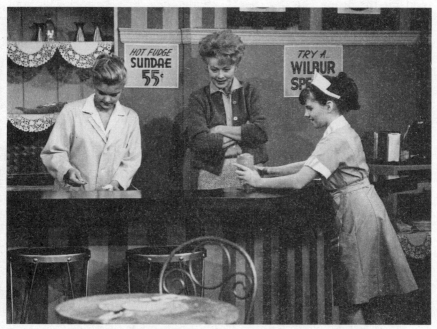

Lucie Arnaz debuts on *The Lucy Show* in "Lucy Is a Soda Jerk."
THOMAS J. WATSON COLLECTION

for a revamped one-hour series featuring the redhead as a studio president. Lucille at the same time claimed she had recently begun writing her memoirs. "Most of it's about Desi," she told *Variety*'s Army Archerd. "Don't worry—our kids will be able to read it."

Simultaneously, CBS's attempts to re-sign Lucille were again thwarted when rumors surfaced that *Greatest Show on Earth* sponsor Henry Kaiser (of Kaiser Jeep) had agreed to Lucille's personal request to continue sponsorship of the high-priced but only moderately successful ABC circus-backdrop series for the 1964–65 season—exacted, however, on his express condition that Ball end her weekly series and instead maintain an active role in *Greatest Show* production. Desperate to keep Desilu Studios afloat and, to that end, eager to sell *The Donald O'Connor Show* pilot to ABC—after CBS and NBC had rejected the property—she made a similar promise to Colgate's television director, George LaBoda, that she would exit CBS (and, in turn, not work for Colgate's competitor, *Lucy Show* sponsor Lever Brothers) if Colgate placed the O'Connor series on the ABC schedule.

Aubrey was so convinced that Ball would not return for another season, he announced the move of *Petticoat Junction* from Tuesday to *Lucy*'s Monday berth, only to incur the wrath of *Petticoat*'s sponsor, Procter & Gamble, and advertising-agency representatives, all incensed at losing the prime Tuesday spot following *The Red Skelton Show* without notification. P&G advertising director Tom Dawson was so enraged that he threatened to remove "all P&G business off CBS as soon as possible." In order to retain multimillion-dollar advertising billings provided by Procter & Gamble, Aubrey had no choice but to return to the negotiating table in hopes of securing Ball's services for 1964–65. Eager to topple CBS's Monday night dominance largely due to the success of *The Lucy Show,* ABC's Leonard Goldenson and Tom Moore were eager to remove Ball from the rival network and negotiated with *Greatest Show on Earth* sponsor Henry Kaiser for the upcoming season.

ABC, however, believing Ball's CBS exit was at this point a *fait accompli,* overplayed its hand by insisting that Kaiser commit to sponsoring more episodes than he had offered; Kaiser abruptly ended negotiations and placed his advertising time with CBS News evening broadcasts with Walter Cronkite. Subsequently, ABC revealed it would only purchase *The Donald O'Connor Show* if the series was fully sponsored; Colgate would only agree to sponsor the program on an alternate-week basis, and no other sponsor was found. As a result, Lucille was no longer bound to exit CBS and, with no Desilu series other than *The Lucy Show* scheduled for the 1964–65 season, Ball and Desilu were in a vulnerable position, and, not surprisingly, Ball said she was again "reconsidering" the CBS offer and might indeed return to weekly television. Her General Foods advertising-agency representative, Bud Barry, flew to the West Coast—without Aubrey's knowledge—and met with Lucille in hopes of convincing her to return to her show. Lucille's relationship with Aubrey—dubbed "the Smiling Cobra" as a description of his charming but particularly ruthless, duplicitous demeanor—ranged, at various times, from adversarial to openly hostile; Bud Barry, on the other hand, was able to mollify the star and convince her to remain with CBS.

She remained bitter over CBS's rejecting five Desilu series—apparently never considering the possibility that her studio's pilot endeavors had been rejected simply as inferior programs. "I thought being a trouper and delivering when you had to deliver counted for something, but it doesn't in this business." Lucille groused. "The kooks who give everybody a bad time seem to do better."

Finally, on March 6, Lucille announced she had signed with CBS for another season—at a record production budget of $90,000 per episode, the highest-priced half-hour series in television history to that point. Although she had previously—and vigorously—denied that her CBS return was largely predicated on the network financing Desilu pilots, her renegotiated pact stipulated that the network would indeed bankroll "a number" of prospective Desilu series ventures.

"I meant it when I said I was going to quit," she steadfastly insisted. I didn't think I wanted to work this hard anymore—just do occasional specials. There were a lot of things involved. One of the most important—the writers."

Perhaps a reflection of Lucille's desire to purge herself of those once close or still strongly allied with ex-husband Desi—and establish a new Desilu regime with husband Gary Morton—*Variety* reported on January 28, 1964, the first of several studio departures: writers Bob Schiller and Bob Weiskopf. Despite plans for the one-hour version of *The Lucy Show* to include three teams of producer-writers, the team had grown weary of creating situation comedy exclusively for Lucille Ball and accepted an offer to write variety-show sketch material for another CBS series, *The Red Skelton Show*.

The most shocking—and unexpected—Desilu departures occurred in March. Ball had disliked the final Madelyn Martin–Bob Carroll, Jr., *Lucy Show* script of the 1963–64 season. The writers dutifully worked through much of the night to fashion an acceptable version. The next morning, they submitted the rewrite to Lucille. Not long after, the star called for them and spit, "What are you trying to do—*ruin my career?*" as she violently threw the script to the floor. Exasperated, the writers attempted to retain their composure by silently retreating to their office to rework their script. Ball, however, chose to interpret their abrupt departure as "walking out" on her—upon their return to Desilu the following morning, Madelyn and Bob discovered their belongings packed up in boxes and moved out of their offices into the hallway for their removal; they had no further contact with Lucille for several years.

"It was all based on fear," assesses Lucie Arnaz. "My mother had a lot more fear about her own ability to do things than even I knew at the time. Insecurity about what she could accomplish, and especially without Desi. I don't think it existed in any sort of tangible way before my father left. After he left, she got very paranoid about her own abilities and just leapt into making decisions and had no one to ask. She couldn't send a script to [Dad in] Del Mar every twenty minutes. And she could be very tactless, very abrupt, with children, with adults, with writers, with producers. My mother had a kind of 'Get on with it' attitude about her whole life and didn't always take the time to be tactful—'What are you upset about? All I did was say you can't *write!* Go back and write *better*, that's all!' "

Ball also began to encourage husband Gary Morton's participation on the show. "The lady was a genius. I got to [know] what was good for Lucy. I stayed every day on the set, learning the three-camera technique, learning the comedy that this lady can teach anyone. She would say, 'Do you think this is good?' I'd say, 'Yes, it is.' Sometimes I was wrong. You get to know what is good for Lucy. There were all these Lucys— there was a 'Lucy,' and there was a Lucille Ball."

Lucille moved quickly to replace her two axed scribes and, less than two weeks following their dismissal, secured veteran comedy writer Milt Josefsberg as *The Lucy Show*'s head writer; Lucille also discarded Martin and Carroll's version of *The Beardsley Story* and commissioned Leonard Spigelgass—writer of her 1941 RKO success *The Big Street*—to create a new version for a summer 1965 filming.

Lucy quickly missed her old writers. "It's easy to become too harsh, but in our TV show we try to keep sympathy for me," she said as she looked toward the 1964–65 *Lucy Show* season. "I don't try to fight my way, I usually resort to tears. You have to watch it in the writing. I've had to throw out a few scripts lately—we have some new writers— where they've made me too harsh and aggressive."

Desilu executive Bernie Weitzman, however, offers other reasons for Ball's change of writers, the casting of Gale Gordon as well as the second-season lesser focus upon Lucy's domestic life with Vance. "She was married, she wasn't really crazy about continuing on the show. We finally had to say to her, 'Look, it's great to have old ladies playing comedy together, but the general public isn't crazy about it.' They were like two dykes together. We said, 'You've gotta change, you have to bring in some male influence to the show.' She had gotten a lot of negative response. That's when she brought in Gale Gordon and changed the writers. She was much happier."

Continuing the Desilu staff exodus, executive producer Elliott Lewis later resigned, followed shortly thereafter by the resignation of producer-creator-writer Cy Howard and the departure of vice president in charge of programming Jerry Thorpe. "Thorpe absolutely left under stress," states Fred Ball, at that time a director of the company. "He was one of the biggest thorns because after Desi left, Jerry Thorpe headed a triumverate that said, 'We're going to take over the studio.' The whole structure, because of Desi's absence, started to break down and deteriorate. And that's where Mickey Rudin came into the picture—he had to get in and manage it, or get the hell out, one of the two. And he got in and did the best he could. Between Rudin and Ed Holly and Art Manella, they kept it going. Management, being an executive, was not Lucy's bag. She had no interest in that. She depended upon the people she worked with, meaning, Desi, Art Manella, Ed Holly, myself, and Mickey Rudin. She had to depend upon these people because she knew that they knew more than she did about the politics of studio management. And she trusted them—she had to. When Desi left, everybody was apprehensive—there was so much at stake for everybody. I had no axes to grind. I was only interested in Lucy, and everybody knew exactly that. I only had one third, fourth, or fifth of Lucy's ear."

Thorpe's successor was twenty-six-year CBS veteran Oscar Katz, who resigned his network position as vice president of program administration. As *Variety* noted, "His job now is to restore Desilu's place in the sun as supplier of network primetime merchandise, the studio's only such series now being the one starring the network's boss." As Katz remembers, "Until the day of her death, Lucy had some positive psychological connection with Desi. Lucy would not allow Desi's office to be used by anybody. With my arrival, Lucy decided she would open it up again. Desi had a huge office, an old Hollywood mogul's office, with mahogany wood paneling, a fireplace, a piano, several sofas, a dining room, and a bathroom with a shower and a massage table. The closet was used to store awards and Emmy statuettes. They were cleaning the closet out when I got there. So I moved into his office."

Subsequently, rising young network executive Herbert F. Solow departed his NBC post as director of daytime programs for at shot at prime-time glory at Desilu as Katz's general program executive. "It was a superior studio under Desi, but there hadn't been anything going on [other than facilities rentals] for a while," says Solow, recalling his arrival on the lot. "It was really dead. It wasn't even a shambles—there wasn't anything to be a shambles. It was a dying studio. Desi was gone. All the shows were gone. The professional image was awful. It was in total disrepair. So we retiled, repainted, relit the stages and rooms."

Katz initially found targeting Desilu winners as challenging as had his predecessors had. His first series project was *The Green Horns,* which which he described as "the most ambitious western on TV." Also unsold were new series attempts for Ethel Merman and the comedy team of Rowan and Martin. Katz then signed Jane Powell, the husband-and-wife team of Julie London and Bobby Troup, and Dorothy Loudon (in a projected *Lucy Show* spin-off) for situation comedies. Signed to development pacts were *Twilight Zone* writer-director Allen Miner and *Playhouse 90* writer Norman Lessing and the writing-producing teams of Arne Sultan and Marvin Worth along with Hal Goodman and Larry Klein. A one-hour adventure series based on the Burt L. Standish "Frank Merriwell" books was also planned. Writer-producer Gene Roddenberry, former MGM-TV producer of the series *The Lieutenant,* was signed to develop and produce three one-hour series, among them a police drama, *Assignment 100,* as well as a science-fiction series, *Star Trek.* Oscar Katz and Lucille heralded a record twenty-two television pilots in various stages of development at the annual August stockholders' meeting—although the only series to eventually materialize was *Star Trek*—and happily imparted news that the company had enjoyed a 1964 net income of $794,261, compared to a 1963 loss of $655,387.

Soon after the stockholders' meeting, Lucy, Gary, DeDe, and Hedda Hopper flew to the East Coast for an August 31 "Lucy Day" at the New York World's Fair—the publicity event pegged on various *Lucy* programs airing in forty-four countries. As she later quipped, "You know, you could be stoned all day there, if you wanted to. I was given Irish coffee at ten-thirty in the morning. Well, after I drank it, that was it for the rest of the day."

After the heady experience of her "Lucy Day" drawing tens of thousands of fans, Lucille returned home to Los Angeles and faced the remainder of a quiet summer hiatus away from the cameras. "She had a shy quality," notes Candy Moore. "I was told that for parties she would have a tutor come over to coach her on current events. She did not want to appear stupid. She had two opposite sides to her. One was the work side, where she was dynamic, extroverted, and secure. She would deal with CBS executives, or the producer or the actors, in a very precise, confident way. Then there was a side to her that I saw at home.

"We went to her house in Palm Springs. I was fourteen at the time and had this fantasy of her life there—Frank Sinatra dropping in, and it was all going to be thrilling and exciting. I could hardly wait to see what she did all weekend, what kind of fascinating, compelling life she led. All I can remember was Gary was off playing golf and Lucy playing solitaire the entire weekend. She seemed distressed at home and thrilled and confident at work. She lived to work. It was as if her sense of self— her oxygen—was cut off when she was at home. She seemed absolutely lost and unhappy."

Chapter Fifteen

"I don't want to be a star—most of the ones I know
are too unhappy."

—Vivian Vance, 1965

The first week of the 1964–65 television season, rumors circulated that an increasingly unhappy Vivian Vance was poised to make her exit from *The Lucy Show*. "We're in negotiation now," said Vivian, "trying to work something out. At present, we've agreed that I will do twenty shows next season, and will be out of the fourth and fifth years altogether. I'm still hoping I can do fewer shows. I have a beautiful life waiting for me in New York, and I'm ready to live it."

Soon after, *The Hollywood Reporter* noted that Ann Sothern "had peeled some thirty pounds" as she planned to go before the cameras for several *Lucy* episodes during that same season to give Ball a female foil during Vance's absences. The headstrong redhead reportedly clashed so often with the equally formidable Sothern that one columnist hinted, "Their pals wish either Lucy Ball or Ann Sothern would pick up the phone and make the first make-up move." Before the on-set battle of temperaments, though, it was widely assumed that Sothern would assume Vance's vacated role or be featured as the same character in a spin-off *Lucy Show* series. Also scuttling the projected Sothern series were late 1965 discussions with producers Cy Feuer and Ernie Martin for Sothern to star in the upcoming Broadway musical *Mame* in a role ultimately won by Angela Lansbury.

For her part, Miss Sothern demurs: "She got mad at me a couple of times, but she knew she was wrong, so we never had grievous fights. Lucy had to take over and be the boss, and sometimes she got a little out of hand, but that's because she had to do it, instead of Desi." Still, Ball's reputation as an on-set taskmaster—if not outright dictator—was widely known throughout Hollywood. "Ethel Merman had done a show with her," recalls Ann. "I saw Ethel at a big party in New York—I had known her for years. She said to me, 'I hear you're working with Lucy.' I said, 'Yes, I am.' Ethel said, 'Well, how do you like her *direction*?' "

NBC optioned pilots for Gene Roddenberry's police drama, *Assignment*

100 (later retitled *Police Story*) and his science-fiction series *Star Trek,* scheduled to go before the Desilu cameras on November 23 starring Jeffrey Hunter as the commander of the starship *Enterprise* space-exploration team, with Susan Oliver set for a guest appearance; by June 1965, the revamped pilot was recast and reshot with William Shatner and Leonard Nimoy. As Oscar Katz recalls, "Gene brought in *Star Trek.* Part of the informal atmosphere around the studio, a guy like Gene could walk into my office and sit down. It wasn't like a network. We take Gene to CBS. They had a big meeting. Gene and I made the pitch. I said to Gene, 'Jesus, it looks like we've got a pretty good chance.' It turns out they were doing a science-fiction show, and they were picking our brains. So we pitched it to NBC, and they liked it."

Since 1961 Lucille had discussed with CBS the possibility of hosting a radio talk program; her revised network pact and the departure of Garry Moore from CBS in 1964 created *Let's Talk to Lucy.* Her new, highly touted ten-minute radio series, however, failed to attract a single sponsor and lasted one season. The talk program—featuring Ball chatting in the studio or on location with fellow performers—premiered September 7, 1964, with Gary Morton as producer. "Not in front of Gary she said, 'I took it so it would give him something to do,'" recalls Cleo Smith of the actual genesis of Lucy's radio program. "So he was producer. She was telling me about the show, and I said, 'That's exactly what I've been looking for.' I had been working for *Look* and was placing their editors and authors on television. I sat down and did a résumé and applied for the job. She called me up and said, 'I got your résumé—I had no idea you did all these things. But you know, I've got Gary, and I've *got* to give him a job.' I said, 'That's all right. Just keep my résumé.' About three weeks later, she called and said, 'How *quickly* can you get here?' Gary didn't know his way around. So we left him as producer."

Simultaneously, Desi Arnaz prepared to return to show business, planning both a television and film-production comeback. Desi, who had spent much of his time since his Desilu retirement breeding horses, was intrigued when he was asked by producer Nick Vanoff to host an episode of ABC's vaudeville-variety series *The Hollywood Palace,* but became infuriated when CBS, on the grounds of contractual exclusivity, refused to allow him to appear on the program. Arnaz had recently reminded the industry of his still-potent charisma when he hosted the Hollywood Press Club's salute to Jimmy Durante. "He was brilliant as emcee," said *The Reporter.* "He looked and sounded great. Silver-haired and silver-tongued, Arnaz ran the gamut from side-splitting humor to moist-eyed drama as he joked with, and praised, the beloved Durante."

As *The Reporter* confirmed on December 15, 1964, "Look for Desi Arnaz to maybe come out of TV retirement. He and long-time manager Don Sharpe are brainstorming a couple of new series ideas."

Rumors shot through Hollywood in early 1965 that upon Twentieth Century–Fox's purchase of the screen rights to the Broadway smash *Hello, Dolly!,* Lucille would eagerly dispose of her weekly series if she landed the plum role of matchmaker Dolly Levi and pointedly told studio mogul Richard Zanuck that she desperately wanted to be considered for the film version of the musical, although he had already announced Doris Day, Shirley MacLaine, Julie Andrews, or Carol Channing, who had originated the role on Broadway, as the leading candidates.

Lucy Show costar Gale Gordon maintains Lucille's yearly decision— and ultimate capitulation—to end her weekly-series run was not a negotiating ploy: "She was seriously wondering if she could keep up the great, high standards. I think it was quite sincere that she had looked forward to having a little rest for a while, and not having the responsibility of having to do a good show every week. She had been at it a long time. And I think she felt entitled to a rest. I don't think she ever did it to say, 'Will I get more money?' God knows, she was making enough."

At the end of the year, General Foods and Lever Brothers announced they wanted another season of *Lucy;* after stalling for several weeks, Ball re-signed with CBS the first week of February. Her $3 million pact provided her with several new fringe benefits; while her weekly per-episode cost jumped only slightly from $90,000 to $93,000—television's highest-priced half-hour series—CBS provided Desilu with a fund to finance pilots and would provide additional revenue for two Lucille Ball solo specials. According to Mike Dann, CBS indulged in the yearly ritual of romancing Ball while convinced from the outset that she would return. "The studio was a terrible burden for her. I don't think she ever enjoyed that role. People were always speaking for her; Mickey Rudin would keep using her show to get them more money or get their shows on the air. I never felt, at any time, that she wanted to give up the show. She didn't want to fire anybody. She hated to fire someone. She hated to have to worry about anything having to do with economics." And to Bernie Weitzman, "Her threat to quit was always a ploy. She really didn't want to. I went back to New York a number of times and said to CBS, 'Well, she's not going to do any more shows.' While she was saying to us, 'You mean it—you really want me to *say* that?' We said, 'Yeah, this is a *negotiation.* What's the worst that can happen?' And she said, 'What if they *agree?*' "

Gary Morton, however, maintains, "She was tired. She felt she wanted to take a rest. She decided she would take it easy for a while. The network, in turn, asked her again. The network wants to bring her back and gives her what they call pilot money—'Would you like to do some pilots?' So she said okay and kept boosting up and bolstering up the Desilu stock and going back to work."

At the time of the network renewal, it was still uncertain if Vivian Vance—at eight thousand dollars per episode—would return for the 1965–66 season. "I don't want anything to happen to my marriage," said Vivian. "All this flying back and forth is difficult. It's no fun working here. I get up, go to the studio, go home, and fall into bed. It's lonely. If I were Lucy, I'd do what she's doing, but I don't own a studio. I just own a beautiful farmhouse and yard filled with flowers that need attention, and I'd like to be there."

Marcia Magill, who worked under John Dodds during his tenure at G. P. Putnam, recalls him as "one of the best-liked people in publishing. He wanted to play more than he wanted to work, because he had a wonderful sense of humor and he was very funny. I've had dinner with John and Viv—they were just incredible together. I've never seen two people enjoy each other more. They were both very funny people, with an intelligent kind of humor, and they amused each other and amused everybody else. John was probably bisexual, and Viv had been married before. I think they both decided they were best friends, and there wasn't anybody else they wanted to be with. It was a special, marvelous love. You felt so good when you were around them because, strange as it may have been, it was a relationship that really worked. Lucy loved John. There was a nice relationship whenever he went out to the Coast. You couldn't help liking him."

Vance's decision to exit the series came when *The Hollywood Reporter*'s Radie Harris announced in summer, "From now on it will be no more TV series for Vivian on the West Coast." As Vance later reflected, "I don't think TV kept me from anything—my ambition was never to be a big star." In a veiled, but still pointed reference to Lucille, she added, "I've seen very few happy stars, and I was determined that that wasn't going to happen to me. The plums hang so high and the vampires beckon, and I knew that if I fell for it, I'd be as unhappy as the other ladies in Hollywood. Ambition doesn't go too well with age or companionship."

Although she initially disliked playing the role of a mother to a ten-year-old son on the series, Vivian quickly warmed to her on-camera offspring: "When you have the misfortune of being childless, as I have had, I don't think it's wrong to try and find a substitute. Playing a mother was a great release for me. They chose Ralph Hart to play my son because he looked liked me, and I really got to love him. In fact, I ended up pleading with his mother to take him *out* of show business."

Lucille was shaken when Viv decided to retire from weekly television. "Lucy cried in private talking to me because she depended on Vivian," reveals Gale Gordon. "She told me she could never do a show without Vivian. Lucy told me that, just prior to the break, Vivian was asking for more money than Lucy was willing to accept. It broke Lucy's heart, really. Vivian thought she was a great, great star. She was wonderful and worked beautifully with Lucy. But she wasn't that great on her own, or as great as she thought she was. She used to embarrass Lucy when she would say things like, 'Well, when you're big stars like us.' And Lucy would cringe. Lucy never thought of herself as a star. Never."

According to Bernie Weitzman, Vivian had demanded nearly half a million dollars to return for another season of *The Lucy Show*. "Lucy came in one day and said, 'I want Vivian to stay. It's very important to me. We have a great personal friendship, so I want her to be more than just an actress.' Lucy didn't have ambitions to direct, but Vivian did. Viv wanted to direct, she wanted to write, she wanted to produce. She wanted to do everything. Lucy said, 'I have no objection to that. She's very helpful to me, consoles me, we have a great relationship.' And she was the last of the old guard. She had been very emotionally involved with her.

"Vivian's agent sits in my office. I say, 'Lucy would be delighted to make an overall deal with Vivian where she can write, produce, and direct. We'll do whatever we can to make her happy. Tell me what she wants.' He gave me some numbers that were out of sight, what she wanted to do, and the control she wanted on the show. I said, 'That's unreasonable. There's no way we can live with that.' He said, 'Vivian doesn't care about doing the show. She's married, she's happy, so if you want her to do the show, if Lucy wants her to do the show, these are her demands.' I said, 'We can't recommend this to Lucy.' I went to Lucy and said, 'Here are the conditions that Vivian wants,' and Lucy says, 'That's outrageous. I can't believe it.' I told her, 'You gotta decide if Vivian Vance is Lucille Ball, because she thinks she's indispensable. That's the decision you have to make, because she wants to own the show.' Lucy made the decision that she was going to do the show without her."

Vance, in her unpublished memoirs, recalled Lucille telephoning her in Connecticut, begging her to return. She responded, " 'Lucille, you mustn't worry. With your talent you mustn't feel that way about any-body.' Yet I was sure she felt I was deserting her. She had a tremendous fear of rejection, and unless she thought it through, it could seem that

I was rejecting her, giving her up after fourteen years of closeness and clowning for a husband and a home I wanted to share with him. She and I would go on chatting together, seeing each other, staying friends, but the relationship inevitably changed."

"She hated being called Ethel, you know," Lucy fondly told Rex Reed years later. "But she was a great show doctor and a wonderful right arm, and when she got married and moved East and quit the show, I never really did recover."

And, it would turn out, neither did *The Lucy Show*.

While Lucy had abandoned her idea the previous season to recast herself in her weekly series as studio president and television performer, she planned to overhaul *The Lucy Show* for the 1965–66 season, and, revealed *The Reporter,* "spotlight her as a very-rich-type, Carole Lombard-like dress designer." When that concept was dropped, "Maury Thompson and I wrote a script for her," says Tommy Thompson, "where she inherited a magazine where Gale Gordon was the managing director. We wrote it so she could be involved in every department of the magazine. We thought it would be terrific. We call her up. She was in her dressing room, doing her nails. She said, 'What is it?' We said, 'We've got a show for you.' She said, 'Who did it?' 'We did.' 'Let me see it.' Now she's doing her nails and turning the pages with her *elbows,* laughing. She says, 'This is wonderful! Who's going to do it?' 'I'm going to produce it, and Maury's going to direct it.' She called Argyle Nelson and Bernie Weitzman. Her eyes were just sparkling. She said, 'Come on down—I want you to meet the new producer and director of the show I'm going to do next season.' She gave it to Milt Josefsberg. He liked it. Everything was fine—and then for some reason, purely financial or residual, I'm sure, it was dropped, and she said she'd go on and do another year of *The Lucy Show*. The show had started to slide down—if we had gone into the magazine-editor format, it would have been an entirely different approach to her humor."

However, Tommy and Maury were, respectively, made producer and director of *The Lucy Show* for 1965–66, and created a slightly revamped format, the star continuing as widow Lucy Carmichael—but relocating her from Connecticut to California and without her on-camera children, Candy Moore and Jimmy Garrett, who have been shunted off, respectively, to college and military school; continuing in the series would be Gale Gordon in his role of banker Mooney, who would concurrently move to the West Coast and hire his redheaded nemesis. In the absence of a sidekick, Ball pursued such top-name guests as Bette Davis, Bing Crosby, John Wayne, and George Burns. Wayne Newton appeared on one episode—along with Gary's mother, who, recalls Maury Thompson, was an extra "right behind Lucille in the recording studio set with Wayne Newton. I asked Lucy, 'Where do you want me to put her? What if she gestures hello to her New York friends during filming?' She said, 'Well, tell her, don't ask me.' I had to go to her and say, 'Now, you're just in the audience. Don't look at Lucy unless she does something funny, like you would naturally.' Lucy's mother, DeDe, wouldn't do the show. She said, 'Aw, *fuck* it. I don't want to do that *shit*—it's not for me!' "

Lucille, who inherited DeDe's abrupt, often unintentionally tactless approach, often rattled some actors guesting on her series. As Maury Thompson remembers, "When we started rehearsing, from ten in the morning until showtime, she used a full voice. She gives you a full show. And so does everyone else, too. Or they're stupid. We had a New York actor. We started to rehearse, and he mumbled his lines. 'Is he speaking?' asks Lucy. 'I can't hear him.' She looks at me: 'What's he saying? Is that his line?' The guy says, 'Well, when the cameras roll, I'll—' She says, 'No, no, no. We don't do that here. I want to hear the voice that I'm going to hear when the camera is rolling. I don't want you to come out here with a bombastic voice and scare the hell out of me. I don't know how to react to you if I haven't heard your voice before. We do full voice on this show.' He made the biggest mistake of his life. He said, 'Well, maybe you'd like to read the lines *for* me.' She screamed, 'Get him out of here. *GET HIM OUT OF HERE RIGHT NOW!*' "

Gale Gordon offers, "Lucy always assumed that if it didn't play, it was her fault. She would get very tense at times. We had some scripts that were very weak. Lucy never tried to be funny. We all played everything we did perfectly straight. She always did everything herself. She never considered using stunt doubles. So she learned the things she didn't know in a few days or in a week. If she had dances to do, she learned a complete routine and would go over it for hours and hours when we weren't around. She'd spend hours at things to get it perfect."

"Claude Akins was a guest on one episode," recounts Tommy Thompson. "Claude's a big, big guy. She reached over and grabbed his arm and said, 'Stay *close* to me—it's a two-shot.' He walked over to me after the rehearsal and said, 'Jesus Christ, look at my arm.' She had nails about an inch long—big nail marks were all over. He said, 'When she wants you to stand close, she means *stand close*.' "

Danny Kaye was not exempt from Lucille's brusque demeanor. "When they were rehearsing, Danny would correct Lucy," says Johny Aitchison. "Lucy would come right back at him. And then it got hot and heavy.

Danny said, 'Just who the hell do you think you are?' She says, 'You're full of *shit*—that's who I am.' "

Lucille—facing the cameras alone without Vivian and without Desi's guidance—revealed to Maury Thompson her deep-seated insecurity. "Lucille really had a soft spot. She protected herself at all times, to be sure she didn't get hurt. She was so afraid that people were going to hurt her. When we were the number-one show, I said, 'What happens now?' She said, 'They'll drag us down. They'll pick until they find something.' She always thought that people were out to get her. I'd say, 'Come on, honey. No one's going to get you.' Even when you'd give her some direction, she'd think, Wait a minute—Is he doing that for *my* benefit? She tried to do it all," he adds. "She thought the job was all on her shoulders. There was no one she could converse with. She just didn't believe anyone. I think she called Desi every night of her life. Even with Gary around, she kept very much in touch with Desi."

Arnaz officially launched his show-business comeback with the purchase of two novels designated for theatrical-feature adaptation. The first property optioned by the newly formed Desi Arnaz Productions was Margaret Culkin Banning's *The Vine and the Olive;* when he optioned the second novel, Theodore Pratt's *Without Consent,* he immediately shelved the Banning book and instead announced a fall 1965 filming for *Without*

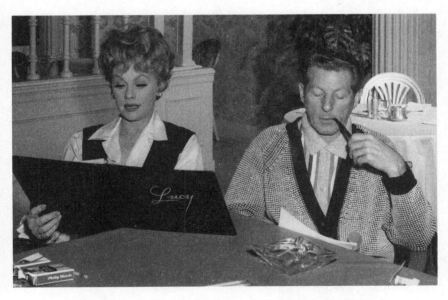

Reading the script for "Lucy Meets Danny Kaye"
THOMAS J. WATSON COLLECTION

Consent, a then-controversial story about rape with a script by Ben Maddow. "I don't want to get involved as an actor," he insisted. "CBS came up with a lot of stuff for me, musical shows which I would emcee, comedies, series which they said I could supervise if I didn't want to be in them. But I don't work that way. I want to do it on my own. If I fail, it will be because of mistakes I made, not because of someone else's." He added, "I'm tired of compromising. I won't do it again. I did it at Desilu on the last year of *The Untouchables* when I let them change the format. I did it because three thousand people depended on me for their livelihood." He promptly checked himself into Cedars of Lebanon for a complete checkup—and to combat recurring intestinal problems—and announced plans to shortly open his new offices at Desilu Culver. "I'm the healthiest son of a bitch on the fifth floor," he told *Variety's* Army Archerd from his hospital bed.

Lucille might well have missed Desi's presence at the August 1965 annual Desilu stockholders' meeting. The proceedings began upon studio president Ball announcing a gross income of $18,997,163 for the fiscal year, a drop amounting to 20 percent from 1964; a net income for 1964 totaled $455,710, a 42 percent decline from the previous year's $794,261; she was quick to note, however, that rental of studio facilities was at a "higher and more profitable level" than during the previous fiscal year. Normal business protocol was disrupted, however, when Los Angeles–based stockholder Helen Barbos criticized Ball for drawing $300,000 in salary and talent fees at a time when the company had suffered a dip in income and refused to pay any dividends to shareholders; she also complained that Desilu stock had dipped from a high of twenty-nine dollars to its then-current level of only seven dollars per share.

Attempting to answer the charges that Ball—paid $100,000 yearly as studio president, and $130,172 as an actress for the company—was grossly overpaid, Mickey Rudin shot back, "She is about two hundred percent underpaid. Lucy, who owns about fifty-two percent of Desilu stock, has continually put [forth] her greatest effort to help the company. Her salary is half of what she is worth as president and top-actress money-maker for the company." Lucille departed from her prepared statement and retorted, "I could make a big show with a tiny dividend. But I'm a conservative. I'm trying to keep the business on an even keel, not make a big show. I make honest reports. I'll remain in as long as I can afford it. We have big land values to help."

At that point, stockholder John Gilbert of New York joined the tumult. He complained that Lucy's income was nearly equal to the loss the company sustained. A hurried attempt was made by Desilu board members—led by Mickey Rudin—to rule Gilbert out of order. The attack on the star—who was almost in tears—prompted Gary Morton to immediately rise to defend his wife and company president—inadvertently further igniting the already volatile situation—by yelling to Gilbert, "Shut up and let Lucy finish her talk!" Chief of security John Reeves was ordered by Rudin to eject Gilbert from the meeting. Reeves and Gilbert began struggling in the aisle, both men doing a pratfall during their violent scuffle.

"Leave him alone," screamed Lucy. "Let him go back to his seat!"

Gilbert was released and sat down; the altercation, however, had prompted fighting to erupt among many of the seventy-five stockholders present, punctuated by catcalls. Ball's flaming temper was clearly evident at several points during the meeting, as she watched Gilbert—well known as a professional stockholder in hundreds of companies who attended such meetings on a regular basis—turn the business meeting into a chaotic shambles. "I've read about him," she said to Rudin. "He's all that they say," to which Gilbert retorted, "Thank you."

The atmosphere in Desilu's Workshop Theater became so heated that one stockholder requested a ten-minute session to "calm down"; during the break, Lucille turned to her highly vocal dissenter, and with her voice slightly shaking asked, "Mister Gilbert, do you mind if I go to the ladies' room?" When Gilbert nodded his approval, Lucy abruptly turned on her heel and went out, slamming the door behind her. She managed to regain her composure upon her return.

When the meeting resumed, Gilbert asked for ballots to vote personally on the election of directors. Lucille sat silently, chain-smoking, and consumed several aspirins while downing a glass of water. "Anyone want an aspirin?" she asked. "Bufferin and water on the house." When a shareholder suggested that Desilu officers be paid only one dollar per year, the remainder of their salaries instead being distributed as dividends to stockholders, Lucille snapped, "How long could I keep these valued advisers at a dollar a year? This isn't *war*—it's the *TV business*." Stockholder Gilbert had the last word. "This has been a real show," he proclaimed at the end of the tumultuous two-hour-and-thirty-five-minute marathon meeting. "Too bad it wasn't shown on television—it might have increased our revenues."

"That really hurt her," offers Bernie Weitzman of the public controversy surrounding Ball's salary. "It really started her thinking, why am I before the public and being scrutinized like this? She was very uncomfortable with people pointing to her and saying, 'Gee, you're making twenty-five thousand dollars an episode, you're president of a company, why aren't you making ten thousand dollars?' She really had nothing to do with the pricing. Whatever we gave her, she took. She was happy because she had all kinds of perks—a car, a nice office, a dressing room, and a maid. From her point of view, she had the world on a string—and getting a lot of money besides."

Not long after, Lucille announced plans to launch Desilu "family-type" feature films, a three-year plan designed to produce fifteen films budgeted at $750,000 each, including her much-postponed *Beardsley Story,* with either Jackie Gleason or Art Carney now favored as her costar in the Desilu–United Artists production. Obviously stung from stock-holders' complaints attacking her salary as performer and company pres-ident, Lucille criticized high-priced salary demands of other actors. "They priced themselves out of the business. I was the first to say, 'I'm not worth it' when my agents told me what they were asking for me.'"

Lucille added that her apparently minuscule *Lucy Show* talent budget precluded her son's currently hot rock group, Dino, Desi & Billy, from appearing on her series; she was prepared to pay four hundred dollars for the guest appearance, while the trio had an established four-thousand-dollar per-guest-shot minimum. "I couldn't blame 'em for turn-ing me down," ruefully admitted the frugal Lucy. "I could get Leonard Bernstein cheaper—he offered to work for free!" Added Desi, Sr., of his son's new career as a teen idol and member of the rock trio, "His mother sent him to me not long ago to see what I thought of him and the boys playing a weekend at one of those teenaged clubs—you know, no liquor or anythin'. I said I guessed it was all right, and said, 'How much you gettin'?' And he tells me four thousand dollars and asks if that's okay. '*Okay!*' I said. 'I never made that much in a week with my bongo band, and there were twenty guys with me!"

Lucille also scotched rumors of an impending Desilu sale, as the value of the three studio lots had been recently appraised at $11 million. "I listen to every offer. Most are merger opportunities—but they always want me to put up the money, do all the work, and still run the place! No, I've got no desire to get rid of it. I've learned a lot in the last three, four years. I can rely on my own judgment now." The fifty-four-year-old star had no plans to retire—"What would I do?"

As Gale Gordon relates, "She was never still. If she had an hour at rehearsals, because something had to be done technically, she'd be play-ing word games or getting anybody to play word games with her, like Scrabble. She was always, always busy doing something—she couldn't sit still and relax. Those sort of things don't interest me at all. She'd get Mary Jane Croft, or anyone who was on the show, and they'd go into her dressing room and go at the word games like mad—anything to keep her mind active. She was just a dynamo. She worked harder than any ten men I've ever known—but she loved it."

"The show was her whole life," concurs Tommy Thompson. "She would call about every other weekend. I'd be sitting at home, and the phone would ring. I'd go crazy when she'd call. Finally, I got smart and I put in a red phone, and the only one who had the number was Lucy. So when I was home on the weekend, the phone would ring, and it wouldn't bother me at all. I knew who it was, and I could handle the situation. I'd pick it up, and she'd say, 'Well, I'm glad I got you. I hope you know we have no show for Monday.' I'd say, 'What's the matter?' She'd say, 'Have you seen the script?' 'Sure.' 'Well, I haven't.' I said, 'Well, Lucy, I don't buy the scripts you haven't seen.' 'Well, I certainly didn't see this one. You sneaked it through on me again, didn't you? You and Milt better get over here right away.' I'd call Milt. We'd get there. She'd say, 'We've got some of the greatest sweet rolls—you've gotta try one. And coffee for the boys. So, what about the script?' We'd say, 'We've got more ideas.' Then she'd say, 'Well, I finished reading it, and it works fine—I remember reading it now—it works fine. Now, what are you two guys doing this weekend?' She just wanted some company."

As the 1965–66 season began, Desilu announced its slate of new pilots targeted for the upcoming television year. Scheduled to go into production were a Jerry Belson–Gary Marshall pilot; a comedy about modern-day Gypsies and an Irish schoolmarm; a Robert Lansing western; and comedies starring Dean Jones, Tony Dow, and Shelley Berman. Also set was a one-hour action-suspense series, *Mission: Impossible,* which creator and executive producer Bruce Geller and producer Joe Gantman originally created as a half-hour serial. Steven Hill—eventually replaced by CBS with Peter Graves—was cast along with Gregg Morris, Peter Lupus, Babara Bain, and, later, her real-life husband, Martin Landau.

"One of the great business decisions I thought Lucy made," says Bernie Weitzman, "was when she had a tremendous development fund. Mickey Rudin and I worked it out with CBS that she could either put half of it in her pocket and do nothing, or spend the whole fund doing programs for Desilu, with CBS having first crack at them. We had six hundred thousand dollars. Whatever she wanted to do with the money was her decision. Bruce Geller was under contract to us and developed *Mission: Impossible*. We took it to CBS. They didn't like it. We came back from the CBS meeting, and Herb Solow said, 'You know, if we could have some of the *Lucy* money to do a presentation of *Mission,* I'm sure CBS would change its mind. So we went to Lucy and said, 'Look, we'd like to spend some of that six hundred thousand dollars, maybe all of it, on this program we believe in.' She said, 'Yeah, I like the show very much. Let's do it.' We took the money, which she could have put in her pocket, and did a semipilot of *Mission: Impossible*. We cast and produced it ourselves."

Lucille pursued Carol Burnett—who had starred the previous season in a ill-fated CBS variety series called *The Entertainers*—to star in a filmed Desilu situation comedy; Carol, however, would not commit to a series until the 1967–68 season, saying, "A live series can be changed every week, through trial and error, to arrive at a perfect format. With a filmed series, you're dead after the debut if the format's wrong." She declined the Desilu offer; *The Carol Burnett Show* premiered in 1967 and enjoyed an eleven-year CBS run. Mentor Ball telephoned Burnett after a *Lucy Show* guest appearance. "Carol, darling, you were *marvelous*," purred Lucille. "I always said you'd make it—if you'd just pay attention."

Simultaneously, *Variety* reported that "Desi Arnaz will get royal treatment when he moves his *Without Consent* feature film company on the Desilu-Culver lot. Lucy gives him the former David O. Selznick offices, plus part of George Stevens' headquarters. Desi is purely a tenant, pays rent like everyone else." Lucille sent him a telegram: HAPPY HOMECOMING. YOU HAVE MY CONSENT TO MAKE "WITHOUT CONSENT" ALL OVER THE PLACE.

Television pioneer Arnaz was quick to comment on the state of mid–1960s television programming: "TV today is not like it was in the old days. We used to try and do something original, but they won't today. At the beginning, nobody knew anything about it, so they had to let you come up with new things. When we did *Lucy,* the shows were based on human emotions—love, greed, fear, ambition—emotions which happen to everybody. I can't believe that all of a sudden, the creative talent is gone—they should take a gamble once in a while." Desi insisted he had no interest in appearing before the cameras. "The one thing I want to do is to be involved with the creative end of the business. I'm seeing Paley in New York next week. But I can't get involved in a series—it takes too much time."

Although Arnaz initially planned to launch his comeback with a motion-picture project, his plans to film *Without Consent* were derailed when, on March 21, 1966, his meetings with Paley and Mike Dann resulted in a contract with CBS and his Desi Arnaz Productions to develop four new program properties. Desi's first small-screen endeavor was to be a one-hour special featuring Mexican star Cantinflas and filmed in Mexico City in August; the program, however, never materialized, nor did his plans to produce a one-hour dramatic series. Also announced, but abandoned, was a situation comedy created by Cy Howard for an *Untouchables* satire, *Joe Sent Me*. Arnaz signed Rory Calhoun (who had earlier teamed with Arnaz for the Desilu series *The Texan*) for his adventure series, *Land's End*.

Upon completion of a number of well-received NBC Dinah Shore specials following their March 1964 Desilu departure, *I Love Lucy* writers Bob Carroll, Jr., and the recently remarried (and rechristened) Madelyn Pugh Davis, were promptly signed by Arnaz to create a trio of television comedy series. With her *Lucy Show* spin-off abandoned, Ann Sothern concurrently discussed plans for a new situation-comedy series with longtime friend Desi Arnaz. Madelyn and Bob created *Gussie, My Girl*, with Ken Murray to essay his real-life role as a camera-toting fan in Hollywood—Arnaz repaying a long-standing debt. Twenty-five years earlier, Arnaz had been signed to his MGM contract directly after Louis B. Mayer attended his showcase appearance in the stage revue *Ken Murray's Blackouts*.

Another Carroll-Davis projected series was *The Carol Channing Show*, a three-camera situation comedy with former *Lucy Show* child star Jimmy Garrett; Channing filmed the pilot while on hiatus from the Broadway production of *Hello, Dolly!* to appear in the Universal musical *Thoroughly Modern Millie*. While Lucille and Gary attended the Channing pilot October filming, they were "unable" to attend the postshow bash with entertainment provided by Bobby Darin; the Mortons did, however, send the Arnazes a perfunctory magnum of champagne.

"Thin's got too big before," reminisced Desi. "There'll be no more studio, and I am very happy just paying rent to Lucy." In a corner of his recently refurbished office, Desi glanced at his old conga drum. "If thin's go wrong," he said, "I've always got that." He then paused and affectionately recalled ex-wife Lucille. "The prettiest girl in the world," he sighed, "and a wonderful woman."

Lucille continued to rely on Desi's advice. "She sent some scripts out to the ranch," recalls Johny Aitchison. "Desi told her, 'Lucy, watch out for the writers. Because you're Lucy, you can make certain things work— they're counting on that. But this is *shit*—you've got to be *very* careful.' He told her, 'They have you, but they still have to do good writing, and there has to be a reason, a motivation, for everything. You just can't do things. It has to be set up.' He warned her, 'Be very careful. Don't let them count on you carrying the whole thing.' "

Despite the concerns he voiced privately to Lucille regarding the writing quality of her series, Desi had, in fact, at least once been asked to intervene on her behalf. During the 1963–64 season, *Lucy Show* scripts plummeted in quality when Desi was no longer present to protect, nurture, and coax the writers into better rewrites. "One day Jim Aubrey gave me a memo from Paley to Jim," recalls CBS executive Bob Lewine. "It said the *Lucy* scripts had suffered, and would I please go to Desi and tell him this? Jim gave it to Hubbell Robinson and said, 'Please take care of this.' Hubbell gave it to me. So I called Desi. I tried to be diplomatic. 'Paley thinks the scripts are losing a great deal of punch. Would you take a look at them?' Desi said, 'Sure.' He took clippings from all the newspapers and sent them to Paley, telling him, 'All raves.' Paley got mad at Jim, who got mad at Hubbell, who got mad at me. Jim said, 'The next time something like this happens, whoever is responsible can say *good-bye* to CBS.' "

Lucille increasingly began to rely on her new husband for professional advice. "Lucy used to give me scripts," recalls Gary Morton. "I guess she was testing me. She'd would say, 'Read this. Let me know what you think.' I read and gave an opinion, and she would say, 'You know, you're right. I didn't realize that.' Then I became very friendly with the writers, Bobby O'Brien, Garry Marshall, and Milt Josefsberg, Ray Singer, all the guys who were writing for us. We had some excellent writers, and I just was fortunate enough to be there with the talent. As I read the scripts, I'd say, 'That's a good idea. I like that.' Don't forget, I had twenty-five or thirty years of comedy myself." For his part, Gale Gordon offers, "Gary was always there—he had some funny ideas. He was a great one to rehearse to. He would laugh at certain things and say, 'Oh, keep that in.' He was very good for Lucille because he was always around. He wasn't a temperamental husband saying, 'Don't do this.' He knew that she knew what she was doing. He was a very good influence on her."

Notes Ball historian Thomas J. Watson, "Lucy had heard that Milt Josefsberg was looking for work, because Jack Benny was going off the air. So, it seemed, who better to write a comedy show than Jack Benny's people? Unfortunately, there's a big difference between sketch comedy, which Jack had been doing, and domestic situation comedy. Milt came on board. It wasn't an immediate change, but it started from that point. Milt wrote gags, and most of the friends that he hired as writers were Jewish writers from the Borscht Belt, and of course, he had a friend because Lucy happened to be married now to a Jewish comedian. And Lucy was upset that none of the writers Milt hired were women. These guys did not understand how to get a housewife into physical stunts, so, essentially, she stopped being a housewife. She became a physical Gracie Allen—as opposed to Lucy Ricardo. The Lucy Ricardo character

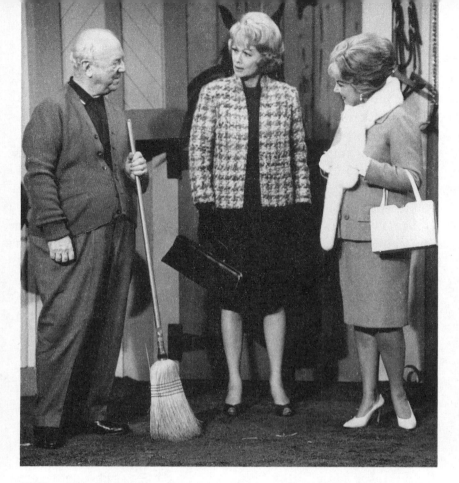

William Frawley made a cameo appearance with Lucille and Ann Sothern on "Lucy and the Countess Have a Horse Guest," first telecast on October 25, 1965. He died the following March.
THOMAS J. WATSON COLLECTION

was zany, but not stupid. Now, she would do stupid things. With Gale Gordon, she became kind of nasty in order to defy him, because he was such a strong character.

"Along with Lucy relying on cue cards, what also changed the series was that they were more concerned with doing a show *Thursday night* than they were with doing the best show possible. And, maybe she got it from *Wildcat,* but she became very concerned with doing the show for the live studio audience and entertaining them, as opposed to making sure the show got into the can right. With *I Love Lucy,* you always had the feeling that you were eavesdropping in on the Ricardos and the Mertzes—with the later *Lucy* shows, you knew she was doing a show. She was presenting it for us. The later shows were simply filmed stage shows, where that studio audience became all-important. It was a major mistake."

By the end of 1965, Lucille began her usual threats to end her weekly series run, at the same time reminded of unpleasant memories when

January brought news that Ann-Margret had been selected for a motion picture version of her ill-fated *Wildcat,* to be a Seven Arts–Ray Stark–Eliott Hyman production; in September 1966, Debbie Reynolds was announced as Ann-Margret's replacement. CBS, however, accustomed to Ball's delays and negotiating tactics, seemed not particularly disturbed at her momentary indecision. The network, though, had an alternate plan to entice Ball to return to the CBS airwaves on a regular basis—*Lucille Ball Presents,* a 1966–67 season anthology series in a rotating format presenting the star headlining every fourth or fifth installment as a comedy hour.

By the end of February—when CBS was close to purchasing Desilu's one-hour espionage series *Mission: Impossible*—Lucille, not surprisingly, warmed to returning to her regular *Lucy Show* format for 1966–67. A few days later, *Variety* announced, SURPRISE! CBS-TV GETS "LUCY" BACK! As the trade paper noted, "It took pleading, the financial demands of Desilu as a corporate entity and a rosy deal to bring Lucille Ball back as the star of her weekly *Lucy Show* next season. It's not without pertinent interest that Desilu also succeeded in selling CBS another hour series, *Mission: Impossible,* slotted in the Saturday night 9–10 period."

According to Ed Holly, Lucille demonstrated particular courage in clinching the *Mission: Impossible* deal with CBS. "One of the biggest decisions that had to be made was when she went against my recommendation and Argyle Nelson's recommendation that had to do with *Star Trek* and *Mission: Impossible.* We had two properties that were both tremendous, we were highly enthused about them. But as we got more and more into the pilot-preparation stage, it was becoming more and more obvious that the executive producers on each show—Gene Roddenberry and Bruce Geller—were inflexible on making compromises that would enable the shows to be produced on an economically sound basis. They were both strong, creative people. According to our estimates, we would lose sixty-five thousand dollars per episode on each series. We didn't have the financial strength to afford that type of show. And we recommended to Lucy and the board that we not do the pilots, much less the series. I told Lucy, 'If we do these and are unfortunate enough to sell them as series, we're going to have to sell the company or go bankrupt.' Lucy deliberated for a bit and then made the decision she wanted to do them." He adds, "If it were not for Lucy, there would be no *Star Trek* today."

While the CBS sale of *Mission: Impossible* allowed Desilu to place less singular dependence upon the venerable *Lucy Show,* the high-budget espionage series did little to improve the studio's less-than-robust financial condition. According to Salvatore Iannucci, "Solow was running their operation. We bought *Mission* for about one hundred thousand dollars per episode and it was costing them one hundred twenty-five thousand dollars or one hundred and thirty thousand dollars to produce. I used to have meetings with Herb—he would show me the numbers and beg us to put up more money, which we refused to do. We never put up more money, so they then were losing substantial money."

"When I presented *Mission: Impossible* to Bill Paley," recalls Mike Dann, "it was a very important project because it was different, it was out of the mold; it came to us right after *Topkapi,* the great caper movie. The problem with the show, though, was that unlike any other program that had been before on the air, it had to have a different location, a different country, different clothing, different cars. So to make up for that, to create the illusion you were in a different country each time, they did the bulk of indoor shooting but still didn't have any permanent sets, except for the burning of the audiotape at the beginning, the tape that self-destructed. And the music was so important. It was a very, very expensive show. It was never a runaway hit—but it was a very solid show. *Mission: Impossible,* for its time, next to *Star Trek,* [was] the most costly [production] possible."

In what *Variety* called "the richest telepix package deal ever made," Lucille's 1966–67 CBS contract involved approximately $12 million, which included production costs of *The Lucy Show* for the upcoming season as well as two Ball specials; her weekly series budget would rise

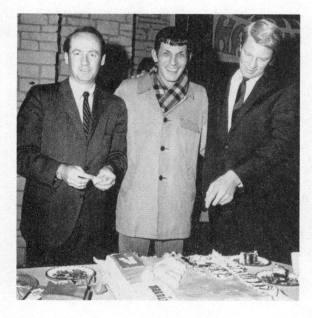

Desilu production executive Herbert F. Solow (*left*) with *Star Trek's* Leonard Nimoy and *Mission: Impossible's* Peter Graves
COURTESY OF HERBERT F. SOLOW

from $93,000 to $100,000 per episode in her twenty-two-week commitment with Desilu receiving an additional $600,000 for sixteen summer repeats. The improved terms also called for CBS to guarantee a *Lucy Show* return buyout minimum of $6 million—or $45,000 per half-hour show, giving Desilu, however, the option to allow CBS to air seven repeats of each episode or put the entire package on the open market to seek better terms, with the network in turn having the right to "substantially" better any other outside offer. Desilu would, in addition, receive "substantial" payment for network daytime reruns of *Lucy*. CBS also would provide Desilu with the $600,000 "pilot fund."

Iannucci counters that the $600,000 had been considered part of total outlay calculated to corral Ball—on paper itemized as a "pilot fund"—in order to entice the star to re-sign with CBS. "It was only money. We knew what we were doing all the time. We were happy she had Desilu. She put herself in a position where she really had to work. We had the leverage because she had the huge overhead of the studio. That gave us the bargaining chip—which we never told her at the time."

With the CBS deal finalized, Lucille moved to further integrate Gary Morton into corporate business affairs and named him vice president in charge of live television programming as well as serving as "production consultant" on *The Lucy Show.* "She helped me," offers Gary Morton. "She's the one who got me involved with Desilu. She had me check out all the studios. There were three of them. She said, 'Would you go over and check this out and check that out?' That's how I learned. Being an executive was not her favorite thing—but she delegated the authority to people who had the experience. She had people who worked with her at RKO and worked with her at MGM. We had two lawyers, and every studio today has twenty-seven lawyers—we had great, great people there. I'm so grateful to the people at Desilu—I learned more about the business from the bottom up from the nicest executives in the industry. And they all absolutely adored her—Ed Holly, Bernie Weitzman, Argyle Nelson—all the people that were just superb to me. They never resented me. As a matter of fact, there was such a wonderful relationship at the beginning of *The Lucy Show,* Desi directed and I was doing the warm-ups."

And, as Ed Holly notes, "Gary had a reputation for being a nice Borscht Belt comedian who was at the point in his career and his life where he could, in essence, drop the rest of his life and make himself Mr. Lucille Ball. He did that. He used to take up a lot of my time, and Argyle Nelson's time, because he wanted to learn everything he could about the business. We spent a lot of time with him, and he didn't have to do that and wouldn't have done it if he wasn't really interested in trying to become more than just Mr. Lucille Ball. I'm sure there are those who resent some of the things Lucy let Gary do in the early years because he took their place away." Bernie Weitzman, however, holds a different perspective: "Lucy put Gary in, but we wouldn't let him in. Because we knew he wasn't capable of managing the company. He was on the periphery. Desi disliked him totally. Everyone else in the company had very little respect for him, because he tried to be what Desi was, without having Desi's authority. He was, at least, smart enough to understand that, and he stayed away from everybody."

And, according to Carole Cook, "In front of the crowd, when we were filming, they would stop the camera for some reason and she would say, 'Should we have that chair there?' And Gary would say from the sidelines—he always laughed louder than anybody else—'Lucy, why don't you move that chair over there?' Then she'd say, 'No, that's not a good idea.' And he'd say, 'That's what I *said*—that's *not* a good idea.' And then he'd laugh. You pay the price."

As part of her renewal pact, Lucille agreed to star in two solo specials during the upcoming season; as her first endeavor, she planned an outing with Mitzi Gaynor—as two nuns touring Europe, the trip enlivened by nun Mitzi's unusual ESP powers. She would then film a *Lucy in Paris* special followed by *Lucy in Arabia*. The French locale was scratched when foreign officials refused to grant cooperation for the Desilu filming. Producer Cleo Smith opted to instead shoot Lucy's special in London; Laurence Olivier along with Anthony Newley—then filming *Doctor Dolittle*—were signed; when Olivier bowed out, the rewritten script—a fast-paced "mod" departure from the weekly series—had Newley costarred with the British rock group the Dave Clark Five.

"France did not want us," says Cleo Smith. "The London special was a first for Desilu—we had never done any foreign filming. We really paved the way for other shows that followed from other companies. We were innovative. It was an exciting time, and Lucy wanted to do it. We were trying to get her to do some other things." Cleo and the cinematographer had a difficult time, however, convincing Lucy to tone down her heavy stage makeup for the outdoor location shooting, which had been somewhat camouflaged by highly filtered *Lucy Show* studio lighting and careful photography.

Lucille had not long before gone under the knife for cosmetic surgery. "I'd tape her up in the back," recalls her makeup artist, Hal King. "She would scar very easily, so I couldn't put the tapes directly near her eyes. But even when I taped her up in the back, she couldn't stand that. They

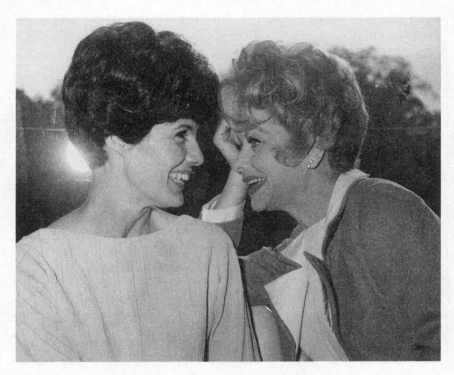

With Cleo Smith, Lucille's cousin but invariably called her "sister" by the redhead, they were so close. The two were in England filming the *Lucy in London* special. Cleo would later become producer of the *Here's Lucy* series.
THOMAS J. WATSON COLLECTION

did as much as they could with photography. She got pretty bad. Her eyelids were beginning to fold, so she had to have them operated on. And they turned lipstick red for years, before the color went away. She didn't heal very well. She couldn't have a full face-lift."

Lucy in London, aired in October 1966, was highly rated but fell victim to bad reviews; *Variety* noted, "What had promised to be one of the season's major specials turned out to be a major disappointment." Poor critical response allowed Lucille the excuse to retreat from her "new image"; as Cleo notes, "She was not happy with the reviews. I had discussed with CBS a three-special deal. After the reviews, she said, 'I *don't* want to do them,' because it didn't get raves."

Reflects Cleo of her executive-producer duties for *Lucy in London:* "Gary didn't look after her best interests. He gave in to her. With me, it wasn't a matter of giving in to her—she would say what she wanted to do, and I would begin to bring in ideas and people and expose these things to her. It was Herb Solow who said, 'Don't let Gary in there, because if it fails, it's going to be *your* thing. And if it does well, it's going to be *his*.'

Jealousy was a big part of it." And, adds Herb Solow, "I never got along with her husband. Don't take from your spouse and use that as your importance. Gary did that. Constantly. Lucy had a big Rolls-Royce, so Gary had a big Rolls-Royce. My business-affairs guy would come in and say, 'Gary came in last night and said Lucy said to add another five thousand dollars to his salary.' "

Carole Cook—among many other of Lucy's intimates spanning back to her days with Desi—soon felt displaced by Gary Morton. "She even called me to come over when the lawyers were at her house and they were signing a prenuptial agreement," recalls Carole. "I couldn't come over that day, but that's when she told me they were going to get married. The first year or so, it was the same, but gradually, he pushed everybody away. He shooed all of her friends away from her. I know he did. We were like a support group for her. I thought he was mean about some of it. And hurtful." And, says Marcella Rabwin, "He tried to root me out, no question about that. He didn't care for anyone who had been important to her. He wanted to be the dominant factor."

With the CBS purchase of *Mission: Impossible* largely the result of Ball's intervention and ongoing network negotiations, Oscar Katz could claim only two series sold to a network—out of twenty-two, primarily Desilu-financed pilots he had commissioned—NBC's *Star Trek* and ABC's *April Savage*. When ABC, however, abruptly dropped plans to place *Savage* on its fall schedule, rumors immediately shot through Hollywood that Katz's Desilu days were numbered; Katz, in fact, shortly announced he

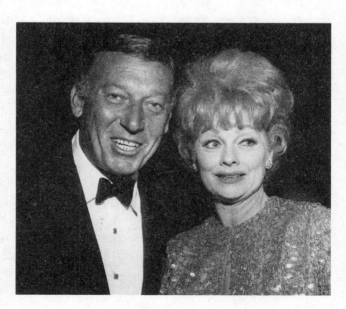

The Mortons
RICK CARL COLLECTION

would leave Desilu on Friday, March 11, 1966. Herb Solow was soon elevated to Desilu programming vice president as his replacement.

"Lucy heard I was looking for a job elsewhere," says Oscar Katz as the reason behind his Desilu dismissal. "She was livid. I told her I would not look for a job under contract; I was offered two jobs while I was there. She was convinced I was out looking for a job." With their relationship strained, he recalls that he requested his two-year contract not be renewed. On his last day at the studio, "Lucy came to my office and closed the door. She was a bit uneasy. I got up and walked around to her. She kissed me and said, 'I want to thank you for the dignified way you ordered this studio. I was very conscious of what used to go on with Desi.' "

However, as Mike Dann offers, "Oscar, who had fine network training, was supposed to be the big white hope, create programming, or select programming concepts that could be sold to the networks. It was a very unsuccessful period."

"The professional image of Desilu was awful," recalls Solow. "Because it had nothing—it was all *Lucy*. Most American half-hour comedy shows that were popular in the States were not popular overseas, but *Lucy* was. Everyone loved to watch *Lucy*. It even worked in England, although their sense of humor was not ours, but they all responded to *Lucy*. Because of that, the name Desilu became very important—Desilu had been as important, at one time, as MGM. But since Desi had left, it was a failing company because Desi was an enormously talented man. Desi had come up with all sorts of superior ideas. And I knew we had to change the current image, that it was a dying studio. Lucy was still puttering away, doing the same thing over and over again. I explained at a meeting, that I wanted to get some new things going. I sent a copy [of a modernized Desilu logo] to Lucy to see. As usual, I never heard from her."

Wary of the anticipated presence of troublesome stockholder John Gilbert at the August 1966 annual stockholders' meeting, Lucille was forearmed with good news that, for the first time, Desilu declared a 5 percent stock dividend. Since she was purportedly stricken with laryngitis, Mickey Rudin on her behalf announced the company posted a net income for the fiscal year of $830,094 as contrasted to 1965's tally of $455,710; 1966's gross revenue was $18,797,502, flat compared to 1965's $18,997,163; corporate revenue had increased due to the sale of *The Lucy Show* to forty-eight countries. Production chief Herb Solow announced a $15 million production budget for the 1967–68 season, including fifteen series pilots.

Gilbert indeed surfaced during the meeting, submitting a proposal to place a ceiling on executive salaries—the move obviously aimed at Lucille's $100,000 Desilu stipend, although it was noted that Ball, obviously stung by Gilbert's attack at the previous year's stockholders' meeting, had amazingly taken a salary cut of $25,000. Studio president Ball, it was also confirmed, had increased her Desilu holdings from 52 percent to 59 percent, providing her with a total of $6 million in company stock. Rudin added that, for the 1966–67 season, the three studio lots would operate at near-to-full capacity with twelve non–Desilu owned series.

On the night of August 30, 1966, Desi, while at his beach house in Del Mar, phoned police to disperse "a rowdy and profane bunch of beach bums"—only to be arrested and placed in jail himself. Desi attested he was in his bathrobe preparing to eat dinner at about nine o'clock when nine youths began a ruckus in the front of his Del Mar beachfront resort. "I have little Lucie, who is now fifteen, and her girlfriend visiting me, and they sleep on the floor. I was worried, and I went out to try to talk to these beach bums. All they did was holler and cuss at me. I put a .38 revolver in my bathrobe pocket. I thought I could scare them by shooting into the sand right at my own feet. I fired two shots. The shots didn't even faze them. They just hollered and cussed some more, even louder. I then went into the house and called the sheriff myself. I told them the situation was getting out of hand and would they please send a car to disperse these kids. I was sitting on my front porch when the sheriff's car drove up. I saw them talking to the youths, and then they came up to me."

As the officers approached his property, Desi proclaimed, "Thank God you're here." His relief vanished in an instant when police surrounded him and suddenly declared, "You're under arrest." Stunned, Desi sputtered, "I'm the guy who *called* the sheriff—you must be *kidding!*"

The deputies, however, advised Arnaz he was charged with assault with a deadly weapon. Desi countered that he had only fired blanks into the sand; the officers searched the sand, found no bullets, but arrested him nonetheless. "I went quietly to jail," said Desi, who posted $1,100 bail. "The gun was a present to me from the cast of the TV series *The Untouchables*. It's all very simple."

"He was obviously three sheets to the wind," recalls neighbor Marcella Rabwin. "Everybody knew where he lived—they'd come to see Desi Arnaz. They were making a lot of noise. He picked up a gun. He went outside on his little porch, and he shot it up into the air. Everyone in that little group thought he was shooting at them. He was pretending to. They called the cops, who took him down to the jailhouse. That's the sort of raucous behavior he would lapse into when he was really drunk."

Upon hearing the horrifying news, a still-protective Lucille immediately went into action. "She arranged for one of her drivers to get some blanks down to Del Mar to make sure that, if there *was* an investigation, Desi had blanks," reveals Johny Aitchison, who adds, "My feeling about their relationship was that they were never *really* divorced—Edie was actually the mistress, and Gary was the boyfriend of Lucille."

Lucille turned her attentions away from the headlines generated by Arnaz's most recent sordid incident and intensely plunged into rehearsals for the 1966–67 season premiere episode of *The Lucy Show* with guest George Burns. "I never worked that hard in my life, and I never met anybody who works as hard as Lucy," grumbled Burns. "She drove me out of my skull. I love to sing, but I love to sit down once in a while, too. I couldn't hide from her during rehearsal. She'd grab me by the arm and go into our dance number. I think she had piano players hidden all around the studio.

"Can you imagine," said Burns as he visibly cringed at the thought, "Lucy getting up in the morning and having somebody tell her, 'Lucy, you're not in show business anymore'?—I wouldn't want to be in the same room."

Chapter Sixteen

★

"In hindsight, everyone can look back, if they want
to, and see how important Desi was."

—Herbert Solow, 1991

★

*S*hortly after the 1966–67 television season premiere of *The Lucy Show*, the star's long-delayed plans to film *The Beardsley Story* finally crystallized when Desilu and producer Robert F. Blumofe entered into a coproduction deal, the film to be financed and released by United Artists. The Ball vehicle would be Blumofe's first project under his exclusive multipicture UA pact, following his recent resignation as the distributor's West Coast operations vice president. Lucille narrowed among her preferred leading man prospects John Wayne, Jackie Gleason, or Art Carney. *The Beardsley Story*—to be filmed by Desilu in the summer of 1967—briefly prompted the studio again to consider entering into feature-film production.

"Desi and Lucy bought it as a feature picture, and they had a series of screenplays written, none of which worked because they were all like *I Love Lucy*," notes Blumofe, initially approached by Mickey Rudin and Bernie Weitzman to develop the property into a viable feature film. Blumofe, in turn, commissioned a new version of *The Beardsley Story* to be scripted by Richard Baer, who, according to Blumofe, "had written for television, and he wrote a script that smacked too much of *I Love Lucy*. The solution was to find a top writer-director who knew comedy and understood what theatrical comedies are, someone like Mel Shavelson. United Artists said, because it's a big investment, we'll do it on one condition—only if you, Lucy, and the writer-director will agree to waive final decision on the screenplay and agree to go forward. I went to Lucy and she said, 'You know, every instinct tells me I should not waive final screenplay approval. I just don't want to make a bad film. But, on the other hand, I like the way you've approached it, and I would like to make it. I'm going to take a chance and say yes, I'll waive final script approval.' That took guts. It was wonderful."

Simultaneously, Desilu Productions began to form its slate of television-pilot productions. Herb Solow's first pilot deal for the 1967–68 season was made with CBS for *Alfred and the Amazon,* an ultimately unsold jungle spoof starring Wally Cox. Also envisioned as a possible CBS series was *Mannix,* a one-hour detective series starring Mike Connors, created by the team of William Link and Richard Levinson and produced by *Mission: Impossible*'s Bruce Geller. "We were given thirteen scripts," offers Gary Morton. "One night, Lucy and myself, upstairs in our bedroom suite in our little office up there, read until three o'clock in the morning. When it was all over, she said, 'What do you think?' I said, 'I like *Mannix.* I liked *Mission: Impossible. Star Trek* was never a script brought to us. I thought *Mannix* was good because there was no hard-hitting, good-looking detective on the air." Yet, according to CBS executive Mike Dann, "They had nothing to do with the making of *Mannix.* We, in a sense, created it. I had seen the film *Harper,* with Paul Newman—I was expecting a straight-on detective movie, and it wasn't like a Mickey Spillane character. He was an honest, handsome guy. I called Perry Lafferty, who was then vice president in charge of the West Coast, and I said to him, 'I've just seen *Harper.* I want to do a pilot based on *Harper.* Pick a nice guy and a great producer.' He said, 'What about Bruce Geller? You can get Bruce Geller over at Desilu.' I said to him, 'Who do we get for the guy?' He said there was a guy, Mike Connors, who had played a private eye, in a series called *Tightrope.* I said, 'Oh, he wasn't very good. I didn't like him. But he was quite attractive.' He said, 'Well, we'll try it in Bruce's hands. Bruce wants Mike Connors.' We gave that show to Desilu and Bruce Geller."

Mannix sold to CBS only a month after the pilot was filmed—largely

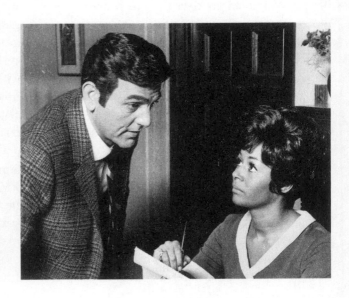

Mike Connors and Gail Fisher in *Mannix*
THOMAS J. WATSON
COLLECTION

the result of Lucille's intervention. "CBS paid for the pilot," notes Bernie Weitzman. "It was very well done. We heard through the grapevine that *Mannix* and another hour show were head-to-head, and one of them was going to be picked over the other—we also heard that the other show had generated a little more enthusiasm by the network than our show. We went to Lucy and said, 'Look, this show is very important to the company's future. We want you to call up CBS. Tell them you feel we have a terrific program, and we want you to buy our show.' She said, 'I can't do that. I've never done that before.' We answered, 'But, Lucy, our whole future may depend on this. CBS will listen to you.' She didn't really believe it. She picked up the phone and called CBS. She said, 'This show is a good show. I'm calling you because I hear this show may not go on the air. And I want you to know I'm supporting this show *one hundred percent*—and I would be *personally* unhappy if CBS passed on this show.' Nine years it was on the air."

Lucille again hesitated signing for another season of *The Lucy Show,* while considered the leading candidate for the supporting role of the tough, aging Broadway musical-comedy star Helen Lawson—a character reportedly based on Ethel Merman—in Twentieth Century–Fox's motion-picture adaptation of Jacqueline Susann's torrid best-seller *Valley of the Dolls,* scheduled to begin filming in early 1967; Ball lost the role to Judy Garland, who, in turn, was replaced by Susan Hayward. Lucille had, in fact, recently reactivated her film career, appearing in a vignette with Art Carney in the Fox film comedy *A Guide for the Married Man.*

Lucille had grown weary of her studio administrative chores, although she continued to handle her responsibilities with aplomb. States Gale Gordon, "Once, Ed Holly came in during rehearsal. He said, 'What are you going to do with the railroad train that you own?' She said, '*What* railroad train?' He said, 'According to the records, when you acquired the studio from RKO, along with the deal you got a railroad diesel engine that is in the Union Station in California that belongs to the studio, so now it belongs to you.' Not-quite-normal business transactions would come up and face her, and she would handle them with such great ease and calm."

At the close of 1966, rumors circulated of a probable Desilu buyout by adjacent Paramount Studios; January 1967 brought confirmation of serious negotiations between the two studios. Paramount Pictures was anxious to expand television production under the new aegis of former CBS executive John Reynolds.

The first week of February brought news that negotiations between

Mickey Rudin, Ed Holly, and Paramount's parent company Gulf + Western board chairman Charles G. Bluhdorn were successfully proceeding. Lucille escaped to Miami to appear with Jackie Gleason on his birthday special—and also avoid her attorney, Mickey Rudin, and the final decision to sell Desilu Studios to Gulf + Western's Paramount Pictures. When Lucille refused to take Rudin's repeated telephone calls, he flew to Florida and found her hiding in a Miami hotel. "Everybody had heard about the merger," she recalled. "I couldn't make up my mind. He had to have an answer, he said. Twenty-four hours or we blow the deal. Well, we went over the whole thing again, and I started to cry. 'I need an hour,' I told him. 'I just gotta have an hour.' More thinking. I said to him, 'Do you know, Mickey, I haven't even *seen* this man?' 'Now, Lucy,' he said, 'I've told you about him. Will you talk to him over the phone?' 'No,' I said. 'I like to see a man's eyes, shake his hand.' Well, I talked to him anyway, and do you know what he said? He said, 'Miss Ball, one of the things I am prepared to like about you is that you care.' I cried again. Then I said yes."

February 15, 1967, brought the announcement of the sale of Desilu Studios to Gulf + Western Industries, Incorporated—new owners of Paramount Pictures since October 1966—for $17 million in a stock-exchange deal. The three-studio, sixty-two-acre Desilu sale provided G + W with a combined studio complex covering several square blocks in Hollywood. Lucille's 60 percent of controlling interest in Desilu stock netted her $10.2 million in Gulf + Western stock. Although it was not reported at the time, furiously bidding for a merger—although essentially a studio buyout—was Danny Thomas. "As far as we were concerned, we had a deal," offers Ronald Jacobs, then executive in charge of production for both Danny Thomas Productions and Sheldon Leonard Productions. "I thought we had Desilu. I thought we were going to own that studio. The deal was in place. Lucy's attorney flew in from New York and met with her that afternoon and said, 'You should sell to Gulf + Western,' and explained to her that she had stock options and that it was a better deal. So she went with Gulf + Western." Another interested Desilu buyer was former Desilu executive Martin Leeds: "I offered Lucy six million dollars cash at the time she was negotiating with Gulf + Western. Mickey Rudin took my offer down to Bluhdorn and squeezed another two million dollars out of Bluhdorn based upon my offer."

Lucille apparently shed few private tears upon ridding herself of Desilu Productions. "I remember seeing my mother lying in bed with her breakfast tray," recalls Lucie Arnaz, "which is pretty much the visual I have of my mother all the time because that's how I spent most of my time with her. And she showed me the paper, and I thought that was a lot of money. I remember feeling a little like the playground was being burned. I don't think she showed much emotion about it. She said, 'Well, we sold the studio today.' To me, the big thing was when they separated—everything after that was, who *cares?* I was still recuperating from that."

A display of corporate unity was effected on July 26, 1967, when Lucille—flanked by Bluhdorn—wielded scissors at a ribbon-cutting ceremony, the giant 70mm film-stock ribbon stretched between the adjacent Desilu-Gower and Paramount Pictures studio lots—a wall had divided the two properties for forty-two years. "Lucy," said Charles Bluhdorn, "It's good to be with you. I love you."

"Charlie," countered Lucille, "I couldn't have made a better choice." She could not resist the temptation to add, "I was offered more money, you know."

A radiant Lucille enthused, "Mr. Bluhdorn is interested in keeping the lots alive, not inactive, and that is what I want. It's a natural marriage, and I was happy to make it." When asked if Paramount and Desilu would coproduce television and motion-picture properties, Bluhdorn promised, "We'll cooperate in everything."

Underscoring the importance of Lucille's continuing role in the Paramount operation, Charlie Bluhdorn suddenly told a group of top-level executives during a management meeting, "We better go over and pay our respects to Miss Ball." The blue-suited group promptly marched down the street to Desilu Studios for an anticipated ten-minute visit that stretched into a two-hour business meeting. "He was charming," recalled Lucille of Bluhdorn's unexpected appearance. "He travels fast, talks fast, and acts on impulse." She then cracked, "I just hope he stays alive."

Not long after, she voiced her relief at divesting herself of her multiple administrative responsibilities, also deeply stung by male-directed criticism of her unique role as the only female having presided over a film studio. "Listen, honey," she told Rex Reed, "If I was going to turn into a man, I would've done it a long time ago. I've been in awe of men most of my life. It never occurred to me how an executive should be. I've been told. But when I took over this job I decided to do it my way. My ability comes from a fairness and a knowledge of people. The rules were here before I took over. I never wanted to be an executive, but when my marriage to Desi broke up after nineteen years, I couldn't just walk away from my obligations and say forget it. We were an institution. So I took on all the responsibilities. Now I've just sold the whole damn thing to a bigger corporation, and pretty soon they'll take my name off the door and I'll be free."

Gulf + Western soon realized the extent of Desilu's bleak financial state. As Ed Holly recalls, "Just a week or so after the merger, when Bluhdorn had started seeing the cost figures, he called me in the middle of the night. All I heard was 'What did you sell me? I'm going to the poorhouse!' I said, 'Charlie, you must be looking at *Star Trek* and *Mission: Impossible*. Those shows are costing almost to the dollar what our projections showed they would cost. You and your people made the judgment that that was all right.' "

Desi Arnaz, under his new Desi Arnaz Productions banner, continued to assemble a multitude of his projected series candidates. He was initially buoyed by reports that CBS was seriously considering purchasing his General Foods–financed pilot, *The Carol Channing Show,* but soon after passed on the series, following the recent single-season flop of a similarly highly touted situation comedy series starring Jean Arthur that General Foods had also urged the network to purchase. When NBC and ABC both rejected the comedy, Arnaz was forced to abandon it.

Desi had not discarded his plans to film the novel *Without Consent.* "He wanted Spencer Tracy to be the defense attorney," notes Arnaz's business adviser Howard Sheppard. "Desi put out fifty thousand dollars for the first script. Then there were a number of rewrites." Then, according to Marcella Rabwin, "Desi tried to write the script. I kept saying, 'Desi, it's such a repulsive subject—a young girl who was raped and then afterwards falls in love with the boy, all the details of the rape.' He started the script and wrote about fifteen or twenty pages and called me and said, 'See what you think of this.' He had written it quite well. He told me the rest of the story and said, 'I don't write as well as I should. I don't spell and I don't type. You want to help me?' I said, 'Sure, I'll help you.' He had tremendous enthusiasm for it. A large part of what I did was to put down his thoughts and rearrange them as scenes. The script was never completed. He never could sell it."

Arnaz turned to another Madelyn Pugh Davis–Bob Carroll, Jr., comedy pilot, *The Mothers-in-Law,* a vehicle originally created to star former Desilu stalwarts Eve Arden and Ann Sothern as battling in-laws. After it was determined that Arden's and Sothern's styles were too similar to provide sufficient basis for conflict, Sothern's role was recast with Kaye Ballard. Herbert Rudley and Roger C. Carmel were chosen to play their spouses, and cast as the newlywed offspring were Jerry Fogel and Deborah Walley. Former *Lucy Show* producer Elliott Lewis was signed to develop television properties and eventually served as *Mothers-in-Law* producer. Although the Procter & Gamble–funded *Mothers-in-Law* pilot was part of Arnaz's CBS deal, when the network failed to purchase the series, Desi promptly offered it to NBC, which bought the series upon the strong recommendation of Procter & Gamble. Bitterly noted Kaye Ballard, "There was no loyalty to Desi or to Eve Arden, who had both made so much money for CBS in the past. Even with the sponsor insistent on the show, they still said no. So we went to NBC."

Desi championed—and protected—his writers as he had during their days together on *I Love Lucy*. "When we were doing *Mothers-in-Law*," recalls Madelyn, "We wrote a script and one of the advertising [account executives] called me at home and said, 'This script is terrible.' I was crushed. It was sent to the agency for their approval. I called Desi. I said, 'What do we do? Rewrite?' He said, 'I'll handle it. Don't worry about it.' I later learned he said to her, 'Don't ever call the writers. You call *me,* and I'll take care of it. Don't you ever do that again.' "

Recalls Kaye Ballard, "Desi was brilliant. Vivian Vance told me he was the greatest script editor. Someone had mentioned my name for the part. Desi asked Lucille for advice, and she said, 'Oh, yeah, I think she'd be good.' Desi worshiped her. I was always a little self-conscious, because he'd say, '*Lucy* would do it *this* way.' I'd say, 'I'm *not* Lucy.' He always compared everything to Lucy."

And, as Madelyn notes, "We'd be in his office having a meeting. Whenever the phone would ring and he would begin talking, I *always* knew if it was Lucy, because his voice changed. You can tell a lot by the way a man talks to his wife—or his ex-wife—from the office, whether he liked her. And it was always very, very sweet. He really cared about her. And some part of her cared about him."

During Ballard's tenure on *The Mothers-in-Law,* Lucille would often call on her in Palm Springs. "She'd pedal over or ride a little Honda scooter and have a few drinks. We'd sit and talk. I knew it was because she was curious about Desi. I still don't believe there was any other great love of her life. He was a class act. He was charming. He taught me so much. He took me to the racetrack, taught me how to gamble—the important things in life. He did know how to live. He made you feel important. He had that quality. Lucille could be wonderful. But she was a difficult person. If you knew Desi, it was to love Desi. He had that ability of making you just adore him. Especially women. I had women knocking on my door years later, asking, 'Is Desi still here?' Because I bought Desi's house. He made that possible. I, who never saved a penny in my life, bought his house because Desi was sick, and he knew how much I loved it. His wife, Edie, was one of the great women of all time,

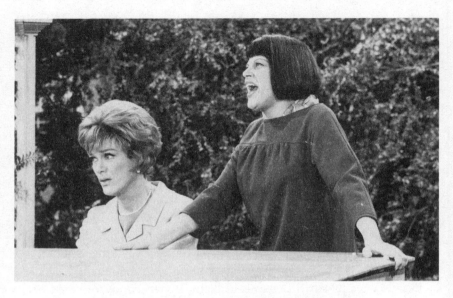

Mothers-in-Law Eve Arden (*left*) and Kaye Ballard
THOMAS J. WATSON COLLECTION

and she knew I loved it. They let me buy it without even a down payment. Edie was an unhappy woman because she loved him so much. In her heart, she knew Lucy was the first love of his life and she was the second."

Kaye recalls another Palm Springs visit: "Lucy and I were riding bikes when a dog came out of the woods, foaming at the mouth. She just looked at the dog and yelled, 'GET THE FUCK *OUT* OF HERE!' The dog ran back into the woods. I turned to her and said, 'That is why you are queen of the world and I am nothing!' "

The Mortons formed a tightly knit—though ever-changing—circle of friends, carefully selected—and many purposely not part of her earlier life with Desi. "Lucy loved Desi totally," says biographer Thomas J. Watson. "And in some ways, I think Desi abused her. Not physically, necessarily. But psychologically. So when Gary came along, and he openly adored this woman and worshiped her, she needed a little worshiping about that time. Gary surrounded her with people that were in awe of her or adored her. Because, as much as she could be very strong, and strong-willed, she was also very fragile. And Gary saw that. So she became a little unapproachable insofar as there was nobody willing to sit her down and say, 'Look, Lucy, you're *wrong*. For your benefit, I'm going to *tell* you why you're wrong.' A few people did on a few occasions—and she did not fight it."

"My mother was very regimented in what she liked to do, what she liked to see and what she liked to eat," offers Lucie. "She had her likes and dislikes. A night at my mother's was never going to be a surprise. It would be backgammon, maybe a movie and dinner—which would be one of five menus. But it was great, real suburbia. But then something would happen—'It was something I did. I never heard from her again.' Friends disappeared over the years who adored them both, who would have killed for them. And it was reduced to a few people who got used to the routine." Echoes Lucy's cousin Cleo, "When she was disenchanted for some reason—it could be the smallest thing in the world—she'd close off."

"There's no question about it," says Marcella Rabwin. "Lucille became harder. Living with Gary Morton, she developed some of the mannerisms, some of the same modes of thinking. Desi was not intellectual, but he was very, very bright. Gary was not intellectual, but he was very, very shrewd. There's a difference."

Lucille's already pronounced frugality apparently blossomed even more in her second marriage, despite her recent ten million-dollar Desilu sale. "One night I had to make her up. It was about six o'clock," recounts Hal King. "I went over to her house. She said, 'Sit down. We're going to have some dinner, and then you can go upstairs and make me up. We're having lobster tail, but we've got *hamburger* for you.' So I ate hamburger. Now, that was a sickness." Adds Maury Thompson, "One year, she gave us little portable radios. Gary got them somewhere for nothing. Five of us all got the same thing. It was October, way before Christmas. She called me into her dressing room and had the radio plugged in. She says, 'What do you think of this?' I said, 'What, the *radio?* Oh, it's a nice little radio.' 'Well, *that's* what you're getting for Christmas.'"

Mary Wickes, on the other hand, notes, "She was a very giving person. She took care of a lot of people other people didn't know about. Lucille took care of Eddie Sedgwick's widow, Ebba. I know of a dialysis machine she bought for someone who had been a dancer at MGM when she was under contract there." And, according to her *Wildcat* supporting player Swen Swenson, Lucille not only convinced him to relocate to Los Angeles to help bolster his career, she also jumped into action when his beloved pet dog suddenly became "desperately ill. She was just about to die. It was on a weekend. I called Lucy and said, 'I know I can't get through to a vet. Could you possibly get through to *your* vet?' She said, 'Oh, of course. I'll get right on it.' She gave me the address of the vet's office, saying, 'He'll meet you there.' I went flying down to the vet's office, and Lucy is there, and I knew she had a phobia about leaving home. And also, she seldom drove herself or seldom ever went out without makeup. And she had come there to support me. I never forgot that. She really came through for me."

Maury Thompson—who had loyally remained with Desilu since the very first *I Love Lucy* episode, elevated from script clerk to camera coordinator to *Lucy Show* director—irrevocably severed his association with Ball at the close of the 1966–67 season, despite his careful handling of the star. "I couldn't *dare* sass her back, or I'd lose my job," he admits. "If I did try and sass her, I'd try and do it in a funny way." His break with Lucille came, as had Madelyn Pugh Davis's and Bob Carroll, Jr.'s, during the final episode of the season: "We had a whole group of dancers. In rehearsal, I looked over, and way off to the side against the burlap stage wall were Lucille and Gale, looking around the corner. I thought, Well, that's kind of cute. We could cut to them. So I said, 'Pan over, and let's see what we've got.' She says, 'This is *not* the show. This is the *rehearsal*. I *don't* want them taking a picture of us.' I said 'Honey, look, we can light it. We don't have to worry about the set. It would be the backstage of a theater. It's just perfect.' She said '*Cut! Hold it!*' And I screamed, 'No!' I thought I was going to faint. I looked over, and she was gone. She knew she had gone too far. After the show, I'm a wreck. Here she comes in her terry-cloth robe. There's no audience. She said, 'Well, honey, we finally got it. Good show, wasn't it? What are you *crying* for?' I said, 'I'm just tired Lucille.' Well, you'd better get some rest.' That's what she would say to Desi when he would blow up— 'What's the *matter* with you? You better go lie down somewhere.' "

The exhausted director promptly made plans for a South American vacation. "I went to my agent and said, 'Look, if she wants me, then I want a raise in salary. Because it's gotten to the point where I just can't please her. But wait until I get back.' The agent called her the next morning and said, 'What about Maury?' She said, 'What *about* Maury?' 'Well, if you want him to stay with you, he wants a raise.' She said, 'Tell him to go *fuck* himself.' I found out from Tommy Thompson later that she picked up the phone and said, 'Jack Donohue, you got a job? Okay, you have one now.' When I came back from vacation, my nameplate was off the door. I said, 'Who stole my nameplate?' The secretary says, 'Have you spoken with Tommy?' She called him over. Tommy says, 'Guess what? You're fired.' "

CBS was eager to re-sign Lucille and presented her with a $12 million package for the 1967–68 season, the revised contract calling for the network to pay Desilu a record $7.8 million for future CBS reruns of *The Lucy Show,* the 156 half hours (including shows yet to be filmed for the upcoming season) scheduled to begin a five-year run of network daytime repeats in 1968 before entering the syndication market. Ball had earned $15,000–$16,000 per show as star of 110 episodes of *The Lucy Show,* with her tax-shelter arrangement stipulating that Desilu owed her a deferred payment of $1.1 million for past seasons; as part of her new CBS pact, the network would assume that obligation and thus save Desilu more than $1 million. Her total salary of $384,000 for twenty-four episodes of *Lucy* for the 1967–68 season would be partially deferred as a tax shelter, with the star paid $180,000 of that amount in 1968 and also in 1969, with $84,000 due in 1970.

Procter & Gamble agreed to finance the Arnaz-directed pilot for his half-hour outdoor adventure series *Land's End,* created by Arnaz's one-time Desilu associate Mort Briskin. Arnaz signed his former Desilu editorial chief Dann Cahn as associate producer. "Mort wanted to use Victor Mature, but Desi insisted on Rory Calhoun. Marty Milner had been in a *Desilu Playhouse,* and Desi decided that because he was such a sweet guy, he'd be the bad guy. Rory Calhoun is the star, and his pal is an aging movie star, Sonny Tufts, which was sort of a joke. As the cop, Desi picked Gilbert Roland to give it that Latin flavor. Rory was going to run Land's End, a vacation fishing place. For the girl in the show, they came up with Lee Chapman, a rather stunning girl. We all went to Texas. Mort had written a pretty good script, but Desi was improvising the script, too. Desi was going nuts. He was acting a little irrational, shooting all kinds of shots. He was making improper decisions governed by his ego and a little help from the alcohol. The only ones that could really calm him down were Bob and Madelyn. They were part of the unit, but they weren't on this show."

"One night, we're all having dinner. Lee wanted some aspirin. She was under a lot of stress. I went to my room to get what looked like pills, and I bring them to the table and give them to Lee Chapman. Desi thinks I'm giving her drugs, so he picks up the whole plate of food and throws it at me, yelling and screaming at me. He finally calmed down. The next morning, I'm watching the sun rise, and out of the shower comes Desi, cold sober, we're philosophizing, and within eight hours, the whole thing was forgotten and we're pals again."

Cahn recalls the disastrous December 31, 1966, screening of *Land's End* for network and advertising-agency executives: "We had all these people from William Morris in Selznick's projection room [at Desilu-Culver]. It was long, and there were problems. Desi had shot so much stuff, when we ran it, it was about forty-five minutes. It was no half hour. Desi didn't want to cut it down—and it wasn't that great. Desi's telling them they have a one-hour show. They kept saying, 'Desi, we only have a half hour. You've gotta make it a half hour.' It was frustrating him. It was New Year's Eve, and everyone wanted to get out of there. Something came up, and I shot my mouth off. Desi came at me, in front of the whole group, and said, 'Goddamn you, you *cocksucker,* you're wrong!' He started this tirade. I walked out. That night the phone rings, and he starts on me again. He says, 'I relied on you, and I brought you back with me.' I said, 'Desi, I've been loyal to you. The problem is, they only want a half-hour show.' In the end, I hung up on him. In my mind, I knew I couldn't stay. I wanted to be his younger brother. I really loved him."

In an impressive final bid for glory, Desilu Productions garnered fourteen Emmy nominations for the 1966–67 season—including *Mission: Impossible* and *Star Trek* sharing nominations for "Outstanding Dramatic Series"; Martin Landau, Barbara Bain, writer Bruce Geller, and composer Lalo Schifrin for *Mission: Impossible;* Leonard Nimoy and art director Jim Rugg for *Star Trek;* and Lucille Ball, Gale Gordon, and director Maury Thompson winning *Lucy Show* nominations. While *Star Trek* failed to win any awards, the June 4, 1967, nineteenth annual Emmy Award ceremonies cited *Mission: Impossible* as "Outstanding Dramatic Series," with star Barbara Bain, writer Geller, and series film and sound editors also honored. And, although Gale Gordon and director Thompson lost Emmy bids, an emotional—and obviously stunned—Lucille Ball was named "Best Comedy Actress," a feat she would also accomplish the following year for the final season of *The Lucy Show.*

"I can't believe it," she earnestly said, clutching her 1966–67 Emmy. "I honestly *cannot* believe it. I don't have *one* thing prepared to say, because I just didn't *expect* it. It's been a long, long time." Clearly touched—and perhaps recalling her *I Love Lucy* prime and the lack of industry recognition in subsequent years—Lucille poignantly noted, "It left a long time ago. I'm glad it's back. The last time I got it, I thought they gave it to me because I had a baby—and that baby is fourteen years old now. I love my work. Thank you for giving me this for it."

The evening was not a pleasant one for Maury Thompson, who enjoyed the distinction of being the only *Lucy* director ever nominated for an Emmy: "She had already fired me. So I'm not sitting at her table, I'm sitting with Sid Caesar. Lucille's at the center table, and there's nothing between their table and where I sat. At her table was just Gary and Lucy, Tommy Thompson and his wife. She knew I was nominated. It would have been nice if she had arranged to have me sit at the *Lucy* table. But no. I looked over a couple of times. The winner was the director of *The*

Monkees. At the end of the evening, she comes running by and goes right past me. She had a thing around her neck that flew right past my face. She didn't stop and say, 'Maury, I'm sorry. Maybe next time.'" Herb Solow also recalls Lucille's lack of graciousness: "There were two camps at Desilu: The *Lucy* camp and the rest of us. We won eleven or fifteen Emmys—I *never* heard from Lucy."

With the redhead set to return to *The Lucy Show* for the 1967–68 season, Ball began production on *The Beardsley Story*, soon retitled *His, Hers and Theirs* and, finally, *Yours, Mine and Ours*. Finally chosen to play opposite Lucille was her RKO *Big Street* leading man, Henry Fonda, along with Van Johnson in a supporting role. Recalls Blumofe, "I was going to call him when suddenly I get a call from New York, and it's Hank on the phone. He said, 'I read about it in the trades. I'd like to play the male role. I remind you that Lucy and I worked together years ago.' I said, 'Lucy and I would both love to have you, Hank, but I have to tell you one thing—we have waived screenplay approval, and we're going ahead. I can't give you screenplay approval.' He said, 'If it's good enough for Lucy and you, it's good enough for me.' Mel Shavelson on his own had brought in Mort Lachman to write the screenplay with him. Mort was Bob Hope's top writer. In six weeks, they turned in a screenplay that was so good no changes were necessary. Lucy was very happy with the screenplay—she loved it—because it gave her a chance to show she was a much more versatile actress than the television shows. It was a wonderful role."

Notes Shavelson, "She tried to get Lucie and Desi, Jr., into the picture.

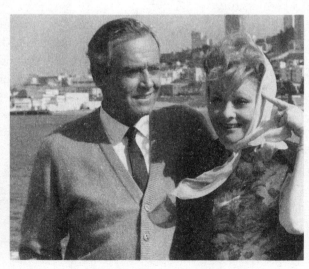

Henry Fonda and Lucille on location in San Francisco for *Yours, Mine and Ours*
THOMAS J. WATSON COLLECTION

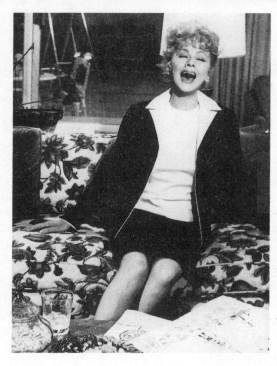

The drunk scene in *Yours, Mine and Ours*
THOMAS J. WATSON COLLECTION

I turned them down. She was a smart enough mother to see they weren't quite right. She didn't force it. My feeling was that her two kids would've thrown a different kind of feel into the whole family situation, and I had enough problems without having to worry about that. And Gary was on the sidelines all the time."

"There was a big scene in which Hank's kids spike her drink and she becomes drunk," recalls Blumofe. "She practically orchestrated it herself. She went from laughter to tears from laughter, back and forth. It was a brilliant tour de force." However, according to Shavelson, "She wouldn't play the scene. She said, 'I can't do that.' It took about an hour of arguing to get her to go out and try it. And it was one of her best performances. She was afraid of combining the drama with the laughter. On the other hand, nobody else could have done it like she did."

Lucille constantly attempted to override the director throughout filming. After shooting one scene with Henry Fonda, she ordered, "*Cut!* Let's do it *again*. There's a shadow on Hank's chin, Mel, move that light three inches to the left. Now stay where you are, Hank." After they filmed another take, Lucy immediately announced, "I liked the first one, Mel, but I'll look at both of them in the projection room." Following a take, Fonda affectionately kissed her, as co-star Van Johnson smiled and remarked, "She's the same girl she was at MGM."

"Lucy was a big problem on the picture," reveals Shavelson, "basically because she was Lucy. She had her own highly successful television show, and she was used to running every department of it. And I wouldn't let her run the movie. There were a lot of battles. She had tremendous talent, but she wanted to be the cameraman, the director, the lighting expert, and everything else. The problem with Lucy was that she was *too* smart—she knew everything, she *could* do it. But I couldn't let her if it was going to be my picture. So when I made the final shot of the picture, which was a close-up of Lucy, she said, 'Mel, now that it's over, how did you enjoy working with me?' I said, 'Lucy, it's the first time I ever made a picture with *nineteen* children.' She burst into tears and didn't talk to me until the grosses started coming in. She liked to be patted on the back—she didn't like anybody to oppose her." He adds, however, "She was smart enough to see things that I didn't see. If I had a good point to make, I could haggle it out with her."

Despite heavy theatrical makeup, adhesives to cosmetically lift her face, and a collection of wigs, the fifty-six-year-old Lucille—portraying a childbearing woman at least a decade younger—presented considerable photographic challenges. "She had a basic lighting problem, and she knew it, and she knew a great deal about her lighting," recalls Mel Shavelson. "You had to frontlight her and photograph her from the front so that the wrinkles did not show. Lucy's skin had gone to pieces because of the years and years of makeup. It took not only time to light her, but also care to shoot a scene so that she was not shown from an unflattering angle."

Lucille—who had taken to the habit of greeting fans from a considerable distance backstage at *The Lucy Show* to preserve the illusion of youthful middle age—had no such protection to hide her natural, aging appearance during a *Yours, Mine and Ours* promotional junket. "We were in some town," recalls Shavelson. "A little girl came up to Lucy to get her autograph. She looked up and said, 'Lucy, what happened to your *face?*' And Lucy turned away and couldn't talk to anyone for the rest of the day. Because nobody would mention it but a child."

The film—deemed "socko family entertainment" by *Variety*—was an enormous popular and critical success. According to Blumofe, "It was one of the top-grossing films of 1968 and was United Artists' number-one grossing picture for that year. We made the whole picture for one million, seven hundred thousand dollars. The way the profits were divided, it went one fourth to Paramount because Lucy had sold the rights to Paramount as part of the sale of the studio; one fourth to United Artists, which distributed and financed; a fourth to Lucy, and one fourth to me. Paramount was after the studios. The film just fell into the grab bag." And, adds Shavelson, "It grossed well over twenty-five million dollars. She said, 'Why didn't you *warn* me?' "

Although Bluhdorn maintained Desilu would continue as a separate entity—with Lucille continuing as the company's president—it was ultimately absorbed into Paramount Television. Bluhdorn swiftly instructed switchboard operators to greet Desilu callers with a new "Paramount Gower" identification—"Sometimes I call my office from the house," ruefully mused Lucille, "and the operators ask me, 'Lucy WHO?' " According to Gary Morton, "It was really like any company that buys another company. They always promise you the sun and the world, and then they walk in and bring their own people in and do their own thing. Once a sale is over, they can promise things, but it's not on paper. What Lucy wanted to do was keep her people, and there was a verbal okay—but knowing Charlie Bluhdorn as we got to know later—his word was *not* his bond."

Rumors circulated that upon the dissolution of the Desilu-Paramount association, the star would form her own independent production company. Herb Solow resigned his post as production vice president to become head of production of Paramount Television Productions—the company move not even requiring him to change offices when Paramount Television relocated to Desilu Gower. "I didn't know Desilu was sold until the day it was announced," notes Solow. "I knew John Reynolds, the new head of Paramount Television, from CBS. He said, 'Do you want to come over and be in charge of television for Paramount?' About two weeks later, it's announced that Gulf + Western bought Desilu. It's now Paramount—and I'm in the same office. Nothing changed—same office, same parking space." Not long after, though, he departed to MGM. "It became very rigid, not the old place." On March 29, 1967, CBS had announced it was irrevocably removing all 180 half-hour episodes of *I Love Lucy* from its weekday schedule and, through its CBS Films subsidiary, offering the series in the syndication market. In contrast to other by-then-dated 1950s TV shows, a new generation was by 1967 discovering the original *I Love Lucy* series, and from the distance of a decade, it was evident that Lucille was becoming a bona fide show-business legend—and more appreciated by the younger generation for her long-past series than for her current efforts. The clout the old series still wielded was evinced by a recent network controversy, CBS opting to beam a daytime *Lucy* rerun instead of airing a Senate Foreign Relations Committee hearing on the Vietnam War, a decision that so infuriated CBS news president Fred Friendly that he tendered his immediate resignation; Lucille opposed CBS and squarely sided with the former news director—whom she said "had a good old squawk—they throw in the old *I Love Lucy*s instead of something vital."

In contrast, Jess Oppenheimer found his *I Love Lucy* contract extremely important in the wake of the upcoming highly lucrative network daytime run—and subsequent syndication sale—of *The Lucy Show*. He slapped a Superior Court lawsuit against Desilu, CBS, Lucille Ball Productions, and Gulf + Western Industries, stemming from an alleged breach of his *I Love Lucy* contract.

The basis of his suit was in his claim that Lucille Ball's characterization on *The Lucy Show*—purportedly based on the book *Life Without George*—was actually derived from his "Lucy Ricardo" *I Love Lucy* character. Under the terms of his December 21, 1954, Desilu contract, Oppenheimer claimed that he was to be paid three quarters of 1 percent of the Desilu gross for the original television broadcast of *any* program "based upon" the allegedly protected material, plus 2.5 percent of the Desilu gross for "each reuse telecast thereof."

"They bought the book, *Life Without George,* and changed her name," confirms Bob Schiller, "but it was the same character. So Jess sued. I had occasion to look at our *Lucy Show* contract. I don't remember the exact words, but it said, 'You will fashion the character of Lucy Carmichael on Lucy Ricardo.' Jess had hired us—he was our friend. So I called Jess. He won his lawsuit." According to Thomas J. Watson, "They settled out of court. It wasn't that Lucille resented paying him. She resented anybody suing in public, particularly a friend. Her way of treating a friend when a friend had done her wrong was simply to ignore him. She learned that from Desi. He said that was the 'Cuban way'— 'You cross me, I won't get even. You simply don't *exist.*' "

Lucille's millions derived from the sale of Desilu and the elimination of multiple studio responsibilities only intensified her focus upon the final season of *The Lucy Show*. The last to arrive at one early Monday morning midseason script conference, she marched in, booming, "Things have sure changed since Charlie Bluhdorn took over! Why aren't the pencils sharp?" Calling for her secretary, she demanded, "Where's Wanda? We could have her shot!" As the group read the script, Lucy stopped when she reached page twelve and complained to head writer Milt Josefsberg, "That's awfully *radio!* It's just radio exposition! I kept hoping there'd be a joke coming up, not a lot of words!" Turning to Josefsberg, she barked, "Let's go! Don't just sit there with your chin on your expensive hand!" Gary, who had remained silent in the background, quietly offered a one-liner. "Where did *that* line come from?" asked Lucille. "I was just thinking by myself over here," said Gary as he retreated. "*No,* darling," she replied. At a later session, she emptied ashtrays and told her head writer, "Now, Milt, that precious joke of yours is going out." When Josefsberg hastily reminded her that he had four other jokes to read her as possible substitutes, she brusquely snapped, "There's no time now—you can give them to me for Christmas. You never know what to give me. Now, don't worry, fellas, I'll simply *do* something."

Following a lunch interview with *TV Guide*'s Dick Hobson ("Don't mind the hair curlers, honey—just pretend you're married to me"), Lucille returned to her office, where Josefsberg interrupted to show her the latest Nielsen ratings, which ranked *The Lucy Show* as the number-one program on the air. "This is a joke," exclaimed Lucy. "Isn't it?" Then, from an outside window, Gary called, "Lucy! Lucy! Can you come out and play?" She went to the window and, in a little-girl voice, replied, "I'd like to come out and play, but I have to do the dishes." Pleading, Gary replied, "Your mother said it's all right." "Later, sweetheart," she ordered.

"Somebody once referred to Gary in *TV Guide* as a 'third-rate comic,' " recalls writer Dan Jenkins. "Lucy called me and started bawling me out. She felt I had something to do with it, but I convinced her I hadn't. The story was written by a free-lance writer. But she let him know, now and again, in very certain terms exactly who he was and who she was— which he understood. The editor of *TV Guide* wanted to see Lucy, so we went up to the house for tea. Gary was dropping names like you wouldn't believe—no last names, all first names. It was getting rather obnoxious. Somehow the conversation got on to architecture, and some-body mentioned the house that Frank Lloyd Wright had built in West Hollywood. Gary said, 'I know that house—I could never understand what *Frank* had in mind.' "

Among the final episodes filmed for the season was a two-part Vivian Vance reunion, the first installment of which featured the longtime costars recalling past adventures via flashbacks largely derived from the superior 1962–63 season of *The Lucy Show*. When a reporter, visiting Lucille and Vivian as they screened footage for possible use in the show, suggested including clips from *I Love Lucy,* Lucille flatly dismissed the idea, stating, "It's another era, and I prefer not getting into it."

The second reunion episode centered around a guest appearance by Joan Crawford, in a script originally designed for Gloria Swanson. Craw-ford infuriated Ball during rehearsals, often forgetting her lines, terrified at the thought of performing in front of a live audience. During one run-through, Lucille reportedly discovered Joan with her nose buried in her purse. "What'cha got in there?" Lucy asked, opening Crawford's pocketbook and discovering that Joan was actually swilling 100-proof Smirnoff's vodka from a brown paper bag—with two straws.

"Lucille had great deal of respect for actors if they knew what they were doing," notes Gale Gordon. "The only time she would get impatient was when people would slough off or not pay attention. She was the only person in the world who ever fired Joan Crawford. She was very, very late for rehearsal. Lucy called her up and said, 'Be on time.' The next day, ten o'clock came and then eleven. Joan hadn't called or shown up. Lucy called her on the phone from her dressing room on the stage, and the door was open. So we heard the conversation. She got some lame excuse from Joan that she overslept or something. Lucy said to her, 'Well, *listen,* if you're not here tomorrow morning at ten on the nose, you're *fired.* You *get* that? Fired!' Lucy hung up. She came out of her dressing room. Her eyes were as big as saucers, her hair was standing on end, she was so mad. She said, 'You know what that broad *said* to me just before we hung up? Joan cried, "No one has ever fired me!"' And Joan was there at ten o'clock sharp the next day, never said a word, knew her lines, worked terribly hard. Crawford never made a peep, because she respected Lucy and realized she was being a bit of a stupid woman since there were only four days to rehearse and do the show."

Then, according to Lucy's *Dream Girl* director, Herb Kenwith, "When Joan came on the set, she called me and said, 'Herbert, I'm *terrified* of this lady. Would you come down tomorrow?' I said, 'Yes, but if you acknowledge me as an outside director, on her set, she'll be very angry and take it out on you and not on me. Let's wait for *her* to introduce us. Let us be total strangers.' She said okay. I got there, and every secretary on the lot was in the bleachers—it was Joan Crawford, the Queen of Hollywood. Joan had her hair pulled back in a bun and wore a black dress. Joan came out of her dressing room and came right over to me. Lucy said, 'How long have *you* known each other?' Joan said, 'For many, many years. Herbert's my neighbor in New York.' They started working. Joan had to do a Charleston. Jack Donohue was the director. A black man was playing the piano. Joan was dancing, and Lucy was watching. She clapped her hands and said, 'Stop, stop, *stop!* You're not even *moving* with the music.' Joan said, 'Well, I've never worked with him before. I don't know his tempo, he doesn't know mine. Let's try it again.' They did it again. Lucy stopped her again. She said, 'I don't like the way you're dancing—how *did* you win a Charleston contest in Texas? You *can't* dance!' She always picked the vulnerable spot. If you were a singer, you can't sing—if you were an actress, you can't act. Joan said, 'Could you let me try it again?' She was acting so subservient—she was shaking. Finally, Lucy said, 'Okay, we'll do it *once* more. But if you *don't* get it this time, it's *out—finished.*'

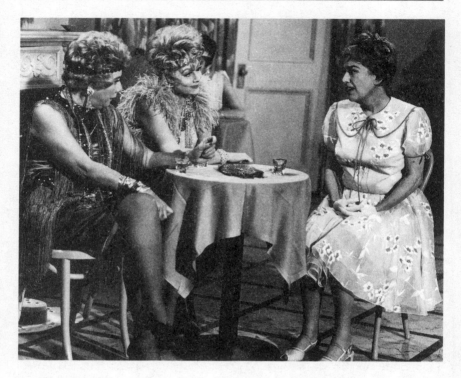

Flappers Vivian and Lucille with a virginal, teetotaling Joan Crawford
CBS INC.

"I got Joan to a corner of the set and tried to do it with her. Joan couldn't even lift her feet off the floor. Lucy said, 'Okay, *cut* it!' And she walked away. Joan ran off into her dressing room. I ran after her. Here was this big motion-picture star, stretched out on the floor crying. I had her face in my lap. I said, 'Don't let her bother you. She does this to everyone. It's a test, Joan.' She said, 'I don't *want* to be tested. I've *been* tested. I don't want to be on this half-hour show to endure this.' I said, 'You're absolutely right. Go out and pretend nothing happened.' 'How *can* I? She's embarrassed me in front of all these people.' I said, 'The first thing we're going to do is fix your hair. Let's get you made up like Joan Crawford. Change your clothes.' I had the makeup lady come in. Lucy called for Joan. I said, 'Miss Crawford will be ready in about one hour. You'll just have to *wait*. No more calls.' After an hour, Joan emerged as Joan Crawford, looking wonderful. People in the bleachers, who waited, started to applaud. They went on with the show. But Lucy criticized everything she did. Jack Benny told me the same thing. Jack called me after doing one show with her and said, 'Herbert, you ought to call a psychiatrist for her.' " After the filming, Crawford announced, "My God, they tell me *I'm* a bitch—Lucy can outbitch me *any* day of the week!"

Lucille occasionally deferred to performers she respected—or those unafraid to confront the formidable star. "She directed me in a parody of *The Untouchables* on one of her shows," Robert Stack told *TV Collector* editor Diane L. Albert. "Normally, I'd pick up the bottle, I'd smell the booze, take a sip, and spit it out, and I'd say, 'Yeah, that's it.' Only this time, I picked up the bottle, smelled the booze, and *drank* it, and got *loaded* as Eliot Ness. And she was very strong, you know. She was my boss. She owned Desilu Studios, and she and Desi cast me as Eliot Ness in the first place. So she started to say, 'Well, I think that maybe . . .' I looked at her. I said, 'Lucy, I played this part one hundred twenty times—if I can't play Eliot Ness by now, I shouldn't even be in the business.' She said, 'You're absolutely right. Keep doing what you're doing.' "

While *The Lucy Show* was television's highest-rated program at the close of 1967, Desi Arnaz's single series on the air, *The Mothers-in-Law,* had failed to make the Top Twenty Nielsen count. Although the series had performed well—if not spectacularly—in the ratings through the year, it was uncertain whether Procter & Gamble, which had repeatedly complained about the "old hat" quality of the scripts, and NBC would renew the situation comedy for a second year. Dan Jenkins was hired to handle publicity duties: "Eve was the star. Kaye was concerned about the ratings. Roger Carmel was the one with the ego. Herb Rudley needed the work. The girl, Deborah Walley, left Columbia because she wanted to work with Desi, the expert on comedy. She didn't know what she was getting into—he chased everybody, but on that show he was after her. But when there were other people around, it was sort of done in a fatherly, big-brother sort of way. He'd put his arm around her and give her a hug. But it was quite obvious what the hell he was up to."

Desi's deteriorating physical and emotional state sparked infrequent but significant problems during production. "Desi was not well," offers Dan Jenkins. "He had a colostomy. He was still wearing the bag. He had lost a lot of weight and looked like hell. I made the mistake of telling him so at a press party, I thought, in a nice way. I said, 'Gee, I hate to see you looking like this.' That's when he just turned on me—everything was my fault. We were like two dogs in the middle of the ring. Everybody was around us in a huge circle. He was laying into me that the promotion had been no good and the publicity had been no good. It was all my fault. He knocked a drink out of my hand. Then we edged over to the side. By the time we got over to the bar, he had his arm around me, and he was slobbering, 'Oh, buddy.' It was a whole different scene. It was funny in a way, but also pathetic."

Although another year seemed doubtful when NBC in January announced plans to drop the series, interest by ABC in acquiring the series prompted NBC—upon P&G's threat of pulling all its business—to reconsider and schedule *The Mothers-in-Law* for its second—and final—season. Arnaz's fervently desired second-season NBC order of *The Mothers-in-Law,* however, sparked considerable backstage turmoil. When Desi learned that Procter & Gamble agreed to sponsor another year on the condition that there would be no production-budget increases—or significant salary hikes—he flew into a rage and telephoned his P&G advertising-agency representative. "I told them to go to hell," said Arnaz.

His William Morris agent quickly intervened and begged Desi to reconsider, since the still-lucrative new deal called for a full season twenty-six-episode commitment and summer-repeat revenue. Desi recanted, and producer Lewis, the writers, and the actors agreed to the deal—with the exception of Kaye Ballard's on-screen spouse, Roger C. Carmel, whose demand for a hefty salary increase infuriated Desi. "He could have deprived one hundred people with the series of work," complained Arnaz. "Where else is he going to make two thousand dollars a week?" Carmel countered, "Desi called me and put it on a personal basis. I didn't feel it should be done that way—it was very unfair of him. Then Desi and the Morris agency threatened I would be replaced. Kaye Ballard and Eve Arden also called me and asked me to go along, but I wouldn't." Arnaz promptly recast Carmel's role with Richard Deacon.

Further distancing her from Paramount Pictures, reports at the same time surfaced that Lucille would likely relocate her still unoffically announced film and television production company to Universal Studios, the resulting of "persistent bidding," said *Variety,* by former Desilu executive Bernie Weitzman, who had recently moved to Universal. Days later, CBS announced it had re-signed Lucille for another year of a weekly situation comedy in a still-undecided new format. Soon after came the announcement of the formation of Lucille Ball Productions—with Lucille installed as president and Gary Morton named vice-president—which would remain based at Paramount, although it moved to Universal several seasons later.

While in London promoting *Yours, Mine and Ours* in late February 1968, she announced that the revamped series—with Gary Morton as executive producer—cast her as working mother "Lucy Carter" with seventeen-year-old Lucie and fifteen-year-old Desi IV portraying her on-camera children. Gale Gordon was to return in the new series—titled *Here's Lucy*—as the blustering, pompous owner of an employment agency where his widowed sister-in-law, Lucy, also worked. Lucie and Desi, Jr., were each signed to three-year contracts with an initial annual salary of $17,600, escalating to $20,400 and, in the third year, $25,200. "They couldn't *believe* it when I told them," said Lucille.

"We went to Hawaii, and I believe it was Milt Josefsberg who said they had an idea to bring her kids in," recounts Gary Morton. "We let the writers sit with her children, to see if they wanted to do it. We never asked them to do it. They said, yes, they'd like to do it. That's how it happened. It was never a decision on Lucy's part to put her children to work." Of her decision to return in a new format following *The Lucy Show,* Morton says, "She had mixed emotions—as long as the kids wanted to do it, then she said, 'Okay, that'll be fun.' "

Yet, according to Lucie Arnaz, "Mother *never* intended to quit. She *always* intended to do another season, either with me or with some other actors. But that's not what she told *us.* She literally said to us at dinner one night, 'I'm thinking of quitting.' And we all said, 'You're going to quit? *Wow.* What *happened?*' 'Oh, nothing, It's just that Vivian doesn't want to work anymore, and I've run the course of the series. Someone suggested that we change the format, that I have a different set of children and be Lucy Somebody Else. But I told them, unless my *own* children play those roles—which you'd both be very good at—I'm really not interested. I think I've done it enough.' I said, 'You've done it enough? What are you talking about? You look terrific, it's not time to quit!' I was just in my first year and a half of high school, so I said, 'When are you talking about doing this?' 'In the fall—you'd have to start in the summer.' 'What about my school?' 'If you decided this was something you'd want to do, you'd go to school on the set. You'd have a tutor every day for three hours, like you did when you played those other little parts.' 'Oh.' She said, 'So think about it and let me know.' I asked, 'When do you have to know?' '*Tomorrow.*'

"So Desi and I said, 'Could we be *excused?*' and we went into the den and shut the door. I looked at him and said, 'Is this something you want to do?' He kind of shrugged his shoulders. He had Dino, Desi and Billy already, so he'd been semi–show biz. I was very, very shy. Much shier than Desi. He said, 'I guess. I don't know.' I said, 'Well, I don't know if I want to do it. I'm going to lay down some laws.' It was the first adult thing I did. I marched back in and said, 'Listen, everybody's going to say I got this part because I'm Lucille Ball's daughter. And I *did* get this part because I *am* Lucille Ball's daughter, so what do I tell them?' And she said, 'I'll make a deal with you. We'll do *one* season, and if the reviewers and the word of mouth are that the kids aren't adding anything to this show, I *promise* I will have you written out cleverly—you'll have a lovely exit, and I'll continue on.' I said, '*Promise?* Because I would like to do this for a living, maybe, and I will be *destroying* my career.' We got okay reviews, and the word of mouth progressively got a little bit better. Reviews didn't say we were the finds of the universe, but they said it was cute, it was okay. It got better and better, so I stayed, but I was *petrified* to go on that show. I would never in a million years have asked her to do that."

And, reveals Lucie Arnaz of hesitantly agreeing to appear with her mother on *Here's Lucy,* "I felt *totally* responsible for Lucille Ball being on television or *never* being on television again—and that the world would *hate* me if I said no."

Chapter Seventeen

"Women's Lib? Oh, I'm afraid it doesn't interest me one bit. I've been so liberated it hurts."

—Lucille Ball, 1972

"*I*'ve always prided myself in knowing when to get off," reflected Lucille of her 1968–74 series, *Here's Lucy*, "and I think I waited three years too long. I was ready to quit five years before I did. I was getting too old to be yelled at by 'Uncle Harry' for doing idiotic things." She reluctantly admitted, however, "Nobody twisted my arm but myself."

While his children adjusted to the demands of weekly television, Desi Arnaz faced certain cancellation of *The Mothers-in-Law*, his series invariably in last place opposite the combined formidable competition of ABC's Quinn Martin series *The FBI*, and CBS's long-running *Ed Sullivan Show*. Also battling failing health, in late 1968 he was rushed to Cedars of Lebanon for diverticulitis surgery. Bolstered by a personal note of support from President Lyndon Johnson, Desi recuperated at Del Mar with Edie at his side. While he did not particularly encourage his children to accept Lucy's offer to appear on her series, Desi remained supportive as he recovered from surgery: "As long as they keep up their grades at school, I don't care. We both feel the same way. When Desi first started the trio with Dean Martin's son, Dino, and Billy Hinsche, Lucy and I told them that, and Dean told them the same thing. If they kept up their grades in school, that was fine with us. It's good for them to have another interest in life, an outside interest. But I told him, 'You let your grades fail, no more trio, no more drums. I don't want a stupid drummer around the house.' Lucy and I both have the same ultimate aim for both of them—bring them up as well as we can, teach them all we can—how to behave, and how to conduct their personal lives. Nothing in life comes before my kids."

Milt Josefberg and Bob O'Brien's *Here's Lucy* premise attempted to comically present the "generation gap" struggle between working-mother Lucille and her two increasingly independent teenagers—the markedly strident and belabored scripts mired in an already-dated 1950s sensibility far removed from America's sweeping social changes involving morality,

317

drugs, music, civil rights, and a sexual revolution that marked the close of the decade and much of the 1970s. The pilot episode's preposterous premise, in fact, had Lucy scheming to land her children jobs entertaining at a posh birthday bash; daughter Kim loses her voice, and the fifty-seven-year-old substitutes, at the last minute, for her teenaged daughter in son Craig's rock-'n'-roll band—partygoers unaware of the switch.

The premiere of *Here's Lucy* met with tepid-to-poor notices. Said *Variety,* "Lucie and Desi Arnaz, Jr., play nicely against mama's japes. Otherwise, the show truly belongs to Lucy as a dizzy employment agency staffer and Gale Gordon as her uncle-boss. They manage to put a nice sheen on some hoary slapstick routines." *TV Guide's* Cleveland Amory blasted, "While we loved *I Love Lucy,* we can't even make friends with this show." Rex Reed, in *Women's Wear Daily,* called the show "terrible" and added, "I love Lucy, but these scripts have got to get better."

Desi Arnaz, however, preferred to view the program from a highly personal perspective: "I think the wonderful surprise to everyone is my daughter," said Desi after viewing the first *Here's Lucy* installment. "Everyone already had known about Desi with his trio. But nobody had seen Lucie do anything. I knew she was loaded with talent. She has a great sense of rhythm and a wonderful sense of humor—which is obviously inherited. She's got a lot of her mother in her." Desi phoned Lucille after the premiere broadcast. "Honey, regardless of whether they're our children or not, they were just great. I just wanted you to know how proud I was of the kids—and of you." Lucy interrupted him and emotionally said, "Stop that, you troublemaker—Are you trying to get me to ruin my dress with tears?"

Desi had phoned Lucille before filming the first show and good-naturedly admonished, "Now, Lucy, you play that part good—I don't want you to louse up the kids' show!" Following the series premiere episode, proud father Desi placed a full-page ad in both *Variety* and *The Hollywood Reporter:* LUCIE AND DESI: I AM SO PROUD. LOVE, DAD. P.S.—THAT RED-HEADED GAL PLAYING YOUR MOTHER IS THE GREATEST.

His waist swathed in bandages following his abdominal surgery, a reflective Desi mused about the trade advertisement, admitting to veteran television reporter Will Tusher, "Well, it's only the truth—she is the greatest. I love Lucy. I *do* love her. Lucy and I were married for a long time, and we're still very fond of each other. We lived together for twenty years—you can't stay together that long unless there's something there. Lucy and I are very good friends. We talk every day. We behave like any good friends would behave. The lines are open all the time. We talk about the kids, and we talk about our problems in the business or what

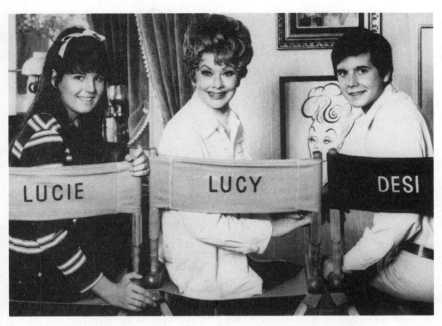

Lucie, Lucille, and Desi, Jr., promote the premiere of *Here's Lucy*.
THOMAS J. WATSON COLLECTION

I am doing with my shows. In general, I guess, like two friends do."

"My father is Latin and terribly sentimental," remarked Desi, Jr., in 1971. "My dad should have stayed in Cuba and had a little house and a boat. Simple things like home and family and honesty turn him on. Business doesn't, so when he got totally hung up on things that were fairly low on his scale of importance, he ended up hating himself—and that's when he got himself in trouble." He added, "Mom is still hung up in the excitement of what she's doing. Not that it isn't meaningful—she gives pleasure to millions of people every week. But sometimes, it seems to be making up for a void somewhere. At work, she is totally engrossed, a perfectionist to whom nothing else matters. As a business-woman, she's good instinctively, but not technically. She's fantastic at home when she's calm—when she isn't worried about working or what everybody outside is thinking. She tackles cooking a dinner the same way she does putting on a TV show, as if it were the most important thing in the world at that moment. She makes a bed the same way—like which camera is on me? I suppose it's because when she's doing these things, she feels insecure—and she isn't accustomed to that feeling."

To revitalize her series, Lucille instigated several changes for the second season, hiring George Marshall—who had directed her in 1942's *Valley of the Sun* and again in 1950 for *Fancy Pants*—as well as *Dream*

Girl's Herbert Kenwith. She continued with her plans to utilize a mobile-truck production unit and shoot several episodes in various locations across the country; after filming on-location programs at Los Angeles International Airport, Colorado Springs, and Las Vegas, remaining location shows were canceled when costs proved "too excessive."

Lucille activated discussions with Avco-Embassy mogul Joseph Levine on filming her much-delayed Lillian Russell–"Diamond" Jim Brady property, the project abruptly scuttled when Jackie Gleason insisted on shooting the feature entirely at his own Florida studios, where he taped his weekly CBS variety series. Paramount's original casting choices for the motion-picture adaptation of Neil Simon's hit play *Plaza Suite,* to be filmed in early 1969, called for the teams of George C. Scott and Maureen Stapleton; Peter Sellers and Barbra Streisand; and Lucille Ball and Walter Matthau—ultimately, only Matthau and Stapleton appeared in the 1971 release.

To give CBS a more modern image and attract advertisers eager to bankroll new programming attracting the highly desirable younger audience demographic, network chief Fred Silverman stunned industry insiders when he unceremoniously canceled the highly rated *Petticoat Junction* as well as still-popular variety programs headlined by television institutions Red Skelton and Jackie Gleason. While Ball's series remained on the CBS schedule, the star became furious when the new New York–based network executive attempted to tamper with her venerable brand of comedy. Silverman flew to Los Angeles expressly to meet with Ball, greeting her with the pronouncement, "I'd like to suggest some ways to improve the show." Lucy excused herself and telephoned CBS founder and chairman William S. Paley in New York. When she reached him on the phone, she said, "Bill, would you do me a favor?" Paley responded, "For you, Lucy? Anything." Lucy said, "I have a young man here from New York. He wants to tell me how to improve my show. Would you get on the phone with him and tell him to get the fuck *out* of here?"

Unfortunately, Paley intervened on Ball's behalf, and *Here's Lucy* remained frozen, the aging star unwilling to improve an increasingly creaky and vastly inferior vehicle. "I have no intention of ever changing," she insisted. "I want someplace on the dial you can turn to and know what to expect. I haven't let changing times affect my writers. I'm trying to stay in the same old rut. My audiences are three generations in every home. I want it to stay that way." She tellingly added, "Out of all those millions, there must be a couple who want things to stay as they are. Me? I still like *Amos 'n' Andy.*"

Lucille swiftly moved to replace producer Tommy Thompson with her cousin Cleo Smith for *Here's Lucy*'s second season. "Suddenly, she was disenchanted with Tommy," notes Smith. "I had been his confidante. He had been telling me, 'She's not happy with me, can you get me some time with her?' She just closed off. I said to him, 'I can't get you time with her, she won't do anything. You've got so much going for you, why the hell should you care? Don't take it, walk away.' Then they came to me and said, 'Lucy wants you to produce.' When he found out, Tommy said, 'Oh, sure. *UH-HUH. "Walk away!"* ' It was the furthest thing from my mind to produce the show. I was married to Cecil and had two small children. I said, 'I can't.' They said, 'Talk to her.' So I did. I said, 'I'm so bowled over, but I feel so inadequate.' She said, 'What is it that you think you don't know?' I said, 'I don't know the first thing about this.' She said, 'You're going to *learn*.' "

Adds Cleo, "She wanted me because her children were teenagers. If they had little parental talks the night before, the next day, Lucy would say, 'You go in and see Auntie Cleo.' They'd come into my office. I felt exactly like a school vice principal. I served a purpose no other producer could have served—I was also a confidante, I was trusted and in the inner family circle. What happened at home the night before could be thrashed out on my carpet. I did learn to love it. She would tell me she wanted to do things she had never done. Milt Josefsberg was very gag-oriented. I went out and searched for new writers."

Director Herbert Kenwith, who often socialized with Lucille in the intervening years following their 1948 *Dream Girl* summer-stock success, was asked to come aboard *Here's Lucy* in the 1969–70 season. Recalls Kenwith, "She would invite me to dinner. One night, DeDe was there. I adored her mother. At dinner, Lucy said, 'Herbert, I would like you to direct some of the *Lucy* shows.' I said to her, 'I guess I'd be interested in doing your show.' And DeDe said, 'Herbert, my daughter's a *bitch*—it will be the *end* of your friendship!' I said, 'No, I think I can handle her.' Lucy says, 'Oh, you *think* so? You think you have the balls to handle me?' I said, 'Yeah, I do.' She says, 'Okay, just for that alone, I want you to do the show.' I said, 'Okay.'

"The first show, I gave Lucy direction, and she charged at me, just ran up to me, nose-to-nose, and screamed at me, '*Why?*' I kept my nose against hers, and I said, 'Because I said so!' We both stood there like that for about five seconds, but it seemed like five hours. She walked away and said, 'I'll try it.' So she did it. It was just a challenge. While she was doing it, she said, 'You know, that's not so bad. Why don't I try this?' And I said, 'Absolutely—try whatever you want. Feel that within the framework of what I say, you can do other things.' "

During the first week of *Here's Lucy* rehearsals, Kenwith had another confrontation with the star: "When camera day came, I noticed she was looking all around the cameras. She'd have a scene with the actors, but would never look at them. She was reading cue cards all the time. She kept looking at the cameras, back and forth, and I got very upset with her, because the other actors were not having any contact with her. I came out of the booth and said, 'Okay, I'd like the four cameras to all come together here.' Lucy said, 'What are you doing?' I said, 'Just a moment, Lucy.' She was standing, leaning against a doorway. I said, 'Lucy, will you come over here and sit down, please?' She said, 'What for?' I said, 'I want you to look at all those cameras till you get sick and tired of looking at them, because you're always looking at the cameras.' She stormed off the stage, slammed her door so hard that I thought the ceiling would fall down. There was such a silence you could hear people blinking their eyes. I went about my business, checking props, deliberately making myself busy. Eventually, I said to the stage manager, 'Will you get Lucy, please?' He said, '*I'm* not going to get her—*you* get her!' I went to her dressing-room door and knocked. 'Who is it?' I said, 'It's Herbert. And I'd like you back onstage.' She didn't answer, but she flung the door open, walked past me without saying a word, went out on the stage, rehearsed, and everything fell back into place. That night, after the show, Lucy said to me, 'Gary and I would like you to join us for dinner at Matteo's.' I waited until I knew she would be there. I walked in, and Lucy's first remark to me was, 'Herbert, you *do* have balls—no one has ever treated me like that except Desi. I want to tell you something—I *liked* it.' "

Kenwith directed an episode that featured Lawrence Welk and also served as the annual visit of Vivian Vance. "Vivian and I had a very nice reunion, which Lucy didn't like," recounts Kenwith. "We had such fun doing *Voice of the Turtle,* we sort of had our own thing, a lot of kisses. Lucy was sitting, watching us. We got around to reading the script, sitting around the table. Every time Vivian had a good laugh line, Lucy would say, 'Okay, let's *cut* that!' When we were finished with all the cutting, Vivian said to her, 'Okay, Lucy, you've cut *all* my lines. I've learned them. And I'm *doing* them, whether you answer me or not. I'm doing *every* line that I got from this script while I was in Connecticut.' Lucy said, 'You *can't.*' Viv said, 'I *can*—and I *will.* So either put the lines back in *now,* or just *stand* there with egg on your face while I do my lines!' She wasn't taking any crap from her—and she did her lines and did them all."

George Marshall departed after directing only twelve episodes. "She tore directors apart," says Kenwith. "She tore Marshall to shreds. He wore a hard hat on the set all the time because he couldn't contend with her—she was so impossible. All the toughness was now coming through. That wonderful inner humor was gone. She was on guard all the time and suspicious of people, constantly suspicious." Several observers suggest that Lucille's social drinking had increased by this point— some further claiming she even drank on the set—and that this may well have contributed to her volatile behavior.

About Lucille's performance on the shows, Kenwith recalls, "After dinner she'd get up and put on the television. I'd say, 'What are you going to watch?' She'd say, 'My show.' I'd say, 'I've seen it in editing. I've seen enough of it.' So I used to sit in the living room while she sat in the den and watched the show. Maybe it was a constant learning process of some sort, which is admirable. But she was performing by rote, reading her lines. I don't think she ever saw the other dimension."

A chance meeting between Lucille and Richard Burton and wife Elizabeth Taylor would result in *Here's Lucy*'s 1970–71 season premiere, a highly publicized event that won an impressive 52 audience-share rating and ranked as the second-highest-rated *Lucy* show in television history. As Cleo Smith recalls, "Lucy and Gary came into work the next morning after a party. She said, 'We were sitting there, and across the room, Richard Burton said, 'I want to work with you.' I said, 'You want to work with *me?*' That was one of the funny things—Lucy never had the feeling she was a star. Gary went in, got the information, and said, 'Burton and Taylor *do* want to do an episode with us.' Everyone gone, just Lucille and me. I said, 'Who do you have in mind to write the script?' She said, 'That's Milt's department.' I said, 'How about Bob and Madelyn for a good old *I Love Lucy* show?' She said, 'I don't think they'd be interested.' I had kept in touch with Bob and Madelyn. I said, 'Oh, Lucy, if they knew you wanted them, that would delight them so.' She said, 'If you think so, go ahead.' I went right over. Bob and Madelyn were still with Desi. I said, 'Would you?' They said, 'Lucy *wants* us?' I said, 'I wouldn't be here otherwise.' Everyone had their little hurts. I set up a lunch date. Bob and Madelyn came to the studio. It was the first time they had seen each other in years. And it was lovely. They gave us a funny script. It was so funny, there was so much laughter, it stretched out to forty-five minutes. We asked CBS if it could go longer than a half hour. We worked on that for days. We were turned down. So we had to cut the first act."

The script had Burton donning a plumber's outfit to escape zealous fans; unaware it is indeed the Welsh actor, Lucille drags him to her office to fix a leaky faucet. After she learns his true identity, he leaves, and Lucy finds Elizabeth's famous sixty-nine-carat, $1.1 million diamond ring in the pocket of his discarded coveralls. She is unable to resist trying it on, and the ring becomes stuck on her finger just as Burton returns to retrieve it, only hours before Elizabeth is to display the gem at a press conference. Borrowing a physical-comedy bit from *I Love Lucy* (and reprised on *The Lucy Show*), Lucy hides behind a curtain, still wearing the ring, and presents her own hand—which takes on a life of its own— as Liz's as the unsuspecting members of the press corps greet her in a receiving line.

Variety called the Madelyn Pugh Davis–Bob Carroll, Jr., script directed by Jerry Paris "a great yockfest, a fine example of situation comedy played to the hilt, broad comedy laced with crackling one-liners and Miss Ball and Burton were particularly fine. Burton matched her step-by-step in a sharply etched parody of himself, and belting over his punch lines with great skill." Taskmaster Ball, however, had intervened early in the week of rehearsals to instruct Burton not only how to recite Shakespeare for one scene but also with instructions to improve his comedic delivery—which she increasingly had come to believe required high-decibel recitation. "When the English are doing a comedy, they throw it away," she said. "They do not stress. They really have a penchant for throwing funny lines away. Not just upstage, but away! Well, *we* don't work that way. It so happened the writers had written a hell of a first scene for him. They had written marvelous looks and takes and waits and dialogue and, by God, he turned his back, talked upstage, mumbled his words, threw them away. I sat there for three days, and

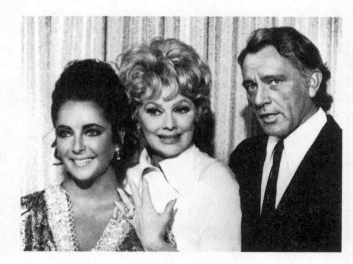

With Elizabeth Taylor, Richard Burton, and The Ring
THOMAS J. WATSON COLLECTION

then we had the dress rehearsal. Finally, I went into his dressing room and knocked on his door. He said, 'What is it, luv?' I said, very nervously, that I had counted eleven laughs he was throwing away. 'Eleven laughs?' he said. 'Throwing away eleven laughs?' Well, came time for the show, and he was terrific, faced the audience, enunciated his lines. Between scenes, he came up to me and said, '*Fifteen*—I got *fifteen* laughs!' "

Jerry Paris had signed to direct six episodes of the 1970–71 season; the strong-willed, aggressive former actor—who had begun his directing career with *The Dick Van Dyke Show*—departed, however, after his initial episode with Burton and Taylor following frequent, stormy clashes with Lucille. "Lucy took over the direction," according to Herbert Kenwith. "He argued with her. She called him a horse's ass. He said, 'Well, the horse's ass is *leaving*.' And he left. They were all standing there with egg on their face. Someone went out after him and begged him to come back. He came back in, but he wouldn't put up with name-calling. I don't think she really thought it out. I think she was very impulsive. Her anger bubbled up. It controlled everything she was doing—she exercised no control." Paris later said, "She runs her own ship. That's a pity. Experienced actresses need good directors. I think if she'd given it a chance more with me, we'd have swung together. But she's not used to a good director, so she didn't recognize one."

And, adds Cleo Smith, "The worst problem we had was Jerry Paris. He came on so strong. Lucy just cut him off at the knees. They blew up on the set. I took them outside. I said, 'Fellows, we have *guests*— two big stars—this is *not* professional conduct. Do what you want to do in your office, not on your set.' I was always the monitor—I think that was my main function as producer."

To perhaps solidify their recently mended relationship with the star, Madelyn and Bob promptly placed full-page ads in the trades: DEAR LUCY—THANK YOU FOR DOING SUCH A WONDERFUL JOB WITH OUR SCRIPT LAST NIGHT. PLEASE GIVE OUR THANKS TO ELIZABETH TAYLOR AND RICHARD BURTON, AND GIVE OUR LOVE TO THE RING. After their highly successful reunion on the Burton-Taylor episode, "She asked if we would come back," recalls Madelyn Davis, "and we did about a third of them for three years." Their *Here's Lucy* experience was, however, not always particularly satisfying or pleasant. As Bob Carroll, Jr., notes, "The big thing was that Gary was in complete charge by then. Now you've gotta go and pitch stories to him. That was too bad."

Following a long-standing friendship between the Mortons and Jayne Meadows and husband Steve Allen, Lucille invited her to guest on the episode filmed directly after the Burton-Taylor half hour; Jayne fell victim not only to Lucy's on-set tyranny but also an admittedly poor script. "Here was this woman who had come to our house, had done our radio show, had invited us to parties at her house, and she came to our parties. I really loved Lucy off the set. We were very good friends. I turn up for the first day of rehearsals, and she walked right past me. Didn't speak to me. We sat down at the table, and she sat at one end. I had most of my scenes with Gale Gordon, so they told me to sit at the other end. Suddenly, Lucy is now the boss lady. I've never *seen* anybody so bossy. No longer the friend—it was Jekyll and Hyde. When you worked with her, a whole screen came down, and it was a different human being. The rehearsal was very painful. I didn't know if she was a little deaf, but she made everybody scream. '*Louder, louder!*' she'd scream. She talked very loud herself when she acted—never talked in a conversational tone. Her shows were all screaming conversation. After all the days of her screaming at us, 'Louder, louder,' the microphones came in, but I didn't know it. I kept talking as loudly as she wanted me to talk. Then she said, 'Don't *scream*—we've got the microphones!' I was doing a scene with Gale Gordon, and she was watching it. She said, 'Gale, for *God*'s sake, look what she's *doing*—she's *completely* upstaging you!' Gale said, 'Lucy, *how* can she upstage me—we don't have any cameras yet!' We were just sitting opposite each other. Gary would stand there with a sad, embarrassed look on his face, wishing she wouldn't do it.

"Because they had spent so much money on the Richard Burton–Elizabeth Taylor script and everything else they had to spend for that show, she said, 'This is our meat-and-potatoes show. We bought this script off the market and paid very little for it. I have to apologize for

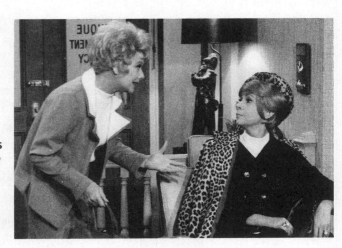

Jayne Meadows guested on the "Lucy Stops a Marriage" episode of *Here's Lucy.* THOMAS J. WATSON COLLECTION

this script—there aren't many good jokes.' We sat down to read, and Lucy would read a line wrong, or she would stop and say, 'Oh, *God, that's not* funny.' And little Lucie would say, '*Mom,* it's *funny.* Say it *right.*' I did notice how talented the daughter was. Her daughter knew every single move and reading to make in that show. But Lucy would read another line and say, 'What does *this* mean?' She didn't seem to have any idea of what was funny or how to do things. We got on our feet, and there was a scene where she had to do a funny physical thing— they wanted her to fall over a little swinging door in the office. She couldn't get it or understand it. She turned to the director, Jack Donohue, and said, 'Show me, Jack.' And then she did it. She controlled *every* move I made, every move Gale Gordon made, every move her children made. As far as what I call professionalism, her daughter knew more than she did. And Lucy was very, very hard on the son in front of the public. She stopped one scene and said, 'This won't do at *all,* Desi. That's *no* good. We'll start it from the top and shoot the whole scene over again!'

"Lucy ran that show—and she was tough, really tough," adds Meadows. "She was the most driven actress I have ever known—we *never* had a break, not even for coffee, until you went almost crazy. We'd all have to go into her dressing room and go over and over the lines—so Lucy could *learn* them. I realized later it might have been because she was getting a little older. Lucy would call for the wardrobe mistress and look at all the costumes she had bought. I had to supply my own clothes—they wouldn't supply you with a *handkerchief.* She would look at the price tags. One price tag for a scarf, she went, 'God!' I looked at it before I walked out of her trailer—it was three dollars and twenty-four cents—she acted like it was three thousand dollars. Lucy was *very* cheap—she *was* what Jack Benny *played.*"

"Mary Wickes was hired for one episode I directed," recalls Herbert Kenwith. "I used to do the salary lists. I said to Lucy, 'Is there a mistake here? You gave Mary Wickes only *six hundred dollars* for a full week?' It was her *best* friend. She said, 'Oh, yes.' "

"I came home," concludes Jayne, "and thought, *Why* is my *friend* acting this way? I spoke to everyone I knew who had worked on her show, and they all told me the exact same stories. Jack Benny—who never said a bad word about anybody—said, 'She's tough, *very* tough.' Milton Berle told me, 'She's just so *bossy.*' The only thing I can attribute it to is deep-rooted insecurity. When you worked with her, you were no longer a friend—you're her *enemy.* You might steal the scene from her."

And, as Bernie Weitzman offers, "With all her talent, she didn't really believe she had that much talent. She couldn't do half of the things she did unless somebody said to her, 'Try it.' She'd say, 'I can't jump around on a pogo stick—I've never done it before.' 'Well, try it.' And she could do it. She had a great natural talent—but she also lost it. It's difficult for a woman almost sixty to act like a kid. You have to move into another area. She didn't have the support anymore, she didn't have the writers, the directors, she should have had. I blame Gary for a lot of it. People didn't want to work with him, they didn't respect him. Talented people want to surround themselves with talented people; they knew she was talented and wanted to work with her. But he brought her down again and again. She was so loyal to him. He was there at her side. He had brought her back from this terrible tragedy that had befallen her. She treated her family and friends as the most important people around her. She could have surrounded herself with a lot of important people. She couldn't keep someone who was truly talented with her—either because of Gary or her own lack of interest."

According to Cleo, "Gary finally got to the point with props, costumes, and other departments where he got control. He knew how to manipulate it so they wouldn't go to Lucy. He'd say, 'You want anything, you come to me.' She might even say, 'I didn't know about that—you'd better see Gary.' So she began also to give him control. So they knew he could hire and fire. She didn't really protect [her employees] when the chips were down. She wanted to give him balls. That's really what it came down to."

Adds Lucie, "I don't think anyone thought he was 'Mister Ball,' really. He proved himself to be able to run the company. I don't think he was a creative genius at picking scripts. I think he should have said yes to a few things he said no to, or talked her into doing a few things she was scared to do, because she was always scared to do things. But instead of saying, 'Come on, you know you can do this,' he'd say, 'Okay, okay.' " Lucie, however, further stresses, "Some people don't like him. I don't know why. He's always been nothing but kind and generous to us."

At eighteen, Lucie left home and moved into her own apartment; in 1971 she married actor Phil Vandervort. "I was already madly in love with Phil when I was fifteen, but my mother kept urging me to date other men," reflected Lucie Arnaz a decade later. "I understand that now. I was very young, and she thought, He's a good guy, but she shouldn't get married. And sure enough, I did. I was a married lady, and a year later an estranged wife, before I had found out anything about myself."

Plagued by admitted alcohol and drug problems, Desi IV left *Here's*

Lucy as a series regular at the close of the 1970–71 season to launch his film career in Hal Wallis's *Red Sky at Morning*. "Mom and I started to fight," admitted Desi, Jr. "She worried that success had come too easily to me and got angry when I ignored my schoolwork and brought home failing grades. She pleaded with me to get help for my drinking and drug habits. But I felt indestructible. We argued a lot and sometimes stopped speaking to each other for weeks. I spent more and more time at Dad's house. He had a love for life that I admired, and his own drinking problem prevented him from coming down too hard on me."

Desi romanced Liza Minnelli following the dissolution of a brief—but widely publicized—affair with Patty Duke, culminating with the birth of a son she initially claimed to be Desi's, although years later she insisted the child had been fathered by John Astin. Lucille revealed her fury at her son's affair with the twenty-five-year-old former child star by remarking, "I worked for years for a quiet personal life. I brought Patty to the house, feeling very maternal about her, saying, Look at this clever girl, what a big talent she is. Now I can thank her for useless notoriety. She's living in some fantastic dreamworld, and we're the victims of it. Desi being the tender age of seventeen when they met, she used him. She hasn't proved or asked for anything. I asked Desi if he wanted to marry her, and he said no. My daughter helped outfit the baby, which Patty brought to the house—but did she ever say thank you?"

According to Herb Kenwith, "When Desi was with Patty, they were both on drugs very badly. She used to come to rehearsals wrapped up in a blanket—nothing underneath. Lucy never wanted her around. Desi took the apartment next to me. He used to come over for dinner every once in a while. Patty had the baby. One day while I was going down to the elevator, the doors opened, and a woman in a black veil gets off. Lucy wore a perfume that I knew, and I could still see the reddish hair through the black veil. I said, 'Oh, hi, Lucy.' She stopped and said, 'What are *you* doing here?' I said, 'I live here—next door to Desi and Patty.' She said, 'Oh,' and with that walked away from me. I'm now waiting for an elevator to take me down. She went in, and I knew she was visiting the baby."

"The basic concern of my mother and stepfather has been protection of the family name—don't do or say anything that might expose us in a bad light," said Desi, Jr., at the time. "I never felt it was all that important—and neither did my dad, who hasn't done too well on this score."

Lucille subjected longtime friend and neighbor Jack Benny to con-

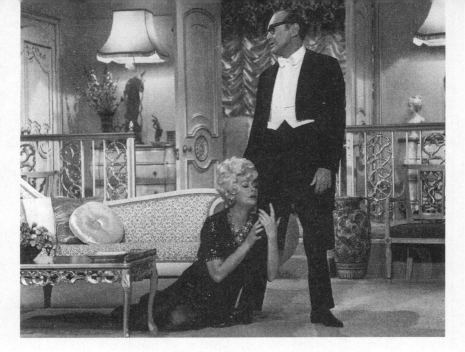

The "Lucy and Jack Benny's Biography" episode
THOMAS J. WATSON COLLECTION

siderable discomfort during a subsequent *Here's Lucy* episode. According to Kenwith, "She kept giving Jack line readings until Jack, very calmly, said, 'Lucy, I've been doing this before you were born. *Don't* tell me how to read my lines!' She didn't want him to take his pause, that long pause on his '*Well!* . . .' She didn't want that in, she wanted it shorter. He said, 'I *know* the timing—I *know* the kind of laugh I should get.' She said, 'Okay, *do* it that way. We'll take care of it in editing.' And she did.

"There was a scene where Jack is dreaming about a romance with Lucy. I had the whole set done in white. He was in a black suit, and she was in a white gown and had on a white wig. I had a love seat covered in satin, so when Lucy sat on the arm, she could slide right down it. She loved the idea. Jack had to sit in a certain place so that when she slid down, their thighs were almost one. Then Jack had to get up and get away from her. As he does, Lucy grabs him by one pant leg, and the pants come off—it was fixed, of course. Jack, at the first rehearsal, couldn't hold his balance, and he had to hold on to the love seat, and it turned him upstage. After the rehearsal, he said, 'Herbert, can you put a small table there? I feel I'm going to fall because I don't have balance—I could grab onto the table.' I said, 'Sure, no problem.'

"I had the table painted white. Lucy immediately saw it—her powers of observation were unbelievable. She came on the set and said, 'What's that doing there?' I said, 'So Jack won't fall.' She said, 'He won't fall— take it away.' I said, 'Lucy, you *can't*. This is an old man. He cannot stand on one leg while you're pulling on the other leg.' 'Take it away.

330

I *don't* want it there.' Jack came out of his dressing room. They started rehearsing, and he said, 'I *thought* you were going to get me a table.' I said, 'I did, but Lucy doesn't want it there.' 'Well, I *want* it.' I said, 'You talk to her. I can't get into the middle of this.' He talked to her, and she said, 'You try it without the table, and let's see how it works.' He did and fell flat on his face. It was so sad to see this man on the floor. It was terrible."

Sammy Davis, Jr., according to Kenwith, did not escape similar treatment. "Sammy was blind in his left eye. The scene had Sammy come into the employment agency holding an ice bag over his eye. As he came in, Lucy was to hit him with the door. And she wanted to hit him in the right eye, the good eye. He didn't want that. Of course, he couldn't put the ice bag over his good eye. She would say to him, 'I would like you over here!' and he would say, 'I can't *see* out of this eye. I *have* to stand over here to see what I'm doing.' But she insisted he put the bag over his other eye. He finally won out with my help. She was very annoyed by that. It was so cruel to do that to him. She knew he couldn't see. He *cried* later on, because she was very cruel and criticized him while he was singing."

The star's attacks were apparently not confided to her soundstage. Kenwith vividly recalls one incident: "One of the [attorneys], a nice man, had an office on the lot, right on the street as you went through the gates. I passed by one day and heard Lucy screaming. She said such terrible things to this man that I cried. I felt such compassion for him. She called him a toilet, she called him everything. The cruel things she said to him, personally cruel. You could hear it all over the lot, it was so loud. No one interrupted her. She didn't stop. Her wrath went on and on. That evening, when I saw him on the show, I said to him, 'I just want you to know I heard that argument this afternoon.' And he said, 'How dare she talk to me like that—me, a grandfather.' While he's telling me this, he burst into tears. That man got a verbal beating like I have never heard anyone get in my life. It was terrible."

Paradoxically, although she often targeted coworkers and crew members with cruelty and blistering verbal assaults, according to Gale Gordon, "I've seen her break down and cry many times. A thoughtless remark from someone whom she was fond of could destroy her." Despite clashes with directors and performers, Gale Gordon maintains, "She took advice from anyone because she recognized good advice when she heard it. She was not above asking for advice. When anyone needed advice, they went to her, because she knew the television business better than anybody. She knew every angle of it. She was, in my view, a genius."

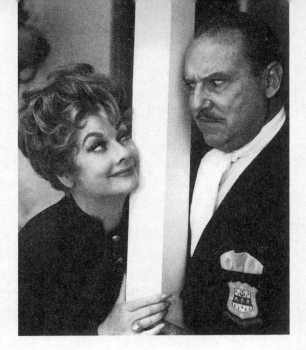

Lucy and Gale Gordon
RICK CARL COLLECTION

Lucille occasionally attempted to lighten the somber atmosphere she herself created in her misplaced bid to retain total control on the set. "We were doing a scene," once recalled Gale Gordon, "and she tried to break me up by changing a phrase like, 'I don't think you should' to 'I'll be damned if you will.' I promptly let go with a long, long string of swear words. She'd never heard me even say '*damn*' before, and it just broke her up completely. She'd say, 'Well, if you want to hear *swearing*, you ought to hear *this* man when he gets going!' "

Removed from the controlling, dictatorial role she played on her soundstage, Lucille could still exhibit a softer, kinder demeanor. Then twenty-year-old aspiring actor Michael Yakaitis attended a *Here's Lucy* filming and met the star backstage after the show. "She said I looked like someone she went to school with in Jamestown. She laughed and said, 'He doesn't look that way *now*—he's *bald!*' I told her I had to go back to Chicago because I was being drafted. She told me her son was also going through that right then, and she was worried about him—we were both trying to get out of the draft. I said good-bye and left. The bus had already gone. I decided to go back the way I had come in to see if someone would help me. I ran into into Lucy again. She said, '*Now* what?' I told her I had missed my bus. She said, 'Don't worry about it. My car's going to leave in a few minutes. Get in.' Lucy jumped in the backseat of her station wagon, which had her logo on the side. She invited me to watch a rehearsal. She asked me how I was doing. She even asked me if I needed any money." He attended a rehearsal the next week. "Midway through the afternoon, Lucy took a break and had a Popsicle. She was kind enough to bring me one. She didn't ask if I *wanted* one—she came to me and said, '*Here!*' Later in the day, I ran into her again as I was about to leave. She said, 'How are you going to get home?' I said, 'I'm going to take the bus.' 'Don't be *silly*. I'll give you a ride.' I said, 'Isn't Beverly Hills one way and Hollywood the other direction?' She said, 'It doesn't matter. I can take you. It's no problem.' It was *such* a surprise, after seeing this tough woman running the show on the set, to then find this motherly type character in her come out."

And, according to Gale Gordon, "She was completely loyal to people. We had a carpenter who had been with her since way back until he was forced to retire. The labor union insisted that people at the age of sixty-five in the studio retire. When he did retire, she gave a party for him at the studio. We were then at Universal. It was the most wonderful party in the world. He, a little carpenter, that's all he ever was, but he was the star of the evening. He would have laid down his life for Lucy at any moment. When we greeted each other in the morning on the first day of rehearsal, everybody, from the carpenters to the painters, the sweepers, they all said hello as if it was a family. I think that's one of the reasons for her great success. She worked harder than anyone, and she loved people who felt the same way as she did. She was always trying to do the best she could do, and she expected it from other people. She was very unpopular with some people who didn't like to work for their money. She had no time for people like that."

Despite his frequent clashes with the star, Kenwith often reflected on a much different, much gentler Lucille he knew in early, apparently happier times. "I was working at NBC in New York. I had two weeks off. I came to Hollywood and spent time with Lucy and Desi. I told her I had to go home. She said, 'Do you need any money?' I said no. She said, 'Here, you take this and stay on in California.' She didn't realize I was going back to my job in New York. She wrote me a check for *ten thousand dollars*. I said I didn't need it. I was very touched. I gave her back the check, telling her I was working and had money, that I was fine. I said, 'Thanks, I'll never forget it.' That was *very* generous. She used to laugh a lot. She was amused about things. I remember visiting them at the Desilu ranch in Chatsworth when Lucy was pregnant. Once, she grabbed my hand and said, 'Oh, *feel!*' I didn't like the sensation of feeling someone's stomach moving like that. I pulled my hand away like it was on a hot plate. She said, 'Oh, don't do that—it's *wonderful!*' "

After the cancellation of *The Mothers-in-Law* and his failure to produce *Without Consent* or any other television series, Desi again attempted another comeback—this time in front of the cameras—in the summer of 1970, when he signed to guest on an episode of the western series, *The Men from Shiloh,* a revamped version of *The Virginian.* "Everybody, but everybody, was sure I had cancer," he remarked following bouts with diverticulitis and hematoma. "The reason was because they heard I had surgery four times during the last two years. Actually, I haven't felt better in fifteen years. I've put on about twenty-fi' pounds, but that's because I haven't been doing anytheeng but fishing and dreenking beer since I sol' my interest in Desilu Studios." He had recently sold his thoroughbred breeding farm in Corona, built a fishing hideaway in Las Cruces—about thirty miles south of La Paz, Mexico—and settled in his Del Mar retreat. Explaining his return to television, Desi quipped, "The simple truth is I was getting tired of seeing Ricardo Montalban and Fernando Lamas in all these Mexican roles."

Arnaz would attempt another unsuccessful comeback a few years later in *Doctor Domingo,* an unsold spin-off pilot from the Raymond Burr detective series *Ironside,* after entering into a development deal with MCA-Universal mogul Lew Wasserman that included an unsold series, *Chairman of the Board,* starring Elke Sommer. Desi's final screen appearance came in 1982, a small role as a crooked politician in the Francis Ford Coppola-produced box-office failure *The Escape Artist.*

"I don't think Desi wanted to leave the industry," reveals Bernie Weitzman. "I think the industry left him. After he did *The Mothers-in-Law*—which was sixty episodes and not too thrilling a series—people weren't knocking on his door. I brought Lucy over to Universal, and I tried to bring Desi over there. He wanted to. We just couldn't find a vehicle that would work. The networks just weren't crazy about him. They didn't want him. And he was one of the great television stars of all time. Sometimes, people as part of a team work well and as individuals they don't. Desi—after *I Love Lucy*—never did anything important."

And, notes Lucie Arnaz, "He was depressed and disappointed in later years that that was all there was, *I Love Lucy,* and when it was over, the industry didn't trust him the way they used to. But that's a lot of denial, too, because they didn't trust him because the last image they had of him was in the last years. They tried to trust him a long time, but when you're drinking and making bad decisions, people lose their trust. Until he could acknowledge that he had a problem, he could never rejuvenate his career. It was such a tragedy. Had he had the ability to say, 'Look, I've got a problem,' there would have been a second life for Desi Arnaz. He wouldn't just have been some 'has-been' from the old *I Love Lucy* show.

"Her humor was that fast-talkin' broad of the thirties, and his was to see life as funnier than it really was, a joyous thing, with a kinder laughter, to survive. When he'd get mad, he'd blow up real fast with that Cuban temper and then laugh about it. We'd all be shaking in our boots because he'd be screaming so loudly. Normally, he didn't do it when he was sober. When he was sober, he was one of the funniest people in the world. When he got mad, he could hang on to his humor. He would hear himself saying things and make a joke in the middle of it. That's why it's such a tragedy that he didn't stay himself, that he changed his personality with alcohol the way he did.

"Humor didn't save their marriage," offers Lucie, "but it saved them to a point and created that incredible show. Otherwise, what would they have done? She would have been 'Queen of the B's' forever, and he would have been onstage at nightclubs until nightclubs died and the Latin craze was gone—and they would have been nobodies."

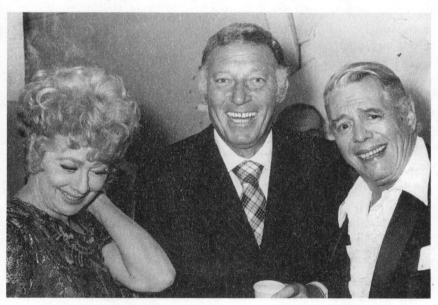

Lucille, Gary Morton, and Desi at a Hollywood Bowl benefit,
August 27, 1971
THOMAS J. WATSON COLLECTION

Chapter Eighteen

★

"It's funny—Lucy and I get along better now than we did when we were married."

—Desi Arnaz, 1970

★

"Desi was always very protective of her," offers Bernie Weitzman. "He told her not to do *Mame*. He was very careful about the things she should do. He fought for her, and he fought with her to do good things. Her taste was limited. She wasn't interested in everything else—she was interested only in what was good for her."

In January 1968, Warner–Seven Arts purchased motion-picture rights to the long-running Broadway hit musical scored by Jerry Herman and written by Jerome Lawrence and Robert E. Lee for $3 million, in addition to 30 percent of the film's gross profits paid to the stage production's producers, Robert Fryer and and Lawrence Carr. Under the terms of the deal, however, the picture could not be released until 1971 in order to avoid competition with Broadway or national touring productions. The star of the stage musical *Mame*, Angela Lansbury, openly coveted the motion picture role—"If they're going to do my *Mame*, then I'll *have* to do the film!" she admitted in 1968—and although she was the first choice of producers Fryer and Carr, her perceived lack of strong motion-picture box-office marquee value prompted rumors in 1969 that Lansbury would be cast by Warner–Seven Arts only if front-runner Elizabeth Taylor declined the role; when she proved unavailable, Lansbury suddenly found herself the following year in competition with another unexpected, unlikely but formidable candidate—Lucille Ball.

On December 28, 1971, syndicated columnist Joyce Haber revealed, "Now it's official. It has been decided unofficially for months—Lucy has it."

Lucille's keen desire to conquer the singing-and-dancing, tour-de-force role of the outrageous, eccentric Mame Dennis in the lavish $12 million feature—and the continuation of *Here's Lucy*—seemed suddenly dashed when she broke her leg skiing the first week of January during the Mortons' holiday vacation at their Snowmass, Colorado, condominium. At age of sixty, the indomitable Lucille had only recently taken

336

up the sport. Only a month after she signed for *Mame,* as Lucille stood on the sidelines of a slope talking, another skier barreled into her pole, causing her to fall. Lucy heard her leg crack and was taken down the mountain on a toboggan stretcher. She convalesced in Palm Springs and threatened to end her weekly series and cancel her *Mame* feature-film return.

"I'll never work again," she vowed. "To hell with it. To hell with it all."

Producer Robert Fryer rushed to Palm Springs and assured her he would hold up production of *Mame* until her leg healed. "I'm not sure I can even walk, much less dance," she said cautiously. "We want *you,*" he said. "We'll wait until you're ready to play her." Gary attempted to bolster Lucille's flagging spirits, bringing in her meal trays while doing an exaggerated Bette Davis impression, enlisting friends to visit Palm Springs to play word games with her to pass the time.

On the mend, a revitalized Lucille decided to return to *Here's Lucy* and retain *Mame.* "Gary pulled me through," she said not long after. "I never realized what a guy he is until that ordeal. He's somethin' else."

Warner Bros. postponed shooting until January 1973, with a projected Easter 1974 release date. Ball's broken leg was perhaps an omen that *Mame* was doomed from the start. While it was announced in 1970 that Leonard Gershe (*Funny Face* and *Silk Stockings*) had signed to write the film adaptation, the shooting script was ultimately written by the talented—but ill-suited—*The Effects of Gamma Rays on Man-in-the-Moon Marigolds* 1971 Pulitzer Prize–winning playwright Paul Zindel. George Cukor was initially sought as director but reportedly was unavailable due to the lengthy sixteen-month filming delay while Lucille's leg mended. Gene Saks, director of the original stage production, was ultimately signed. He was also the husband of Beatrice Arthur, who prior to being cast in the picture—despite the avid pursuit of the film role by Bette Davis—had played opposite Lansbury as aging actress Vera Charles, Mame's acerbic and perenially besotted "bosom buddy."

Ball—armed with casting approval and a percentage of the film's profit—caused considerable dissension during rehearsals. Until the trade paper eventually printed a retraction, she threatened to sue *The Hollywood Reporter* when columnist Radie Harris announced that Arthur had abruptly exited the production resulting from "conceptual differences over her handling of the part she had created on Broadway." When Joyce Haber approached Ball and asked if her if her mental state had improved following *The Reporter*'s retraction, a livid Lucy shot back, "How can you be fine with Radie Harris up your ass?" She further insisted,

"I love Bea Arthur. There's nobody else for that part. I can't think of one name."

While Bea Arthur remained in *Mame,* Madeline Kahn did not. The actress had been cast by producers Robert Fryer and James Cresson as Agnes Gooch—the neurotic spinster eventually blossoming under Mame's guidance—following her well-received appearance in Peter Bogdanovich's screwball comedy *What's Up, Doc?* "I waited five weeks in rehearsal for her to become Gooch," Lucille later remarked. "Finally, I said, 'Madeline, this is the fifth week of rehearsals, we start shooting in three days. When *are* you going to show us Gooch?' She said, 'I *have.*' She got them for fifty grand, and she knew that all she had to do was play it cool—she would get paid off and go to work immediately on *Blazing Saddles.* She had no intention of giving me Gooch."

Kahn counters, "I never had any conflict. The producers explained a few things and let me go, wishing I could have stayed. They came to me one day and said, 'Would you mind while we go out to lunch putting on a semblance of the costume? It isn't quite ready yet, but would you mind—the hat covering up your hair and the glasses. When we come back from lunch, be in rehearsal in that costume.' They wanted to see if she could recognize me. I put the costume on, and she walked right past me. I don't think she even recognized me, but it somehow failed to change her mind. It was devastating. It didn't turn out to be a tragedy—it cleared me to be available for *Blazing Saddles*—but it felt really, really bad at the time. Having only seen me in one film, *What's Up, Doc?*, I was covered with a wig and dresses which enhanced the fact that I was a little plump then. Her impression of me was totally based on that. Gooch was a real character role, far removed from me. I think she might have been surprised what I looked like in person. Possibly, she was unnerved by my presence. And there was an age difference."

Throughout filming, despite careful photography and the use of temporary lifts, Lucille was terrified that the large screen would brutally reveal her heavily lined face—her insecurity ending her professional relationship with Hal King, who had first served as her RKO makeup artist in 1937. "It was toward the end of shooting *Mame,*" he reveals. "I came to the studio. I had been ill. I said, 'Lucy, the doctor said that I should take a week off and rest.' She didn't say anything. She hauled off and hit me in the face. Broke my jaw. 'Who the hell is going to make me up?' she yelled. I said, 'Well, Lucy, after this, I don't care.' She was so afraid she wasn't going to look good. I used a liquid adhesive, and she couldn't wear it all day long. It would hurt her, so I'd have to take it off, and then, in the afternoon, start again. It was awfully hard toward the end to make Lucy look good."

Lucille occasionally took a humorous view at the great lengths enlisted to present the illusion of Mame's youthful maturity. As a cameraman set up for a close-up, the star cracked, "Wait until they put on the 'twenty-five-year-old' lens."

A nervous Lucy refused to watch the first forty minutes of a rough-cut version of the film. Gary attended the screening and reportedly was so moved he wept. "What good is your opinion?" cracked Lucy. "You cry at basketball games."

Prior to the film's release, Lucille bubbled with enthusiasm for *Mame*—fully expecting to drop her weekly series and embark on a new motion-picture career. "It's beautifully done," she gushed. "I hope this film is a success. People are always saying they want good, family entertainment, something different from all this distasteful sex and violence. I'm really going to go out to sell this picture. I have lots of Lucy fans, and I think they will come out for me. I hope so."

Reviews for *Mame,* however, were so uniformly brutal that Lucille forever fled motion pictures. "After forty years in movies and TV," asked *The New Yorker,* "did she discover in herself an unfulfilled ambition to be a flaming drag queen?" Said *Time,* "Miss Ball had been molded over the years into some sort of a national monument and she performs like one too. Her grace, her timing, her vigor have all vanished." Added *The New Republic,* "Had she made this film fifteen years ago, she would have been terrific. But she is now too old, too stringy in the legs, too basso in the voice, and too creaky in the joints."

Criticism blasting the film was matched by blistering attacks on the extreme—and unsuccessful—efforts made to camouflage Ball's aged appearance. As one critic noted, "Gene Saks accommodates the elderly star's wrinkles by shooting her in close-ups so soft-focus—so gauzy you think you're in a hospital." Lucille broke down during an interview with film critic Gene Siskel, following an unflattering *People* magazine profile and a Chicago *Sun-Times* story that stated that she "good-naturedly admonishes the photographers to 'back up about 18 feet.' " "It's not that I'm tired," she sobbed as tears rolled down her face. "It's the pictures they've taken and what they've written about me. The studio spent plenty of money to get the best photographs of me in *Mame,* so why do the newspapers have to send people just so they can take ugly pictures of me?" Now shouting, she defensively raged, "So I look my age—what's wrong with that? These stories make me feel wrong and old."

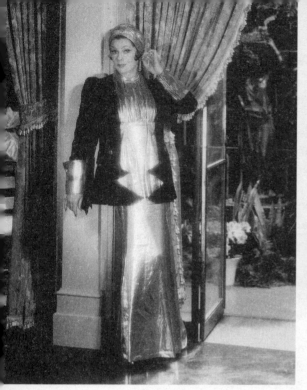

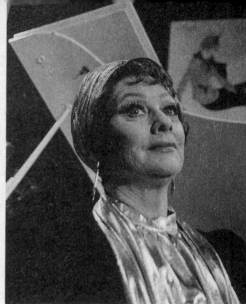

Lucille promoting *Mame*
RICK CARL COLLECTION

Lucille as *Mame*
THOMAS J. WATSON COLLECTION

"I was shocked at the notices she got," notes Onna White, who choreographed both the original stage production and the film version. "I think it broke her heart." And, adds Robert Osborne, "She thought she was going to win the Oscar. Although she loved television, she wanted to be a movie star, because that's the era she grew up in, when movie stars were the important people in Hollywood." Of her near-obsessive need to camouflage her age before the cameras, he notes, "It's not vanity as much as it is survival. It's knowing the town so well and how Hollywood gets rid of you with age, and she wanted to work."

Lucille's 1973–74 return to *Here's Lucy* was as ill-advised as her motion-picture comeback, marking the first time a Ball series had dropped below the Top Twenty. And while the star announced her weekly-series "retirement" at the close of the 1973–74 season in favor of headlining occasional CBS specials, the network had, in fact, canceled *Here's Lucy*. "I've got six years of product," she wistfully noted at a May 1974 testimonial dinner. "We really don't need it. CBS doesn't seem to need it. They wanted us to do some specials, but it won't be as much fun as what we had done every day for so long." She later admitted how greatly her injury had impeded her performances during her last season. "After I broke my leg, the writers were coming up with great comedy that I couldn't do. I was disheartened. I couldn't jump on a horse, I

340

couldn't roller-skate. I couldn't ice-skate. That finished me. I cried my heart out."

"Lucy was willing to do another season," notes Thomas Watson, "but CBS knew that the *Here's Lucy* format was essentially shot. Everybody knew that the series was not going to make it into a seventh year, including Lucy's own people. She wanted to do another series, another variation, but wanted a multiple-year pickup. She didn't want to do just one season. CBS didn't want to commit to another six-year run of the fourth *Lucy* show. Her major turning point was when she broke her leg. It changed her psychologically, as well as physically. Physically, it slowed her down. Psychologically, it made her aware of the fact that she was human and vulnerable. Her leg never did heal totally. That meant she couldn't do all the wonderful, split-second-timing moves that she wanted to. She couldn't dance like she wanted to. It took a toll on her. It made her mad. The other thing that changed her persona was her voice, when she stopped being Lucy Ricardo and started sounding like Broderick Crawford. Not only did she have a lot of baritone, there were no subtleties and variations in her voice. It all came out the same."

Lucille remained devastated by the cancellation of her series. "It was almost like losing my identity after all those years," she admitted. "It was a helluva jolt to find myself unemployed with nothing to do after more than twenty-five years of steady work. I think the fact that I love housework saved my sanity. The first thing I did was fire the household help that I'd had for twelve years. Then I set about to clean my house. It took me six months, but I cleaned everything." Adds Marcella Rabwin, "She used to call me every day. She was in tears all the time, very depressed. She said, 'I cleaned the whole house. When I got finished, I *still* didn't know what to do with myself, so I went over to Desi [Jr.]'s and cleaned *his* house."

The handful of CBS specials that followed *Here's Lucy,* although highly rated, were, for the most part, poorly received and contributed to the dissolution of her long-standing relationship with the network by the close of the decade. For her first CBS special, she teamed with Art Carney for a comedy-drama titled *Happy Anniversary and Goodbye.* The teleplay detailing the dissolution and reunion of middle-aged marrieds Ball and Carney, said *Variety,* was undermined by "dusty zingers and ancient sitcom humor to hammer home a story whose sensitive message gets buried in the accumulation of cornball." A subsequent Las Vegas–based comedy special teaming the *Lucy* character with Dean Martin (*Lucy Gets Lucky*) had *Variety* to dismiss the Bob O'Brien script—and the production—as "old hat." For the 1975–76 season, Lucille first teamed with Jackie Gleason in the comedy-drama *Three for Two*—which *Variety* blasted as "a dismal trio of one-act plays about unpleasant and stupid people." Her second hour of the season—*What Now, Catherine Curtis?*— was her most successful postseries effort, a comedy-drama trilogy under the guidance of former MGM director Chuck Walters, and, praised *Variety,* delivered "an outstanding performance as a middle-aged divorcée emotionally shattered by the end of a twenty-year marriage." Ball's CBS nadir, however, was a subsequent Grand Old Opry special, *Lucy Comes to Nashville.*

Bernie Weitzman notes, "I don't want to blame Gary totally for her demise as a star, but I think he had a lot to do with it, because he tried to protect her and keep her away from everybody. He insisted that he review everything before she would see it, and therefore it was very difficult for any top-notch creative people to want to give him something because they never knew whether he thought it was good or bad, or whether he would take credit for it or not, or whether she would actually see it. It became very, very difficult to get material to her."

Her most successful special following *Here's Lucy* was not a current effort, but rather a glowing retrospective titled *CBS Salutes Lucy—The First 25 Years.* The salute showcased clips from *I Love Lucy, The Lucy Show,* and *Here's Lucy,* as well as including tributes from dozens of fellow performers—including Desi Arnaz, Sr., and Vivian Vance—along with CBS founder William Paley. While the tribute was well received, *Variety* commented, "The two-hour special was produced by Lucille Ball's production company, which made the format a little awkward."

Desi Arnaz also reached into the past with the release of his autobiography, *A Book,* written under the guidance of his William Morrow and Company editor Howard Cady and onetime Desilu press agent Ken Morgan. The best-seller concluded with his 1960 divorce from Lucille; a planned sequel, *Another Book,* detailing his break from Desilu Productions and show business, failed to materialize. While promoting his autobiography, the fifty-nine-year-old Arnaz frequently reflected on his ex-wife. "I still love Lucy very much," he admitted. "It's ironic we spent half of our married life trying to work together and in the end were both working too hard and, perhaps, seeing too much of each other."

Lucille returned to her brand of 1960s broad slapstick comedy in a one-hour 1977 CBS special, *Lucy Calls the President,* with *I Love Lucy* director Marc Daniels and a script by Madelyn Davis and Bob Carroll, Jr. Featured were Vivian Vance, Gale Gordon, Mary Wickes, Mary Jane Croft, Steve Allen, Ed Mahon (as Lucy's husband), and a brief appearance by Lillian

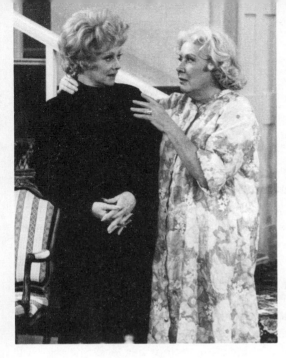

Lucille and Vivian reunite
for the last time on the
CBS special "Lucy Calls
the President."
THOMAS J. WATSON COLLECTION

Carter. "I've been doing specials that were different kinds of comedy-dramas than the *Lucy* shows," she said, "trying to act my age, trying to do something that they would believe and buy. Well, they didn't buy it—not really. What the people seemed to want was Lucy again. Then I decided, the hell with anything different—I'll do a *Lucy* show."

DeDe Ball had died in July at age eighty-five, and, as Madelyn Davis once noted, "Lucy's mother had always been in the audience from the very first *I Love Lucy* days. When Lucy would go onstage to greet the audience, she'd call out 'Hi, Mother,' and then say, 'I want you to meet my beautiful mother, DeDe.' It was a lovely moment. The two of them had been through a lot of hard times, and Lucy was so happy that she'd made her mother proud of her." During the taping of the special, "When Lucy went onstage as usual to greet the audience, I could see for a moment that she felt utterly lost. It only lasted a moment, but the pain was there."

At the same time, Vivian Vance battled rapidly failing health, a recent stroke leaving one side of her face partially immoblized as she also attempted to combat advancing cancer with chemotherapy treatments. "Vivian was very brave," recalls Gale, "because she knew she had cancer and never said anything to anybody."

Lucille apparently vented her unfocused rage resulting from the agonizing loss of her beloved mother during rehearsals for the reunion special. As one observer recalls, "Lucy was so incredibly mean to everyone at dress rehearsal. There wasn't a full audience, just a few people. My seat was next to her off-camera makeup table. She yelled at everyone—the wardrobe lady, the makeup man, everyone. She kept screaming

343

at Gary Morton, '*Shut up!*' whenever he tried to say something. Then she would tell him to go away, yelling at him the whole while. Once, Vivian Vance came over to her. She didn't look well. It was after her stroke, you could see she was very ill and obviously on some type of medication. Holding up two dresses, she asked Lucy nicely, 'Which one do you think I should wear?' Lucy looked at her with complete disgust and yelled, 'What *difference* does it make? You look like a *cow* in anything you wear!' Vivian ran away in tears. A few days later, in front of an audience, Lucy was a different person, all sweetness and light and 'My dear Viv.' "

That same year, Lucille made a guest appearance on Donny and Marie Osmond's ABC variety series. Recalls the show's choreographer, Carl Jablonski, "Lucy had great legs, and she loved to show them off. We were going to do a number and shoot it in a mirror so there would be a chorus line of Lucys and nothing showing but her legs. She was still recuperating from the bad skiing accident, so we knew not to put too much stress on that one leg. Lucy came into rehearsal, and I presented the number. She said, 'Oh, yeah, that's good.' The moment we talked about a musical number, she lit up like a Christmas tree. Lucy wanted to sing and dance, but couldn't. I started teaching her, and she would scream with pain. I said, 'Lucy, are you okay? I'll change the routine.' She said, 'No, no, no. Don't you change *one* thing.' She would let out such yelps, it was pitiful, saying, 'I'm *not* gonna quit, I'm gonna do this.' And she did. Lucy had a rehearsal studio in back of her house and called to ask, 'Would you come over and work with me on this?' We worked an entire afternoon. She was absolutely grand. We were like two gypsies. She loved singing and dancing. She was so concerned about her work. She wanted it to be right. There was no bullshit with her, and to some that was being brusque or rude, but I never saw anything but a consummate professional."

In the summer of 1979, Lucille flew to San Francisco for a poignant last visit with Vivian Vance, her terminal cancer in its final stages. "I was in a play there," says Mary Wickes, "and we rented a limousine and went out to see Vivian. I told the nurse when she came to the door, 'Now, you give us the high sign so we don't stay too long. We don't want to wear Vivian out.' Well, we were there for two hours and laughed. I sort of stayed in the corner, because Lucy and Viv had so much to talk about. Finally, I said, 'I think we'd better go, we're gonna wear Viv out,' and she said, 'Oh, no!' Vivian loved it. We left and cried all the way back."

Following the dissolution of her CBS pact, in 1980 Lucille signed with NBC to headline specials and develop a slate of comedy programming. The single project to result from the widely heralded but quickly abandoned pact was a low-rated, critically assailed ninety-minute special, *Lucy Comes to NBC*. Reaching back into her Desilu past, Lucille presented a fictionalized version of herself—a television-company president (flanked by assistant Gale Gordon) asked by the network to produce a situation comedy, which she promptly cast with faded screen stars Donald O'Connor and Gloria DeHaven. The dated "generation gap" *Coogan's Music Mart* premise between former Big Band musician O'Connor and fledgling rock-star son Scotty Plummer was, in fact, an actual projected (and unsold) series done under the Lucille Ball Productions banner. Critical response was tepid. As *Variety* offered, "Most of this activity had a definitely old-timey look and flavor."

"I don't see the networks really ready for anything that I have to give," she sadly conceded. "They asked me to give, so I tried again. I don't know if my era will ever come back. I don't have that much hope for anything that I do."

Her break with CBS and the much-heralded but suddenly aborted NBC contract plunged Lucille into deep melancholy. "She was at NBC," recalls Carole Cook, "and I was doing a guest shot, so I went over to see her. We were chatting, and she said, 'I only want to live five more years.' I said, 'You've got two kids, you're rich and famous. You've got a husband, and you're happy with him, what is your *problem?*' She was bitter. That woman lived to work. And the work was cut off. She didn't like to travel, she didn't go to the theater, she didn't have hobbies."

"It was so sad," notes one former Desilu executive. "In later years, she became an alcoholic." Family members, however, discount that Lucille drank excessively. "Drinking too much meant losing control, and she would *never* do that," explains Cleo Smith.

The Mortons in 1981 signed with Twentieth Century–Fox Television to develop a situation comedy, two theatrical releases, a twenty-hour miniseries, and an original play, the deal rumored to have been struck as the result of the Mortonses close friendship with then–Fox president Marvin Davis. While Gary Morton announced at the time of the deal's inception, "I think we're ready for the *Lucy* comedy again," the only vehicle to be launched by the Fox-Ball pact was the successful motion picture *All the Right Moves,* with Tom Cruise. Although Ball and Morton were to be credited as the film's executive producers, Lucille was reportedly so distressed at the script's adult language and brief nudity that only Morton's name appeared on the credits.

In 1985 Lucille returned to CBS to make her made-for-television feature dramatic debut in *Stone Pillow,* the Rose Leiman Goldemberg (*Burning Bed*) script of an elderly homeless woman attempting to survive on the streets of Manhattan—Lucille naming her character Florabelle after her beloved grandmother. *Stone Pillow* was the second-highest-rated TV movie of the season; critics generally lauded her performance—if not the actual production or the sentimental script—although Lucille who had allowed herself to appear old and slovenly in the film, failed to win an Emmy nomination. While *Variety* called production "Damon Runyon warmed over without his bite," the paper said, "Lucille brings home the bacon. Physically, Ball does superb work as she flails around in the heavy-duty gear she wears. Tough, gallant, impatient, Florabelle becomes a memorable portrait of pride going after a fall." The Washington *Post,* though, called it "a boulder of a show that even Ball cannot keep from rolling downhill."

Stone Pillow triggered an irreversible decline in Lucille's health. The film was initially scheduled to be shot entirely on location in New York, as Lucy noted, "in the dreariest, coldest weather possible." Just before shooting was to commence in the winter of 1984, Goldemberg's daughter was killed. "We were all ready to go," said Lucy, "except for some work that needed to be done on the script. And we had to leave the poor lady alone, of course, and delay a few months." Manhattan shooting was delayed until May in the midst of a sweltering heat wave. The star—wrapped in layers of clothing to present the illusion of the homeless woman fighting to survive the winter—lost twenty-three pounds during the six-week shoot and was immediately hospitalized for dehydration when she returned to Los Angeles upon the completion of filming; Lucy was told she was allergic to cigarettes and was forced to give up smoking. Despite the ordeal, Ball had refused to halt production. "You just keep going. You get in there and get it over with. There's a whole company around, and they're suffering, too. So you just shut up and do it."

Over the previous several years, Lucille's personal life had presented formidable challenges—and some happiness as well. Her son's 1979 marriage to actress Linda Purl dissolved only one year later reportedly due to his drug and alcohol abuse. In 1982, upon the recommendation of physician Marcus Rabwin, he admitted himself into Scripps Memorial Hospital to battle his chemical dependency.

"Mom was a crucial part in my recovery," recalled Desi, Jr., in 1991. "She endured family-confrontation therapy with five other families. She had no hesitations—but the others couldn't forget her public image. On the first day, everyone was wearing an 'I Love Lucy' button. Mom talked about her feelings of guilt. 'I keep thinking I should have been able to prevent your problems,' she said. 'All I wanted was for you to be happy.' She described how scared she'd felt when she saw me destroying myself. Suddenly, I saw how much I hurt her. I realized I wasn't separate and isolated. That was nine years ago, and I haven't used drugs or alcohol since." Desi, Jr., was remarried in 1987 to Amy Bargiel.

Desi, Sr., sought treatment for substance abuse as well. "He did the tremendous thing of going to the recovery center with Desi [Jr.] and saying, 'I'm Desi, and I'm an alcoholic," recounts Lucie Arnaz. "I stood there next to him when I heard him say that. Oh, I cried. I have enormous pride that he could do that. Unfortunately, he couldn't live up to it, and when the six or eight weeks were up, he locked himself into a room and never went to one meeting. He didn't drink, but he drugged himself to death on every other thing you could think of. 'Oh, my knees hurt, I have sinuses, I have a cough.' Lucky him, he got lung cancer and could have all the morphine he wanted. It was such a tragedy."

Following national tours of *Cabaret* and *Annie Get Your Gun,* daughter Lucie was cast opposite Robert Klein in the Broadway musical *They're Playing Our Song,* to critical acclaim, and subsequently triumphed in *My One and Only* with Tommy Tune. Divorced from Phil Vandervort, in 1980 Lucie had married actor Laurence Luckinbill—having met him while both were starring on Broadway in Neil Simon plays—and would make Lucille a grandmother with the birth of Simon Thomas (named for the playwright) and then, in 1982, Joseph Henry. A third Luckinbill offspring, Kate Desiree, was born to Lucie and Larry in January 1985. "Both of my grandsons were born in December," noted grandfather Desi to columnist Earl Wilson. "I yelled at Lucie and said, 'What's going on— do you and Larry only make love in the *spring?*' "

"My father loved Larry," offers Lucie. "Instinctively. Immediately. 'You love him? He loves you? That's good enough for me.' And he meant it. From that moment on, Larry could do no wrong. He was 'amigo' and 'pardner.' He adored his grandchildren. He was so much fun to be with as a grandpa. You ask them their last memory that they have of their grandpa, and they'll say it's of him walking all the way down from that tilted walkway at his house at Del Mar with a cane. They had kissed him good-bye, but he thought his grandchildren hadn't said good-bye to him. They were already in the car. He hadn't gotten out of bed for weeks, and he forced himself to get up, and he struggled—he had terrible knees—all the way down the walkway. He tried to lean on the station wagon, trying not to fall over, and kiss his grandchildren. And they kissed and hugged him, saying, 'Good-bye, Grandpa, we love you, Grandpa.' He was really big about doing stuff like that.

"That's why I've spent many sleepness nights crying about the things that can very well be said about his drinking and his temper," reveals Lucie. "It's such a shame, as is the case with most alcoholics. This gentle bear was just the dearest man. And *such* a genius, *such* a good business-person. I hear all these stories, and the more I hear them, the more I want to scream, 'Why, *why?*' "

"Lucie was devoted to her father, but he resented her interference in his drinking," says Marcella Rabwin. "After my husband and I went to see Lucie in *They're Playing Our Song,* we all went out for supper. She said, 'You're not much of a friend if you give him a drink when he comes to your house.' He was at my house two or three times a day. I said, 'I can't turn him down. I can't do that to my friend Desi.' She said, 'If you were his friend, you wouldn't give him a drink.' So the next time Desi came to our house, the first thing he did was ask for a glass of wine. I said, 'No more. You don't drink in this house.' He said, 'You've been talking to Lucie.' He turned on his heels and left and didn't talk to me again for months. He had his pills, his drink. He felt he didn't need anybody anymore."

Edie Arnaz died in 1985, following a three-year battle against cancer; Lucille insisted that Desi temporarily move into the Roxbury Drive guest-house under her watchful eye. Desi was diagnosed with lung cancer the following year, and Lucy was devasted at the news. The Mortons's film archivist, Stuart Shostak, recalls, "I dropped by her house to deliver some tapes. She had just gotten off the phone with Desi. She was sobbing and in a daze. She took off her glasses and was wiping her eyes. I asked her, 'Are you okay?' She said, 'Desi's got lung cancer. I just called to wish him happy birthday, and he told me.' "

Following his cancer diagnosis, Desi was frequently hospitalized at Scripps Memorial in La Jolla, California, and endured debilitating ra-diation and chemotherapy treatments. "He still felt he had something to give," offers Rabwin. "But he was despondent. He wasn't the same Desi of the young days of Desilu. That was gone. But he had some humor left in him. He did a lot of reading. Eventually, instead of sitting, he'd go to bed and read. Then, toward the end, he was in bed all the time. He never wanted to get up, which is a real sign of depression. After Edie died, he was a recluse. But he was very, very ill."

In early 1986, it was announced that the seventy-five-year-old redhead would return to weekly television in an ABC situation comedy series, *Life with Lucy,* a coventure between Lucille Ball Productions and Aaron Spelling Productions; Spelling, ironically, had been seen as an actor on *I Love Lucy* and had scripted episodes of *Desilu Playhouse.* In the rush to sign Ball following her highly rated *Stone Pillow* telefilm, ABC sought ratings dominance with Ball's new sitcom, certain to topple such top-rated NBC comedy series as *The Golden Girls* and *The Cosby Show;* to that end, the network gave Ball and Spelling a firm full-season, twenty-two-episode commitment.

The new series materialized following a dinner hosted by Marvin Davis attended by the Mortons and Aaron Spelling, whose then-current programs included *Dynasty, The Love Boat,* and *Charlie's Angels.* Spelling contacted Gary Morton, who hinted Ball "might" consider a return to weekly television "under the right circumstances"—a full-season network commitment; Gale Gordon as her costar; and the hiring of her writer-producers Madelyn Davis and Bob Carroll, Jr. Spelling agreed, contacted ABC, and got "the easiest 'yes' I've ever gotten in my life. This is the first time I've ever sold a series without a pilot"; the producer gave Ball final creative control. "I've never given that to anybody. But I'd be an idiot not to trust Lucy with how to do Lucy."

The star unwisely refused to update her Lucy characterization, or consider appearing in a fresh, contemporary format. Cleo Smith and Tommy Thompson were unsuccessfully approached to join the new series. Along with Peter Baldwin, Marc Daniels, Lucy's original *I Love Lucy* director, was hired. Daniels's successor, Bill Asher, was also asked to direct the new series. "I said, 'There's only one way I can make a contribution—don't do it.' It had disaster written all over it."

Upon signing her ABC pact, Lucille phoned an ailing Desi in Del Mar. "He was all for it," she said. "He said, 'What took you so long to get back to work?'" Lucille clearly relished a return to her cherished "arena"—as she had come to call the various *Lucy* soundstages over which she had reigned over the years. "I refuse to be just an old woman who dyed her hair for attention," she said. "I love my work." *Life With Lucy* executive producer Gary Morton offered, "I think it's absolutely sensational that Lucille is going back to work. We love to work together." He added, "When she's working, she's easier to get along with."

"There were problems from the beginning," says series publicist Thomas Watson, "because they didn't really have a concept for the show. ABC wanted a show on quickly for the fall, so the announcement was that they had Lucy coming back to TV—but there was no show yet." The thin, hastily assembled Davis and Carroll series premise cast Lucy Barker as a jogging, health-food-toting grandmother who moves in with her daughter (Ann Dusenberry), son-in-law (Larry Anderson), and their two young children, played by Jenny Lewis and Philip J. Amelio II; Lucy's foil was eighty-year-old Gale Gordon, adversarial co-owners of a small hardware store. "I thought the country needed to see families getting back together," said Lucille.

Larry Anderson recalls auditioning for the role of Lucy's son-in-law. "It was down to the wire, the last callback. Lucy grabbed me, and with a whisper said, 'Are you nervous?' I said, 'Yes, ma'am.' She said, 'You *should* be!' And then she smiled, with a wink. It broke the ice. She said, 'You'll do good,' turned around, and walked away. It was Lucy's decision to bring in Bob and Madelyn, because of Lucy's fear of change. When the reviews came out, she had second thoughts about whether she had done the right thing, but she was a tremendously loyal person—there was no backing out. They were doing the same kind of scripts they did in the 1950s. We never developed the family, instead of just trying to use us as pawns or foils to build a scene for Lucy to do a slapstick bit. The formula was to get Lucy into what they called 'the blocked scene,' where the reclining chair would go haywire, or she'd be hanging from something. We were cardboard characters."

"*Life With Lucy* shouldn't have happened," reflects writer-producer Bob Carroll, Jr. "It was hard to resist being back with her. We wanted it to be kind of *Lucy: The Granny Years*. Lucy didn't want to do that, didn't want to say she was a grandmother. She wanted Gale Gordon back, whom we loved, but we didn't want him again. She was involved in the casting, the two kids we didn't really want or like. Lucy [had] also lost it by then, and so she couldn't do the routines she used to do, didn't want to rehearse as much, didn't want to do retakes when scenes went poorly. I was very relieved when it went off."

And, notes Gary Morton, "Later on, she said, 'I made a mistake. If I was going to do something new, I should have walked in new all the way.'"

According to Ann Dusenberry, "Lucy would come up against somebody's opinion and say, 'Oh, no, when I was working, it wasn't like that.' She had rules, and they were ingrained in her. She had old ideas. When we talked about moving on a joke, she said, '*Never* move on a line that's gonna bring a laugh!' So we stood there, faced out to the audience, delivering lines that seemed a little like vaudeville. But she would also say, 'There are an awful lot of producers around,' because all the writers took producer credits. She'd say, 'There are just too many producers around—we need some writers.' And she was right."

And, insists Anderson, "She could be abrupt, but that was far less the case than what we saw of her on a normal basis, which was a fun, humorous, unpretentious, giving, generous lady. She came on the set

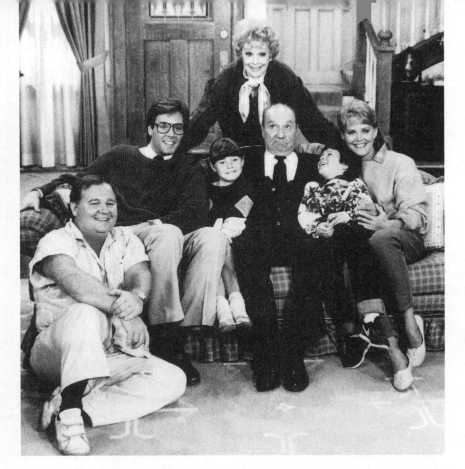

Life With Lucy: (from left) Donovan Scott, Larry Anderson, Jenny Lewis, Gale Gordon, Lucille, Philip J. Amelio II, Ann Dusenberry

RICK CARL COLLECTION

and knew the names of all the crew members. She treated everybody the same—from the lowliest guy sweeping the floor to the director—and cared what was going on in their lives. If someone had a headache or was sick, she would go over and ask them what was wrong. Sometimes she would lose patience or would flat-out say, 'Do it this way.' It would sting a little, but she never meant to be hurtful. When she perceived that somebody might have gotten hurt, she would take them aside and throw her arm around them, and a couple of minutes later, you would see them laughing or telling jokes."

Life With Lucy was an ignominious end to an illustrious television career. "That wasn't Lucy up on the screen," said *Channels*. "It was some elderly impostor. Caked with makeup, she looked mummified. Her voice, deep and hoarse, sounded like a bullfrog's in agony. She gamely attempted her old style of slapstick but her impeccable timing had fled. Worse, what used to be cute and girlish in a younger woman turned

351

out to be embarrassing in a senior citizen today. Her new impossible dream of agelessness only saddened audiences with its intimations of mortality."

Guesting on *The Late Show With Joan Rivers,* Lucille revealed, "I didn't have any idea that I would get chastised for working. I got some lousy notices for coming back to work at all, which I felt was very strange. I was so amazed. I can take critique about the show, and I've done that for years, but to be critiqued for coming back at all—that threw me. I cried, my God, I cried."

"I went to see her on the set," recounts Carole Cook. "She was livid. She said, 'The critics don't want to see anybody over fifty.' By that time, she couldn't see. *The Golden Girls* had become a tremendous hit, but they didn't write like that for her because she wouldn't let them." According to Watson, "Lucy was very leery about the scripts. She'd often say, 'I don't think this script is working at all, but I'm willing to give it a try.' Twelve years had passed since *Here's Lucy,* during which time she had become the Grand Empress of Old Television. Suddenly, the studio audience was allowed to see this woman play Lucy. The people were so in awe that they let her down, because whenever she thought a script was bad, she turned to the studio audience to find out. If a joke wouldn't work, she'd want it out, but they laughed at everything. She'd do little throwaway bits and got huge laughs, which didn't play at all at home. It worked totally against her, and she didn't know it."

Life With Lucy's premiere episode was the highest-rated episode in the run of the series—although, said *Variety,* not the "overpowering success some had expected"—narrowly winning its time slot opposite a *Murder, She Wrote* rerun. The ratings picture the following week was even more alarming, Ball's ratings plummeting 31 percent from the premiere episode, beaten by season premieres of NBC's *Facts of Life* and CBS's *Downtown. Life With Lucy* numbers dropped with each passing week, consistently outranked by its formidable *Facts of Life* competition. In November, *Variety* announced the Ball series was on the "Nielsen critical list." Responding to rumors of imminent cancellation, Lucille turned to ex-husband Desi for counsel. "I talk to him two or three times a week," she admitted. "We talk about the show, and he wishes he was in better health so he could help us."

On November 10, 1986, *Variety* announced, "Lucille Ball's TV series comeback has come to an inglorious end." The ABC cancellation, though, was hardly a surprise—latest Nielsen figures had *Life With Lucy* ranked in the ratings cellar at seventy-first place. "I'm in shock," said Lucille as she and Gary Morton vacated their new offices on the Warner Bros.

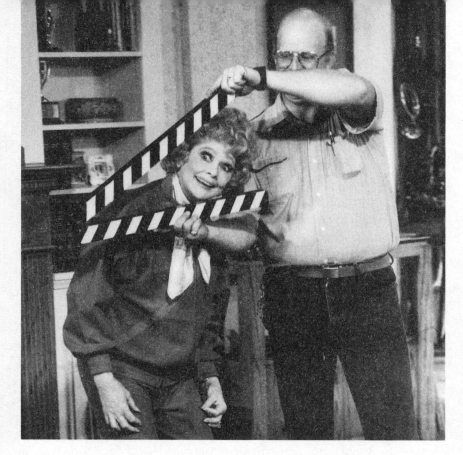

Lucille clowns on the *Life With Lucy* set.
RICK CARL COLLECTION

Hollywood lot. "I don't know what I'm going to do. I give up—but only for the moment. Actually, I'm relieved. I hated to be around, the way things were going. But I'll miss that divine crew and cast."

"I got the notification first," says Morton. "But Lucy already knew it was over. She looked at the ratings and knew we were in trouble. She was very upset about it. She had never failed in television. But she walked out with her head high."

The cancellation proved most costly to ABC. The series, according to Morton's assistant Stuart Shostak, "had the highest per-episode production cost on ABC at the time. Each half-hour cost six hundred seventy-five thousand dollars a week. Out of that, Lucy was paid one hundred and fifty thousand dollars per show, Gary one hundred thousand dollars an episode, and Gale Gordon twenty-five thousand dollars."

The failure of her television comeback was a severe blow from which she never recovered. Gale Gordon notes, "The night we did the thirteenth episode, Gary Morton got a phone call from someone in the Spelling office who said, 'As of now, your show is canceled.' He didn't tell Lucy that night because he got the call just before we were going on in front

353

of the audience to do the show. To have an underling call up to say the show was canceled, not even to have the decency to do it in person, was shocking and awful. That cut her to the quick and rightly so. It was a disgrace." Recalls Larry Anderson, "I helped Lucy clean out her dressing room the day after the cancellation. She was really down, but down as she was, she was trying to bolster me. She said, 'The thing that troubles me the most is that for you kids, it was a big break—I feel much worse for you.' That was very gracious."

For a time, Anderson and Dusenberry remained close with Lucille. "I played backgammon with her a few times," says Ann. "She took me to one of her upstairs rooms and started giving me her clothes, two beautiful outfits. She'd say, 'Put this on, this will look great on you.' She was very, very giving. When she would talk of Vivian Vance and their relationship, her eyes would well up. She loved her and missed her desperately. After Viv was gone, I got the feeling that she was always seeking that kind of connection again. I just think Lucy wanted a friend."

Nearing death and in and out of the hospital throughout the year, Desi returned to his Del Mar retreat for his remaining days. He stubbornly refused to see visitors—particularly Lucy—with his weight now hovering below one hundred pounds and his head nearly bald due to chemotherapy treatments. "Everybody knew his health was very bad," recalls Anderson. "It definitely had her attention through the course of production. I'd say, 'Lucy, are you all right?' She'd say, 'No, Desi's not well.' " On the last episode filmed, Lucille poignantly recited the lyrics to "Sunrise, Sunset" from *Fiddler on the Roof*. "There she was, singing this song, and we knew she was thinking of Desi," offers Dusenberry. "In a quiet moment, she'd let us know that she was hurting about him. She was really thinking about him a lot."

Daughter Lucie steadfastly remained at Desi's side in Del Mar in his final weeks. "The doctors would say, 'It could be any time now.' And you hate hearing that. I would talk to my mother, and she would say, 'If you need me . . . ' and I knew that was her way of saying, 'Don't you need me?' I would say, 'I don't know if I need you to be here, but I think you need to be here.' She'd tell me, 'Oh, he doesn't want to see me. He doesn't want to be seen in his condition. He doesn't like the way he looks.' 'Yeah, that's true, but I think he wants to see you.' Because it was true. He wasn't seeing anybody, even his best friends. A lot of people don't want to be seen looking worse than they've ever looked in their entire life. They don't want to be remembered like that.

"My mother came down once and visited for a brief time. He wasn't feeling so well that day. She came down again, and he was better. They talked, and I was sort of nervous, wondering how they'd keep themselves busy all day. I had brought some tapes for Dad to watch, to keep him busy. So I pulled out a couple *I Love Lucy* videotapes and put them in the machine. And it seemed like the dumbest, corniest thing to do. And it was the best thing that could have happened. First of all, it broke the ice. Then they reminisced. His attitude at that time was, 'God, you were always so good at that,' a lot of accolades. And they laughed and joked. And I just shut the door to let them have their time together. I started them off, like two kids on their first date."

"Lucy always wanted me to tell her about Desi, which I did," offers Del Mar neighbor Marcella Rabwin. "I used to report to her about Desi. I said to him, 'Are you still in love with her?' He said, 'Yeah.' He never stopped loving her."

Lucy and Desi spoke once more in the final days before his death on December 2, 1986. As Lucie remembers, "I got on the phone with my mother and said, 'He's barely speaking. He didn't eat any of the dinner we fixed. He hasn't eaten in three days. I don't even know if he'll understand what you're saying, but I'll put the phone up to his ear.' She said, 'Oh, okay.' She was always trying to be so brave. You could hear her voice cracking. I put the phone up to Dad's ear in the bed. And he gave me a look that said, 'Who is it?' And I said, 'It's the redhead.' He just listened, and I heard what he said. She just said the same thing over and over again. It was muffled, but you could clearly make out it was the same thing over and over again.

"It was, 'I love you. I love you. Desi, I love you.' You could even hear the intonations of the voice change, how she meant each one, the interpretations. And I just sat there, trying not to show him I was listening, because I had to hold the phone. I couldn't get out of the room. He couldn't hold the phone. And he said, 'I love you, too, honey. Good luck with your show.' I had told him in passing, 'Mom's going to be on a variety show tonight, she's going to give somebody an award.' I'm sure he didn't realize what show it was, it was just important for him to say that. I couldn't say anything to her. I just said, 'I'll talk to you later.' And I hung up the phone. Really, my mother was the last person he talked to, because he died about forty-eight hours later.

"Until I went back into my little diary," concludes Lucie, "I never put it together that the date this happened was November 30—the same date as their wedding anniversary."

Epilogue

"I'm happy that I have brought laughter because I have been shown by many the value of it in so many lives, in so many ways."

—Lucille Ball, 1989

"The day Desi died, she and I were doing *Password* together," recalled Betty White. "She was being real funny on the show, but during a break she said, 'You know, it's the damnedest thing. Goddamn it, I didn't think I'd get this upset. There he goes.' It was a funny feeling, kind of a lovely, private moment."

That same morning, Lucille had issued a press statement: "Desi has been ill with cancer for many months, and my family and I have been praying for his release from this terrible ordeal. Desi died early this morning in his daughter's arms. Our relationship has remained very close, very amiable over the years, and now I'm grateful to God that Desi's suffering is over."

Desi Arnaz's singularly significant contribution to the development of the television industry was acknowledged—albeit in somewhat muted fashion—in obituaries. *The New York Times* hailed him as "an important figure in the history of television." On the other hand, *Newsweek,* while recognizing him as "a shrewd businessman and an innovative producer" ultimately concluded that Arnaz was "best known as second banana to wife Lucille Ball."

Lucille and Gary were among the one hundred mourners attending the funeral at St. James Roman Catholic Church near San Diego, the eulogy delivered by former Desilu tenant Danny Thomas. Desi's devoted friend and former personal assistant Johny Aitchison attended the private services. "I saw Madelyn and Marcella Rabwin, so I walked in with them, and little Desi came over and said, 'Oh you're family, sit here.' Lucie gave me a hug. I was sitting with Margie Durante. Lucy was surrounded, of course, so I didn't make any effort to go over, but she came over to me and said, 'I'm delighted you came.'"

By the end of the week, Lucille had flown to Washington, D.C., to accept perhaps the crowning achievement of her career—the prestigious

Kennedy Center Honors, the nation's recognition of performing-arts excellence. Honored along with Lucille at the ninth annual event were Ray Charles, Hume Cronyn and Jessica Tandy, violinist Yehudi Menuhin, and ballet choreographer Anthony Tudor.

At the ceremonies, Lucille was hailed as a "superb clown of infinite range" whose "sidesplitting buffoonery was carved into her bone marrow by an exquisite understanding of the tragic sense of life."

An air of poignancy was cast over the proceedings when Robert Stack took the stage to read a statement from Desi Arnaz, who originally had been approached to appear at the ceremonies. Lucille struggled to maintain her composure as Robert Stack read from Desi's statement: "*The New York Times* asked me to divide the credit for *I Love Lucy*'s success between the writers, the directors, and the cast. I told them, 'Give Lucy ninety percent of the credit—divide the other ten percent among the rest of us. Lucy *was* the show.'"

Apart from the Kennedy Center appearance, Lucille maintained a low profile in the wake of the failure of *Life With Lucy* and Desi's subsequent death. Less-than-enthusiastic critical response to roles other than "Lucy"-based characters had left her wary of trying to broaden her repertoire; at the same time, it had become painfully clear that the world held little interest in embracing a seventy-five-year-old's variation on her Lucy Ricardo characterization. Thus, her few television appearances in her last years were limited to awards shows and guest spots. Her rapidly failing health continued to alarm her. She suffered from high blood pressure and angina attacks; she complained of recurrent pain in her shoulder; and, in January 1988, a cyst was removed from her thyroid.

In early May of that year, Lucille taped an appearance on Bob Hope's eighty-fifth birthday special, to be broadcast on NBC later in the month—performing a song-and-dance number rather ironically titled, "Comedy Ain't No Joke." On Tuesday, May 10, she was hospitalized after suffering a stroke. As devoted friend and backgammon partner Jim Brochu recounted in his book *Lucy in the Afternoon,* "Lucy said, 'I woke up about four-thirty in the morning and went to the bathroom. I didn't turn any lights on since I knew my way in the dark. After a minute I felt this heavy object crash into my lap. I thought a piece of the ceiling fell down, it hit me so hard. I reached into my lap to see what it was and almost screamed when I found an arm there. My own right arm! It had fallen asleep. It was over my head when I got up, and I never felt it or thought anything was wrong until it fell in my lap. I started back to bed, but fell before I got there. Gary picked me up and took me to Cedars–Sinai Medical Center."

Though the stroke left Lucille partially paralyzed, she began immediate therapy and made remarkably rapid progress, a slight facial droop eventually vanishing. Four months after she was stricken, she felt sufficiently recovered to appear on an *All Star Super Password Special*. Listless and slow to respond, *Password* veteran Lucille at one point during the word game completely lost her concentration, prompting a long—and awkward—silence as she failed to provide a single synonym for one of her passwords. *Life with Lucy* costar Ann Dusenberry recalls Lucille being concerned about her mental agility during their own *Password* session: "She would beat herself up for not being sharp enough. When we were rehearsing, she said, 'I'm gonna screw this up. It's not going to work.' She didn't think her brain was working like it should. We'd get off, and she'd go, 'I'm just terrible at this, I'm just *terrible* at this.' I remember thinking, This is like torture to her. I didn't understand why she did it."

Lucille's next major appearance was at the March 29, 1989, telecast of the Academy Awards ceremonies, teamed with Bob Hope to introduce a "Oscar Winners of Tomorrow" production number. Their entrance was met with an extended standing ovation, Lucille appearing vibrant and alert. Bob Hope's publicist Frank Liberman recalls Lucille's great concern about her appearance backstage as she prepared to make her entrance, squarely facing him and asking, "Do my eyes look baggy?" "I told her, 'Don't worry about it. You and Hope have a way of straightening up and dropping thirty years when the lights hit you and you hear the applause.' "

As she left show-business agent Irving "Swifty" Lazar's annual post-Oscar party at Spago restaurant in West Hollywood, Lucille was revitalized when a group of star watchers gathered outside the restaurant cheered her. Mitchell Fink noted in the Los Angeles *Herald-Examiner,* "Lucy suddenly broke into a little dance on the street. The crowd went wild. Then Lucy started hiking up her dress, showing a little more leg, then a little more, and the crowd went wilder. Lucy threw kisses to the crowd, got in the car, and left."

Three weeks later, on the morning of April 18, Lucille began having chest pains and experienced difficulty breathing. She was promptly rushed to Cedars-Sinai, where it was diagnosed that she was suffering from an aortal aneurysm; it was then determined she faced certain death if her aortic valve and part of her aorta were not replaced immediately. In a high-risk seven-hour operation, two heart specialists replaced Lucille's damaged tissue with tissue taken from a recently deceased twenty-seven-year-old donor. She weathered the difficult operation admirably, awaking the next morning and even having sufficient strength to inquire about her beloved pet dog.

News of Lucille's condition was met with an unprecedented outpouring of public sentiment and affection that conclusively confirmed the uniquely intimate—and powerful—impact the actress held throughout the world. Five thousand calls—from such distant corners of the world as Australia and Europe—flooded the Cedars-Sinai switchboard daily. Hospital fax machines became jammed with hundreds of get-well messages, alarming hospital officials, who feared that vital messages would be blocked. Telegrams, mail, and floral arrangements poured in, including an eight-by-four-foot card signed by four thousand residents of Louisiana. Get-well cards by the dozens were taped on the door of her Roxbury Drive home. The Hard Rock Café, situated across the street from the hospital, erected a banner proclaiming love and support for Lucy during her recovery.

"On a scale of one to ten, this is an absolute ten," Cedars-Sinai spokesman Ron Wise said. "Before it's over [the hospital] will look like a combination of the U.S. Post Office and the botanical gardens."

Lucille made steady progress and soon became aware of the public clamor and universal outpouring of love and support. Lucie Arnaz recalls, "They got her up to walk a couple of times. They moved her to a better room with windows, and you could actually see the Hard Rock Café from there. She heard all the incredible reports on television about all the mail pouring in, how much the whole world was hoping for Lucy to get better. And she saw the Hard Rock Café on TV. I said, 'Can you believe what's going on here?' and she said, 'It's *wonderful*.' By that time, we were all in great spirits anyway, and we could kid about it because she was going to get better."

On April 25, Lucie and Desi, Jr., again visited Lucille at the hospital. As she was leaving, Lucie asked her mother if there was anything she needed from the house. "She said, 'My Florida water.' She used to buy it by the case. I kissed her two times on the forehead and told her I'd bring her the Florida water."

The next morning shortly before five o'clock, Lucille was awakened by sharp back pain, losing consciousness moments later. A tear had developed in the abdominal portion of her aorta, about ten inches below the surgically repaired area, resulting in cardiac arrest. A team of a dozen doctors and nurses vainly attempted for over an hour to resuscitate her with respirators, intravenous drugs, and external cardiac compression. She was pronounced dead at 5:47 A.M.

"This was unexpected, sudden, and catastrophic," pronounced one of her heart surgeons, Dr. Robert Kass, said. "She lost a lot of blood, and it happened very suddenly. We could not get a heartbeat, and there was no way to operate."

News bulletins interrupted radio broadcasts and television programming, shock and disbelief overwhelming the public, her death felt as a personal loss akin to losing a beloved relative, a point of reference shared by everyone. In a move usually reserved for such major events as the outbreak of war or the Kennedy assassination, the New York *Post* erected posters at newsstands throughout the city, announcing in bold black letters: LUCY DIES.

The media blitz surrounding her passing continued with an intensity usually only accorded the death of a head of state. *Entertainment Tonight* and ABC's late-night series *Nightline* dedicated entire programs to Lucille, and her death was reported at the top of CBS and ABC's evening newscasts.

Clearly indicating the magnitude of Lucille's significance as an American icon was the preemption of an hour of prime-time network programming for a CBS News special titled *Lucy*. "We lost a member of the family today," noted host Dan Rather, "or maybe she was more like a good friend, the lady next door." Narrating a compilation of *I Love Lucy* clips for the special, Charles Osgood remarked, "We *did* love Lucy. She could make us laugh until we hurt, she was just *so* funny. But there was more to Lucille Ball than comic instincts and timing. Like Charlie Chaplin, her funniness was *art*. And it came out of being like us—human and vulnerable."

In a rare public appearance, eighty-eight-year-old CBS founder William S. Paley took to his network's airwaves to pay tribute to Lucille Ball. "What she meant to CBS—and to broadcasting—can hardly be expressed in words. She was in a class by herself." He further offered, "What you feel right now in this country because she died tells you more than anything else. The whole country seems to be aroused by it. We're all so damned upset about it."

"I always tried my whole life not to think about how famous she was," reflects Lucie Arnaz. "And yet there were certain times when it hit me, when someone big would die, and the hoopla associated with that person dying. And I'd think Oh, my God. It was exactly as I had feared and imagined—days and days of news reports. Actually, it was even more intense because it was the entire week before. The whole *world* knew what I was going through. If someone in your family died and nineteen or one hundred of your closest family friends showed up at the funeral, you'd feel really good. But if it was in the millions of family and friends, you *really* feel supported through the first few months. I must say, it was helpful—I can't see any negative side to having all those people mourn with you. You don't *really* want total privacy. It was nice going to the grocery store and having some checker you don't know touch you on the arm and say, 'I'm *sorry*.' You have to say 'Thank you' a lot—but it was nice. It felt good."

Immediately following Lucy's death, an easel bearing a memorial sign was erected over her Walk of Fame star on Hollywood Boulevard, where a blocklong condolence card was eventually signed by hundreds of fans. The Walk of Fame tribute prompted Candy Moore to recall a curious— and telling—dream Lucille had related to her many years ago during their *Lucy Show* days: "She told me she dreamt she had died. And she came back as a ghost on Hollywood Boulevard. She's walking along as a ghost, and no one remembers her. When she died, that was the first thing I thought of, because you never saw such an outpouring of love, almost obsession. I thought, She would be so proud."

Lucie Arnaz eventually responded to all of the letters of condolence she received, having been taught by her mother to answer her own fan mail. "You know how *many* she had answered personally? Most of them. Especially in later years, when there weren't thousands, but hundreds. I appreciated that." She further notes, "There were almost an equal amount for my father. I thought that was great, because he had really dropped out of sight. People didn't even know where to write. The mail was delivered to all these weird addresses—but they eventually got to me."

Lucille left an estate valued at a reported $22 million—its assets held in the Lucille Ball Morton Trust—with revenues divided equally between her children. Although declining to confirm the amount held in the Morton Trust, her longtime tax attorney Art Manella—and executor of the estate—notes, "We managed her affairs in such a way that it was consistent with her own personality. Lucy's major purpose in life was not to accumulate wealth. Her needs were quite simple. She was always concerned about whether she could afford to do something, and, of course, she could afford to do most things. We talked a lot about her will and her estate. She was concerned about doing well with her children. I always took the position that it was much more important to preserve her economic net worth than to try and double it, because her children were grown and they had done fine."

Manella adds, "Right before she died, I was at her home one day, and we were reviewing something. We had finished, and we were just chatting. She said, 'Arthur, do you know that in all the years you have represented me, you have never *once* asked me for my autograph?' I said, 'That's right, Lucy, I never have. And, you know, in all those same years, you have never asked me for *mine!*' We both laughed. She said, 'I want you to have a picture of me.' Two days later a photo arrived at my office. I'm so glad I have that, because I thought very highly of her. She was such a sound, decent human being."

While Lucille received countless accolades following her passing, one of the most eloquent summations of her career was delivered at a 1984 tribute by Sammy Davis, Jr., who directly faced the star and said: "Be proud, Lucy, of your legacy. . . . The sun never sets on Lucille Ball. All over this worried world tonight, nations of untold millions are watching reruns they also watched the first time around. Joy requires no translation. God wanted the world to laugh, and He invented you. Many are called, but *you* were chosen. Clown you are *not.* All of the funny hats, the baggy pants, the mustaches and the wigs, and the pratfalls and the blacked-out-teeth—they didn't fool us for one minute. We saw through all the disguises, and what we found inside is *more* than we deserve."

But the essence of Lucille Ball when she stood at her dazzling *I Love Lucy* zenith alongside husband Desi Arnaz was perhaps best captured at her Kennedy Center induction, when Walter Matthau attempted to explain the universal appeal of Lucy Ricardo: "There's no dream she wouldn't reach for," he concluded, "and no fall she wouldn't take."

LEONARD NADEL

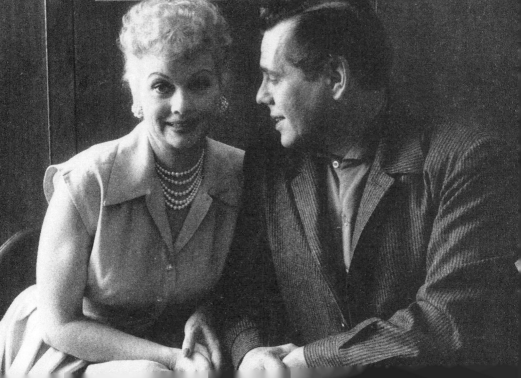

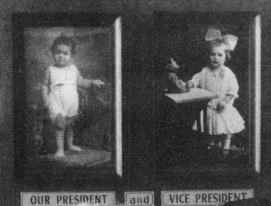

OUR PRESIDENT and VICE PRESIDENT

Bibliography

Andrews, Bart. *Lucy & Ricky & Fred & Ethel*. New York: Dutton, 1976.

Andrews, Bart. *The "I Love Lucy" Book* (revised version of *Lucy & Ricky & Fred & Ethel*). New York: Doubleday, 1985.

Andrews, Bart, and Thomas J. Watson. *Loving Lucy*. New York: St. Martin's Press, 1980.

Arnaz, Desi. *A Book*. New York: William Morrow & Company, 1976.

Brochu, Jim. *Lucy in the Afternoon*. New York: William Morrow & Company, 1990.

Gregory, James. *The Lucille Ball Story*. New York: Signet, 1974.

Harris, Eleanor. *The Real Story of Lucille Ball*. New York: Ballantine, 1954.

Morella, Joe, and Edward Epstein. *Lucy: The Bittersweet Life of Lucille Ball*. New York: Lyle Stuart, 1973.

Morella, Joe, and Edward Epstein. *Forever Lucy* (revised version of *Lucy: The Bittersweet Life of Lucille Ball*). New York: Lyle Stuart, 1986.

Stack, Robert (with Mark Evans). *Straight Shooting*. New York: Macmillan, 1980.

Acknowledgments

★ ★ ★

We wish to thank those who graciously shared memories and insight: Steve Ackerman, Edie Adams, Larry Anderson, Bill Asher, Kaye Ballard, Robert F. Blumofe, Mort Briskin, Herb Browar, Emily Daniels, Dixon Dern, Ann Dusenberry, Jimmy Garrett, Gale Gordon, Joe Harris, June Havoc, Charles Henry, Alexander (Jake) Jaco, Dan Jenkins, Madeline Kahn, Dave Kaufman, Michael Kidd, Hal King, Charles Lane, Ronald Lee, Marjorie Lord, William Luce, Barbara McClay, the late Sam Marx, Bud Molin, Candy Moore, N. Richard Nash, Gregg Oppenheimer, Rose Marie, Bob Schiller, Percy Schultz, Mel Shavelson, Howard Sheppard, Al Simon, Ann Sothern, Ashton Springer, Swen Swenson, Tommy Thompson, Bob Weiskopf, Onna White, and Margaret Whiting. Also greatly adding to the scope of this project were the always enlightening, candid Jayne Meadows and Steve Allen; Al Morley; Michael Yakaitis; former CBS executives Mike Dann, Salvatore Iannucci, and Robert Lewine; Marcia Magill; and the late John Graham, who provided the inspiration for this project several years ago.

A profound debt of gratitude to the following Desilu executives and associates, gentlemen all: Bert Granet, Art Manella, the late George Murphy, Oscar Katz, Herbert Solow, John Strauss, Bernard Weitzman, and especially Edwin Holly, whose photos and news clippings provided a wealth of background and perspective. We are particularly indebted to Martin Leeds for his accessibility, generosity, keen insight, and reference materials.

Special appreciation is owed to Maury Thompson, the value of his great humor and cooperation near incalculable; and to Herbert Kenwith, whose insight and experiences with Lucille helped set the parameters for the book.

For sharing their experiences and offering candor, we also wish to express enormous gratitude to: Robert Osborne, Desilu contract player, *Hollywood Reporter* columnist, official historian of the Academy of Motion Picture Arts and Sciences, and, above all, a kind, generous and exceptional man who opened many doors and provided great insight along the way; and Carole Cook, an extraordinary woman and actress, who generously shared her intimate memories of Lucille for the first time in these pages.

We also extend our appreciation for the particularly generous efforts of: Mary Wickes, Jim Brochu, and Steve Schalchlin, who kindly opened doors to Lucy's inner circle; Madelyn Pugh Davis, whose vote of confidence imbued this project with credibility and established a cornerstone upon which to build; Bob Carroll, Jr., for his unique candor and potent wit; Dann Cahn, whose enthusiasm, generosity, and guidance helped provide the book's foundation; Marcella Rabwin, whose love of truth, and whose selflessness and encouragement, proved inspirational; Frank Gorey, whose patience and kindness added layers of understanding; Wanda Clark, whose unique perspective and compassion provided a standard of fairness against which to weigh information; Johny Aitchison, for his graciousness and generosity; Stuart Shostak, for his boundless energy and willingness to share; and Howard Frank, Leslie Solow, Wallace Seawell, Ron Mandelbaum of Photofest, and particularly Michael McClay, for their significant help in locating and providing photographs.

Also deserving of recognition and appreciation is Ball historian Tom Watson, who offered his unique personal and professional insight into Lucille Ball and generously provided us with his unparalleled resource materials and rare photographs. We are also enormously in debt to Rick Carl, a Ball archivist who also offered friendship and access to his enormous collection of photographs and related materials to enhance this work. Sincere thanks also to kind, generous Martin Silverstein of CBS Photos. A special note of thanks to Denver Stedman for providing author photographs—and friendship.

Special mention must be made of Evelyn Nadel, the widow of photographer Leonard Nadel, whose fine artistry graces the front cover as well as several inside pages. We are most grateful for her generosity in providing these photographs, as well as for support along the way.

We also extend our appreciation to Serge Matt, who graciously allowed us access to and permission to include portions of Vivian Vance's unpublished memoirs in this book, facilitated by the kind assistance of his literary representative, Oscar Collier of Oscar Collier Associates.

We extend our appreciation to Diane L. Albert and Stephen W. Albert, editors of *The TV Collector* magazine: P.O. Box 1088, Easton, Mass., 02334. (Send SASE for information.)

In addition, we express our sincere gratitude to the following people who were invaluable in the preparation of this book: the wise and remarkable Mark Epstein; Todd Reznick; our diligent, accommodating transcriber, Robert Waldron; Richard Jordan; Stephen Spurgeon; Don Azars; Ginny Weissman; Cherie Baker; Jay Platt; Neal Hitchens and Christopher Esposito; Steve Brenner; Marc Courtland; Charles Higham; Tom Troupe; Ned Comstock and Dace Taube of the University of Southern California; the enormously helpful staff of the Margaret Herrick

Library of the Motion Picture Academy of Television Arts and Sciences; William McNeil; Tom Brown and Wayne Kranick; Sy Sher; Tom Jones; Ronald Jacobs; Dale Gonyea; Tom Boghossian; Jack Allen; Carolyn Kozo and her staff at the Los Angeles Public Library; and B & R Graphics in Hollywood. Special thanks to Rain Burns and our friend and fellow biographer Karen Swenson, for vital contributions. A special bow to John Fricke, who supported this project in a myriad of ways; his friendship remains a profound and continuing influence.

Personal thanks to Michael Silverman, Sandy Saka, Stephen West, Richard Bozanich, Kinsey Lowe, Jonathan Taylor, and Tim Gray of *Daily Variety,* whose patience and flexibility eased our paths. Special thanks also to *Variety*'s Syd Silverman, Mark Silverman, Donna Brown, Tony Scott, Doug Galloway, Bruce Brosnan, Frank Stephens, Sylvester Joachim, and Joseph McBride for their individual contributions; to John Ginnelli at *The Hollywood Reporter,* for allowing us to research endlessly and for being a friend—particular thanks also to the *Reporter*'s Robert Dowling, David Robb, and Teri Ritzer; and to *Business Week*'s Joan Warner for leading us to our cover photo. Gratitude also goes to Radie Harris, whose interest and support helped propel the project along, and to Frank Liberman for his myriad suggestions. Also, a note of thanks to Steve Lew and Bernadette Bowman at Universal Studios Hollywood for making their excellent *Lucy: A Tribute* attraction accessible to us on a moment's notice. To the following folks at Paramount Pictures, who helped us piece together the remnants of Desilu Studios, a big note of appreciation: Karen Kearnes, Robert McCracken, Gundy Grandt, and Larry MacAllister.

Thanks indeed to Allison J. Waldman for putting us together in the first place, to Marie Silverman Marich for her indefatigable efforts at the computer, and to Charlie Earle for his enthusiasm and for his very early notion that there would ever be such a book. For their moral support, we also thank: Susan Gilbert, Bob Janssen, Bob Valleau, the late Charlie Willard, Ursula and Joe Warner, Charles Moore, Norma Nannini, Joanne Carson, Ben and Pat Gilbert, Jackie Stroupe, June Morrissey, Gwynn Gilbert, Sher Lee Sommers, Jessica Josell, Frank Meyer, John Madden, Patricia O'Connell, Heidi Myers, Gerry Putzer, the late Guy C. Hall, Marcel Vin Hang, John Bailey, Randy Garrett, Art Christensen, David Harlan, and Alan Salit. And a note of recognition to John and Sheila Stewart, Rob Tesmer, Joan Kreider, Carolyn Olsen, Mark Savoretti, Alex Montaner, Patricia Casey, and Patty Stangby.

A singularly important note of appreciation to Kieth Dodge—without whom this project might never have come to pass.

Special and heartfelt thanks to three people who made this book possible: our peerless agent, Dominick Abel, who stands far above the rest; our incomparable editor at William Morrow, Lisa Drew, who—as always—provided unerring wisdom, understanding, solid advice, and patience; and gratitude also to her assistant, Robert Shuman, who answered the questions, solved the problems, and offered support and friendship along the way. Our appreciation, too, to Morrow's Katherine Boyle.

A major debt of gratitude to Lucy's family: Gary Morton, who graciously lent his unique perspective; Fred and Zo Ball, whose hospitality and straight shooting were refreshing and enlightening; and Cleo Smith, whose intelligence, charm, and vantage point lent an immeasurable amount of depth to our understanding.

Finally, the most gratitude of all to Lucie Arnaz, who so generously shared her memories and her special insight, for the first time participating in a book about her parents. Not only did she add an entirely unexpected dimension to this project, she opened the door to the many loyal family friends and associates who might never otherwise have granted interviews. We also greatly appreciate access to many Arnaz family archive photographs seen throughout the book. Our biggest debt of all to her, however, is for infusing this book with heart—something so very much a part of the whole "Desilu" phenomenon. For her unflinching honesty—and her trust—we are profoundly grateful.

Index

Page numbers in *italics* refer to illustrations.